Increasing Your Influence at Work

All-IN-ONE

by Shamash Alidina and Juliet Adams;
Maria Gamb; Bob Kelleher;
Elizabeth Kuhnke; Vivian Scott and
the Dispute Resolution Center;
Christina Tangora Schlachter, PhD;
Marie Taylor and Steve Crabb; and
Hannah L. Ubl, Lisa X. Walden,
and Debra Arbit

for dummies®

A Wiley Brand

Increasing Your Influence at Work All-in-One For Dummies®

Published by: **John Wiley & Sons, Inc.**, 111 River Street, Hoboken, NJ 07030-5774, www.wiley.com

Copyright © 2018 by John Wiley & Sons, Inc., Hoboken, New Jersey

Published simultaneously in Canada

For general information on our other products and services, please contact our Customer Care Department within the U.S. at 877-762-2974, outside the U.S. at 317-572-3993, or fax 317-572-4002. For technical support, please visit https://hub.wiley.com/community/support/dummies.

Wiley publishes in a variety of print and electronic formats and by print-on-demand. Some material included with standard print versions of this book may not be included in e-books or in print-on-demand. If this book refers to media such as a CD or DVD that is not included in the version you purchased, you may download this material at http://booksupport.wiley.com. For more information about Wiley products, visit www.wiley.com.

Library of Congress Control Number: 2018942935

ISBN 978-1-119-48906-1 (pbk); ISBN 978-1-119-48908-5 (ebk); ISBN 978-1-119-48907-8 (ebk)

Manufactured in the United States of America

V087108_061418

Contents at a Glance

Table of Contents

Introduction

nfluence at work isn't just for CEOs anymore. No matter where you work or what you do, you need influence to get things done and enjoy greater success. *Increasing Your Influence at Work All-in-One For Dummies* is your guide to developing the skills you need — and using them effectively.

About This Book

People who know how to exert influence in the workplace have more control over their work lives and move up the career ladder faster than others do. But you don't need to be your company's head honcho to wield influence; it's a well-kept secret that anyone can build the influence they need to make a greater impact (and income).

Increasing Your Influence at Work All-in-One For Dummies helps you acquire and cultivate some of the most important attributes needed for influence, such as trustworthiness, reliability, and assertiveness. Here, you get pointers on improving your basic communication skills (both verbal and nonverbal), having critical conversations with co-workers, handling conflicts (even the ones you're involved in), engaging teams and departments, exerting influence on co-workers of different generations (including Millennials), and strengthening your leadership skills.

A quick note: Sidebars (shaded boxes of text) dig into the details of a given topic, but they aren't crucial to understanding it. Feel free to read them or skip them. You can pass over the text accompanied by the Technical Stuff icon, too. The text marked with this icon gives some interesting but nonessential information about increasing influence.

One last thing: Within this book, you may note that some web addresses break across two lines of text. If you're reading this book in print and want to visit one of these web pages, simply key in the web address exactly as it's noted in the text, pretending as though the line break doesn't exist. If you're reading this as an e-book, you've got it easy — just click the web address to be taken directly to the web page.

Foolish Assumptions

Here are some assumptions about you, dear reader, and why you're picking up this book:

>> You work in the business world and want to gain the attention and cooperation of your co-workers.

>> You want to gain influence on a team, as a manager, or in meetings so that you can work with others more effectively, become more respected and appreciated, and make your voice more likely to be heard.

>> You want to engage in a more genuine work environment where people can share concerns and ways to collectively solve problems.

>> You want to help make important things happen at work and create and cultivate relationships that matter.

Icons Used in This Book

Like all *For Dummies* books, this book features icons to help you navigate the information. Here's what they mean.

REMEMBER

If you take away anything from this book, it should be the information marked with this icon.

TECHNICAL STUFF

This icon flags information that delves a little deeper than usual into a particular topic.

TIP

This icon highlights especially helpful advice about developing and using the skills you need to exert more influence in the workplace.

WARNING

This icon points out situations and actions to avoid as you strive to increase your influence at work.

Beyond the Book

In addition to the material in the book, this product comes with some access-anywhere goodies that you'll find online. Check out the free Cheat Sheet at dummies.com. Just search for "Increasing Your Influence at Work All-in-One" Cheat Sheet.

Where to Go from Here

You don't have to read this book from cover to cover, but if you're an especially thorough person, feel free to do so! If you just want to find specific information and then get back to work, take a look at the table of contents or the index, and then dive into the chapter or section that interests you.

For example, if you want to strengthen your verbal and nonverbal communication skills, flip to Book 1. If you want to influence co-workers of several different generations, check out Book 4. Or if you want to head straight to the top of your organization, Book 6 on becoming an influential leader is the place to be.

No matter where you start, you'll find the information you need to more effectively influence peers, managers, and subordinates. Good luck!

1

Body Talk: Influencing through Communication and Body Language

Contents at a Glance

Chapter 1

Building Effective Verbal Communication Techniques

I n everyday situations, people rely on the familiar back-and-forth of verbal communication. You probably don't walk down the street in the morning and pause to think about what to say or what to do when a neighbor says hello. Instead, you have a fairly common pattern based on an existing relationship; you smile, say "hi" back, perhaps engage in small talk, and go on with your day. For most of your relationships, this process works fine. During critical work conversations, however, the intent changes the process. For this situation, you need effective and explicit communication techniques to manage the dialogues and to ensure that the results are focused and clear. Building effective communication techniques will catapult the success of a critical conversation.

In this chapter, you get the 4-1-1 on how to communicate clearly and effectively. You discover techniques that help build productivity and improve employee morale with different verbal cues you can use in every conversation, especially the critical ones. Part of this chapter addresses examples of open, authentic, and explicit conversations. Finally, you find out how to turn confrontational language into cooperative discussions that get results.

Great Communicators Are Made, Not Born

Although people have been communicating for most of their lives, critical conversations are different. Critical conversations are deliberate events that are targeted on results. In most cases, the main goal of the critical conversation is to improve working relationships or organizational results. That goal is a lot different from leading a project meeting, sending an email about a status update, or even presenting the company's results to shareowners.

A leader may be a wonderful speaker who communicates frequently and with transparency. But even the best communicators can get caught up in the message when delivering a critical point.

To understand why communication skills are so critical to a successful conversation, briefly walk through what happens when people engage in dialogue. First, the sender has an idea, translates this idea into words, and sends it. Then the receiver gets the message, applies meaning to the idea, and gives feedback, making the receiver the new sender. Every back-and-forth exchange of words (and even nonverbal cues) continues with this process.

REMEMBER

Communication is a transaction in which both parties continuously send and receive messages. Even before the initiator speaks, the receiver is observing nonverbal signals. Verbal communication and nonverbal communication are the building blocks to a successful critical conversation. For more on nonverbal techniques, check out Book 1, Chapter 2.

Now imagine a chain of this communication. Back and forth, each time with the other party interpreting what was or wasn't said and adding meaning to the information. A message's meanings can easily become distorted.

Here's an example to show how the simple act of communicating can turn a bad situation into a horrible one.

Kate: "Hi, John. Thanks for agreeing to meet with me today. I wanted to talk with you about a concern I have with your behavior in team meetings recently."

John (getting a bit defensive): "A concern. What concern?"

Kate: "Well, it's hard for me to believe that you did this because I wasn't in the room, but Kasha came into my office complaining that you have been raising your voice, and —"

John (cutting in): "How can you give me any feedback when you weren't in the meeting?"

Kate: "Sounds like you're mad. If you'll let me speak, I can help."

John promptly rolls his eyes and tunes out the conversation, allowing Kate to speak all she wants.

Right off the bat, Kate sends the message that she has a concern, which may seem like a fair statement. What Kate does wrong is to use words that lead John to believe the problem is entirely on his end ("your behavior"). The situation just gets worse when Kate says "it's hard for me to believe this." Perhaps she's trying to add some humor or use a less accusatory tone, but John interprets this statement as an accusation that his actions are so wrong even his boss can't imagine they happened. (Find out how tone and other nonverbal cues impact a conversation in Book 1, Chapter 2) Words make a giant difference in how the receiver accepts and agrees on the desired result of the critical conversation.

The good news is that with simple strategies, you won't fall into Kate's slip-ups. When you communicate well, participants will be committed to improving their working relationships in the course of improving the business. When you don't communicate correctly, the other parties will be put on the defensive and refuse to engage in the conversation. You can see how the former option gives you a much better outcome.

Verbal Communication: When Words Matter Most

Effective verbal communication employs a number of simple and not-so-simple tools during different situations. The goal of mastering critical conversation is to know what the tools are, without using an overformulaic "toolkit" approach. Success depends on the relationship the two parties have before the conversation takes place and whether they can understand and respect each other. Being interested in and respectful of others' points of view through your choice of words will contribute greatly to open communication and cooperation.

REMEMBER

According to some communication experts, body language and other nonverbal communication skills account for more than 90 percent of the way an individual receives information from a sender. Book 1, Chapters 2 and 3 dive into all the nonverbal cues and body language that facilitate a successful critical conversation.

Facts, opinions, and gossip

Emotions can get high during a discussion, so write down the feedback you want to give. If an employee is late, write down when she was late. If a customer is abusing your employees during customer service calls, write down the specific examples of when the customer stepped over the lines of professionalism. This prep work isn't meant to be a witch-hunt! Quite the opposite. Having facts to back up why you're initiating the conversation helps the receiver know that you care enough to get to the bottom of the problem and that you aren't just presenting hearsay.

But just having the facts doesn't guarantee a successful critical conversation. You have to present the facts as facts; this is when words matter most. During a critical conversation, present factual information and avoid the temptation to use opinion or hearsay. These steps leave no room for question and distrust, which could lead to one of the parties closing off the flow of communication.

REMEMBER

Although this chapter is far from an English lesson (if you need one, check out *English Grammar For Dummies* by Geraldine Woods [John Wiley & Sons, Inc.]), here are some clear-cut definitions to help guide you through what to do (and what not to do) during a critical conversation:

>> **Fact:** An action you witnessed. Use facts during critical conversations — they can't be disputed. Lead with, "When I was in the meeting, you were pacing around the table while everyone else was sitting down."

>> **Opinion:** A personal judgment. Try to avoid opinions as much as possible during critical conversations, because they leave room for misinterpretation and uncertainty. Although your opinion may be right, you have no proof. Believing that someone left the room during a meeting because he thought the meeting was going nowhere, or that he crossed his arms because he didn't agree with the group's opinion, is just that — opinion. Opinions that can wreck a critical conversation include, "The administration believes you lied," or, "People who are usually so angry often aren't good workers."

>> **Gossip:** Anything that comes secondhand or through the rumor mill. Gossip has no place in a critical conversation. Statements like "People have told me that you're a boozehound in the office," or "Lots of people have told me you aren't working that hard," open the conversation to doubt and mistrust.

Pronouns matter and words create meaning

No one wants to be brought into a conversation and told that she's doing things wrong or that she's going against the company. During a critical conversation, limit the words "them" and "they," and stick to "I" and "we."

Think of the different reactions these statements generate:

Situation: A client relationship manager walks into his manager's office right after losing a key customer account.

Manager (who didn't read this book): "Because *you* didn't get along with our client's executive team, *you* lost us a giant amount of business."

Note how this statement immediately pits "you" versus "us."

Manager (using a revised approach): "I realize there were different perspectives on the right approach with Company ABC, especially during the last project. How can we work together to prevent losing another client, and perhaps even get Company ABC back?"

Here's another example to demonstrate the nuances of word choice:

Situation: At an engineering conference, one of the senior engineers partied every night and word got back to her manager.

Manager (not using the right words): "They shouldn't be as sensitive when it comes to how other people behave when they aren't officially in the office, but you really need to watch your behavior when it comes to how you act at conferences."

Here's a double-whammy! The recipient is already on the defensive with "they" and "you," and then is hit again with a conditional verb, "should."

Here's a better approach to the conversation from the previous example:

Manager (making good use of verbal skills): "I know that during conferences, it's important to be social. This has to be balanced with maintaining professional behavior. Can we work together to talk about which activities are better than others?"

REMEMBER

Accusations make people defensive. *Collaboration* makes change possible — and change is the ultimate goal of a critical conversation. During critical conversations, the smallest details, like the use of pronouns, can set a positive tone or create an argumentative or confrontational environment. Using the right inclusive words creates a higher level of commitment to the conversation because all the parties can take part in the discussion instead of being talked to by the other parties.

WARNING

Talking in corporate speak, buzz words, and jargon — even if all parties are part of the same organization — usually results in glazed eyes or, worse, rolling eyes. A critical conversation isn't the time to demonstrate how smart or with-it you are; it's time to get to the point clearly and make sure the message is heard.

TIP

Table 1-1 shows a few key words and phrases that may have negative meanings during a critical conversation. You also see how to turn these phrases into positive ones that can help create an open environment for honest discussion.

TABLE 1-1   **Poor Word Choices and Better Alternatives**

Poor Word Choices	Examples	Why It's a Poor Choice	Better Alternatives
"You should . . ." or "You could . . ."	"You should work harder." "You could do things differently."	The words "should" and "could" may be taken as an order and put the recipient on the defensive. "You should work harder" will derail a conversation faster than the blink of an eye.	"Would you be willing to look at different ways of working?" "Based on this feedback, can we agree on how to create more positive results?"
"You need to . . ."	"You need to change your behavior and listen to me."	Letting someone else know that she needs to do anything may put her on the defensive. Instead of telling someone what she needs to do, focus on talking about why changing is good and focus on the positive.	"Can we look at ways to make a more positive impact with the behavior I mentioned?"
"They" and "them"	"They told me you are a bad presenter." "I heard issues with your presentation style from them."	Using "them" or "they" instead of "us" or "we" can create a competitive environment. Instead, try focusing on what people can achieve together.	"I'd like to share some presentation examples I saw in last week's meeting."
"Horrible" and "bad"	"You have a horrible presentation style." "Your communication skills are bad."	Although someone's behavior may truly be horrible, these negative adjectives tend to create a defensive environment. Instead, try to focus on positive solutions rather than problems. If in doubt, simply drop the negative adjective.	"I want to talk about your presentation style." "Are you willing to discuss your communication skills?"

Cooperative Language: Verbal Communication at Its Finest

Although the goal of some communication may be to excite or shock the audience, the intent of critical conversations is to engage and perhaps educate all parties on how to work together more effectively in the future. Cooperative language is the cornerstone of critical conversations.

The polar opposite of cooperative language is confrontational and argumentative language. When a difference of opinion arises, many people want to win while the other person loses. In some situations and cultures, arguing or using rank to influence is seen as a sign of strength. Critical conversation is not one of these times.

REMEMBER

Don't think that critical conversations will never involve a debate about the best possible solution. Parties will have to discuss (and even debate) during a critical conversation; the tone and words of the debate, however, are most productive when they're cooperative rather than confrontational.

Keeping out confrontational language

When you have a difference of opinion on how to solve a problem or concern, getting caught up in the moment is easy to do. One misinterpretation or difference of opinion can cause someone to lose her cool, causing the conversation to spiral out of control. Just like that, a critical confrontation — rather than a critical conversation — begins.

Confrontational language blocks each party from listening to the other's interests and needs. The focus becomes protecting or standing your ground rather than finding a common and agreeable ground. Confrontational language is often emotionally charged or even defensive, and lets the other parties in the conversation know that you're not there to help build relationships and create something better; you're there to win.

Here's an example of a critical conversation that starts as a simple misunderstanding between two peers about who was responsible for doing a final review of a proposal document before it went to a customer. Notice how one piece of confrontational language can belly flop an entire conversation.

> **Erin:** "Julian, I'm not sure if you knew this, but the final proposal that went to the client didn't include all the answers we had developed. What were you thinking?"
>
> **Julian:** "What do you mean, 'What was I thinking?' I've been at this company 15 years, and in all my life I've never seen such a mess. The lawyers changed the meaning of all our responses in the document. It wasn't my fault. It was their fault. You really need to tone down your attitude and stop accusing me of things."
>
> **Erin:** "Attitude? I don't care how long you've been at this company; if you read the proposal before it went out to the customer, this wouldn't have happened."
>
> **Julian:** "It isn't my job to proofread what the lawyers said."

You can almost feel the negative force escalating in the conversation. Taking a step back, the goal of the conversation is to find out what happened to the document, where the process broke down, and perhaps even solve the problem. All Julian hears was that he was wrong ("What were you thinking?"), and the conversation tumbles downward from the beginning.

Table 1-2 shows you the areas that turn the conversation sour. In this example, you can see two of those confrontational triggers:

TABLE 1-2 **Spotting Confrontational Language (and Turning It Around)**

Confrontational Triggers	Examples	Why It's Confrontational	Better Alternatives
One individual or party thinks she's unconditionally right	"What were you thinking?" "If you read . . ."	Because one individual thinks she's right, that person is unwilling to consider other opinions, ideas, or positions.	"Are you willing to work together and explore other ideas that may work?"
A lot of blame	"What were you thinking?"	Because the individual believes she's right, the only solution is for the other party to agree. This ultimatum leaves little room for finding a common ground in a solution all parties can agree to work with in the future.	"Let's focus on the solution. What can we do to avoid the situation from happening again?"
Attacks	"Fine, talk with my supervisor." "I don't care." "You're wrong."	Confrontational language that's emotionally charged puts people on the defensive and shuts down collaboration, period.	"I want to resolve the issue, but if you do want to talk with my supervisor, I can help you do that." "I may not agree with your actions, but let's talk about how we can create a positive solution."
Absolutes ("always" and "never")	"We always do it this way." "You never show up to work."	Saying something always happens or never happens leaves no room for discussion or interpretation. It is better to state a fact in place of absolutes.	"That's different from how I usually solve this concern." "Based on this week's time report, I noticed that you didn't come into work all week."

» Erin thinks she's right, and she says so by accusing Julian with "What were you thinking?" and "If you read . . ." Erin goes as far as saying, "I don't care." It doesn't matter what comes next — this language immediately signals Julian to give up or get defensive, neither of which is good for a critical conversation. Giving up is one of several defensive reactions.

» Blame starts from the very beginning with Erin saying, "What were you thinking?" which can be interpreted as, "Why did you do this?" This conversation has plenty of blame to go around, and the blame isn't just between Julian and Erin. By the end of this simple conversation, Julian is fed up and starts sharing the blame. The only solution Erin presents is for Julian to recognize that if he had "read the proposal before it went out to the customer, this wouldn't have happened."

Confrontational language can also give the impression that a party's only choice is to fight back, just like Julian starts doing as soon as Erin asks what he was thinking. The principles of physics can be applied to the principles of conversation: For every action there is an equal and opposite reaction. If one person tells another person that he's wrong, the second individual has a choice to either combat one negative with another negative, or to react in an equal but more positive way.

In the previous example, Erin and Julian are going back and forth with negative force in the conversation. The conversation goes in a completely different (and better) direction when Erin starts the discussion like this:

Erin: "Hi, Julian. We just sent out that proposal to the client, and the final version wasn't the same version we created last week. Can we sit down and find out how we can correct it?"

Julian: "Yes. Let's sit down and find out how we can fix it."

Erin may also choose to use an "I" statement, like "The proposal just went to the client, and after it was sent, I noticed it wasn't the same version we created last week. Can we sit down and find out how we can correct it?"

Unless Julian saw Erin rewrite the proposal and press send, blaming her for the error is not only premature, but also does nothing to correct the situation now or in the future. In almost all critical conversations, what's done is done — the parties can't go back in history to redo the events. Create an open and honest environment to help direct the future rather than try to find out who should be blamed.

The good news is that even if one individual begins to use confrontational language, the other individual can respond in an equal but more positive manner. The next section shows how to turn confrontational language into accommodating words that get results.

Turning confrontational words into accommodating words

The goal of critical conversation isn't to win, but to approach a problem as a collaborative effort and seek solutions that are beneficial to all parties involved. Whether you're kicking off the critical conversation or on the receiving end of a potentially confrontational situation, moving from argument to collaboration will create more positive results.

With a little practice, almost any confrontational situation can be flipped into a collaborative and accommodating discussion. The following sections give you some ways to turn confrontational words into more accommodating ones.

Tip #1: Focus on the process and the future, not the person and the past

One pointer for having a collaborative discussion is to focus on the process and the future rather than the person and the past. Here's an example:

> **Argumentative:** "I never received any emails. You must have made a mistake."

> **Accommodating:** "I don't remember receiving the email. If you like, I would be happy to look into the process together and find out what happened and how we can fix it."

What changed and why: In one sentence, you can see three big changes. First, "you made a mistake" turns into presenting an opportunity to work together. Second, instead of accusing a person, the focus of the meeting is on the process and how it can be fixed. Third, rather than accusing the other party of doing anything wrong, the accommodating sentence focuses on the future and how to prevent the problem from happening again.

Tip #2: Lead with fact and options

Starting with facts can get a conversation off on the right foot (see the earlier section "Facts, opinions, and gossip" for more information). Here's an example:

> **Argumentative:** "You have to change your behavior."

> **Accommodating:** "Emotions were high last week in the office. I noticed that the yelling in the office made team members withdraw and stop sharing their ideas on the customer meeting."

What changed and why: Keep in mind that no one needs to do anything during a critical conversation, so telling someone that she has to change anything, especially her behavior, could easily be met with hostility. Instead, state the facts and their impact from an objective point of view. It can also be helpful to turn possibly harsh statements into questions. Genuine questions help gather more information and open a dialogue, which is perfect for a critical conversation.

WARNING

When using questions to turn possibly hostile conversations into cooperative ones, be careful not to start the Spanish Inquisition. Come to the conversation with a genuine desire to make things better, not to sarcastically or critically accuse someone. A comment isn't necessarily cooperative just because you add a question mark to the end.

Tip #3: Things are always possible, even if they aren't probable

Avoid absolutes to encourage an accommodating conversation. Here's an example:

> **Argumentative:** "That's just not possible."

> **Accommodating:** "That's different from how we usually solve problems. Are you willing to look at other alternative solutions?"

What changed and why: Using the words "never" or "not possible" immediately closes the discussion and limits the number of solutions that are possible.

Using five key phrases that get results

No one has a magic wand to make all critical conversations go perfectly, but you can draw on key phases to get the discussion going in the right direction and redirect the discussion if it gets off track.

Using the five key phrases in the following sections when they're appropriate lets the other parties know you want to help make the situation better. Although all these phrases (and all the tactics in this chapter) need to come from a genuine desire to help, using them signals to the other parties that you want to create a critical dialogue to solve the issue instead of giving a one-way lecture on what needs to change.

Why don't we work together to solve . . .

In the heat of a debate or emotional discussion, having at least one common goal helps the conversation move forward. "Why don't we work together on . . ." gives the other individual an opportunity to have some control in the discussion. She can control whether or not she's there, and she can have a voice in the conversation. This phrase is also helpful to go back to as common ground if the conversation gets off track. For example, you may say, "It seems like we may have gotten off track. In the beginning of the conversation we agreed to work together to solve the problem. Can we keep doing that?"

It's difficult to . . .

When providing critical information during a conversation that may not be well received, you'll probably feel stressed. Opening up can help set a genuine tone that you're there to help. This openness can neutralize confrontational individuals so you can move toward talking about the real issues. As the initiator of the conversation, you may begin with, "It's difficult to deliver bad news to a great employee, and this situation is no different."

WARNING

Don't use this phrase if you don't genuinely feel the situation is hard. For example, if your job is to fire people, saying "It's hard to fire you" could be seen as insincere. If it's true, you can say, "I'm in a position to deliver tough news more often than others, but that doesn't make the situation any easier. I can understand how you may be feeling."

The receiver of the information may also use this tactic. "It's hard to hear this information. I'm feeling a bit overwhelmed with the information you provided. Do you mind if we walk through that example again?"

Were you aware . . .

Asking another individual whether she was aware of behavior, rules, or policies is one of the most underutilized tools during a critical conversation — and in communication in general. At times, information may just go unnoticed. A person may really not be aware of the impact a behavior has on the team. A customer may not be aware of a policy. "Awareness" is a safe word that helps the other party to save face, and it provides a great opportunity to give critical information or education.

REMEMBER

A critical conversation should open the doors of communication and create an honest environment for discussion. If one individual feels that she lost the discussion and the other person won, or if any party feels embarrassed, the safe environment of conversation can quickly deteriorate.

WARNING

Don't phrase this statement as "Did you know . . ." Meeting space tends to be ego space, and asking "Did you know . . ." can be interpreted as the other individual not having the intelligence or ability.

That is different from . . .

Saying "That is different from the way other situations have been solved" is a great and positive alternative to saying that something will never happen or isn't possible. Using the phrase "that is different" doesn't accuse or blame; it simply states a fact. Suppose a customer is complaining on the phone and demanding more than a customer has received in the past. Rather than saying that what the customer wants is impossible, simply say, "That is different from the way we usually work through problems." The information the customer gave has been acknowledged, and the customer service representative has refocused the conversation on the solution. Maybe you have a magic wand for making critical conversation productive after all!

REMEMBER

If someone is outright lying about a situation, make sure you focus on the ethical issue at hand. Chapter 4 in Book 2 covers dealing with ethical issues in more detail and addresses how a mediator may help in tricky situations.

How might [problems] be solved?

Keeping the conversation focused on the future keeps the discussion positive. This phrase is especially useful when a conversation is focusing on excuses or things that have happened in the past that can't be changed. Although looking at facts is important for making critical conversations successful, the goal of a critical conversation is to change behavior — not just to present information. This phrase also takes the burden off the initiator of the conversation. One person doesn't need to have all the solutions to every problem, so asking for other alternatives is a good way to get buy-in and agreement on what will happen after the conversation ends.

Chapter **2**

Grasping Nonverbal Cues

onverbal cues during conversations include everything from body language to the use of space, and from moments of silence to eye contact. Nonverbal cues can be defined as broadly as almost anything that's not verbally communicated, and they can be interpreted in just as many ways.

This chapter introduces nonverbal techniques that speak volumes during a critical work conversation. It then walks you through the process of active listening and gives you examples to make sure you can really hear the concerns in the room. This chapter gives many examples of how to become more aware of the way nonverbal cues are perceived and how they can help (or hinder!) a critical conversation. (For even more information devoted specifically to body language, check out Book 1, Chapter 3.)

Noting Nonverbal Techniques that Speak Volumes

Nonverbal techniques in communication encompass everything from how you sit or stand, your facial expressions, eye contact, nerves and stress, dress and appearance, and even voice quality. Nonverbal cues often reflect emotions and may be unconscious and unintentional. For example, blushing often means embarrassment, and clearing the throat or a cracking voice can mean nervousness. Even the most positive critical conversation needs the right unspoken communication methods to make sure the message is delivered appropriately and understood.

The following is an example that uses just a few of the nonverbal elements that can influence a conversation:

Sally is moving an employee into a new position after the employee did not get a promotion. If you were the employee, which conversation, noted in Table 2-1, would make you more likely to want to accept the offer?

TABLE 2-1   ### Considering Nonverbal Elements in Conversation

Conversation Element	Conversation One	Conversation Two
What is said	"Jim, I know you've wanted the manager position. I have another opportunity I would like you to consider . . ."	"Jim, I know you've wanted the manager position. I have another opportunity I would like you to consider . . ."
Body language	Sally's arms and legs are crossed, or her hands are tightly clasped.	Sally is sitting at a round table, both feet on the ground, shoulders relaxed.
Eye contact	Sally switches from looking at Jim to looking at her phone every five to ten seconds.	Sally is leaning in slightly, looking at Jim as he talks.
Dress and appearance	Sally just got back from the gym over lunch hour and is running late.	Sally is poised and dressed in work clothes.

Even though the words are exactly the same in conversations one and two, you may think that the Sally in conversation one is just too busy to care about an employee and simply wants to fill a role in the organization. Conversation two, on the other hand, has more sincere nonverbal cues and genuine interest. In conversation two, it seems like Sally really cares about the conversation — the key ingredient of critical conversations! What you don't say is just as important as what you do.

Expressions that count

A key to unlocking the nonverbal cues treasure chest is to be mindful of how you're expressing your message. Pay attention to facial expressions, the way you display nerves and stress, and voice quality. The upcoming sections help you master these nonverbal languages. Table 2-2 is a handy guide on effective nonverbal expressions during a critical conversation.

TABLE 2-2   Comparing Effective and Ineffective Nonverbal Expressions

Nonverbal Expression	Supportive and Positive	Unsupportive and Negative
Body language (lower body)	Feet on ground, ankles crossed slightly	Legs crossed
Body language (upper body)	Sitting up straight, relaxed shoulders, arms on the table — ideally at waist height	Slouched shoulders, hands in front of mouth, leaning against a wall, waving arms around, pointing fingers
Eye contact	Looking at the other individual or individuals as they talk; concentrating on their voice, movement, and eyes	Staring at the other individuals or never looking at their eyes during the conversation
Dress and appearance	Dressing appropriately; holding the conversation in a clutter-free zone	Rushing from one meeting to the next; papers everywhere; being flustered; food on face or clothes (this really does happen!); wearing outdoor gear when you're inside (rain jacket, wool coat, hat, gloves)
Facial expressions	Smiling appropriately	Raising eyebrows, smirking, grimacing, resting or putting your head in your hands
Voice quality	Steady and clear, may be a bit slower than your usual conversation speed but not exaggeratedly slow	High, fast, too soft, too slow; using *um, ah, you know*, and *like*
Nerves and stress	Taking a deep breath and being aware of sudden changes in body language or nervous habits	Tightly crossing hands; toes/hands tapping; legs shaking; pacing the room; spinning pens or pencils between your fingers; jingling loose change in your pocket; vocal sighs, *hmmms*, and throat-clearing

WARNING

Most of the body language techniques in Table 2-2 are common in some Western cultures, but be careful not to make assumptions about the meaning of non-verbal cues in all geographic or organizational cultures. Nodding a head in one culture may mean agreement, while in another culture it may simply mean that you're being heard. *Cross-Cultural Selling For Dummies*, by Michael Soon Lee, Ralph R. Roberts, and Joe Kraynak (John Wiley & Sons, Inc.), can help with ideas on how to adapt your message and get a crash course in building multicultural rapport.

TIP

With so many expressions to be attentive of, becoming overwhelmed is easy to do. But nonverbal expressions don't need to be overwhelming if you find ways to become aware of them. Improving nonverbal techniques takes practice. Try this exercise during a non–critical conversation, such as a relaxed talk with a col-league. Notice how you sit; what you do with your hands, arms, and legs; how you physically change when the other person is talking; and how often you look away to check what's outside the window or who's texting you on the phone. Although few communicators are ever perfect at all these expressions, little changes can make a big difference during a conversation.

TIP

Bring a light jacket or sweater to a critical conversation! No, your mother isn't writing this book. But crossing your arms can signal a number of reactions: being uninterested in the conversation, disdain for the topic or person, or anxiousness. Crossed arms can also just mean that you're trying to stay warm in an air-conditioned meeting room. Be sure not to cross signals, and if you happen to get cold quickly, keep a light jacket or sweater on hand. Sounds simple and perhaps silly, but it will be one less thing you need to be aware of during a conversation — and that's significant.

Keep your body relaxed, but don't be a slouch

Think back to your primary school teacher and sit straight and confident, but don't be tense. Crossing your arms can give the impression that you're guarding some piece of information. Remain open to giving and receiving information during the conversation by sitting straight, either with both feet on the floor or your ankles crossed, and keeping your arms open and shoulders down.

IMITATION IS THE BEST FORM OF FLATTERY

A good way to increase the comfort level of the other party is to focus on your own nonverbal cues when you're listening to and delivering a message. People not only listen to you during a critical conversation, but also watch you and can even start mirroring your behavior. If you have your hands relaxed on the desk and are listening intently, the other individual may begin to do the same thing. This imitation often is unconscious, so try not to force the issue by overemphasizing the behavior you want the other individual to imitate. For example, if you want the other person to slow down the pace, slow down your own pace slightly, but don't go into extreme slow motion. If you do, the other person may focus on the pace of the conversation rather than the conversation itself. As with all nonverbal techniques, moderation is the key.

Mirroring positive nonverbal communication from the other party can also relax everyone in the conversation. For example, if the other party is gently leaning toward you (often a sign of interest), you may want to lean your head toward the other party as well. If you see the other party backing away, you may tone down your own arm or body movements and perhaps even take a step back to show respect for the other individual's desire for space.

Maintain appropriate eye contact

Being in a deadlock stare with another individual during a conversation can be intimidating or downright creepy. Look at the other person's eyes and mouth throughout the conversation, but move your eyes every three to five seconds to avoid making the conversation feel like a police investigation rather than a critical conversation. Sometimes gently nodding helps to maintain the appropriate level of eye contact as well — but be sure to keep it in moderation. Nodding is good; being a bobble-head doll is annoying.

TIP

When you create eye contact, you aren't just doing it because this book told you to. Eye contact helps you look for signals like fidgeting (the other person is nervous), darting glares (an individual may be getting defensive), and glancing at the clock (the person is distracted). All these signals indicate that you may need to make an adjustment in the conversation.

Use genuine facial expressions

Even during tough conversations, relaxing is okay. A gentle smile and leaning your head in slightly can help put the other person at ease. When you make an agreement during the conversation, a smile can be appropriate to show a sincere appreciation for the way the conversation is progressing. Be sure not to touch your face or lay your head in your hands in a show of frustration or desperation — both are distracting and can indicate that you're nervous.

Keep dress and appearance professional

You don't need to go out and buy a nice suit, but tuck in your shirt, don't leave old coffee cups out on the table, and have enough empty space to avoid distractions. When your outward appearance and the location for the conversation are professional, the recipient of the conversation knows that you're taking the matter seriously. As simple as it may sound, looking in the mirror before having a critical conversation may help catch a piece of food between your teeth. Limit visual distractions from a critical conversation.

Acknowledge and control nerves

Every critical conversation comes with some nerves and stress. If appropriate, acknowledge these reactions verbally, and then control them physically. For example, if you find your voice cracking and your hands shaking, simply say, "I'm a little nervous about this conversation," and then move on. Make sure your shoulders stay relaxed, keep your hands unclenched, and try not to shake your legs or tap your fingers. If you tend to talk with your hands, don't change your body language to look like Frankenstein's monster. Instead, use moderate gestures or even point to a part in the notes you may be taking.

TIP

You have some nonverbal options, as a facilitator, to alleviate the stress and manage high stakes and high emotions during a critical conversation:

>> **Support the discussion.** Acknowledge that all parties in the room are critical to the success of the discussion. Let the other person know that you need her to be involved verbally by saying that she's part of the discussion, not just the recipient of the discussion. Then back up your words with nonverbal cues like sitting around an open, round table rather than behind a desk or try uncrossing your arms as the discussion occurs.

>> **Provide gentle relief.** An executive doesn't have to be a comedian, but if a little humor fits the situation, it can help all the parties let off some steam. For example, if you realize there is more tension in the room than you expected, you may say something like, "I feel the tension in the room may be growing, not decreasing. We don't have a massage therapist in the room, so are there other ideas on how to relieve this tension?" Don't go for slapstick comedy, but humility and honesty can do wonders to bring relief to a stressful situation. If humor isn't a forte (or if humor starts hiding the seriousness of the conversation), a simple smile and nod of the head can also add relief to the room.

Know how your voice sounds

Vocal quality is a lot more than the words you choose during a conversation. Watch out for extremes in volume, pace, pitch, and diction. You don't need a speech coach, but nervous tension can tighten your body and vocal cords, so remember to breathe and take time for the conversation instead of being rushed through it. These techniques help in the overall presentation of the critical message. Finish one statement before starting another, and leave plenty of time between the two, especially when emotions and nerves are high.

REMEMBER

The way you use your voice dictates how recipients listen to the message: a fast delivery can make individuals nervous or overly stimulated, while a delivery that's too slow may seem a bit dramatic and controlled.

Use of voice

Your voice can work wonders in creating a safe and productive environment for the conversation. It's important to plan and prepare for a conversation, but the use of voice sets the tone (literally) of the meeting. Tone can either build rapport and trust, or put up an iron curtain.

Using the right style and tone of voice is directly related to how the receiver perceives your point of view on the conversation. Open, enthusiastic, and patient use of voice leads to trust and collaboration. And you probably don't need to be reminded of what pessimism, sarcasm, and a rushed tone do to the conversation! The following sections give you a look at how tone can influence the conversation.

TIP

One cue can help turn around almost any professional critical conversation: keeping a genuine, positive attitude. A genuine desire to help the situation not only drives the tone of the conversation but also makes a big difference in body language and other nonverbal cues. And it goes both ways. Smiling and listening to other people creates sincerity.

Friendly and open

Is your voice friendly and open? You don't have to be best friends with the other parties in the conversation, but if you offer information, the recipient is more likely to offer information back to you. This openness establishes a constructive dialogue.

Even in black and white, you can hear the use of voice in these examples:

> **Good use of tone:** "I understand there is a difference of opinion on the team, and the goal of the conversation is to find a solution we can all live with and work toward."

> **Questionable use of tone:** "There is a difference of opinion and we need to solve it."

Appropriately enthusiastic

Simply having a genuine desire to help change the situation creates a positive environment with the appropriate level of enthusiasm needed for the discussion. If you are watching every minute tick by during the conversation or thinking that you would much rather be playing a game on your phone, your interest for the topic at hand is probably fairly low. On the other hand, if you genuinely are interested in working with the other parties, all the parties involved will see and hear that you care and they will be more inclined to mirror your positive behavior. You don't have to be a cheerleader or oddly excited to be enthusiastic.

Here are a few examples of what the right level of enthusiasm could sound like:

> **Overenthusiastic:** You can imagine the reaction to a chipper boss saying, "Hey everyone, I asked you to come to this meeting to let you know your paychecks are cut in half! Yeah! Sis-boom-bah!"

> **Underenthusiastic:** On the other hand, having a critical conversation at 5 p.m. on a Friday after a long week of deadlines may not be the best time. "Thanks for working so hard this week. I'm so exhausted from the week too (yawn). Your paychecks are cut," won't go over well either.

Appropriately enthusiastic: A better use of voice (and choice of words) may be, "I know everyone has been putting in long days during the recession to keep our company in business. It's hard to let you know this, but even with the extra work, we need to make pay cuts. I'd like to walk through the details to answer the many questions you may have right now."

Patient and calm

Perhaps the easiest use of voice to control is making your voice patient and calm. Because many critical conversations deliver a message that could lead to disagreement or focus on a difficult topic, try to slow down your words and not rush the recipients. Being rushed can make people nervous. Rushed conversations can also be seen as blunt or tactless.

TIP

The easiest way to slow down the conversation — especially if you're prone to speaking and acting fast — is to be clear and leave enough time for discussion. Don't schedule back-to-back meetings, and don't hold the meeting right before lunch hour or at 5 p.m. If you find yourself rushing through a conversation, take a breath or take a break. Taking a break to slow down doesn't mean going out for a coffee or taking a walk. Simply allow the other party to speak. For example, "Let me take a break and let you do some of the talking. Can you tell me any more about how the meeting went with our customer?" Although these may seem like minor details, they can make a big difference.

Silence is golden, space is priceless

Two other nonverbal techniques can keep a critical conversation on target for success. The first is silence and the second is space.

Giving pause for silence

Listening is very important in a critical conversation, but listening and silence are two different things. Silence does one thing that no other verbal or nonverbal technique can do: It gives everyone time to process information and to think.

Silence doesn't need to be long, and if it is, it may seem unnatural. Use silence between thoughts, before responding to a question, or when you feel yourself getting impatient or nervous. You need only three seconds to take a breath, allow words to sink in, and clearly think about what to do next.

Making good use of space

Look around you and notice how the space is being used during the conversation — both the physical space of the room and the space around your body. Try to keep the space suitable for the conversation. If the conversation is happening between two groups, don't try to cram everyone into the only tiny conference room available. A circular table immediately conveys inclusion, while a boardroom table can signal intimidation. When looking at how you use the space around you, try to lean in to the conversation, but don't tumble over. Leaning in signals interest, leaning back signals indifference, and leaning in too far can feel like intimidation.

Also consider where you sit or stand during the conversation. Standing too close to someone can cut into her personal space, but having a critical conversation from across the room becomes a critical yelling match. Bottom line with the use of space: Use moderation and practice what's comfortable.

Nonverbal no-no's

It's nice to think that although critical conversations may be stressful, they will at least be professional. Unfortunately, not everyone thinks this way or acts this way. Emotions can be expressed by words, but they're often first exhibited through nonverbal cues.

REMEMBER

If you find yourself making the following nonverbal mistakes, or if you're the recipient of them, stop the conversation immediately and either redirect it or call in a mediator (see Chapter 4 in Book 2):

>> **Disrespect:** Rolling eyes, smirking, interrupting, and audible sighs are not only annoying but also disrespectful. Come to the conversation with a genuine desire to help make the situation better, and this type of disrespect for the other party in the conversation quickly disappears.

>> **Anger and hostility:** Nonverbal examples of these emotions include pounding on a desk or table or hitting a wall. Critical conversations aren't always pleasant, but violence and anger should never be part of the discussion.

>> **Intimidation:** Waving a finger in someone's face is one of the more subtle examples of nonverbal intimidation. Also, if you see someone getting up close and personal, it signals that she may be trying to bully the conversation.

>> **Destruction:** Throwing things or ripping paper or other property is a not-so-subtle signal that tells you to redirect the conversation, most likely with a mediator involved.

TIP

Balancing focus and flexibility when you're faced with resistance is the name of the game. If you tell someone who's already being difficult that she has to do something or act a certain way, 999 times out of 1,000, she'll put her feet on the ground and do exactly the opposite. But just letting the meeting go astray isn't a good option either. Think of focus and flexibility as the out-of-bounds line in a soccer match. Players, as long as they follow some general rules, have a lot of flexibility to move one way or the other as long as they stay inbounds. In a critical conversation, make those boundaries clear and then let the other parties know where they have flexibility in the discussion. Here are two easy ways to show flexibility with boundaries:

>> **State what is and isn't acceptable.** Being flexible doesn't mean you need to let someone walk all over you. If someone's behavior is unacceptable — like abusive language — you may say, "I ask that you treat me as a professional and stop using abusive language. I want to work with you, and I'm flexible with how we proceed, but first we need to both talk to one another with respect."

>> **Set ground rules.** If you think boundaries may need to be established during a conversation, set them now, and show flexibility when you set these rules. Before the conversation even starts, you may want to say, "I want to propose some ground rules for our conversation, but I would like to first ask if you have any ground rules you want us to both follow." Some ground rules may be agreeing to stick with an agenda, speaking the truth, staying on time, or using a professional tone throughout the conversation.

Becoming an Expert in Active Listening

When people say they have trouble communicating, they often mean that they're having trouble understanding the other person's perspective or opinion. The best way to understand what the other person is saying is to actively pay attention to the speaker's verbal words and nonverbal cues. Doing so is called *active listening*. As an active listener, you use nonverbal cues to show your interest and understanding when the other party is talking.

You'll discover a few differences between listening and active listening. Take a look at Table 2-3 for an explanation.

TABLE 2-3

Listening versus Active Listening

Listening	Active Listening
To determine whether or not you agree with the other person's point of view: When you're listening, you may begin judging the value of the other party's statements before she has a chance to finish saying what she's saying.	**To understand the other person's point of view:** Hold back forming an opinion until the individual is done talking. If someone is nervous, her first words may not be perfectly stated. Often the real meaning comes out in the second half of a statement. Actively listen so you can hear everything being said — not just selective words.
To decide what to say next: When someone else is talking, you may be thinking about your next statement rather than listening to what the other person has to say.	**To hear what the other individual has to say, and then respond to her statement:** Active listening slows down the pace of the conversation, engages the other person in a discussion of what to do next, and eliminates the other individual thinking "Did that person not listen to a word I said?"
To decide what to say and when to say something based only on the words being said: Often this kind of listening happens during phone calls because nonverbal cues aren't available.	**To deal with the topic at hand by taking into account verbal and nonverbal cues:** Active listening gives you feedback on how the message is being received. For example, if the speaker is saying, "I totally agree with you," but her body language is closed and he's looking at the clock, she may just be saying he agrees to try to end the conversation as quickly as possible.

Grasping Nonverbal Cues

REMEMBER

Because active listening can also help a leader decide how to move a discussion forward, it's a good skill to have during a critical conversation.

Use the active listening process to clarify ambivalence to an issue. Actively listen to what someone *doesn't* say, as well as to what she does say. Active listening involves three steps:

1. **Engage in active silence while the other individual is talking.**

2. **Reflect before responding.**

3. **Ask to confirm that you received the right message.**

REMEMBER

Active listening ends when the listener becomes the speaker. After the listen-reflect-clarify cycle is completed, respond to the message. The cycle of active listening may have multiple repetitions. Note that this repetition is normal and valuable to the conversation. Spending more time clarifying words, emotions, and intentions up-front is better than making assumptions and stalling the conversation later.

Practicing active silence

During active listening, one party is speaking and the other is using active silence to understand what the first individual is trying to communicate. Although you need a lot of practice to be an expert in silence, the first step is to simply be present. Here are some additional hints:

>> Try to maintain eye contact and an engaged posture.

>> Look at the other party, lean in slightly, and focus on what the other party is saying.

>> Try to use only small gestures that are appropriate for the conversation.

>> Keep hands and arms at waist height and try to control any nervous activity (see the earlier section "Expressions that count" for more details).

>> Make sure the environment is conducive to engaged silence. Having a critical conversation in a loud coffee house or in a meeting room with large glass windows is just begging for distraction.

These nonverbal techniques will help create an interested silence that helps you listen for content and emotions. You may detect a difference in what's being said and the emotions being felt. If the other party is nodding her head in agreement and saying, "Yes, I understand," but tears are building up in her eyes or her face is turning red with either anger or embarrassment, her emotions and words aren't the same. Use the verbal questioning techniques from Book 1, Chapter 1 to find out what the individual is really thinking before moving on with the conversation.

Active silence isn't easy, and the numbers prove it. People can talk at a rate of 120 or more words per minute, but most individuals can comprehend about 300 to 400 words per minute. When you listen to someone speak, you're using only part of your brain's capability, which makes it easy to tune out and think of other things. Really focusing on 120 words per minute takes a good amount of mental effort. Use the extra processing space in the brain to pay attention to intent and emotions. You can clarify the intent later in the active listening process, but often, the intent and emotions clarify the message more than the content of the message does.

Reflecting before responding

For some people, silence isn't comfortable. Many people think that silence shows weakness or ignorance. During active listening, you need some time for silence so that you can reflect on what was said. If the listening party is paying attention to what's being said by being present (not thinking about what to say next), silence is the necessary processing time to reflect on what to do or say next. A bit of natural silence helps to keep the conversation at a steady but unhurried pace. The time doesn't need to be uncomfortably long; you can imagine how odd the conversation would be if a speaker took 30-second pauses after every sentence.

Reflection also ensures that the speaker can finish her thoughts. Jumping in to respond may interrupt the speaker in the middle of a thought, intentionally or unintentionally.

Asking to clarify what you heard

After you really listen and take time to reflect on the information, clarify what you heard. The goal of clarifying questions is to confirm that the message, intent, and emotions you heard and noticed were the message the speaker intended to convey. You have a few ways to clarify information:

>> **Paraphrase, don't parrot:** Repeating the speaker's exact words is annoying to most people. Instead, rephrase the statement by using your own words.

Suppose Sam comes to you (his manager) and says, "I'm feeling really upset about this layoff."

Don't say: "So, Sam, what I heard is you are feeling really upset about this layoff?" *(Polly wants a cracker! Squawk, squawk.)*

Do say: "Sam, it's natural to feel upset about this process. I'm going to do everything I can to help."

>> **Perception check:** Having biases and opinions is only human, but those biases and opinions often lead you to jump to conclusions, especially if a critical conversation is long overdue. As hard as it may seem, suspend judgment for the conversation and use reflection, hearing the other party out. When clarifying perceptions, don't blame or accuse. Instead, simply state what you observe.

Don't say: "It's obvious you're disappointed."

Do say: "It sounds like you're disappointed."

>> **Open-ended question:** Use open-ended questions to clarify the message, intent, or emotions so that you don't jump to conclusions (see the previous bullet). You can also use open-ended questions to probe for more information when the message is unclear.

Don't say: "It seems like you're not open to any of my ideas to improve the team's performance."

Do say: "What ideas do you have to improve the team's performance?"

TIP Try to keep the clarifying statements and questions in manageable chunks of one or two sentences. Anything more makes it difficult for the other party to adequately reflect when he's bombarded with questions and statements.

ASSESSING OTHERS' UNSPOKEN CUES THROUGH ACTIVE LISTENING

Nonverbal communication isn't just about the speaker's behavior. Being aware of how the other party is responding, both verbally and nonverbally, provides insight into how your message is being received. Don't jump to conclusions, however, when you're looking at nonverbal cues. Active listening helps you assess how the other party is receiving the message and her emotional reaction to the message.

When assessing nonverbal communication, keep in mind the situational context and how behavior changes during the conversation.

- **Situational context:** Thinking that someone will start jumping for joy when you give him bad news is unreasonable. Some nonverbal cues can be expected during a conversation, but keep the environment and the situation in mind. Feet tapping on the ground may just show expected nervousness, but feet tapping, legs swinging, and fingers tapping probably mean that you need to address an emotional side of the issue before moving forward.

- **Changes over the course of the conversation:** One nonverbal communication assessment technique that leaves little to interpretation is how behavior changes over the course of the conversation. Is the person open and smiling when he walks in and then quickly becomes upset and irrational after hearing the message? This change probably indicates that her emotions are high. Is the person agitated from the beginning? This behavior may be fueled by the conversation, but it could also mean that he's simply having a bad day.

Chapter 3

Defining Body Language

I n the big scheme of things, the scientific study of body language is a fairly recent phenomenon, with documented research covering only the last 80 years or so. In order to better understand the thoughts and emotions behind human behavior, psychologists, zoologists, and social anthropologists have conducted detailed investigations into the use and components of body language — part of the larger family known as nonverbal behavior (introduced in Book 1, Chapter 2).

When you take the time to focus on your own and others' physical movements and expressions at work, you can spot and interpret unspoken thoughts, feelings, and intentions that reveal more about a person than that individual may want you to know. You can even identify some people by a particular gesture or expression such as pursed lips, swaying hips, fiddling fingers, or an arched brow.

By observing people's body language you can detect their inner state. Are they despondent, in turmoil, or feeling cool, calm, and collected? Through a twitch of the mouth, flare of a nostril, or change of posture, people unconsciously reveal their thoughts, intentions, and feelings. In this chapter, you begin discovering how to interpret nonverbal body language, and you explore the gestures and actions that reveal attitudes, thoughts, and intentions. In addition, you find out how you can use gestures to enhance your relationships and improve your communications at work and beyond.

Discovering How Body Language Conveys Messages

When cave dwellers discovered how to decipher grunts and to create words to convey their messages, their lives became a lot more complex. Before verbal communication, they relied on their bodies to communicate. Their simple brains informed their faces, torsos, and limbs. They instinctively knew that fear, surprise, love, hunger, and annoyance were different attitudes requiring different movements and facial expressions. Emotions were less complex then, and so were gestures.

Speech is a relatively new introduction to the communication process and is used to persuade and influence others and to convey information, including facts and data. Body language, on the other hand, has been around forever. Without relying on the spoken word for confirmation, the body's movements also persuade and influence others by conveying feelings, thoughts, and intentions. Like it or not, your body speaks through signs and signals.

According to research conducted by Professor Albert Mehrabian at the University of California, Los Angeles, 55 percent of the message in face-to-face communication is relayed through body language when the message contains emotional content. You only have to experience any of the following gestures or expressions to know how true is the adage "Actions speak louder than words":

>> Someone raising her fist to you

>> A warm embrace

>> A finger wagging in your face

>> A pout

>> A frown

>> A parent's look of worry

>> An exuberant smile

>> Your hand placed over your heart

Creating an impression within moments

You can tell within the first seven seconds of meeting someone how she feels about herself by the expression on her face and the way she moves her body. Whether she knows it or not, she's transmitting messages through her gestures and actions.

EARLY OBSERVATIONS ABOUT BODY LANGUAGE

Before the 20th century, only a few forays were made into identifying and analyzing movement and gesture. The first known work exclusively addressing body language is John Bulwer's *Chirologia: or the Natural Language of the Hand,* published in 1644. By the 19th century, directors and teachers of drama and pantomime were instructing their actors and students how to convey emotion and attitude through movement and gesture.

In *The Expression of the Emotions in Man and Animals* (1872), Charles Darwin explores the connection between humans, apes, and monkeys. These species use similar facial expressions, inherited from a common ancestor, to express specific emotions. Out of Darwin's work grew an interest in *ethology* — the study of animal behavior.

In the late 1960s, Desmond Morris created a sensation when his interpretations of human behavior, based on ethological research, were published in *The Naked Ape* and *Manwatching.* Further publications and media presentations continue to reveal how much our nonverbal behavior is based on human animal nature.

You walk into a room of strangers and, from their stance, movements, and expressions, you receive messages about their feelings, moods, thoughts, and intentions. Look at the man standing in the corner. From his slouching shoulders, his lowered head, and the way his hands fidget over his stomach, you can tell that he isn't a happy camper.

A young woman in this room of strangers is standing amongst a group of contemporaries. Her eyes twinkle, she throws back her head as she laughs, her hands and arms move with ease and openness, and her weight is evenly distributed between her feet, which are placed beneath her, hip width apart. This woman is projecting an image of self-confidence and joie de vivre that draws people to her.

Like it or not, how you position your head, shoulders, torso, arms, hands, legs, and feet, and how your eyes, mouth, fingers, and toes move, tell an observer more about your state of being than any words you can say.

Transmitting messages unconsciously

In addition to your ability to consciously choose precise gestures and actions to convey a particular message, your body sends out signals without your awareness. Dilated or contracted pupils and the unconscious movements of your hands and feet indicate an inner emotion that you may want to conceal. For example, if you notice that the pupils of someone's eyes are dilated, and you know that she's not under the influence of drugs, you'd be correct in assuming that whatever she's looking at is giving her pleasure. If the pupils are contracted, the opposite is true.

WARNING

Even though body language speaks volumes, be careful when ascribing feelings and attitudes based solely on nonverbal behavior. Individual signals can be easily overlooked or misidentified if they're taken out of their social context. Look for clusters of gestures and expressions that involve several parts of the body. Also observe breathing patterns to gauge someone's internal state. At times, you may want to conceal your thoughts and feelings, so you behave in a way that you believe hides your true emotions. And then, wouldn't you know it, out pops a giveaway gesture, barely perceptible to the untrained eye, sending a signal that all's not what it appears. Don't kid yourself that no one notices. Just because these micro-gestures and -expressions are fleeting doesn't mean that they don't send powerful messages.

TECHNICAL STUFF

In the 1970s, Paul Ekman and Wallace V. Friesen developed the Facial Action Coding System (FACS) to measure, describe, and interpret facial behaviors. This instrument is designed to gauge even the slightest facial muscle contractions and determine what category or categories each facial action fits into. It detects what the naked eye can't and is used by the police, film animators, and researchers of human behavior.

According to research conducted by Professor Mehrabian, when people are discussing feelings and emotions in a face-to-face setting and an incongruity exists between the words themselves and the way you deliver them, 7 percent of the message received is conveyed through your words, 38 percent is revealed through your vocal quality, and a whopping 55 percent of your message is expressed through your gestures, expression, and posture. Mehrabian's premise is that your nonverbal behaviors are directly tied to your feelings, whether you're conscious of the connection or not. Although skeptics contest Mehrabian's figures, the point remains that body language and vocal quality significantly contribute to the meaning of the message.

Here's an example from the workplace: Gunther is the CFO of a global corporation and is a charming, successful, and popular man. In addition, he is used to getting what he wants, when he wants it. You know the time has come to hurry up when Gunther points his index finger in your direction, raises his chin, lifts his eyebrows, and barks out a rapid-fire command, even if he has a smile on his face.

Substituting gestures for the spoken word

Sometimes a gesture is more effective in conveying a message than any words you can say. Signals expressing love and support, pleasure and pain, fear, loathing, and disappointment are clear to decipher and require few, if any, words for clarification. Approval, complicity, or insults are commonly communicated without a sound passing between lips. When you frown, smile, or sneer you don't need words to clarify your meaning.

When words aren't enough or the word mustn't be spoken out loud, you can gesture to convey your meaning. For example:

>> Putting your index finger in front of your mouth while at the same time pursing your lips is a common signal for silence.

>> Putting your hand up sharply with your fingers held tightly together and your palm facing forward means "Stop!"

Here's an example of gestures in action at work: Nick and Holly were involved in a tough business negotiation. At one point during the meeting, Nick started to give away too much information. Holly calmly placed her index finger over her lips while resting her chin on her thumb. This was a sign to Nick for him to listen more and talk less.

Gesturing to illustrate what you're saying

When you describe an object, you frequently use gestures to illustrate what the object is like. Your listener finds it easier to understand what you're saying when your body creates a picture of the object rather than relying on words alone. For example:

>> If you're describing a round object, like a ball, you may hold your hands in front of yourself with your fingers arched upward and your thumbs pointing down.

>> When describing a square building, you may draw vertical and horizontal lines with a flat hand, cutting through the space like a knife.

>> If you're telling someone about a turbulent ride on a boat or plane, your arms and hands may beat up and down in rhythmic fashion.

>> You may hold your arms out wide when describing a large object and hold your fingers close together when you're illustrating a small point.

The point is that gesturing is a practical way to convey visual information.

TIP

Because some people are more comfortable processing information through the visual channel, illustrate your messages through gestures. Doing so helps create a clear picture and adds energy to your voice.

Physically supporting the spoken word

Appropriate gestures add emphasis to your voice, clarify your meaning, and give impact to your message. Whether you're sending out signals of interest or signs of disgust, when your body movements reflect your emotions you help your listener understand how you're feeling.

In addition to reinforcing your message, specific hand signals reflect your desire to communicate clearly. Watch well-schooled politicians standing at the podium. See how their hands move in a precise, controlled manner — no wasted gestures, just those specific ones that tell the tale they want you to believe.

TIP

When you're making a formal presentation, use illustrative gestures to help your audience remember the points you're making. During the introduction to your presentation, as you establish the points to be covered, list them separately on your fingers. You may hold your fingers up in front of you or touch them individually on one hand with a finger from your other hand as you say the point. When talking about point one in your presentation, point to the first finger, or gesture to it; when you reach point two, point or gesture to your second finger, and so on. This technique helps both you and your listener focus on the subject and stay on track. (*Note:* Many American and British people begin counting with their index finger. Many Europeans begin counting with their thumb.)

Experienced lawyers, celebrities, and anyone else who takes their public persona seriously strive to emphasize their messages through considered movements, gestures, and facial expressions. By carefully timing, focusing, and controlling their actions, they court the people they want by using open, welcoming gestures and dismiss others with a flick of the wrist.

Revealing feelings, attitudes, and beliefs

You don't have to tell people how you're feeling for them to know. Look at someone deep in thought. As she leans forward, looks downward, wrinkling her forehead in contemplation, and rests her chin on her hand, she's replicating Rodin's sculpture, *The Thinker*. Equally so, a child throwing a tantrum with stomping feet, clenched fists, and a screwed up face is letting you know that she's not happy. The body says it all.

Think of your body as if it were a movie screen. The information you project derives from your inner life of thoughts, feelings, and intentions. Your physical body is the vehicle onto which the information is displayed. Whether you're anxious, excited, happy, or sad, your movements and expressions tell your tale. Here are some examples:

>> People who feel threatened or unsure of themselves touch their bodies as a means of self-comfort or self-restraint. Gestures such as rubbing their foreheads, crossing their arms, and holding or rubbing their fingers in front of their mouths provide comfort and protection.

>> People in a state of elation often breathe in deeply and gesture outward with expanded arms. Pictures of winning athletes frequently show them in the open position with their arms extended, their heads thrown back, and their mouths and eyes opened in ecstasy.

>> People who are despondent, or feeling down and depressed, reveal their feelings by the slouch in their step, their drooping heads, limp lips, and downward-cast eyes. Positive people, on the other hand, reveal their feelings with an upright stance, a bounce in their step, lifted lips, and eyes that twinkle with liveliness and engagement.

>> Not every bent head signals depression. Sometimes it just means that you're reflecting, thinking, or absorbing information. If you're thinking hard for example, your head most likely rests in your hand or on your fingertips unless you're pacing the room as you consider your options, in which case you still might rest your chin on your thumb as you stroke your cheeks and lips with your index finger.

>> Holding your hands over or near your heart is an expression of how much something means to you. You often see this gesture when people give and receive compliments.

Examining Key Types of Gestures

Humans are blessed with the ability to create a wide variety of gestures and expressions from the top of the head to the tips of the toes. Gestures can show intention, such as leaning forward just before rising out of a chair, and no intention, such as crossing arms and legs. Certain gestures, frequently referred to as *signature gestures*, are acts you perform and by which you are identified. Others are *displacement gestures*: you perform them for no reason other than to shift some energy. Local customs call for specific gestures and other gestures are universal, performed, and interpreted the same way across the globe.

Unintentional gestures

Unintentional gestures are types of body language that inhibit your ability to act. They hold you back from speaking and make it hard for your body to budge. As opposed to intentional gestures — those movements you specifically choose to support your spoken message — unintentional gestures usually surface without conscious thought.

Examples of unintentional gestures are as follows:

>> Folded arms

>> Lips pressed together

>> A hand or finger in front of the mouth

>> Crossed legs

When your arms are folded, you can't strike out. When your lips are sealed, your thoughts remain silent. When your legs are crossed, you can't run away. These gestures prevent you from moving and speaking, which may not be such a bad thing. Standing or sitting with your legs crossed is no position to take if you want to get somewhere quickly. The scissor stance is a prime example of a gesture that keeps you in your place. One leg is crossed over the other, rendering you immobile. When someone adopts this position, you know she's staying put.

TECHNICAL
STUFF

Because the scissor stance contains no sign of impatience, the gesture can come across as submissive. You take up less space as you make yourself smaller. Men seldom adopt this stance while women frequently do. Physiological reasons make the pose more or less comfortable for the two genders. People who move freely, not locking themselves into awkward physical positions, are considered to be more dominant than those who are constrained and hesitant in their movements.

Signature gestures

A signature gesture is one that you become known by, a common gesture that you perform in a particular way. Some examples include:

>> Twirling your hair around your finger

>> Pointing your finger

>> Sticking your tongue out

>> Patting your eyebrows

>> Stroking your throat

>> Winking

You provide clues about your personality through your signature gestures. They set you apart from others and draw their attention to you.

Here's an example of signature gestures at work: Toby is a quiet, task-orientated, focused man. His boss, Annie, is highly energetic with a mind that skips and leaps from one project to the next. Frequently, Annie asks Toby to do one task, only to interrupt his concentration by asking him to do something else, often unrelated. When Toby pats his eyebrows with the tips of his fingers, Annie recognizes his signature gesture of impatience and frustration and quickly backs off, letting him get on with what he has to do.

TECHNICAL STUFF

Frequently referred to as the Power Pose, in which you put your hands in front of your stomach, thumbs pointing upwards and fingertips touching, with your thumbs and index fingers forming a rough diamond shape, this action is one of German Chancellor Angela Merkel's most recognized poses. Known in Germany as the Merkel-Raute (The Triangle of Power), this posture is synonymous with Merkel's reputation for strong leadership and a safe pair of hands. The gesture has been used by Merkel's party, the Christian Democratic Union (CDU), for publicity purposes and the emoticon <> referencing the gesture is used in its Internet communications.

Fake gestures

Fake gestures are designed to camouflage, conceal, and fool. They pretend to be something when they're actually something else. You're able to tell a fake gesture from a real one because some of the genuine gesture's parts are missing.

Some gestures that are commonly faked include the following:

>> Smiling

>> Frowning

>> Sighing

>> Crying

>> Holding your body as if in pain

Consider this work-related example: Anna is a highly motivated, recently qualified lawyer in a large urban firm. She knows that, in part, her success depends on her ability to get on well with clients and colleagues. One day, her supervising partner invited her to attend a client meeting and to put together the remaining briefs that a previous trainee had begun and hadn't had time to finish. Anna, already overloaded with work, stayed at the office until well past midnight. Despite little sleep and more than an hour's commute, she arrived, shortly before the meeting's 8 a.m. start looking smart and ready to go. At one point during the session, the client remarked that some information seemed to be missing. The partner shot Anna a glance of annoyance before covering up his feelings with the hearty remark, "Well, she's new on the job. We'll let her get away with it just this once." To cover her fury and shame, Anna put on what she calls her "smiley face," a big toothy grin, and offered to find the missing materials. Anna's teeth were clenched, and her eyes didn't crinkle, which they would have were her smile sincere. She was tired, hurt, and humiliated and anyone paying attention would have seen that her grin was fake.

To avoid being fooled by a fake gesture, observe all the signals.

Micro-gestures

Teeny weeny, so small that they sometimes take highly specialized equipment to see them, micro-gestures flicker and flash across your face faster than a speeding bullet. Unfortunately, you're at the mercy of your micro-expressions as you don't choose them and they tell an observer a lot about your internal state at that moment.

Although you may choose to smile, pout, or frown, you may not want a micro-gesture of fear, loathing, love, or disgust to flicker across your face. The good news is, if you're a careful observer you can figure out how someone's feeling from their micro-expressions. The bad news is, an adept observer can spot your emotions through the same channel.

A list of the more common micro-gestures includes the following:

>> Movement around the mouth

>> Tension at the eyes

>> Flaring of the nostrils

Here's an example from the workplace: Erik is the newly appointed CEO of a global corporation. In his position, he's used to being the center of attention. Erik recently entered a room where two colleagues were speaking to each other. Erik winked and smiled as he asked if they were talking about him. Although he robustly said, "Good, I'm glad" when they told him that they weren't, they noticed a momentary flicker of surprise cross his face.

Displacement gestures

When you experience conflicting emotions, you may engage in self-directed gestures that release nervous energy and provide a temporary feeling of comfort. Drumming fingers, flicking feet, fetching a glass of water when you're not even thirsty — these are the types of behavior of someone who's looking to refocus or vent some pent up energy. Called *displacement activities*, they're a conduit for excess energy that's looking for somewhere to go.

Here are some examples of displacement gestures:

>> Fiddling with objects

>> Tugging at your earlobe

>> Straightening your clothes

>> Stroking your chin

>> Running your fingers through your hair

>> Eating

REMEMBER

Words convey information. Gestures reveal emotions. If someone's feeling anxious, she may fiddle with her keys, twist the ring on her finger, or pull at her clothes to manage her discomfort.

TIP

If you see someone being scrutinized, look to see what her hands are doing. If she's gently rubbing her stomach, stroking her sternum, or running her fingers up and down her throat, you may assume that she's feeling the pressure and is doing her best to calm and comfort herself without calling attention to it.

Universal gestures

Universal gestures, such as blushing, smiling, and the wide-eyed expression of fear mean the same thing around the world. These gestures stem from human biological make-up, which is why you can easily recognize the signs.

Smiling

From the sands of the Middle East to the shores of Malibu, humans are born with the ability to smile. From the earliest days in a baby's life, her facial muscles can form the upward turn of the lips and the crinkling around the outer edges of the eyes to create a recognizable grin. Anyone with working facial muscles who's conveying a genuine smile lifts her lips in pleasure while the outer muscles around her eyes crinkle.

TIP

In Western cultures people smile as a sign of recognition and acknowledgment, whether they know you or not. In China, don't feel left out if no one smiles at you as you walk through their towns. The Japanese smile when they're confused, angry, or embarrassed. In the former USSR you're perceived as suspicious if you smile at strangers in public.

Blushing

Blushing, caused by blood flowing to your chest and face, is a universal response when feeling passionate or embarrassed. No matter where your passport takes you, when you see someone blush you know she's consumed with embarrassment.

TIP

To control the blushing take several slow, deep breaths from your diaphragm to steady your nerves and control the blood flow.

Crying

Crying is a universal sign of sadness. One of a healthy baby's first actions is to let out a walloping great cry when she first enters this world, having been torn from the comfort and safety of her mother's womb. No one had to teach her how to cry; she was born with the innate ability to express her unhappiness.

TIP

If you feel tears well up in your eyes and you want to stop them from flowing down your face, fix your gaze at the point where the ceiling and wall meet. Performing this action focuses your attention onto a meaningless and unrelated subject and frees your mind of upsetting thoughts. Another way to prevent your tears from flowing is to press your tongue firmly against the roof of your mouth as you remind yourself that in a few moments what's troubling you will be over. If, however, you feel the salt of your tears about to splash down your face, you could acknowledge what's happening and move on. Sometimes accepting what's about to occur is enough to make it stop.

Shrugging

Shrugging is a gesture that people use when they need to protect or distance themselves from something they'd rather avoid. In the full shrug your head dips into your rising shoulders, the sides of your mouth turn down, and your palms turn upwards as you raise your eyebrows.

TELEVISION VERSUS RADIO

In the early 1960s, little was known about body language. Yet John F. Kennedy intuitively knew how to use it. Prior to their first televised debate in 1960, JFK and Richard Nixon posed for a media photo call. Kennedy placed himself to the right of Nixon and shook Nixon's hand. The resulting photograph showed Kennedy applying the upper-hand position, causing Nixon to appear diminished in stature. This was one of Kennedy's favorite gestures. The Nixon–Kennedy election debate that followed this photo call was a further testimonial to the power of body language. Most of the Americans who heard the debate on the radio believed that Nixon out-performed Kennedy. However, the majority of those who saw the debate on television believed Kennedy was the victor. The media savvy Kennedy knew how to use his body to manipulate public perception and did it with grace, charm, and ease.

The shrug can indicate any of the following:

>> Indifference

>> Disdain

>> Lack of knowledge

>> Embarrassment

To know which attitude is being expressed, you have to identify what the other body parts are doing at the same time.

Here's a work-related example: Anne, a French woman, heads up her organization's public relations department. Chad, one of her internal clients, makes Anne's life difficult because he frequently fails to prepare for the presentations Anne writes for him, is late in responding to her requests for information, and often argues with her directives. When Anne was asked how she finds working with Chad, she closed her eyes, pursed her lips, raised her shoulders holding her palms upward, and uttered the dismissive "puh" sound as a quick blast of air escaped from her mouth. "I don't think much of him" was her message.

Getting the Most Out of Body Language

People in powerful positions know how to use their bodies to greatest effect. They stand tall, chests open, shoulders back and down, and, when they move, they do so with purpose. They choose their gestures with care to reflect their sense of who they are and how they want to be perceived.

Powerful people know where to position themselves in relation to others. They know that if they stand too close they're perceived as overwhelming or threatening, while if they stand too far away they come across as distant. They know that the gestures they use and how they use them have a powerful impact.

REMEMBER

A major part of your message is conveyed through your posture, movements, and facial expressions. Being aware of the impact of your body language enables you to act confidently, knowing that your message is received in the way you intend.

Becoming spatially aware

Understanding how to position yourself in relation to other people is a skill that some people just don't seem to have. Someone is either up so close and personal that you can smell her coffee breath, or she stands just slightly too far away, making her appear uninterested and disengaged. Others know just how close to come. They understand and respect the different parameters people place around themselves, and being with them is comfortable.

Think of yourself as having a personal, individual space bubble that you stand, sit, and move in. This invisible space expands and contracts depending on circumstances. For example, when you're with people you like, you tend to close the gap between yourselves. When you're with people you don't know well or whose company you don't enjoy, you may find that you're more comfortable when you expand the space. People who grew up in the country and now live in crowded cities frequently complain about lack of space while people who were raised in metropolitan areas adapt to confined conditions more readily.

TECHNICAL STUFF

The study of *proxemics* — how people use and relate to the space around them for purposes of communication — was pioneered by Edward T. Hall, an American anthropologist, in the 1960s. His findings reveal the different amounts of personal space that people feel they need depending on their social situation. Robert Sommer, an American psychologist, coined the term "personal space" in 1969. He defined it as the "comfortable separation zone" people like to have around them.

Anticipating movements

If you're able to anticipate another person's movements, you can predict what they're going to do next, giving you the upper hand by eliminating the element of surprise.

An American anthropologist, Ray Birdwhistell, pioneered *kinesics* — the study of body movement and verbal communication. Replaying in slow motion films of people in conversation, Birdwhistell was able to analyze people's actions, gestures, and facial expressions.

Consider these examples:

>> Spotting the subtle gestures a person makes in preparation for rising from a seated position lets you know that it's time to move on.

>> Seeing that someone wants to speak enables you to give them the chance to be heard.

REMEMBER

Anticipating a movement can save your life, keep you from harm, and even bring you great happiness. By predicting gestures, you gain the upper hand in figuring out your response before the other person has completed her action.

Creating rapport through reflecting gestures

In order to establish rapport — a state of understanding feelings and communicating well — you accept and connect with other people, treating one another with respect. Rapport assures that your communications are effective and lead to results that satisfy both parties' needs.

You can create rapport in many ways, including touch, word choice, and eye contact. You can also create rapport by reflecting another person's movements. By mirroring and matching the other person's gestures and behaviors, you're demonstrating that you know what it feels, sounds, and looks like to be in her shoes. If connecting with others and behaving respectfully is important to you, mirroring and matching their behavior helps you achieve that goal. For more information about the benefit of mirroring and matching others' actions, check out Book 1, Chapter 6.

WARNING

A fine line exists between reflecting another person's gestures and mimicking her. People who are being mimicked quickly figure out what you're doing, recognize your insincerity, and question your motives.

Becoming who you want to be

How you present yourself, how you move and gesture, and how you stand, sit, and walk all play their part in creating the image you present and determining people's perceptions of you. By developing an arsenal of postures, positions, gestures, and expressions, you can project a plethora of attitudes. Positive body language — through which you establish eye contact and move with purpose — comes across as strong, engaged, and vibrant. Negative body language — whereby you avoid looking at another person and fold into yourself — communicates weakness, dullness, and a disconnect between yourself and others. How you move your head, face, torso, and limbs determines how you're perceived and the results you achieve.

TECHNICAL STUFF

Actors know how to create a character from both within — the character's history, present life, beliefs, attitudes, thoughts, and feelings — and without — her physical attributes, including how she looks and behaves. They draw upon the technique of acting "as if," that is, behaving as if they were the character. Working from the outside in, actors consider how their character sounds, moves, and gestures. They ask themselves:

>> **How would the character walk, sit, and stand?** Would she move like a gazelle, lumber along like a sleepy bear, or stagger in a zigzag pattern like someone who's had one drink too many? Is her posture upright and erect or slouched and limp?

>> **What gestures would convey a particular mood or emotion?** Slow, deliberate, and carefully timed gestures create a different impression from those that are quick, spontaneous, and unfocused.

By adopting the appropriate behaviors, the actor creates an attitude, emotion, or feeling that the audience recognizes and understands. The same is true for the layperson. By acting in a particular manner you can create an image and become that character. As Cary Grant said, "I pretended to be someone I wanted to be until finally I became that person."

REMEMBER

The way you act makes an impression. How you're perceived — champion of the people or chairman of the board — is up to you. The key is to adopt the appropriate behaviors. To do that, keep these points in mind:

>> **Make sure that your gestures reinforce the impression you want to make.** For example, the higher up the command chain, the more contained the gesture (which is why you never see the chief executive running down the hall).

>> **You can modify your gestures to suit the situation.** When you're hanging out with friends, your body language is loose and relaxed. When meeting a client for the first time, your body language is more contained and formal. Follow the lead of the other person and reflect what you're observing to create rapport.

TIP

Pick an attitude that you want to project. Determine the appropriate gestures and expressions. If you struggle to come up with ideas of your own, model the gestures of someone you think successfully conveys the image you want to portray.

Reading the signs and responding appropriately

Recognizing, interpreting, and responding to other people's body language is a stepping stone to effective communication. By observing how people move and gesture, you get a glimpse into their thoughts, emotions, and intentions. You can tell, for example, how someone is feeling by the way she stands. You can see what kind of mood a person is in by the speed of her gestures. You can spot someone's attitude by the tilt of her head. By having an insight into someone's thoughts and emotions, you're forewarned and forearmed for whatever may happen next.

Here's a work-related example: Holly unexpectedly stopped by to have a chat with her colleague, Tony. Tony was rushing to complete a project and had little time to stop for a gossip. Because they're friends, Tony looked up at Holly and smiled and nodded when he saw her. He also stayed seated at his desk and didn't maintain eye contact. He kept his fingers on his keyboard, looked back at his computer screen, and resumed typing. Holly sensed from Tony's body language that now wasn't a convenient time for them to speak, and she quickly left.

Appreciating Cultural Differences

How much more exciting, interesting, and stimulating it is to live in a world with difference and diversity, rather than one in which everything's the same. Even though you appreciate the differences between cultures and nationalities, you may sometimes find yourself confused, scared, or even repelled by displays of body language that are very different from what you're used to.

Because people in one culture act differently to people in another doesn't suggest that one is right and the other wrong. When it comes to cultural differences, the operative verbs are "to respect" and "to value." Valuing behaviors that vary so much from those that you grew up with, and were taught to believe in, can be hard. To create respectful, positive relationships between different cultures and nationalities, you need to expand the way you think and work. If you remember nothing else from this paragraph, remember that in multicultural encounters, respect for others' ways of being is paramount. That doesn't mean having to agree with all the behaviors you see in your travels. Instead, accept that differences do exist, and then decide how best to respond.

REMEMBER

People of different nationalities and cultures use their bodies differently. An acceptable gesture in one country may land you in jail in another. Before visiting or moving to another country, do your homework and find out what's suitable and what's not.

Chapter 4

Working with Different Communication Styles

I f everyone talked alike, had the same communication habits, and understood messages similarly, you wouldn't need information on critical conversations at work or the progression of an entire industry on how to communicate effectively. Back in reality, you'll find as many different styles of communication as people communicating.

The differences in communication style make work and life interesting. Although there is no one right way to communicate all the time, there are definitely wrong ways to communicate. This chapter walks you through the pros and cons of being overly assertive or passive when communicating. You also go over a model of assertive communication that works wonders during a critical conversation. Because understanding your personal style of communication helps others respond better to different situations and environments, you get an opportunity to discover more about your own communication strengths and weaknesses. Finally, you find out how to avoid making assumptions about different communication styles. By adapting the approach to communication and assumptions, each critical conversation can conclude objectively.

Taking On Direct and Passive Communication Styles

Effectively delivering a message comes down to style. This isn't a reference to the style on runways each season; style is the way you deliver the message, not necessarily which words you deliver.

Individual style and behaviors can greatly impact the message. Most individuals have to adapt their personal style during conversations, or at least be aware of their own style. This chapter uncovers the three main types of styles out there: direct, passive, and assertive.

REMEMBER

The message you deliver and the way you deliver it are equally important.

TIP

This chapter provides high-level groups of communication styles. To better understand your own style and how to best use and adapt it, turn to the many communication and conflict assessments that provide specific insights and compatibility recommendations when working with other styles. A few of the more common assessments include Myers-Briggs, DiSC, and the Thomas-Kilmann Conflict Mode assessment.

Direct communicators

People who are direct communicators often tell it like it is, with very few exceptions. They also like to drive action and continue forward momentum during meetings and discussions. At times they may argue just for the sake of arguing. Although direct communicators can be seen as aggressive or forceful, their behavior is often driven by a passion about what they believe is right or wrong.

Perhaps unsurprisingly, politicians and executives who seem decisive and driven are direct communicators. Direct communicators are nearly perfect at public speaking because they can energize others with their passion. During critical conversations, however, the direct style can come across as a bit overbearing. Because the goal of critical conversations is to make meaningful change to behaviors or to create a mutual agreement toward a behavior change, being driven to get immediate results isn't always the best policy.

If the other party thinks you have a one-track mind for the right way things are done, she may feel that her opinions and ideas don't matter. How do you know you're working with a direct communicator and what can you do to balance such a powerful communication personality? Table 4-1 gives you a few ideas on how to balance directing and driving results with getting mutual agreements that make behaviors change. A direct communicator may naturally do some or all of the behaviors in the table.

TABLE 4-1   ## Behaviors of a Direct Communicator

Behavior	What You May Observe	How to Adapt If You See This Behavior	What to Do If You Behave This Way
Talking fast and moving fast	Few breaths, a rapid conversation pace, quickly moving from one topic to another, perhaps even pacing around the room. Conversation is deadline — or action — focused.	Clearly state the end goal of the conversation up front. If the other party is pushing for action before agreement on the problem, meet her halfway by letting her know the goals or next steps will more likely be achieved if everyone agrees on them first.	Count to two before jumping into the conversation to allow a few seconds of silence between thoughts. Let the other parties know it's okay to slow you down or ask questions.
Using intense body language	Large hand movements, banging hands on the desk or waving them around in the air, big gestures.	Keep your own actions subtle and calm to balance the energy in the room.	Look at how others in the room are moving and using space and mirror their behaviors. Find out more about ideal body language and other nonverbal cues during a critical conversation (introduced in Book 1, Chapter 2).
Talking more than listening	Direct communicators are often so busy expressing their own opinion that they miss the opinion of others. This doesn't mean that they don't care.	Slow down the pace. Step in frequently to make sure all parties have mutual agreements and an understanding of next steps.	Be aware of your pace. Allow others to voice ideas or concerns. Ask for input at the end of each thought. You may practice saying, "Let me take a break from talking and ask for your ideas."

Some people may be intimidated by the intensity of direct communicators and therefore they may not naturally want to speak up during a conversation with them. Direct communicators may benefit from having a trusted peer or coach give them feedback on how their communication style is working or not working, and work together to think of ways to adapt behaviors in the future.

REMEMBER

Don't make an assumption. Direct communicators aren't necessarily aggressive or hostile people. Passion, purpose, and drive often fuel this communication style.

Passive communicators

People who are passive communicators resemble introverts; they may speak more slowly and be more careful of how and what they say. Often, they don't voice their own needs and opinions. Passive communicators often avoid expressing their ideas or feelings.

Passive communicators are almost the polar opposite of direct communicators, often using a calm and quiet voice, reserved body gestures, and listening more than talking. All these traits are wonderful in a genuine leader, but because critical conversations focus on mutual agreements that move behaviors and relationships forward, not speaking up for your own point of view can impede a critical conversation.

Although passive communicators may want to work on expressing their ideas, other styles can learn great qualities from this communication style. They're often seen as polite, allowing others to speak and ask many questions. As an expert critical communicator, your goal is to make sure their voices and opinions are heard and not pushed to the side.

Here's what a critical conversation may look like if one party is a passive communicator:

> **Messenger Marvin:** "Hi, Paul. I wanted to talk with you about a potential problem with the project."
>
> **Passive Paul:** "Okay."
>
> **Marvin:** "Based on the numbers from last quarter, we're going to have to cut the spending by 30 percent."
>
> **Paul:** "I understand. What can I do to help you?"
>
> **Marvin:** "I think you'll need to cut all your contractors out of the budget. Can you do that?"
>
> **Paul:** "Of course. Anything to help."

At face value, this conversation looks civilized and really not that critical. After all, no one's emotions get out of hand, and Paul seems to be in complete agreement with Marvin. Unfortunately, Paul never gives an alternative idea, even though he may have better ways to save the money. Passive communicators often feel that their needs aren't as important as the needs of others. Although this approach may be great for avoiding conflict, it doesn't work well for developing mutual agreements that make a difference.

If Paul steps out of his passive style and becomes more assertive (see the next section), here's how the conversation may go:

Messenger Marvin: "Hi, Paul. I wanted to talk with you about a potential problem with the project."

Passive Paul: "I'm happy to discuss the problem. What's your concern?"

Marvin: "Based on the numbers from last quarter, we're going to have to cut the spending by 30 percent."

Paul: "I understand. I have some ideas that may help cut the spending."

Marvin: "I'm listening."

Paul: "Based on our results, it looks like our project scope has gotten out of control. The team is putting in overtime because we're trying to implement two solutions, when originally we were just doing one . . . ."

Paul still maintains his gentle approach, but with one sentence he speaks up for his ideas and concerns, instead of letting another individual drive the entire conversation.

If you're a passive communicator, or if you're working with a passive communicator, Table 4-2 offers a few tips to make sure that everyone hears the passive voices.

TABLE 4-2   **Behaviors of a Passive Communicator**

Behavior	What You May Observe	How to Adapt If You See This Behavior	What to Do If You Behave This Way
Silence or little active participation	Sitting quietly, not speaking up or chiming in with ideas.	In a group setting, during a break ask for any questions or ideas one on one. In one-on-one situations, let the silence happen because passive communicators often like to process complete thoughts before talking.	Come prepared. If you're leading a conversation, have notes on what message you want to deliver. If you're on the receiving end of a conversation, ask what information you can contribute to the conversation. Perhaps ask, "I'm not sure what to say. Can you let me know what information I can provide?"
Complete agreement, avoiding any conflict	Sometimes passive communicators nod along in agreement instead of speaking up.	Ask probing questions like, "This looks like a good solution. What's missing?" or, "I think this is a great path to take. Can we think of an alternative to compare it to?" Asking for options can be intimidating to a conflict-adverse passive communicator, so try to use the terms *other* or *alternative* rather than *best* or *better*.	Speak up. If you're afraid to voice your opinion, ask others what can be done to strengthen agreements.

TIP

If you're working with passive communicators, try to minimize the risk for them to participate. Passive communicators often feel that their needs and ideas aren't as important as others. They may also feel that voicing their concerns will cause conflict. Create a safe environment during the conversation by establishing that the information you discuss stays in the room. You may also want to encourage parties to participate in the conversation by holding a brainstorming session to get ideas rolling.

WARNING

Watch out for passive-aggressive behavior. Although passive communicators tend to avoid conflict and often go with the good of the group, some passive communicators repress feelings of anger or resentment. The passive-aggressive style may agree in the moment but sabotage the solution later. Gaining agreements throughout the conversation on next steps and clarifying that the message is understood can help prevent this sabotage.

Saying Yes to Assertiveness

No matter what communication style you have, trying to use assertiveness and trying to get your employees to use assertiveness is the key to successful communication. During a critical conversation, assertive communication styles deliver the message in a firm yet professional manner. Assertiveness during a critical conversation is about making sure everyone's needs are met rather than getting just one person's point across. Assertive techniques during a critical conversation are geared toward getting other individuals to speak openly and provide ideas and solutions, and then making sure the solutions work for everyone.

Checking out assertive qualities

Assertive communicators have these qualities:

>> **They ask questions to spur discussion.** During a critical conversation, assertive communicators ask for the other party's perspective first and then use their own perspective to help generate discussion, instead of simply supplying the ultimate answer.

>> **They are flexible with the means, agreeing on the end goal.** Assertive communicators remain flexible with the needs of all the parties and the way to reach agreement. Although assertive styles don't back down from their own needs and values, they can be open to finding new ways to achieve the goals.

>> **They take time to build agreement and find solutions that benefit all parties.** Assertive communicators approach conversations as a problem solving opportunity instead of trying to rush to solutions. They clarify information frequently while they build agreements. For example, an assertive communicator may say, "These three next steps look good. How about making sure we both understand what's on this list. Any items here you would like clarified?"

Here's what an assertive style may look like during a critical conversation:

Situation: Sam has been the product development director at GamesOnline for 23 years. Sam is a passive communicator, sometimes passive-aggressive. A new manager, Alex, was recently hired as the director of Sales and Marketing. He has an assertive style and his goal is to hit the sales targets out of the park and eventually run the company. Alex needs Sam's team to work with Sales and Marketing, but it's not happening. Watch how Alex uses assertive styles to get Sam to come up with ideas to help the team.

Assertive Alex: "Hi, Sam. Thanks for meeting today. As I mentioned to you last week, I want to search for ways that our teams can work together to achieve our company goals for next year. Are you willing to work together on this?"

Passive Sam: "Okay."

Alex: "Great. I noticed last year that both teams were working around the clock to meet our targets, and many people were exhausted after that heroic push. Have you seen or heard of different alternatives to the last-minute rush that have worked in the past?"

Sam: "Not really. We can do whatever you want to."

Alex: "I would love to come up with some ideas together. I would be happy to have you start, or I can put the first one out there."

Sam: "Oh, I'm happy to just help."

Alex: "Okay. One idea may be to ask our teams to sit next to one another in the office, opening up the communication between groups."

Sam: "Sounds great."

Alex: "Finding multiple options could help both teams find even more ways to collaborate. Can we brainstorm an alternative idea?"

Sam: "Sure. You know one thing that we used to do was have quarterly production targets. Not sure why we don't anymore . . ."

Critical communication experts dream about this conversation as an example for everyone to follow. Alex directly states the reason for the discussion and asks for agreement. Asking Sam whether he was willing to work on the issue takes time but builds a key agreement. When Sam responds, "Not really," Alex is flexible in his approach, providing information and then asking more questions to spur discussion. Assertive communicators are more than facilitators or managers — they can be magicians! On the third try, Sam brings up new information, which may never have been discussed if not for Alex's open style.

REMEMBER

The goal of a critical conversation is to positively build mutual agreements that solve tough, emotionally charged issues. Using an assertive style helps the other parties provide their points of view to help build a solution everyone can agree on and work toward. Assertive communication may not be your natural style, but practice and feedback from others can help create a balanced assertive style that gets results that everyone can agree to work on the in the future.

Using assertive styles to move to action

If you were a fly on the wall during the conversation in the example between Sam and Alex (see the previous section), you may wonder why Alex tries so hard to get Sam to talk and give ideas. If only one person talks or only one person gives ideas during a critical conversation, chances are good that the idea will never see the light of day after the conversation is over. After all, the parties don't reach an agreement. If a critical conversation is over and nothing changes, you had no consensus and the time was wasted. By probing for ideas and asking for commitment, Alex starts to develop actionable agreements.

REMEMBER

Direct or aggressive communicators may get their points across, but later find out find out that everyone was listening but no one agreed. Passive communicators may just let the conversation happen while nodding their heads, but have no commitment to the end goal after the conversation is done.

An assertive communication style advocates the perspective of the speaker and gathers information from other parties. If you make sure the parties discuss all the information and views, you have a higher chance for action after the conversation closes because everyone's views have been heard and incorporated into the final outcome.

Knowing Your Communication Style

Knowing you own communication style helps you create awareness, increase your strengths, and deliver a more productive message that gets results during a conversation. When you enter a conversation, critical or not, do you come with the desire to get a goal accomplished or to get everyone to agree to the goal to be accomplished? Do you use sarcasm and humor to avoid or confront tough issues? Take this eight-question quiz to find out.

Think of the last conversation you had that involved a disagreement or conflict. Did you . . .

1. Feel genuinely concerned about other people's ideas and thoughts?

2. Ask others questions about what they think, feel, or need?

3. Pause for two to three seconds before responding to questions?

4. Avoid confrontation during the conversation?

5. Solve everyone else's problems during the meeting, leaving your own issues for later?

6. Say it like it is?

7. Finish people's conversations?

8. Use sarcasm or clever comments to get your point across?

If you answered "yes" to questions 1, 2, and 3, well done. You use an assertive communication style that facilitates agreements during tough conversations — good for you!

If you answered "yes" to questions 4 and 5, you may be putting your views last. If so, think about how to stop sitting passively during a conversation. Next time you're in a conversation (critical or not), practice stating how you feel and your view of the situation. Don't worry whether your idea is the best one or not — just state that you have another idea or a different opinion. You may be surprised to find that your ideas are the ones that have been missing from the discussion all along.

Did you answer "yes" to 6 and 7? A direct, or even aggressive, style may be standing in the way of getting results. Next time you find yourself in a critical conversation, try to ask others for their opinions and ideas before voicing your own. Try waiting for a few seconds before jumping in to make sure you aren't cutting off another person's thoughts. Aggressive styles can get work done quickly, but assertive styles that build mutual agreements often result in more long-term results everyone can agree on.

Did you answer "yes" to question 8? Humor can help relax a conversation, but too much joking or sarcasm may mean that you're passively pushing your ideas down, leading to passive-aggressive communication styles. Instead of joking about the end result, try using one of the tools in this book — like silence and space in Book 1, Chapter 2, or the "we" and "us" phrases in Book 1, Chapter 1.

REMEMBER

Knowing your own style can help you adapt in nearly all situations, not just critical conversations. If you develop the ability to proactively and assertively facilitate discussions to reach meaningful agreements, you will more easily create action after the conversation ends.

Sharpening Your Communication Style

Even the best communicators can find ways to constantly improve. No matter what style you're most comfortable with during conversations, gaining insight from those around you will improve the way you communicate.

Sharpening your communication style will help make every conversation more productive. To sharpen your style, you have to know what you want to work on. The good news is that these areas aren't that hard to find with a little digging. Three ways to improve your style (outside of reading this book, of course) are to:

>> Ask for feedback.

>> Manage your style during stressful times.

>> Learn more about assumptions you making during conversations.

Gaining insight from your peers

Having a little bird that watches every communication and gives feedback in a positive and productive way would be wonderful. In absence of a little bird watching over you, asking for feedback is the best alternative.

Some individuals may not be comfortable providing candid feedback, especially if they've never given feedback before. Keep the process simple by asking these questions:

>> What am I currently doing well when it comes to communicating?

>> What do I need to do differently?

>> What should I prioritize first to keep doing well and to improve on?

After directing these questions to a small group of peers, employees, and managers, you'll probably start seeing key themes and common issues. These themes and issues then become an action plan for your own development. Take each of the themes and turn them into actions by asking yourself the question, "What does this mean I have to deliver?" Spend some time exploring the actions that you need in order to improve your own communication style. Make sure the actions are SMART (specific, measurable, actionable and agreed-on, realistic, and time bound).

TIP

Don't get too stressed out about making sure your conversation style is perfect before holding a critical conversation. Having a good conversation is better than having no conversation. If you still need to work on your tone of voice, work on it during the conversation. Just knowing the areas you can develop will help throughout the conversation. Recognize that it takes commitment and practice to adapt your style, but anytime you open the lines of communication with a genuine desire to help the situation, you help to create a more positive environment.

WARNING

Here are two of the biggest problems facing communicators:

>> Being unaware of how others perceive their conversation style.

>> Not fully recognizing their own biases in communication.

These problems don't crop up because leaders don't care. They're simply a result of the fact that so few people have been given the opportunity to gather multiple perspectives. Some leaders benefit greatly from a 360-degree communication review. A 360-degree feedback session is when a facilitator asks the leader's employees, managers, and peers for feedback and then provides this information back to the leader. This review is a chance to get feedback from the people you work with most closely, to better understand your conversation style through the eyes of others, and to see what biases you may bring to a conversation.

Managing your style under stress

After reading this entire chapter, you're ready to develop a communication style that can deliver critical conversations perfectly. Yeah! But wait, what's that you hear? Quarterly results aren't as good as expected? A project deadline is moved up a month? Your best employee just quit? Argh — talk about stress. Read on to discover how each of the three communication styles in this chapter can deal with stress.

Putting an assertive style to the test

In perfect situations with little stress, using an assertive communication style and remaining patient throughout the critical conversation process is easy. But when push comes to shove, stress can make a conversation turn into a screaming match. Look at the eight-question quiz in the earlier section "Knowing Your Communication Style" and answer the questions while thinking about the last highly stressful conversation you had. The results may be different. This exercise can help you see how your conversation style changes when emotions are high and stress levels are higher.

Challenging direct communicators

Direct communicators may benefit from taking control and directing the process, not the discussion. For example, some direct communicators feel that unless they're being directive and dictating the course of action, they're not being a leader and nothing will happen. Under stress, these leaders may believe that collaborative conversations make them look weak or are just a waste of time. If this is the case, try to direct the process for conversations by exploring, deciding, getting into the action, and evaluating the success of the conversation instead of directing the results. These tools will build actions that all parties are committed to rather than actions that all parties just agree with and ignore after the conversation is done.

Pumping up passive communicators

Passive communicators may withdraw when stressed. This habit can make passive communicators seem indifferent or even uncaring, which is often not the case. Under stress, passive communicators may benefit from actively inviting discussion by first giving their perspective and then inviting dialogue. For example, under stress (or anytime!), a passive communicator could kick off a critical conversation with, "Jim, I feel like our team isn't talking with one another. Our last three meetings seem to have focused on solving the same issue again and again. Do you feel the same way?" Starting with this statement makes sure a passive communicator's feelings and thoughts are heard first.

REMEMBER

Passive communicators often have one big advantage they can use during stressful times — they tend to stay calm in the face of high-stress situations. Because these communicators don't jump in and try to fix the conversation while ignoring others, a passive communicator may be a pro at promoting an environment of respect during high-stress times.

Clarifying assumptions

As communicators, leaders are continually observing the actions and interactions of those around them. After a few observations or experiences, you may start seeing patterns emerge. Most people tend to place their own meaning on the behaviors they observe and to make inferences about these patterns. Making assumptions about people's actions or personalities can lead to problems and work against productivity.

Here's an example of someone making an assumption and the consequences that follow:

> *Situation:* David observes Mike talking loudly to employees and often ending calls in a screaming match or with frustration.
>
> *David's assumption:* Mike doesn't know how to control his temper.
>
> *David's conclusion:* David doesn't want to work with Mike.
>
> *David's action:* Never be part of Mike's work teams.

The first problem with this inference of Mike's behavior is that David never initiated a critical conversation to find out why Mike's behavior was happening. You can fix this problem by working through a conversation that's probably long overdue. The second — and perhaps more serious — problem with this conclusion is that David may not want to be on teams with anyone who talks loudly because he associates loud talking with Mike's behavior.

A better way for David to approach Mike's loud talking would be to simply ask, "Hey, Mike, I heard some loud voices earlier today when you were on the phone. I'm wondering whether we can have a discussion on how you and I can work together in such a small office space. Would you be able to have a discussion later today?" Critical conversation tools can help avoid assumptions about what is going to happen in the future, and instead gain agreement on what is going to happen in the future.

REMEMBER

Interpretations are inevitable, but rather than attribute meaning to behaviors, ask for the meaning.

Chapter **5**

Influencing through Communication

H umans are the chatty, social species, and masters of communication. Even during brief moments of silence, people speak volumes. Over generations, humans have developed the ability to communicate across the boundaries of gender, age, race, and culture, enabling everyone to create alliances for the greater good, as well as evil.

This chapter focuses on the underlying patterns of communication. You discover how to inform, engage, and influence ethically, as well as be better able to recognize when someone else is trying to influence you.

Understanding the Importance of Effective Communication

Underlying communications are common patterns, concepts, and principles that influence social behavior. Understanding and being able to use these concepts and principles enable you to become a better communicator and master of persuasion and to influence in multiple business contexts. Effective communication is increasingly recognized as a key determinant of business success.

Specializations like copywriting, media presentations, presenting to audiences, sales, customer service, negotiation, and arbitration all influence human behavior, and what is common to all these programs is:

>> How people internally process communication

>> How people are influenced by communication to make decisions

These concepts of communication are used in many business contexts, such as the following:

>> Marketing:

- Capturing customer attention and engaging people in conversations that lead to business.

- Influencing behaviors and the resultant actions and decisions that people make.

- Creating powerful brand associations.

>> Selling:

- Getting people to say yes and to mean it.

- Overcoming objections to propositions.

>> Negotiating and resolving conflicts:

- Bridging seemingly insurmountable differences of opinion.

- Creating situations where differences don't matter.

>> Gaining compliance:

- Ensuring that people listen to learn.

- Getting people to follow up on declarations.

>> Striving for greater understanding:

- Imparting information to ensure that people understand your communications.

- Informing people so they take specifically desired actions.

Communicating Quicker than the Speed of Conscious Thought

Here are two concepts about how the mind processes communication received by the listener (or receiver), which ultimately affects and influences behavior:

» **Communication is verbal and nonverbal.** The mind processes millions of bits of data per second, way beyond the conscious ability to process all the incoming information; yet it's all being processed at some unconscious level. Everything you see, hear, feel, smell, and taste is being processed, even if you aren't consciously aware of it. Whether you like it, the external is influencing how you perceive, think, feel, and act.

Research shows that while processing verbal communications, people are aware of and influenced 7 percent by the spoken word (what's said), 38 percent by voice and tonality (how those words are said), and 55 percent by body language (what's not said). Nonverbal communication, which includes the 55 percent body language, also includes other forms such as visual aids (graphs, charts, and models), as well as information conveyed through the senses of touch, taste, and smell. (Flip to Book 1, Chapters 1, 2, and 3 for an introduction to both verbal and nonverbal communication.)

» **You cannot not process the communication.** As soon as the verbal or nonverbal communication is made, the listener processes it regardless of whether he is consciously aware of it. The package of information has been delivered. (See the nearby sidebar "Every communication counts" for an example of this concept.)

For example, think of a situation where you have said to colleagues, "Just imagine how successful this venture will be." In order to make sense of the sentence, colleagues have to first make a picture in their minds of how they imagine a successful venture would look. You influence others by everything you say and do, whether they (or you) are consciously aware of the degree of influence or not. With your communication, you're getting them to create pictures in their minds and are, therefore, influencing their behaviors. They're also doing the same with customers, suppliers, and colleagues with every communication in all formats and media.

TIP

If people want to engage, inform, and influence, they have to first get the attention of the listener (receivers). A simple way to get this attention is to ask a question that forces listeners to become engaged in the communication so they're now in a state of curiosity. Get their attention first; then build up interest (curiosity) and desire; then instruct them what action to take. This sequential chaining of states moving toward a desired action is known by the acronym AIDA, short for attention, interest, desire, action.

EVERY COMMUNICATION COUNTS

On UK TV, Derren Brown gives a powerful demonstration of the power of unconscious communication to influence people. In one episode, he gave two designers a brief: They had half an hour to create a logo for a pet cemetery.

When they had created their logo, Derren unveiled one he had prepared earlier, which was a mirror image of theirs using all the design elements they had used. The designers were dumbfounded at the uncanny similarities.

On the cab journey to the studio, images had been strategically placed throughout the journey to influence their decisions. There were stickers of teddy bears and posters of angel wings. They drove past iron gates — all of which later appeared in their design proposal. Although the designers were not consciously aware of the images, they had processed them nonetheless and been influenced to use them.

Understanding the power of these two concepts — whereby communication both verbal and nonverbal is processed unconsciously and that the communication goes in regardless of whether the receiver is aware of it — opens up a whole toolbox of communication tools and concepts available to you.

Nudge theory (credited to Professor Richard Thaler of the University of Chicago) is a concept that argues that positive reinforcement and indirect suggestions influence the decision-making of groups and individuals, at least as effectively as, if not more effectively than, enforcement, a direct instruction, or legislation. Consider in your business where you've directed staff to take actions that have either been ignored or at least resisted. Nudge uses the concept of unconscious communication discussed in this chapter to direct people to take a desired course of action where it seems they have made the choice themselves instead of being influenced.

When the person being influenced (or nudged) feels he has made the decision to take a course of action under his own volition, he feels he has ownership of his actions and then tends to defend his decision by being consistent with his actions. Consider where this approach would be useful in your organization in order to make behavioral changes instead of using traditional top-down management directives.

Understanding Why People Say Yes

Imagine an open fridge door. Inside is celery and cheesecake. Which do you choose? Behind the decision to choose the obvious answer, which is undoubtedly cheesecake, is a lot of internal processing of information.

What people say yes to and what they say no to (two sides of the same coin) are influenced by a number of key questions the mind asks itself:

>> What do I value, or what's important to me?

>> What do I move away from to avoid? (This is also known as pain, which can be in the forms of physical, sexual, social, financial, and emotional.)

>> What do I move toward to gain? (This is also known as pleasure, whether physical, sexual, social, financial, or emotional.)

The mind processes these variables and presents the answer. The processing happens in a fraction of a second, and the answer is given in the form of mind pictures. In the fridge scenario, if the answer is celery (as unlikely as that may be), the mind picture of celery and what it means to the individual will seem more appealing than the way cheesecake is represented.

Mind pictures come with picture qualities and details that affect the impact they have on people's feelings. These qualities are known as *submodalities*. Here are a few key visual submodalities:

>> Location in space, size, and distance from the observer.

>> Associated (in the image) or disassociated (being an observer of the image).

>> Still picture or moving.

>> Color or black and white.

>> Two-dimensional (2D) or three-dimensional (3D).

Two aspects to submodalities are critical to understanding how they influence what people say yes to:

>> **Comparative analysis:** When presented with choices, people unconsciously process the options, and the comparative analysis of the submodalities of the choices (the differences between the choices) determines their decisions. One choice will appeal more than the other: It may be bigger, brighter, more colorful, in 3D or a movie compared to small, dull, monochrome, 2D, and a still image. If clear distinctions exist between the choices, then the decision literally "appears obvious." If the distinctions are similar, people often find it difficult to make a choice.

>> **Seeing a desired outcome:** People say "yes" when they see the outcome of the decision and it makes them feel good. The submodalities of the mind pictures can be static or moving but will generally be associated and create feelings of desire, comfort, or a sense of certainty.

These two unconscious decision-making processes are exploited in negotiation, advertising, and selling, although most people in these professions have no awareness that what they do and say influences and changes the submodalities in people's minds. For example:

>> The negotiator may point out the pain and costs of someone sticking to a position and build up a picture of desire by discussing the benefits of agreeing to a new position.

>> The salesperson often describes the financial pain of missing out on an offer and the pleasure and benefits of buying the product, often getting people to hold the product or try out the service so they effectively experience the desired outcome.

>> The advertisers create lifestyle images so the viewer literally imagines living the dream or owning the product — stepping into the pictures painted and becoming associated with the product.

TIP

These processes are just two ways to influence people's actions and decisions and to get them to say yes:

>> If they have choices, use your communication to diminish the mind pictures of the choice or choices you would prefer them not to take and then enhance the desired choice.

>> Use verbal and nonverbal communication to create mind pictures in people's heads where they see a desired outcome that makes them feel good.

If You Have the Need to Influence, You Get to Do All the Work

Have you ever been communicating with people and had the sense that you were talking to yourself and they weren't hearing the communication? Anyone with teenage children will be familiar with this notion. If you are the communicator and you want the listener (receiver) to be engaged, informed, and influenced, start by taking total responsibility for doing all the work. Don't expect listeners to adjust what they're doing; they have no need to. The person with the need gets to do the work.

If someone is unwilling to listen or receive the communication, then you need to adjust what you're doing and do something else to engage him (for more on this, see the "If You Aren't Getting the Desired Results, Change Your Communication" section at the end of the chapter).

ENEMIES OF LEARNING

When discovering new things, many people experience what's called *enemies of learning*. These unconscious behaviors block people from trying new things for the sake of comfort and familiarity. The concept of enemies of learning applies to all forms of communication where the intention is to influence. Here are some common enemies of learning:

- **Is this the same as that?** Humans are pattern-matching machines. They look for the sequences and familiarity in everything as a means to learn about the world. Is this like that? Is that like this? If someone operates by assuming what's being presented is the same as what he already knows, he's closing his mind to new ideas.

- **I've heard this before.** If a person assumes he's heard this before, the open mind closes. Suppose you're sitting in a training session, listening to a presenter tell a story. Although you've heard the story a good 30 times before at previous training sessions, you suddenly hear a *new* message. You can always find something to learn.

- **Do you know who I am?** Professional experts, senior executives, high earners, and high achievers can often let their perceived status block them from learning in a coaching conversation. The person who thinks he's the finished article, who's reached his potential because of a title or qualification, has a cup that's overflowing.

- **I don't have time for this.** Everyone is busy. Unless someone values the time and effort involved in a process, he may be resistant from the start.

- **This is all highly amusing.** Fun is a great state for learning. But a distinction exists between having fun and making light of the work. Playing the joker is often a way to camouflage insecurity. When someone is trying to disengage by using humor for fear of not being good enough, of not being able to learn, or of changes that may come about, humor becomes a problem.

Navigating the Political Landscape

The political landscape of every business is totally unique and idiosyncratic and changes over time. No two businesses are alike. When preparing any communications with the intentions to engage, inform, and influence, keep in mind that communication is more than simply one person talking and another listening. Instead, the communication happens within the context of the political landscape of the listener. The listener is operating in a complex world that affects how he perceives the communication, what it means to him, and ultimately the actions he takes.

The elegant and effective communicator takes the landscape into consideration before crafting his communications. Consider a diagnostic tool called the Information Grid, which can be used to transform great visions into workable plans. Parts of the Information Grid can also be used to bring order into the complex political landscape within which communication happens.

TIP

When creating communications — whether a newsletter, speech, sales pitch, website, or report — consider the listener's perspective and political landscape before crafting the message or messages. Ask the following questions:

>> What's important to the listener? What does he value?

>> What may the listener object to (move away from)?

>> What may appeal to the listener (moving toward)?

>> What would the listener need to see, hear, and feel in order to say yes?

Then use parts of the Information Grid (listed as follows) to consider the wider context within which the listener operates and ask this question for each part: "What may affect the listener and prevent him from agreeing or saying yes?" Could it be:

>> Time

>> Money

>> Effort

>> People

>> Beliefs and values

>> Skills

>> Capabilities

>> Environment

>> Ecology

>> Legal

TIP

People are wise to spend time researching and finding out from prospective listeners what they would have to hear in order to be influenced. Market research, surveys, and think tanks give valuable information enabling communications to be crafted specifically to meet the needs of the listener.

REVEALING HIDDEN RESISTANCE TO BEING INFLUENCED

Colin was CEO of a property development group. At one point, he raised a problem that he and his team were struggling with. They had negotiated an "in principle" deal with Stuart, a farmer, to redevelop a parcel of agricultural land for mixed light-industrial and part residential units. Over an 18-month period, they had finally obtained planning consent, yet Stuart was unwilling to sign the contract so work could commence. Colin and his team had a good relationship with Stuart, who was unable to explain his reluctance to sign.

It was suggested to Colin that Stuart's resistance was caused by an unconscious factor. After imagining seeing things from Stuart's perspective and asking the question "What may be affecting Stuart and preventing him from agreeing and saying yes?," Colin was instructed to further examine two categories with Stuart to find out what unknown influences were causing the resistance. These influences were:

- **Beliefs and values:** What would selling the land mean to Stuart?
- **Ecology:** What else and who else in Stuart's world would be affected by the sale of the land?

Colin arranged a meeting with Stuart and got to the bottom of Stuart's reluctance, and the project was now off the table. Colin discussed with Stuart what selling the land would mean to him and what and who else would be affected by the sale. After a moment's reflection, Stuart had a "light bulb" moment of insight. Stuart was the descendant of a long line of landowners, and although he needed the money from the sale of the land, he realized that he didn't want to be known as the first in his family for generations to have to sell land. He would see himself as a failure and was sure that others would see him that way, too. Had this resistance, hidden deep within the political landscape of Stuart's life, been identified earlier, it would've been easier to address at the start of the negotiations or, if found to be an insurmountable obstacle from the start, Colin would have let the project go and saved the business considerable time, money, and effort.

With the knowledge of what the resistance was, a meeting was arranged with Stuart to offer him a restructured deal giving him a small percentage part ownership of the project for less money. Stuart was able to release valuable equity from the sale and still be the landowner for future generations to come.

Ethically Influencing and Persuading for Results

When looking to influence and persuade, always keep the end goal in mind and consider what could be an obstacle or resistance to reaching it.

REMEMBER

Always think, what does my language do to the submodalities of the listener or receiver?

The word *manipulation* is emotionally charged, especially in the context of influencing and persuasion. For many people, it implies being underhanded. The word *manipulation* means "to use or change (numbers, information, and so on) in a skillful way or for a particular purpose." If we add "or to move in a particular direction" to this definition, it becomes clear that without moving customers, colleagues, or suppliers in the direction of saying yes, no business would ever happen. The intention behind the manipulation is what's important.

Like any tools, persuasion and influence can be used for good as well as harm. Many of the principles and concepts in this chapter have been misused by many people and even been used for evil. They have been used for speed seduction, unethical selling, politics, warmongering, and radicalization, but that does not make the tools themselves evil. It's an unfortunate fact of life that there are people who see these tools as ways to persuade others to make decisions that are not in their best interests.

TIP

Use this simple model to decide whether persuasion and influence are being used ethically. If the results are:

>> **Win** (for the communicator) and **win** (for the listener), the answer is **yes**.

>> **Win** (for the communicator) and **lose** (for the listener), the answer is **no**.

>> **Lose** (for the communicator) and **win** (for the listener), the answer is **no**.

The term *toxic leadership* has been used to describe the failure rate of CEOs. In the past two decades, 30 percent of Fortune 500 CEOs have lasted less than three years, with studies showing CEO failure rates ranging from 30 percent to 75 percent in the first three years of tenure. Toxic leadership is a phenomenon that operates from the win/lose perspective and is driven by hubris, ego, and a lack of emotional intelligence.

REMEMBER

Valuing the importance of a win/win relationship with colleagues, staff, customers, and suppliers will increase your value at work, your effectiveness, and your longevity.

It Takes Two to Influence

Think of engaging, informing, and influencing as an elegant interaction, like a dance between the communicator and the receiver. The communicator is the one leading the dance, manipulating and taking the receiver gently in a desired direction. The communicator pays attention to how the receiver reacts to his lead, and if the receiver starts to go off-track, the communicator gently guides him around by changing his communication so he follows. This process is known as *pacing and leading*.

TIP

The key to great influencing is to pay attention to the feedback from the listener or receiver of the communication and to test that you're getting the desired results or at least going in the right general direction. (For more on changing the direction, see the later section "If You Aren't Getting the Desired Results, Change Your Communication.")

The following tools all manipulate. When used in a win-win scenario, it would be irresponsible for people not to use them to get others to say yes.

Paying attention

The following exercise on the power of paying attention can help improve your communication skills.

1. **Sit facing a partner and ask him to talk to you about a hobby or activity that he loves and to keep going for three minutes.**

This conversation should be one-way with only him speaking.

2. **For the first minute, pay undivided attention with your whole physiology. Add in lots of nodding, smiles, and agreeable sounds without commenting.**

3. **After one minute, start to fidget and be distracted: Yawn, pick dust off your trousers, clean under your fingernails, or glance at your cell phone.**

REMEMBER

At all times, while feigning distraction, pay attention to what he's saying so you can replay it back to him at the end of the exercise.

One of two things will happen. He may talk to you more intently in an attempt to get your attention, but this happens rarely. The normal response is that he'll stop talking because you aren't paying attention.

4. **Instruct him to keep talking and remind him that you're listening.**

He will reluctantly continue.

5. **Resume the distracted behavior while listening intently.**

6. **After a minute, return your physiology back to paying full attention for the remainder of the time.**

7. **Then call a halt to the exercise.**

8. **Debrief him about his experience.**

   Common feedback is "While you weren't listening, I felt uncomfortable," "I was unable to talk," or "I was annoyed." Then relate to him all that was said while you were seemingly paying no attention; he'll be shocked that you were listening.

This exercise teaches people two valuable influencing lessons. First, they find out about the power of paying full attention when someone is communicating — if people feel someone isn't listening, they tend to switch off. Second, they discover how easy it can be to misinterpret whether someone is paying attention.

REMEMBER

Be sure to:

>> Fully pay attention when someone is communicating.

>> Not make assumptions about whether someone has heard the meaning of your communication. Test his understanding. Test by asking questions and, if appropriate, get him to repeat back to you what's been said. This testing is invaluable during meetings when quite often people have been given instructions but haven't really heard what was said or have interpreted them differently from the way they were meant.

These two skills are essential, especially for negotiators, salespeople, and customer service people, to master.

Listening actively

You can call this exercise "Parrot phrase not para-phrase":

1. **Imagine that you're a property agent, and you have a partner describe to you an ideal house.**

   Instruct him to describe the size, location, rooms, and features of the property.

2. **While describing, listen for and make notes of the following two things:**

   • The sequence and order he asks for the features in.

   • The words he uses to describe how important and necessary they are. These words are called *modal operators*, or MOs. The words to listen out for are *wish, like, want, need, have/has/hasn't, must/must not, can/could, couldn't, will,* and *should/shouldn't.*

3. **When he has described his ideal property, read back the list three times, and each time ask how the information is received. How does it sound and feel? Are you describing the ideal property?**

   For example, he says, "I want a two-story house; it must be in the country; it should have four bedrooms with two en-suite bathrooms. It has to be within a 30-minute drive of my office. I would like it to have an open-plan kitchen, and it must have a large garden, preferably with a patio for sitting outside in the evening."

4. **First, change the sequence around and test his reaction to the description.**

   "So, it has to be within a 30-minute drive of your office; it must be in the country; it should have four bedrooms; it must have a large garden, preferably with a patio for sitting outside in the evening. You would like it to have an open-plan kitchen. And you want a two-story house with two en-suite bathrooms. Is that correct?"

5. **Second, repeat the original sequence, change the modal operators and test his reaction to the description.**

   "So, you'd like a two-story house. It could be in the country; it might have four bedrooms with two en-suite bathrooms; and you want it to be within a 30-minute drive of your office. It needs to have an open-plan kitchen, and you would like it to have a large garden, which might have a patio for sitting outside in the evening. Is that correct?"

6. **Third, repeat the original sequence and use the modal operators as he presented them and test his reaction to the description.**

   "So you want a two-story house. It must be in the country. It should have four bedrooms with two en-suite bathrooms. It has to be within a 30-minute drive of your office, and you'd like it to have an open-plan kitchen. It must have a large garden, preferably with a patio for sitting outside in the evening."

With the first two descriptions, he'll struggle to recognize the ideal property and may even adamantly reject what you've said because, simply put, it's not what he asked for. You weren't listening. By changing the sequence and the modal operators, you're giving a clear message that "I've heard what you've said, but I'm not really listening and I'll now change it." This description is the verbal equivalent of flicking dust off your trousers during a conversation. With the third description, you'll see him visibly relax as he recognizes your description to be the ideal property he described.

GIVING SOMEONE WHAT HE ASKED FOR

In customer service and sales, as well as negotiations, being able to listen purposefully and communicate exactly back to the listener so he feels you understand is an essential skill. It creates rapport between two individuals and demonstrates understanding.

Have your coffee just as you like it:

- **Customer:** "I would like a large latte with soymilk, extra hot, with an extra shot of coffee, in a to-go cup, and two pumps of hazelnut syrup please. Oh, and a doughnut."

- **Barista:** "So, you want a doughnut with a large latte with an extra shot to go, and two pumps of hazelnut syrup. You'd like it made extra hot with soymilk. Is that correct?"

- **Customer:** "I have no idea. I'll just have a glass of water!"

I'm not angry, I just want to be heard:

- **Customer:** "I'm calling not to complain but because I'm disappointed that my refrigerator was delivered at 1 p.m. You had promised a morning delivery, and I thought you would appreciate the feedback."

- **Customer service:** "I'm sorry to hear you're upset. I will let our delivery team know that they wasted your morning."

- **Customer:** "Well, they didn't waste my morning. I had the day off. I just thought you would want to know that I didn't get the text message as promised. If the delivery was going to be delayed, I would have liked to have known so I could step out if I wanted to."

- **Customer service:** "Yes, that shouldn't have happened, and I'm sorry you're angry. Sometimes the text messages are delayed. I'll pass your complaint on to the delivery department. If it was important and you needed to go out, I understand why you're upset."

- **Customer:** "Listen to me. I wasn't angry, or complaining, or upset . . . but I am now."

Building rapport

Communicating to engage, inform, and influence is easier when a rapport is evident between the communicator and receiver. *Rapport* is when you have trust and harmony in a relationship. Think of rapport as part of the dance — where the communicator who has the need to influence extends his hand as an invitation to dance. If the receiver feels comfortable, he extends his and gives the communicator permission to lead the dance. The communicator gains rapport in order to lead the receiver in a purposeful direction to the point of agreeing or saying yes.

Influencing is a four-step process:

1. **Rapport:** Gain rapport. Ways to do so are covered in the following sections.

2. **Understanding:** When rapport has been established, trust and harmony are present so the receiver feels understood.

3. **Permission:** Because the receiver feels understood, he (unconsciously) gives permission to be led. He is willing to engage in the communication.

4. **Influence:** He is now more willing to be influenced by the communication.

Creating rapport elegantly

Here are a number of ways in which humans naturally experience and demonstrate rapport between individuals and groups:

>> **Identity:** People who share the same perceived identity often have natural rapport, whether that's gender, race, religion, or members of social groups, a team, or an organization.

>> **Beliefs and values:** Consider all the people you spend time with. At some level, you must have rapport in what you believe and value or you wouldn't associate with them. This concept is openly used by business when values statements are made public. An example is that of "ethical" or "fair trade," where companies proclaim ethical practice allowing customers who have matching values the opportunity to decide to use their products and services.

>> **Skills and capabilities:** People with qualifications or in the same professions demonstrate natural rapport by their credentials.

>> **Environment:** Generally, people like places they're familiar with or that match their expectations and make them feel comfortable. In terms of rapport, consider a professional business coach who operates from a business center; has training credentials on the wall; has a nice, clean, tidy professional office; and dresses professionally. Compare this scenario to that of an equally skilled and qualified business coach who works from his living room at home with family photographs on display and dresses casually. A client who visits the home office may value the more relaxed approach and have similar family values and find the family photographs create rapport, but generally it's best to create an environment that meets the environmental expectations of the majority.

WARNING

Don't try to create rapport with identity, beliefs, and values if none exists. Pretending to be what you're not is never a good strategy for creating trust. When no natural rapport exists, the easiest way to create rapport is with skills, capabilities, and particularly behaviors.

TIP

Here are four ways to gain rapport at a behavioral level:

>> Matching language patterns.

>> Matching body movements and gestures.

>> Matching voice tonality, volume, and tempo.

>> With dress and attire.

REMEMBER

The purpose of creating rapport is to create a relationship so the receiver feels trust (even at an unconscious level) and understood so he gives permission to be influenced.

Understanding preferred representation systems

We all communicate using a combination of language that represents the five senses — visual (sight), auditory (hearing), kinesthetic (touch), olfactory (smell), and gustatory (taste). These are known as the *representation systems*. The sensory words that people use in communication to represent their experience are called *predicates*.

Most people have a preferred representation system, one they use more often and are comfortable with. If a person whose preferred representation system is visual and tends to communicate using predominantly visual predicates talks with someone whose preferred representation system is auditory, at times they may as well be talking different languages because they're out of rapport. For example:

Manager: "I keep telling you, but you keep saying you don't see what I mean." (Preferred representation system is auditory.)

Supervisor: "I hear what you're saying, but it still doesn't appear clear to me." (Preferred representation system is visual.)

TIP

Listen actively to the words people use in their language because they leave clues as to their preferred representation system by the predicates they commonly use. Table 5-1 lists some predicates that people commonly use in the business world.

TABLE 5-1 **Commonly Used Sensory Words**

Visual	Auditory	Kinesthetic	Olfactory	Gustatory
Analyze	Announce	Active	Aroma	Bitter
Appear	Articulate	Charge	Bouquet	Bland
Clarity	Converse	Concrete	Essence	Delicious
Examine	Discuss	Emotional	Fragrance	Flat
Focus	Enunciate	Feel	Musty	Salty
Foresee	Hear	Firm grasp	Odor	Sharp
Illustrate	Listen	Grip	Pungent	Sour
Look	Mention	Hold	Rotten	Sweet
Notice	Noise	Intuition	Smells	Tangy
Observe	Proclaim	Motion	Stench	Tasty
Perception	Pronounce	Pressure	Stinks	Zesty
Scope	Remark	Sensitive	Sweet	
Show	Say	Shift		
Survey	State	Stir		
View	Tell	Support		
Vision	Utter	Touch		
Watch	Voice			

Mastering rapport skills takes practice. Here are four exercises for you to practice in the great laboratory of normal life. These skills take practice but are powerful for creating rapport where there may be none. You'll begin to see examples of people naturally in rapport whether linguistically or with their physiology all around you.

To identify preferred representation systems, try this exercise:

1. **Divide a piece of paper into five columns headed Visual, Auditory, Kinesthetic, Olfactory, and Gustatory (as in Table 5-1).**

2. **Work with a partner and ask him to talk to you for five minutes about a subject he loves.**

3. **Make a mark under the respective column when you hear, notice, or get a sense that he has used a sensory predicate word.**

4. **After five minutes, simply count up the predicate scores for each sense.**

The sense he has used most in his language is his preferred representation system.

TIP

If possible, have two or more people doing the tally so you can compare the totals. Generally, the two people will agree, with perhaps a few discrepancies. To improve your ability to identify someone's preferred representation system so it becomes second nature, watch and listen to TV and keep a tally.

To match someone's preferred representation systems, try this exercise:

1. **Work with someone whom you have already identified has a predominant representation system.**

If, for example, he was predominantly visual, talk to him for two minutes about a subject you like using predominantly visual predicates.

2. **After a few minutes, stop and repeat the conversation using other sensory predicates.**

3. **Debrief your partner about his experience.**

Which of the two conversations did he prefer? Although the subject matter was the same, the partner almost certainly preferred the first version because you have been talking his language.

Try this exercise to match body movements and gestures:

1. **Go to a quiet place like a library and choose an unsuspecting partner. Sit at a distance so you can observe him without being observed yourself.**

2. **Notice his rate of breathing.**

This is best done by watching for the rise and fall of the shoulders.

3. **Match your breathing to his.**

4. **Do this breathing for a few minutes so breathing is synchronized and then slowly speed up or slow down your rate of breathing.**

The unsuspecting partner will follow your lead. Although he will be unconscious of this phenomenon, he is in rapport with you.

5. **Match breathing for a few more minutes; then make a gesture and wait for him to follow your gesture.**

With practice, you can have people following your lead.

CREATING RAPPORT WITH A STRANGER

On persuasion and influence training in Florida, Steve was having breakfast in the hotel restaurant and decided to practice some of the skills that would be taught over the course. He sat back and, out of his peripheral vision six tables away, saw a well-built man with a lumberjack shirt and large, bushy beard having breakfast.

Steve matched his breathing and movements, lifting food to his mouth to match the man, drinking when he drank, turning his paper when the man turned his. Then Steve ran his fingers through his hair, and the man followed the gesture. Steve scratched his nose; the man followed again.

After a few minutes of this, the man closed his newspaper and stood up, looked across the room, and headed toward Steve. Focusing intently on reading his newspaper, Steve cautiously looked up to see this giant of a man standing in front of him. "Excuse me," he said, "I don't mean to interrupt your breakfast, but I have really strong sense that I know you from somewhere. Have we met before?"

In this exercise, you match voice tonality, volume, and tempo:

1. **Engage in a conversation with a colleague, paying careful attention first to his rate of breathing.**
2. **Then become aware of the speed and volume that he talks.**
3. **Match his breathing and talk to him at the same speed and volume that he talks.**
4. **Slowly reduce your volume and speed of conversation so he begins to also slow down.**

Choosing words that could, should, might make a difference

Have you ever met someone who said he would do something but didn't follow through with his actions? This sorry state of affairs is not uncommon in business, especially after meetings when instructions have been given or agreements have been made but people still don't do their part. This section explores how modal operators give clues as to why this inactivity sets in and how you can listen carefully to others' communication and change their language in order to influence people to deliver on promises made.

Modal operators can be thought of as "moody operators." They juice up the motivational desire to take action by changing the submodalities of the mind pictures. Thoughts precede actions, and when people can literally see themselves taking the action in the movie in their mind and see the movie run to the end with a successful outcome, they'll engage in the activity.

This exercise is called "Juicing up the motivation to take action." Use this exercise to personally experience how changing one word in a sentence has an influence on how you feel about taking action and how you're likely to behave.

1. **Play the following sentences, one at a time, inside your head using your own internal voice.**

   Say each sentence, stop, and notice the feelings you get.

2. **As you go through the exercise, compare the feelings from one sentence to another.**

   On a motivational scale of 0 to 10 where 0 is no motivation to take action and 10 is totally motivated, note the motivation for each sentence.

   Start by making an assumption that, regardless of the reality and circumstances of your life, it is within your power to take Monday off work and say to yourself:

   - "I *wish* I could take Monday off." Notice the motivational feeling and rate it 0 to 10.

   - "I'd *like* to take Monday off." Notice the motivational feeling and rate it 0 to 10.

   - "I *want* to take Monday off." Notice the motivational feeling and rate it 0 to 10.

   - "I *need* to take Monday off." Notice the motivational feeling and rate it 0 to 10.

   - "I *must* take Monday off." Notice the motivational feeling and rate it 0 to 10.

   - "I *can* take Monday off." Notice the motivational feeling and rate it 0 to 10.

   - "I *will* take Monday off." Notice the motivational feeling and rate it 0 to 10.

   - "I'm *going* to take Monday off." Notice the motivational feeling and rate it 0 to 10.

Notice that simply by changing one word in the sentence, you experience a different degree of motivation. Generally, for most people, as they progress down the list, they feel more motivated.

REMEMBER

These language patterns and humans are all unique, so some people won't comply exactly with the usual patterns. Always work with whatever the unique individual human you're communicating with presents to you.

Now, do the same exercise again, but this time pay attention to the mind pictures that you make as you say the sentences, becoming aware of which submodalities change.

Generally, the sentences at the top of the list are described as unclear or wishy-washy; people experience low levels of motivation and the activity is not likely to happen. As people progress down the list, the images become clearer and more active, and more motivation is present to take the desired action.

Try one further sentence and notice what happens. If someone were to say to you, "You *should* take Monday off," what happens to the picture? For most people, when someone else tells them what they should do, the mind picture disappears. Tell people what they *should* do and you're literally erasing the very thoughts from their mind. No thought = no action.

With this knowledge about how language changes the motivation and desire to take action, consider these sentences and whether the person saying them is likely to deliver or get others to deliver on their promise. Against each sentence is a reworked sentence using language designed to influence the listener and get the desired results.

>> "I would like the report to be concluded by Monday" versus "The report must be concluded and delivered to my office on Monday."

>> "We want to finish this project by the end of the month" versus "Let's aim to finish this project and see it done by the end of the month."

>> "The customers must be told they have to return the signed contracts before we can ship the product" versus "Tell the customer to return the signed contracts and the product will be shipped to them by return."

TIP

To improve your success rate in influencing people to take action, where possible completely remove the modal operators from the communication or use more motivating ones.

INFLUENCING OTHERS BY DEMONSTRATING WHAT YOU CAN DO FOR THEM

Steve was invited by an international TV and film company to review a series of TV commercials promoting a new series of documentaries. The brief was to appraise the commercials from a "persuasion and influence perspective." The client wanted to know two things:

- Could the commercials be improved to encourage viewers to stay on the channel during the ads, rather than channel-hop?

- Could anything be done to improve the viewers' recall about what the upcoming shows were and when they were being aired?

The commercials had been failing to retain viewer attention in viewer research samples; not only were an unusually high number of viewers switching over when the commercials came on, but those who did watch the commercials were unable to recall what or when the documentaries were being aired.

After viewing the commercials, Steve asked the client, "Do you want the bad news first or the really bad news, which is really the good news?" The client was understandably confused and a little upset by this frank feedback but curious as to what Steve meant.

The client group was made up of senior executives as well as the team who had designed and filmed the commercials. First, Steve explained to the group that from a persuasion and influence perspective, all communication is processed by the viewer whether consciously or not. In the first part of the commercials, there was a sharp red arrow with a high-pitched musical accompaniment that flew through a beautiful series of landscapes and finished by aiming directly at the viewer. Although it looked artistic and the landscape was aesthetically pleasing, the human mind reacts negatively to fast-moving, sharp objects flying toward it, even if only on a screen. The red color, which is unconsciously associated with threat and danger, and the sharp staccato sound only amplified this reaction.

Research has shown the impact on the neurology of sharp objects moving toward the body. By using tests with cutlery, it was discovered that sharp metal objects caused increased heart rates, as well as increases in adrenaline. Steve was later able to demonstrate this effect by setting up tests using heart-rate monitors and software that showed that viewers experienced elevated stress levels while watching the first part of the commercial. This was one reason for large numbers of viewers changing channels or heading to the kitchen for a snack. The first part of the commercial made them feel stressed, and what people perceive as stress, they tend to move away from and avoid.

In the second part of the commercial, the main character in the new documentary appeared onscreen looking to the upper-left corner of the monitor, while the show logo and scheduled viewing time appeared in the opposite upper-right corner. The viewer would naturally follow the nonverbal communication of the character onscreen and gaze where his eyes looked, totally missing the logo and time. This was one reason why viewers could not recall the name or timing of the show. They hadn't looked at it; they'd been misdirected.

In the commercial, the show logo at the upper right of the screen flashed on and off and then exploded into fragments and disappeared over the horizon, all highly dramatic and visually pleasing. However, this animation had the same effect as giving the viewers virtual amnesia for the show and schedule. Steve demonstrated the effectiveness of this technique with Charles, the commercial director, by having him think of a problem he had been worrying about unnecessarily and that he'd like to forget about. After doing the technique for five minutes, Charles found it difficult to recall what the problem was.

In summary, the first part of the commercial made people feel stressed, which was bad. The really bad news was they would then feel bad by association about the upcoming show, but the good news was those who stayed on the channel, although they were feeling bad, wouldn't remember what the show was anyway.

Although the group of executives were upset to hear the negative impact of their artistic creation, they now understood why their research figures for these commercials were so poor and why the ads were failing to have the desired effects of engaging the audience, informing them of the upcoming show, and influencing them to switch on at the aired time. The commercials were changed by making the accompanying music less physically uncomfortable, by blunting the end of the arrow, and by reducing the bright red color down to a pastel shade. The main figure on the screen was reversed so he looked up toward the show name and time so the viewers' eyes naturally followed the nonverbal communication of his gaze. The show details were kept static for a few seconds, enabling the viewers to imprint these details into their memory. The research statistics for viewing retention during the commercial break and recall of the show afterward both increased dramatically.

If You Aren't Getting the Desired Results, Change Your Communication

Do you know the saying, "The meaning of the communication is the response you get"? The more variety people have in the way they communicate their ideas, the more success they have in achieving their desired results.

Social psychology experiments confirm that our decisions and behaviors are influenced by many things beyond our conscious awareness. In Robert Cialdini's book *Influence: The Psychology of Persuasion* (Harper Business), he identifies six principles as influencing decisions unconsciously, all of which were tested and validated through social experiments.

Using these principles gives you a wide variety of ways to influence. With each principle, you're given examples of how to use it effectively in business. The principles are as follows:

>> **Reciprocity:** People tend to return a favor. Businesses that offer free samples use this principle to influence potential buyers to feel that they owe a favor.

- *Offer something first.* Allow someone to feel indebted to you.

- *Offer something exclusive.* This allows someone to feel special.

- *Personalize the offer.* Make sure they know the offer comes from you.

>> **Commitment and consistency:** If people make a verbal commitment, they're more likely to follow through with an action because they want their actions to remain congruent and consistent with their word.

- *Ask people to start from small actions.* If they take the first action, they're more likely to take the next action.

- *Encourage public commitments.* People are less likely to back out of an agreement if they've made a public declaration.

>> **Social proof:** People do things that they see others doing.

- *Users:* Approval from current/past users, use ratings, reviews, and testimonials.

- *Peers:* Approval from friends and people similar to the listener.

>> **Authority:** People tend to obey or comply with authority figures, perceived experts, and celebrities:

- *Experts:* Approval from credible experts in the relevant field.

- *Celebrities:* Approval or endorsements from people who are widely admired.

>> **Liking:** People are easily persuaded by people they like (see the "Building rapport" section earlier in this chapter). This fact can be due to

- *Physical attractiveness:* People are influenced by looks. This unfortunate fact of life is clearly demonstrated throughout the advertising world.

- *Similarity:* Behave like a friend, not a brand. Show people that you can relate to and understand them.

» **Scarcity:** If a perceived scarcity for a product or service exists, this scarcity generates a demand such as the following:

- *Limited number:* The item is in short supply and won't be available when it runs out.

- *Limited time:* The item is only available during a fixed time period.

- *Competition:* The inclination is to want things more because other people also want them. This tendency can be used in auctions, bids, or countdowns that show a diminishing supply.

These principles are well known and used in business, especially in online marketing and selling where the Internet and emails provide cost-effective platforms to offer incentives and multiple communications including all or some of the six principles.

REMEMBER

The principles work because they unconsciously influence the decisions of the person receiving the communication. What we're unconscious of is difficult to disagree with because it bypasses any conscious resistance.

Chapter **6**

Influencing through Body Language

How you perceive and project yourself determines how people perceive and receive you. If you want to be seen as positive, powerful, and influential at work, you have to act the part. Your gestures, actions, and expressions need to celebrate and reflect your strengths and abilities. Based on what you reveal in the way you appear and move, people want to know more — or close the door on you.

From the moment you enter the work environment to your last day on the job, you're being watched. Make sure that the way you're moving, gesturing, and behaving projects the image you desire. The higher up the hierarchy you go, the more focused your actions and the more contained your gestures need to be, in order to project the expected authority. You never see chief executives running down the hall or senior partners flapping their hands. You never see presidents sitting with their backs to the door.

REMEMBER

Self-awareness is paramount if you're to work your way successfully through the office maze.

This chapter looks at how you can make a positive impact all the way to the final exit. You discover that how you position your body impacts how people perceive you, and you gain skills to display confidence, commitment, and credibility. (Flip to Book 1, Chapter 5 for techniques on influencing specifically through verbal communication.)

Creating a Positive Environment

If you want to get ahead at work, you need to treat people with respect. Not everyone you work with is going to be the same as you — thankfully — or even like you (which you may find hard to believe, being the likeable person that you are). But each person brings a unique quality that can contribute to the success of an organization when steered with sensitivity and compassion.

As well as treating people with respect, aim to establish rapport. When two or more people are reading from the same page and playing with the same goal in mind, miracles can happen. Or at least, deadlines can be met.

Demonstrating respect

People often say that what they really want at work is to be treated with dignity and respect. Consider the following:

» **Treat people with courtesy and kindness.** Keep your body in an open position — where your weight is evenly distributed and your muscles are relaxed — to allow a free flow of information, inviting people to feel comfortable in your presence.

» **Encourage colleagues and staff to express their ideas and opinions.** Look them in the eye as they speak, and appear interested. Pay attention to people's facial expressions — are they frowning or smiling, are their lips taut or trembling? Refrain from multitasking when someone's speaking: fiddling with your phone and playing with paper, pens, or pencils is rude and potentially distracting. If you don't agree with what you hear, keep your facial expressions and gestures neutral.

» **Listen to what others have to say before expressing your opinions.** Never interrupt or butt in while someone else is speaking. If you struggle not to interrupt, make a conscious effort to keep your mouth closed while others speak. Refrain from clenching your teeth, however, as doing so creates tension in your mouth, mind, and body. Allow your lips to lie lightly together and your tongue to float gently in your mouth. Make sure that your eyes are open and not burrowed in a frown.

» **Encourage someone who offers an idea that may improve current conditions.** Lean forward, look them in the eye, and smile as you speak if you want to let them and others know that you think they're making sense.

» **Never insult, bully, or disparage someone or their ideas.** Raising your nostrils as if you're smelling something past its prime, pulling up your upper lip, laughing with derision, or physically prodding or pushing another person is rude, unproductive, and about as far away from demonstrating respect as a person can get.

» **Praise more often than you criticize.** Encourage a culture of praise and recognition among employees as well as from management. When you praise people, look at them face to face and smile. Doing so may feel uncomfortable at first because many people shy away from giving and receiving praise. To see the benefits, persevere.

» **Practice giving and receiving praise.** When you offer praise, be sure that you believe what you're saying or the person you're praising won't believe you. Like animals, people can pick up on physical vibrations including facial expressions and bodily tension. Nod as you speak in confirmation of what you're saying. Look the other person in the eye. Smile with pleasure as you give and receive the praise.

» **Treat others as they want to be treated.** Maintain an open mind and reflect your attitude in your open body language. Nobody wants to be spoken to in tense tones accompanied by tight gestures.

Establishing rapport

When you're in rapport, you feel a harmonious connection between yourself and others. All's right in the world and communication flows. You might even find yourself smiling and nodding in agreement as you converse.

The word *rapport* derives from the French word *rapporter*, which translates as "to return or bring back." English dictionaries define rapport as "a sympathetic relationship or understanding." The result is that people in rapport can create outstanding results.

When you have rapport with someone, taking on that person's style of behavior — also called *mirroring* and *matching* — helps you become highly tuned to the way the other person thinks and experiences the world. Your whole body becomes involved in the observation process. *Mirroring* is a direct replication of the other person's movements while *matching* is more about moving in sync with them. Be attuned to the difference between moving in rhythm with someone and mimicking their actions, though, because people know when you're making fun of them or being insincere.

Mirroring

People who are in rapport tend to reflect one another's physical patterns. They move in time with each other and mirror behavior that they observe.

Research on rapport indicates that, from an evolutionary perspective, mirroring body language facilitates interaction between people. When you mirror people — whether in the way they speak or move — you're unconsciously reproducing their state of mind within yourself. The more effectively you can do so, the more able you are to understand the other person's perspective.

WARNING

When you're reflecting other people's behavior back to them, avoid mimicry. If you recreate muscle movement for muscle movement and replicate exact gestures and expressions with precision, the other person feels mocked and disinclined to engage in a meaningful conversation with you.

Matching

Matching someone's behavior indicates that you're in sync with one another, experiencing similar feelings and emotions. When you're matching someone's behavior, you create a similar state to the other person that helps you understand their point of view.

Try to match the other person's

» Body postures and gestures.

» Breathing rates.

» Rhythm of movement and energy levels.

» Voice tonality, including pitch, pace, and volume.

Using effective gazes in business situations

If you're uncomfortable looking people directly in the eye and you want to come across as a person to be taken seriously, keep your gaze in the triangular area between the eyes and the center of the forehead. As long as your eyes remain in that space and you keep control of the interaction, the other person reckons that you're someone who means business. The following are other tricks that come in handy in business situations.

AT LAST, A WAY TO SHORTEN BUSINESS MEETINGS!

One study showed that in presentations where visual aids are used, 83 percent of the information is absorbed visually, 11 percent through the audio channel, and 6 percent through the other three senses. A study conducted at the Wharton School of the University of Pennsylvania found that in presentations that relied solely on the spoken word, only 10 percent of the information was retained. For a verbal presentation to be effective, key points must be repeated frequently. When a visual element is added to a verbal presentation, the retention rate increases to 50 percent. By including visual aids in your presentations, you achieve a 400 percent increase in efficiency. Further findings show that when visual aids are used in business meetings, on average they last 18.6 minutes as opposed to 25.7 minutes — equating to a time saving of 28 percent.

Controlling a bore

Looking a tedious, dull, and mind-numbing windbag straight in the eyes without flinching is a highly effective way of stopping her in her tracks. If you fix your eyes directly in the business gaze triangle without a flicker of an eye, you may be amazed at how quickly she comes to a halt.

The power lift

If you want to get your message across when you're presenting visual information during a meeting, guide the audience's attention to where you want it to look. A simple way of controlling your listeners' attention is to use a pen. Point to your material and verbalize what you're showing. Then lift the pen off the page and hold it between your eyes and those of your listeners. This movement works like a magnet as your listeners lift their heads, look directly at you, and, while both hearing and seeing what you're saying, absorb your message. While you continue to speak, keep the palm of your other hand open.

Standing tall and holding your ground

Having a superior position carries with it an implied authority. The same goes for tall people: they can command respect as a result of their height. Others have to look up to them and, because of their physiological make-up, they look down on others.

Some people don't feel comfortable being taller than others, so they stoop or slouch. They diminish themselves in size and stature, giving away their authority. Shorter people have to create an image of height and stature. They do so by standing with their center of gravity deep in their loins while lifting their upper torsos upward and outward. Rather than placing their energy in their upper chests — making themselves top heavy — they place their energy in their pelvic area, giving them a sense of firmness and control. Tom Cruise and Al Pacino, for example, are no taller than 5 feet 7 inches, and yet Cruise's bright smile and Pacino's brooding passion all manage to exude an aura of power.

TIP

To experience what being in control feels and looks like, try this short exercise, practicing from both the seated and standing positions:

>> Visualize another person who's challenging you, at an interview, in a meeting, or at an assessment.

>> Place your feet firmly underneath you, hip width apart.

>> Maintain flexibility in your knees and ankles to avoid becoming stiff.

>> Keep your head upright and maintain eye contact with the other person.

>> Let your arms and hands be visible.

>> Keep your chest open, feeling as if your shoulder blades are gently melting down your back.

>> Keep your mouth closed while you're listening.

>> Inhale from your diaphragm. Breathing deeply from your core grounds you and provides a firm foundation from which you can move, gesture and position yourself.

>> Reflect on what you're going to say before speaking.

>> Remind yourself of your strengths and how you want to be perceived.

>> Respond.

Stooped shoulders, caved-in chest and hands in the fig-leaf position (covering your private bits) are protective signals and indicate that you're subconsciously feeling defensive.

Moving with purpose

Whether you stride into a room with focus and direction, or wander in as though you've forgotten why you're there, you're going to create an impression. Unless you're purposely playing the role of someone from La-La Land, if you want to be noticed in a positive sense, put your muscles into your movement and propel yourself into the fray with focus, direction, and positive energy. Other people then perceive you as vibrant, interesting and engaging.

A NEW WAY OF THINKING

Cecile stands at just over 6 feet tall. As an athlete, she was used to being with people of equal height, and felt comfortable with them. When her sports career ended, she obtained her law degree and joined a city firm. After several months, Cecile noticed that she was hunching her shoulders and sinking into her hips. Her chest caved inward, her head sunk into her neck and she was looking at people from under her eyes.

Cecile was experiencing a lack of confidence and low self-esteem because she was still finding out about the job. Highly competitive, she was uncomfortable, fearing that she was being perceived as lacking in her work. In addition, the male partner she reported to was shorter than Cecile. She discovered that she was purposely making herself smaller to make him look bigger. With practice, Cecile regained her stature. She explored her mental attitude and made the necessary self-perception adjustments. Her new way of thinking and perceiving herself was reflected in the way she stood and gestured. Now, when Cecile sits and stands using her full stature she feels confident, looks credible, and commands respect.

Before projecting yourself into other people's territory, test the waters. Moderate your movements to mirror those of the people you're with (see the earlier section "Establishing rapport"). If you come bounding into a room full of silent, contemplative folk, you may be perceived as a bit of a buffoon, if not an outright annoyance. Reflect back the energy you observe in the room and adapt your behavior to match what you notice, still moving with focus and direction.

REMEMBER

Positive energy draws people, whereas negative energy repels them. You don't have to bounce like Tigger to demonstrate focus and energy. Slow actions performed with a clear intention project authority and command attention.

REMEMBER

An intentionally deliberate movement draws attention to the action and highlights the meaning behind the gesture.

Pointing Your Body in the Right Direction

How you position your body in relation to other people impacts their perception of you, which is particularly relevant in the work environment. If you stand directly in front of them, face to face, hands on hips, and jaw jutted forward, you become a threatening force. Turn your shoulder to people, cross your arms, and look down your nose at them, and you indicate that you think they aren't up to scratch. Turn your back completely on people and you better hope that they don't stick anything in it as a response to your dismissive attitude!

To create a more positive interaction, stand facing another person at a comfortable distance — with your arms open, your hands visible, and a welcoming expression on your face — and see how constructive the mood becomes. Sit or stand side by side at a distance that feels right for your relationship, and sense the connection. Both consciously and subconsciously you're adjusting your body position in response to what's happening in your environment.

TIP

People who sit side by side tend to work in a collaborative way. People sitting across the table from one another are often at odds, relying on the furniture to act as a defensive barrier.

TIP

To make a positive impression, hold your head up, keeping your chin parallel to the ground. Think of something that makes you happy. Let your eyes engage and sparkle. Allow yourself to smile. Free your shoulders and permit your chest to open as if it were a plane about to take off (but don't puff it out, which reveals defensiveness, not strength). Breathe from your diaphragm. Ground yourself by connecting with your environment. Imagine roots coming out from the soles of your feet, providing you with a firm foundation. Pretend that you've a taproot driving deep from the center of your sole, making you solid and strong. In addition, make believe that you've shallow roots coming out from the soles of your feet, providing you with flexibility.

If someone you're engaging with seems distracted, uninterested, or even annoyed, aim to match that person's movements and energy as a means of creating rapport. When the person feels that the two of you are connected, you can more easily lead the conversation in the direction you desire.

Creating a relaxed attitude with the 45-degree angle

The angle at which you position yourself in relation to another person affects the outcome of your communication. If you want your interaction to be comfortable, co-operative, and congenial, place yourself at a 45-degree angle to the other person. This position encourages openness and trust. By positioning yourself at this angle, you form a third point where you avoid being perceived as aggressive or flirtatious. Whereas face-to-face is confrontational, and side-by-side is intimate, placing yourself halfway between the two creates an atmosphere of confidence and equality. Neither confrontational nor intimate, the 45-degree angle allows people to see one another, gesture freely and maintain a comfortable space between themselves.

The 45-degree angle is a co-operative space that encourages discussion and the flow of ideas — it's perceived as neutral territory. The third angle allows another person to join you in the space, creating an equilateral triangle. If a fourth person enters the group they can form a square, and if one or two more people join, they can form a circle or divide themselves into two triangles.

Positioning yourself for co-operation

Say that you're the newly appointed head of a well-established and successful team. One by one, you invite your new colleagues into your office for a 'getting acquainted' session. They may feel a little wary of you and watch to see how you manage the meeting. By placing yourself in the neutral 45-degree zone, you encourage openness and honest discussion. No threatening aspect is associated with this position. Turn 10 degrees in either direction and the dynamics change. If you turn inwards, you indicate that intimacy is in the air. If you angle your body away, you shut out the other person.

Sitting with subordinates

When you want to create a relaxed, informal atmosphere when speaking to a subordinate in your office, open the session with both of you sitting in the 45-degree angle position, directing your bodies to a third point forming a triangle, suggesting agreement. From this position you can reflect the other person's gestures, creating a sense of ease and rapport.

If you want a direct answer to a question and you feel that you're not getting it in the 45-degree pose, shift your position to face directly toward the other person. This action says that you want a direct answer to your direct question.

Taking the pressure off

Positioning your body at a 45-degree angle relieves the potential stress of the meeting. When a sensitive issue needs addressing, go for this position. It takes the pressure off and encourages more open answers to your open questions. Unless, of course, you want to put the pressure on, in which case face the other person directly and look him in the eye.

Facing directly for serious answers

If someone asks you a direct question, look at the person directly — that is, if you want to be taken seriously. If you drop your head, avert your eyes, and peer over your shoulder, you're conveying that you're unsure, doubtful, and perhaps even scared; you've lost your power.

TIP

Serious questions require a serious attitude and so you need to reflect that attitude in your pose. When you're asked a direct question, follow these steps (seated or standing):

1. **Close your mouth.**
2. **Breathe deeply from your lower abdomen.**
3. **Hold your head vertically as if your chin is resting on a calm lake.**
4. **Align your hips and shoulders with your knees.**
5. **Place your knees directly over your ankles, with your feet planted firmly on the ground.**
6. **Open your chest.**
7. **Look the questioner in the eye.**
8. **Pause.**
9. **Answer.**

FROM NERVOUS TO CALM

Emma works in the HR department of a telecoms company. She's ambitious and wants to progress in her career. During her annual appraisal she received disturbing feedback: her superiors weren't taking her seriously because her behavior makes her appear unsure of herself.

Emma was alive with unfocused, nervous energy. She shifted her weight from leg to leg and slouched into her hips. Her shoulders stooped and her hands fidgeted. She tossed her head and frequently giggled. She had difficulty establishing and maintaining eye contact. Her words said that she wanted to progress in her work, but her body language conveyed that she wasn't up to the job.

When Emma saw herself on video she was shocked at the negative impression her gestures and behavior were making. By adjusting her stance, she stood taller. By controlling her breathing, her actions calmed down. By opening her chest, she filled her space. Her fidgeting lessened and she began to project the image she wanted. Emma now comes across as confident, convincing, and credible.

Picking the power seats

At work, stay away from seats that make you look small, awkward, and insignificant. Avoid seats that force you to look upward, lifting your chin and exposing your neck, one of the most vulnerable parts of your body. The person in the other chair is sitting upright and in control. Even if he's leaning back in his chair, he's still in a higher position than you. He can look down on you along the length of his nose. He can lower his glasses, looking over the top at you, sitting in a cramped and awkward position and thus feeling uncomfortable.

Considering the back of the chair

The higher the back of the chair, the higher the status of the person it belongs to. The person with the support behind his back, the protective shield and frame that surrounds him, holds a more powerful position than the person sitting on a stool at his feet. Kings and queens, popes and presidents, chief executives and oligarchs sit in chairs that reflect their power and status. The higher the back of the chair and the more luxurious the fabric, the higher the status of the person.

Rolling on casters

Chairs on casters have a power and mobility that fixed chairs lack. The person sitting in a chair that swivels has more freedom of movement and can cover more space in a shorter time than someone sitting in a fixed chair. The person who's sitting in the chair on wheels, with the arm rests and the high, reclining back, tends to be the person in charge.

Gaining height advantage

Height is associated with status and power: the higher you are, the more authority you hold. Savvy business types know that, by adjusting the seat height of their chairs, they gain a competitive advantage.

TIP

If someone invites you to sit in a chair that puts you at eye level with the other person's desk, politely decline and say that you prefer to stand.

Placing the chair

When you seat yourself directly across the desk or table from another person, face to face, the atmosphere is immediately confrontational. But place the chair at a 45-degree angle in front of the desk and you create a welcoming environment. If you want to reduce a visitor's status, arrange for him to be seated as far away from your desk as possible, into the public zone at least 8 feet away from where you're sitting.

Negotiating Styles

When crunch time arrives and you're at the final stage of a work or business negotiation, you want to win, right? The best negotiations result in everyone feeling like a winner. And to feel that you're a winner you have to look, sound, and behave like one — you must act the part.

TIP

Before you go into any meeting where you want to be seen performing well (interview, negotiation, or assessment), find yourself a quiet spot in which you can gather your thoughts in peace. Five minutes is ample. Reflect on how you want to be perceived and visualize yourself behaving in that manner. See and hear yourself performing at your best and experience the feeling. By creating your desired image, you're able to act the part and convince others that you really are like that. Who knows, you may actually be that person.

Claiming your space

When you enter a negotiation, you need to claim your space right from the start. If you don't, the competition is going to have you for breakfast. *Claiming your space* means that you're taking responsibility for yourself and your actions, and that you act as though you've got the right to be where you are, doing what you're doing. When you walk into a space and make it your own, you're telling others that this territory is yours and woe betide anyone who tries to take it away from you. Dogs spend much of their time marking out their territory in order to let the rest of the pack know that they've been there, and the same applies to people (although in a less obvious manner!). Your intention is to let people know that you own this space and you're to be taken seriously.

ACTING THE PART

The Russian director Constantine Stanislavski popularized a style of acting that became known as *method acting*, which requires actors to base their characterizations on the emotional memory process. The actors immerse themselves in their characters' lives, to experience that life as the characters would. Actors draw upon memories and incidents from their own lives and incorporate them into their roles, enriching and enhancing the portrayal. Devotees of method acting include Dustin Hoffman, Jane Fonda, and Robert De Niro.

In a similar manner, by recalling how you felt and behaved when you negotiated a favorable outcome in the past, and by emulating the behaviors of negotiators you admire, you too can act yourself into the part.

When you claim your space successfully, you can act as if you belong there. Your gestures appear fluid, your posture is upright, and you engage in eye contact with ease. You send out positive signals indicating that you're comfortable and in control.

Getting acquainted with the environment

One way of demonstrating that the space you're in belongs to you is to make contact with an item in the area. Say, for example, that you've been invited to speak at an event attended by many influential people, some of whom you know, others you don't. You want to appear confident and in charge of yourself and your material. To do that, follow these suggestions for getting comfortable in the space and making it your own:

>> Walk into the room where the event is taking place as if you own the space. Move with purpose and authority.

>> If you're expected to sit, pull your chair out and sit down without waiting to be invited. (Be advised, though, that if you do take this action at a first interview, you may be perceived as forward or rude.)

>> Place your notes and pen in front of you with confidence and authority.

>> Establish eye contact and open the discussion clearly and concisely.

Consider this example: Tricia is a highly qualified and respected lawyer. Practicing for her partnership interview, Tricia felt nervous and awkward, as though she didn't belong. She fidgeted with her clothes, avoided eye contact, and played with her jewelry. Her behavior began shifting as she practiced entering the room and taking her seat at the table in front of the imaginary panel. Before Tricia sat, she let her hands rest on the top of the chair's back as if staking her claim to that seat. By making contact with this object, she established a sense of ownership with the room. Her nerves steadied, and she gained an appearance of confidence and credibility.

Choosing a good seat

When attending meetings, arrive early so that you can pick your spot. Sitting facing the door gives you the upper hand. Research shows that people seated with their backs to the door experience stress, increased blood pressure, and shallow, rapid breathing as the body prepares itself for a possible attack from behind. Save this weak and defensive position for your competition.

Filling your space

People who fill their space look more commanding and in control, which can be a challenge for small or slim people, who may appear to be devoured by space. The following tips can help people of smaller stature appear more in command of their territory:

>> Hold your elbows slightly out from your sides when standing or sitting. (People who hold their arms close to their bodies look subservient, timid, and fearful.)

>> Lean forward when seated behind a table, letting your hands, elbows, or lower arms rest on the table's surface.

>> Never pull your arms in close by your sides at a meeting; you're reducing your stature and diminishing your influence.

Large people also need to consider the amount of space they fill, because lolling and ambling along or spreading across their space can be perceived as invasive. You don't need to draw your shoulders and arms in toward yourself. Just be aware that you take up more space than smaller people and that you may need to adjust your position to allow others in.

TIP

To avoid overwhelming others with your large presence, contain your gestures, making them concise and precise.

Displaying confidence

The way you stand and sit, your gestures and expressions, the actions you choose and the way you perform them, all reveal who you are and what you're about. Captains of industry, masters of the universe, and doyennes of the theater instinctively know, and are well trained in, how to project a confident countenance. With eyes clear and focused, posture erect and facial muscles engaged, they create a look of positive expectancy.

TIP

To be perceived as confident, you have to demonstrate confident behavior, which requires that you know what confident behavior looks, sounds, and feels like. To clarify your concept, try the following exercise:

>> Ask yourself, "What's important to me about behaving confidently?"

>> Reflect back on a time when you felt confident. Describe the feeling. What gestures and expressions did you incorporate into your behavior?

>> Think of someone who you believe demonstrates confident behavior and describe how that person acts, including specific gestures, fluidity of movement, eye contact, and facial expressions.

>> Consider what you currently do that's similar to that person's behavior.

>> List the benefits of behaving with confidence.

>> Practice the gestures, postures, and expressions that denote confidence for you and avoid those that don't.

Avoiding nervous gestures

People who fidget and fiddle, pick at their fingernails, and scratch their head, face, neck, and/or chest during a negotiation are displaying nervous gestures and giving the game away. You don't need a microscope to see that such people are in a real state and are creating a nervous environment. Spend too much time with someone who's demonstrating nervous behavior and you start feeling uncomfortable too.

TIP

You can't avoid gesturing nervously unless you're aware that you do it. Watch yourself on video, ask a trusted colleague for feedback, and pay attention to yourself as though you're an outside observer. When you recognize the behavior, you can do something about it.

Replace an anxious gesture with another action. If you're fiddling with a pen, put it down whenever you're not writing. Let your hands rest on the desk or table in front of you. If you don't have a surface that your hands can lie on, rest them in your lap. If you find yourself picking at your fingernails, swap that action for another, such as taking a quick note then folding your hands in your lap. You can also shift the way you're sitting or standing. Repositioning your body from a pose in which you're feeling uncomfortable also results in shifting your thoughts, feelings, and intentions. After you shift your position, settle in. If you're bouncing, you're showing your nervousness.

Changing behaviors takes time, commitment, and practice. In fact, research shows that habits can take anything from 18 to 254 days to form. For example, a relatively simple habit, like drinking a cup of hot water and lemon every morning or going for a 10-minute walk every lunchtime, can take up to 66 days. Changing your habitual behaviors in stressful conditions may take longer.

REMEMBER

In today's highly competitive business world, you need simple strategies to provide the extra *oomph* to get you where you want to be. Being good at what you do is no longer enough; you have to be *seen* to be good. Take stock and evaluate what you do well and where you see room for improvement. Consider your behavior and the impact it has. When you're aware of these things, you can make the necessary adaptations.

Opening or closing your fingers

Short, sharp gestures hold more authority than open hands waving in the air. By keeping your fingers closed and your hands below chin level when gesturing, you look confident and in control, and thus command attention.

TIP

If you want to appear caring, approachable, or subservient, also keep your hands below chin level but gesture with open fingers.

Carrying only what's necessary

Keep your accessories slim and compact. A bulging briefcase indicates that you're the worker bee and not the queen making strategic decisions. They convey the impression that, although you may be buzzing away hard, you're not in control of your time.

REMEMBER

Accessories are meant to enhance your image. Decide what image you want to project and choose your accessories accordingly. Also, to make a positive impression, invest in good quality accessories.

Watching your buttons

Tightly closed jackets indicate a tightly closed point of view. People who button up their jackets while making decisions indicate that they're closed to the idea put forward. When they fold their arms across their chests with their jackets buttoned, they're displaying real negativity. If you notice one or two people unbuttoning their jackets during a meeting, you can safely assume that they're changing their opinions and opening up to what's going on.

2

Exerting Influence through Important Conversations

Contents at a Glance

IN THIS CHAPTER

» **Developing superstar employees**

» **Providing positive feedback**

» **Creating a conversation-ready organizational culture**

» **Giving effective feedback when performance is suffering**

» **Creating clear action plans to support the conversation**

Chapter **1**

Conversations in Good and Bad Times

P eople love communicating good news. Professional athletic coaches usually aren't that stressed doing a television interview when they're holding a championship trophy above their heads with the crowd cheering. Yes, communicating good news is a lot more fun than giving bad news. However, just because it's fun doesn't mean it's easy. Critical conversation skills can make good conversations at work great conversations. Using critical conversation skills in good times makes the good times more likely to continue, especially when you're setting goals with employees.

On the flip side, when an employee just isn't living up to expectations, you have two options: Have a performance discussion to see whether the employee can improve, or decide to part ways if the situation is irresolvable. One option that you should steer clear of is ignoring the situation and hoping that it goes away or corrects itself.

This chapter examines the positive and negative sides of critical conversations:

>> First, you find ways to accelerate the success of exceptional employees (say that three times fast!) with the critical conversation model. Coaching is a prime way to infuse positive critical conversations into the workplace, so you get some information on utilizing this great tool. Next, you discover ways to have critical conversations every day by using positive coaching models and proactive feedback tools. Because critical conversations are only as good as the environment that supports them, you can check out ways to create a conversation-ready culture.

>> You also get the lowdown on how to let employees know that they're just not cutting it. The most logical place to begin is preparing for the performance discussion. You then jump into how to make sure the conversation changes behaviors with a clear action plan. Finally, you see how to make sure everything stays confidential during a critical conversation.

Using Critical Conversation Tools to Develop Superstars

Attracting great employees, developing them, and keeping them are the most likely ways to limit the number of problems in an organization (and to limit cause for subsequent difficult critical conversations). So what's the secret to success? Consider the EDGE model (E: Examining what is happening; D: Deciding on resolution options; G: Get moving and see the results; and E: Evaluating the impact of the conversation). This model creates a perfect structure for critical conversations, and you can use the same model when focusing on more positive conversations as well, like developing current employees into future superstars.

Helping employees soar

To help employees deliver exceptional results, many leaders coach employees as they set goals, check progress along the way, and evaluate the results of their work. Whether you follow a more traditional annual process of employee reviews, or have a culture that's continually reviewing and assessing progress, using critical conversations can provide a consistent structure aimed at results. The performance management process fits perfectly into the last two components of the EDGE model for critical conversations:

>> **Get moving with goal-setting:** Time to explore and examine options for goals and individual perspectives. Ask what employees want to accomplish and how these goals link into the goals of the company. Decide on the specifics by asking three key questions:

- What are you going to do?

- When are you going to do it?

- What support do you need to accomplish the goals?

These first two questions in the goal-setting process are great opportunities to create SMART action plans. These plans and goals have a clear definition and time line for follow-up because they are Specific, Measurable, Action-oriented, Realistic, and Time-bound.

>> **Evaluating:** Encourage employees to get moving and then provide continuous feedback and evaluation about how they're doing. Throughout the performance-management process, a leader provides feedback, and the employee should highlight any red flags or changes to goals that come up as goals are accomplished.

When you're ready to start the check-in and evaluation process, the next section of this chapter focuses on how to give feedback as a coach and mentor. For more on performance management, check out *Performance Appraisals & Phrases For Dummies,* by Ken Lloyd (John Wiley & Sons, Inc.).

TIP

To use the critical conversation model, examine all the success and why it was successful, and then decide on next steps and future goals.

Using words that launch exceptional performance

Wouldn't it be nice if you had a list of questions you could ask that would let you discover superstars with exceptional performance potential? Of course it would be. And, yes, here is one for you. Using the critical conversation model, you can help create conversations that generate exceptional performance for your exceptional employees.

During regular meetings with your employees, devote at least half of the discussion to development and growth. Leave the other half for status updates.

To launch a discussion that helps employees excel at their job, start with these questions:

>> **Examine possibilities:** To open up a world of possibilities, ask, "What would be a new way of doing this?" Even the most ordinary tasks can be improved. Challenge employees to think of a new way of doing their jobs. Another key question could be "How would you like this to turn out?" Sometimes, working backward from where employees want to go is the best way to find out how to reach their goals. For example, if an employee wants a project she's passionate about to turn into a full-time position, what resources, skills, and leadership support would she need? It is also a good idea to ask what is working and what the individual should continue to do. Building on past success encourages future results.

>> **Decide how to move forward:** After you establish goals, decide what to act on. The perfect question to ask is "How can I support you in achieving your goals?" or "What resources do you need to do your best?" When deciding what to do, even the most talented employees may need to acknowledge some constraints (such as budgets, project time line, or customer needs). Identifying constraints and support systems will put your superstars on the path to success.

>> **Gain commitment and get moving:** Although most high performers don't need to be told to get moving and achieve results, closing the growth-and-development discussion with "Okay, now what's next?" is a great way to set an action plan into motion.

>> **Evaluate success:** Employee and manager conversations that happen regularly are the perfect opportunity for continuous development. Asking a superstar employee "What did you learn and how can you apply that in the future?" may be all she needs to hear to start thinking about ways to make the next challenge at work an even bigger success. Of course, even superstar employees can have setbacks. When that happens, as long as the employee recognizes that things didn't go as planned, ask "How can we set you up for success next time?" Most superstar employees don't need to be told that they made a mistake or didn't hit the mark — they usually know it and are ready to make it work the next time around. Asking how to set them up for success the next time will help them do so.

Coaching with Critical Conversations

Coaching is a developmental process designed to help individuals and teams achieve and sustain top performance in support of the organization's goals. Coaches provide feedback and encourage discussion that can influence changes in behavior, performance, or even beliefs. Using coaching along with critical conversation methods can turn any positive dialogue into a five-star discussion.

REMEMBER

Coaching in organizations isn't a time to show superiority. Starting with "I did it this way" or "I know what to do here" is training and lecturing, not coaching. Coaching starts with "This is what I liked about how you handled . . ." or "Is there anything you want to do differently next time?"

TIP

Mentoring is usually defined as an expert sharing information on how to do a task or role better, based on the mentor's experience. Coaches help improve performance by creating a dialogue of what could work — and the ideas could come from the recipient or the coach.

Using coaching methods

Coaching with critical conversation techniques can make your work relationships stronger and improve collaboration within a work group. Here are two ways to approach coaching:

>> **Navigator of information:** In this case, the coach guides an employee through mountains of information and approaches to solving a problem. A navigator coach is like a search engine on the Internet. Imagine if you had to go through every possible website to find out how to lead business change or deliver a critical message to employees. You may be hunting for years! A coach would be able to direct you to the information that meets your needs in an efficient manner.

>> **Giver of feedback:** Provide feedback on the areas the person being coached identifies. This identification is the difference between having a critical conversation to improve performance, behavior, or actions and using critical conversation skills to coach the growth and development of an individual. In coaching, the person being coached identifies what she wants to improve. In critical conversations, the manager or initiator usually identifies the areas of improvement.

Coaching gives you the opportunity to encourage an employee's ambitions or goals. During a regular critical conversation to improve performance, the initiator has a specific goal in mind for the conversation. On the other hand, during a coaching conversation, the person being coached can identify areas she wants to improve. Kick off this discussion by asking, "What issues are you facing that have you stuck? What do you want to achieve through our discussion today?"

REMEMBER

Even though the focus comes from different perspectives, the conversation and process still follow the same steps: examine what options are out there, decide what to do next, go and do it, and then evaluate how it went.

Coaching with critical conversations is different than a traditional manager-to-employee discussion, and even different than one-way feedback. Table 1-1 shows some of these differences.

TABLE 1-1   **Managing Employees versus Coaching with Critical Conversations**

Task	Managing Employees Traditionally	Coaching with Critical Conversation Skills
Solving problems	Manager tells employee what to do. Can control solutions and next steps.	Coach explores and brainstorms options with employees, and together they create a plan of action.
Feedback	Manager lets an employee know what she did wrong or right.	Coach asks the employee what she felt she did well and what she would do differently.
Development and training	Manager informs employee of what she needs to improve. Focus on results and bottom-line fiscal improvement.	Coach encourages the employee to explore options for doing things differently; coach and employee reflect on the results and make adjustments.

REMEMBER

A coaching conversation is a partnership, not a lecture. In a manager-to-employee discussion, the manager is usually in control and communicates to the employee. In a coaching conversation, the manager and employee engage in two-way conversation; you encourage the employee to share ideas, concerns, and experiences. The coach may share ideas to help steer a discussion, and the person being coached will process this information and apply it to her day-to-day work. For example, the coach may say, "Your way of handling customer complaints is a great strength. What do you think? How do you want to use this strength as you move into a leadership role in the company?" In this case, the coach helps guide the discussion. If the person being coached asks for feedback or ideas, the coach steps in to provide options for improvement or continued growth.

Although not all situations are right for coaching, you can see how coaching can create a positive partnership, rather than a hierarchical relationship.

Here are the two different approaches to conversation in action. Burt, the boss, just promoted Arnie, the employee, to be the head of compensation and benefits. Everyone is happy, at least for now. Burt walks into Arnie's new office and says, "Congratulations, Arnie," and then . . .

> **The approach: Managing the employee.** Burt says, "I would like to walk through your action plan for the next few months. As the manager, I would like you to make sure you do all the weekly employee reports and production reports. I would also

like you to fill out this incentive compensation report 42 times between now and the next board meeting; you can find it on the shared drive. If you have any questions, let me know. Once again, congratulations on your promotion."

The approach: Coaching the employee with critical conversations. Burt says, "I would like to spend some time exploring what you think needs to happen in this role." Arnie replies, "Thanks, Burt. I am so happy to have this opportunity. You know, I do have some ideas. Oscar was in this role for 20 years before he retired; he had some great methods, but there are a few things I'd like to do differently. I would love to share some ideas with you and get your feedback."

Asking Arnie what he wants to accomplish and how he wants to approach a problem generates a number of ideas and discussion opportunities. It also creates a partnership and a shared responsibility for getting things done.

Using the "management tells you what to do" strategy often does little to drive long-term performance. Can anyone expect others to embrace solutions and ideas if they had little or no input? On the other hand, a partnership, using critical conversation skills, opens up the flow of information and helps create ownership. The latter option is usually the preferred choice when an organization values innovation and teamwork.

You may notice a theme in the coaching model: the coach starts with exploring what's possible and the options available. This is the same first step of development in a successful critical conversation.

Finding coachable moments

Many of the examples in this book are those moments that are fairly big deals: landing a client, behavior that's stopping team productivity, and recurrent performance issues. When using critical conversations, however, the event doesn't need to be monumental — almost anything can be a coachable moment. *Coachable moments* are simply times when you observe a behavior or action and can either tie that action or behavior to consequences or potential growth. Here are some examples of coachable moments that can help keep a top performer motivated:

>> **Coachable moment: Results.** An employee accomplished a task that helped the organization meet its goals. This moment is the most common for positive feedback. Keep the energy flowing by providing specific details on the outcomes and tying them to specific organizational goals. These coachable moments are great chances to link the big picture or the big organizational goals to the work that your high performers are doing every day.

» **Coachable moment: Innovation.** Did an employee use resources creatively or reengineer a process? If an organization values innovation, provide positive feedback when an employee creates a better and more effective way to do something.

» **Coachable moment: Commitment and motivation.** Although results are important, don't forget to provide feedback on the process and commitment an employee has to the organization. If the team came together to solve a tough issue during a tight deadline, thank the employees for showing commitment to the goals.

REMEMBER

Finding coachable moments isn't just a tool to help employees keep performing like superstars; it's also a way to give attention and support to high performers. Often, the low performers can take the majority of your time and energy. Using critical conversations in a positive way makes sure you give high and low performers consistent guidance and input.

Making Everyday Conversations Count

Delivering tough messages in a critical conversation takes planning and organization. But if you want to avoid those tough conversations in the first place, it's the day-to-day conversations that matter most. Day-to-day discussions with employees and peers can solve many difficulties before they become problems that need a critical conversation and catch employees when they do something right.

Changing day-to-day talks into motivating moments

Everyday moments like a morning greeting or walking back to your office after a meeting can be moments for positive critical conversations. Simply add a specific example, why you thought it was positive, and then ask for the other person's perspective to turn a casual hello into a coachable moment.

For example, in the morning you may say, "Hi, John. I just wanted to let you know you handled that customer call perfectly yesterday. You kept calm and asked how you could help a number of times. I am so thrilled you are excelling in this role. How did you feel after the discussion?"

This simple hello has now opened the conversation and has reinforced desired behaviors. In this example, John now knows that asking a number of questions on how to help the customer is something he should repeat again. He also knows you feel he is doing well in his role. And finally, now John has the opportunity to talk about what went well and create a positive development opportunity, and even ask for feedback on another topic.

Using feedback to create results

Many people hear the word *feedback* and immediately think: oh no, I did something wrong. This view of feedback is just plain wrong. Feedback is a powerful tool that employees can use with one another, managers can use with employees, and employees can use with their managers. But feedback must first be positioned as information an employee can use to develop. And it must also become part of everyday conversations. If you give feedback only when something goes wrong, well, yes, feedback will probably be seen as a negative event. However, if you can give feedback when things go right, well, you guessed it — feedback can create a productive and motivated workforce.

A mistake many managers make is providing positive feedback with little substance. Saying "good job" or sending an employee his favorite bottle of scotch for landing a dream client is nice. Really nice. But it does little to support ongoing development and continued success. Rewards and recognition are important, but when an employee does something great, make the connection between specific actions and how to replicate the success again in the future.

REMEMBER

Using positive feedback to create results is just as important as giving developmental feedback when things go wrong. Luckily, feedback is feedback. To master the art of feedback, you can follow the same rules in any situation:

>> **Rule #1: Always be specific.** Talk about tangible behaviors that the employee can control — not general feelings or impressions. Instead of just saying, "You built a good relationship with the client," say, "I see that you're always spending extra time to understand the client's needs." Another specific form of feedback is "I know many employees just email clients or call them. I can see that you go the extra mile and make that professional connection face-to-face."

>> **Rule #2: Draw connections.** Describing what happened as a result of the actions can help your employees repeat the specific action in the future. In the case of landing that dream client, the manager may tell the employee, "Visibly letting the client know you're there for them was a key part of us getting the contract."

>> **Rule #3: Focus on the most important behaviors.** Even if your employee is perfect, to the extent that she can walk on water while juggling everything the client asks for, overloading the feedback can be overwhelming. Try to group

the positive aspects into themes. Going into the smallest detail of everything an employee did right can dilute the message just as much as it does when giving an employee negative feedback.

» **Rule #4: Check for understanding.** Yes, of course people just love hearing how great they are — but as you close the conversation, give the most amazing employee in the world a chance to ask for clarification and respond with other ideas. Asking "Is there anything else you need from me?" can open the discussion for clarifying anything. Asking "Do you have any ideas about how we can spread this type of behavior out to the rest of the organization?" demonstrates that you value opinions and ideas, and that you have an understanding of the exact behavior that was simply awesome.

» **Rule #5: Make feedback a two-way street.** Even great employees may feel a bit awkward giving feedback to a boss or peer. When giving positive feedback, ask the other person whether she has any feedback you can use. And of course, if someone gives you feedback, go through the critical communication steps to create a plan to act on it! This two-way street creates a positive and open environment and mutual respect.

Opening Your Culture to Conversation

Organizational culture is simply the personality of the organization. But culture is perhaps one of the most complex challenges and greatest resources an organization has. Culture is seen, felt, and heard, and an organizational culture that supports critical conversations is as close as you may find to organizational Shangri-la.

Often organizational culture experts talk about norms, values, and artifacts when describing an organizational culture. But you have a much more straightforward way of looking at how cultures value conversation. Look at how knowledge is shared, what values employees have in common, how decisions are made, and what behavior is rewarded. These essentials are central parts of an organizational culture. All these elements can influence conversation skills.

REMEMBER

If leaders can create a culture of conversation in the good times, handling tough situations or difficult news in the bad times (as explained later in this chapter) becomes much easier. To create a culture that's open to critical conversations rather than one that's closed to any exchange of ideas or information, ask these questions (and note the ideal answers):

» **How is knowledge shared?** Information and knowledge, and how they're shared, influence a culture of communication. Are individuals slow to share information or only hoard it, or do individuals ask and provide information to help the team reach its goals? In a culture open to conversation, information is free flowing.

>> **What values are shared?** In a conversation-ready culture, trust and honesty are encouraged, accepted, and rewarded. Employees and leaders in conversation-ready cultures open their doors to people if they have differing opinions or questions and give the attention they expect to receive.

>> **How are decisions made?** In conversation-ready cultures, employees and leaders decide together. Although leadership may give constraints to what can and can't be done (especially with budgets and other resources), decision-making happens at all levels of the organization.

>> **What behaviors are rewards?** Conversation-ready environments not only have a culture of rewarding what people say they will do, but also make sure everyone knows what type of behaviors will be rewarded. And these rewards are consistently applied. Conversation-ready environments expect and reward managers who spend time giving feedback to employees, and these cultures reward employees who listen and use the feedback to improve performance. Finally, rewards in conversation-ready environments value both what is done and how it is done. That means it isn't enough just to complete a project or meet the numbers. In conversation-ready environments, a project team is rewarded for completing the project under budget if the team also worked together and valued different opinions.

Table 1–2 provides a quick reference of the conversation–resistant and conversation–ready cultures discussed in this chapter.

TABLE 1-2   **Conversation-Resistant versus Conversation-Ready Cultures**

Element	Conversation-Resistant Cultures	Conversation-Ready Cultures
Knowledge	Information is stored as data.	Information is shared through discussion and supported with open technology.
Values	Values what work is done, like meeting sales targets or a project coming in on budget.	Values what is done and how it is done. Employees need to get the work done, and do so in a collaborative and genuine manner.
Rewards	Employees are rewarded for working their way up the ranks by doing what they are told to do.	People are rewarded for creating and discovering new ways of doing things.
Decisions	Decisions are made by leaders deciding and announcing a decision or by leaders gathering opinions and then deciding what to do.	Leaders work with teams to gather information before making a decision or let teams make decisions based on information.

Preparing for a Performance Conversation

To conduct a meaningful performance conversation, be prepared to explain why the conversation is happening in a clear way. State the purpose of the discussion to set the tone and focus, and briefly define why the conversation is important to the employee and the organization. The purpose portion of the conversation should include a compelling reason why performance is important to the organization and to their career. For example, you may balance how completing tasks leads to higher productivity in the organization, and completing tasks on time demonstrates the individual is valuable to the company and has career potential.

The key to a good performance conversation is to have the sender of the information be crystal clear on the message. To do this, ask yourself (the sender), "What message do I want to send to my employee and why?" Is it that the employee needs to be on time to work, or is it that when the employee comes into work late the rest of the team feels disrespected because the team is picking up the employee's work? After you know the message and why the message needs to be delivered in a critical conversation, you can create an agenda that gets the message across clearly but with compassion.

The next preparation step is to define the desired outcomes in advance. During the critical conversation, both the initiator and the receiver of the information work on action plans (discussed in the later section "Moving toward action") to change behaviors and work styles. But you don't need to come into the discussion with a completely blank sheet of paper when it comes to what you want to get out of the discussion. Write down the goals that *you* want to achieve. These goals could be focused on the conversation, like delivering feedback effectively, and overall performance goals, like improving an employee's performance in the next two weeks, making a team operate more effectively during the next project, or knowing that when work is given to an employee, it will get done. The goals that you come into the conversation with will be the benchmarks for the action plan that you create together during the discussion.

Having Conversations When Performance Is Suffering

Giving an unfavorable performance review is right up there with getting a cavity filled at the dentist. It's something you know you need to do but really wish you just didn't have to do. But just like that cavity, the quicker you get the performance review done, the quicker you can go on with your life. And, just like that nasty cavity, you really want it done the right way the first time so you don't have to go back again and again.

Before you see how to do the conversation right, here's an example of a performance review that went horribly wrong:

> **Manager Maggie:** "Hi, Joe. Thanks for meeting with me. [The conversation then turns into 15 minutes of small talk or status updates.] So, Joe, I know it's been a while since we've had a meeting. I'm really sorry about that. [Nervous laughter.] But the real reason I asked for this meeting is to let you know that you aren't performing well. Your numbers are bad. I expect much more from a senior manager. I just need you to do a better job."
>
> **Joe:** "Okay. Yes, it has been a few months since we talked. I didn't expect the conversation to go like this. I didn't know my performance was that bad."
>
> **Maggie:** [Cutting Joe off.] "Don't you read your email? I sent you your numbers last week."
>
> **Joe:** "Um, yes, but . . ."
>
> **Maggie:** [Cutting Joe off again.] "Well, listen, you need to improve it. Can you do that ASAP?"
>
> **Joe:** "Of course. I'll get right on it."

The positive part of the conversation is that Maggie had a conversation with Joe in the first place. Well, at least she scheduled it and kicked the conversation off. Unfortunately, Maggie fell into the trap that many managers fall into when they have to give a critical conversation around poor performance. They may have the intent to make a change, but managers tend to dance around the issues and never help the employee develop an action plan that creates better results. There is a better way to get results. Critical conversations can improve if you examine the facts, decide how to move forward, gain commitment to get employees moving in the right productive direction, and then evaluate the performance after the conversation ends (the components of the EDGE model).

Clarifying what's not working

During a critical conversation focused on performance, start with the facts and avoid dillydallying around the issue. Simply put the facts out there. Step 1 of the EDGE model is to examine the facts.

WARNING

You don't need to dive into the conversation without any human interaction, but making excuses or being unclear about what the real problem is doesn't serve anyone. In fact, it can make everyone a bit more nervous.

Giving clear and consistent feedback on how well an employee is performing is preferably done on a regular basis (biweekly or monthly is ideal). But even if you haven't been providing feedback on a regular basis, talk specifically about how the employee's performance is not meeting standards and expected outcomes. As you discuss the issues, state the facts in a clear and coherent way.

In Maggie's case, a better conversation may have gone like this:

> **Manager Maggie:** "Hi, Joe. Thanks for meeting with me. I know it's been a while since we've had a meeting, but I wanted us to start a conversation about your contributions to the team. I see by the numbers over the past few months that your performance has been decreasing. A specific and recent example is last week's sales numbers . . ."

In this case, even though Maggie hadn't been meeting with her employee, she talks about a trend in downward performance and then goes right into a relevant example.

WARNING

Bringing up issues from months earlier can put an employee off guard. The employee may wonder why you didn't bring up the issue earlier. This is not to say you cannot bring up issues from the past, but, if you do, be aware it may put the employee off guard and potentially make the employee defensive or question why you were hiding this information for so long. To counter this reaction, start with the most recent examples and then say, "This may potentially be a trend. Four months ago I recall a similar example (and then state the example). I don't want to bring up things from so long ago, but I do want to make sure we can resolve any concerns so we can start focusing on the future."

Here are a few other situations in which you may find yourself. Use these tips to present negative feedback in a positive, fact-focused way:

» **When you don't have hard numbers:** "Last month you committed to doing _____ and you did _____." This statement is an efficient way to introduce poor performance when you don't have any hard data like sales targets or customer service ratings. Use this statement when working with individuals who haven't met deadlines or who aren't doing what they say they'll do.

» **When performance disrupts a team environment:** "Our organizational goal for this year is _____. In the beginning of the year, we set your goal as _____. You're not on target to meet that goal." This set-up is a good way to introduce goals and how they impact a team environment. If an employee's performance is just starting to go off track, making him aware of the consequences to the team and organization can help turn performance around.

>> **When performance spirals downward quickly:** "Our minimum standard is _____. Based on the past month, you're performing below that. These are the benchmarks needed for your role." This is a constructive way of letting employees know that they need to focus on their individual performance or their job could be at risk. Don't threaten an employee with job loss. Simply put the information out there and let the employee know the expectations for his role.

WARNING

Never come to a performance discussion reading a laundry list of poor performances. Imagine the employee's reaction if a manager started a conversation with "I'm not sure I've made your role on this team clear. Let's go over your job description and I'll rate your performance on a scale of 1 to 10 on each item." A leader has every right to have an opinion, but opinions need to be backed up with facts. Letting an employee know he's a 1 out of 10 on everything he's supposed to be doing is simply demoralizing. Keep the conversation focused on the most important areas to improve and the areas for which you have the most relevant facts.

BEING HELD ACCOUNTABLE

Holding employees accountable is a clear way to make all the parties in the conversation answerable to a common and clear definition of success. Sometimes employees aren't aware of their own roles or what effects their performance may have. Asking the following questions can help guide the agenda and message of a critical conversation, and may even help prevent a poor performance critical conversation in the future:

- **Does the employee have a defined role?** So many performance issues begin with employees having absolutely no idea what they're supposed to be doing. Make sure each employee has a clearly defined job description. You can't hold someone accountable for something he doesn't know he's responsible for doing. Give the employee the opportunity to ask for clarification about your expectations for the role.

- **Are expectations in writing?** You don't need to document every minute of an employee's day, but you should have a working plan or written job description for an employee. At the very least, write down and share with an employee the expected skills he should have and the competencies he should exhibit as he does his job.

- **Does the employee have clear consequences?** Consequences for doing or not doing the job need to be clear. No, don't threaten an employee's job the second he mistypes an email or has a bad day, but let the employee know that if expectations aren't met within a certain time frame, you may need to consider whether he's the right fit for the job.

Coming to the conversation with a genuine desire to help, even when performance is poor, can be hard. Sometimes you may be shocked by just how little an employee does or how much an employee expects from the organization with little in return. But this isn't the time for lecturing and finger pointing. A critical conversation is the time to present facts and then create action plans to turn around behavior.

Looking for options

Step 2 of the EDGE model is to decide on options and find ways to move forward. Use the following questions as ways to prompt positive actions:

>> **"What do you think about approaching the problem from this angle?"** Deciding on the plan of action may be hard for an employee who hasn't been stepping up to the plate. Giving him a few options to consider may help, especially if you'll accept only one or two ways of approaching an issue. For example, if a software engineer isn't completing user testing on time, you may ask him to approach the issue from one of two angles, both which will help complete their action plan. You may say, "What do you think about working with the senior engineer to review the user testing plan or presenting your time line to the team in the next meeting?" You aren't trying to back the employee into a forced answer; you're simply giving him the two options he has to do his job.

>> **"What have you tried in the past? What worked and what didn't?"** The best teacher is always experience. Even though an employee may be getting a less than stellar grade right now, chances are good that this employee once was successful at something. Try your best to find out what experience may have been successful in the past and then tie it to how the employee can improve his current performance. For example, if a team member is having trouble with the quality of work, you may ask, "Can we talk about a time when you were most satisfied with the quality of work you did on another project?"

>> **"What is your first step? What is your next step?"** Critical conversations should create a culture of independence, not dependence. Balance between telling employees exactly what to do and letting them think for themselves. Asking about the first step and the step after that will help the employee start thinking of what he should do to improve his performance. You can do this most simply by asking, "What do you think is the first step?" and when the employee develops the first step, add in another question, "And what do you think should happen next?" And that's better for long-term success than just telling him what to do to improve his performance.

The "deciding what to do next" phase sets the stage for employee improvement to start happening right after the critical conversation. Setting goals that are specific, measurable, actionable, realistic, and time-bound (SMART) helps reinforce the critical conversation message and gives an employee work he can immediately start accomplishing. Coming up with ideas for the action plan together, rather than having the employee create the plan alone or the manager handing over a detailed to-do list, also shows the support necessary to turn around performance. A critical conversation must end with a clear action plan if a positive change in behavior is expected to happen. With no action plan, the conversation may as well have been just a bunch of words.

Moving toward action

Time for action: Step 3 of the EDGE model is to get moving. Put the action plan into place so the receiver of the information can get his performance back on track.

Although some critical conversations solve the problem then and there, performance issues aren't as easy or quick to solve. That doesn't mean you need to keep the critical conversation cycle going on forever — especially if you don't see results in the first few weeks. Action plans should include items that can be accomplished in the short term (within two weeks) and longer term (within four to six weeks).

Figure 1-1 shows what an action plan may look like with two-week, six-week, and twelve-week goals for a manager who isn't making the grade. Notice how all the items are specific, measurable, actionable, realistic, and time-bound (SMART), even when you don't have hard numbers to measure performance against.

2 weeks	6 weeks	12 weeks
• Develop a list of recommended metrics to measure team performance. • Develop plans to address concerns from employee satisfaction surveys. • Set up regular one-on-one meetings with staff.	• Begin tracking measurements for team improvement. • Meet with region partners to review goals. • Deploy at least three improvements that are tied back to the employee engagement survey.	• Track measures against goals, reviewed regularly. • Review employee engagement progress with regional director.

FIGURE 1-1: Two-week, six-week, and twelve-week action plans.

© John Wiley & Sons, Inc.

TIP

After you create and agree on an action plan, you can further help an employee succeed by asking the following two questions:

>> **"What are the barriers to accomplishing the goals on the action plan?"**
Even the best intentions can get sidetracked by unexpected obstacles.
Encourage poor performers to think about what to do if something gets in the way of being able to accomplish the goal. For example, ask your employee to think about where he could find information if his first source isn't available or doesn't have all the answers.

>> **"How will you let me know if things are going well or if you need help removing additional barriers?"** This question is the perfect closing question after you develop SMART goals. Asking an employee how she will update you outside of these meetings puts responsibility in the hands of the employee. It makes her accountable for the success of the action plan and encourages her to speak up when she may have a problem. Also establish regular check-ins as status updates, but this question takes status updates to the next level.

Creating the action plan together is more effective than dictating the plan because the employee has contributed, feels valued, and is more likely to follow through with the plan. This collaboration also helps the manager understand the employee's perception of what is required to get the job done. This give-and-take discussion can result in new and better ideas. Plus, during follow-up coaching sessions, the manager can remind the employee of their contribution to the solution.

Assessing the conversation's impact

Critical conversations that generate positive results do more than just create healthy dialogue during the meeting — these conversations have immediate and lasting impact after the talking is done. Although this chapter is all about the conversation, the real change happens after the conversation ends. So now is the time to measure how marvelously the conversation went by using Step 4 of the EDGE model, evaluating the impact of the conversation.

After the initial critical conversation, schedule another meeting for two or three days later. That gives the employee time to think through what he needs to deliver to be successful.

After these two conversations end, and the action plan is being carried out (Step 3 of EDGE: Get moving), check-ins with the employee (using an abbreviated critical conversation model) ensure that the conversation has a positive and lasting impact.

Regular check-ins assess the conversation and adjust course as necessary. Assessing progress along the way also gives managers an opportunity to reward improvement in real time. If an employee does want to turn around his performance and the critical conversation kicks off that turnaround, giving acknowledgement of the effort can go a long way toward making the new behaviors stick.

During the post–critical conversation assessments look for three key things: an ability to do the job, willingness to improve, and improvement.

Ability

During the critical conversation, employees may agree to complete an action plan, but as the employee starts to work on the plan, it may become obvious to all parties that the poor performer simply doesn't have the ability to complete the task. Even when the desire to improve and the work ethic are solid, some tasks are just beyond an individual's ability or knowledge. If this scenario happens, you have two options:

>> Give the employee training on the task that needs to be completed. Some of these skills gaps may have been highlighted in the action plan during the critical conversation, but others may not be known until the work gets underway.

>> Stop the action plan and determine if there are tasks that the employee can complete. If an employee cannot complete the tasks necessary for the job, one option is to terminate. The other option is to try to find a job that the employee can do. If the employee is willing to improve, you may want to consider if there are other jobs in the organization the employee can perform. This may not always be an option, but doing so does show a genuine desire to help the employee rather than just firing them.

Willingness to improve

Willingness to improve and actual improvement are both needed to turn an employee's performance around, but the willingness to improve comes first. If, after the critical conversation, an employee does nothing on the action plan, be open and honest with the employee by saying, "What you said you would do and what you are doing don't match. What is going to happen differently in the next week?" Willingness to help is a commitment to making a difference. If an employee isn't willing to do whatever it takes to hit or exceed the goals, it may be time for the employee to find another job.

Improvement

If the results are improving with time, and the employee is performing what he's capable of, you can almost guarantee that you aced that first critical conversation. Luckily, measuring improvement against a critical conversation action plan is one of the easiest parts of the conversation. Here are a few questions to ask as you evaluate progress after the critical conversation:

>> "Were the tasks on the action plan completed?"

>> "What is the progress?"

>> "When will this action be finished?"

>> "How can we keep the discussion going between now and next week to make sure the goals are accomplished?"

>> You may also want to focus on how work will be different when the action plan is done by asking, "What will it feel like to have this completed? What's going to happen if you do not take this action?"

>> You may follow up with asking the employee, "Were there any areas of concern when working through the plan?"

REMEMBER

This list of questions opens up the critical conversation cycle again: Examine what happened, decide what to do next, and then get commitment to get moving. Here are the three questions critical conversations repeat again and again: "What happened?" "What are we going to do?" "How are you doing?" When performance goes off track, getting back to what happened and what is going to happen next quickly redirects performance.

Turning Poor Performers into Productive Performers

Don't miss out on a great opportunity for harnessing the positive energy of improved performance. Instead, use it to find ways to help the employee continually learn and develop. Yes, fix the problem of performance first, but don't end on a negative note.

To keep the discussion going, first make sure the employee knows this specific performance improvement is complete, and your intent with kicking off development is to help the employee excel in the future. Your job is to be more of a sounding board, rather than a manager of performance. During the performance improvement process, you may have taken a heavy hand in directing what needed to be done to help the employee get up to an expected level of performance. Now you can turn the tables and ask challenging and provocative questions, while you ask the employee to help focus the discussion.

After the employee has completed the initial action plans to improve performance, offer to sit down with him and find ways to help him develop in the future. This is where coaching fits in (discover more on how to coach with the critical conversation method earlier in this chapter). To help a once-poor performer to start thinking of what's possible now that his performance has improved, ask the following questions:

>> "What opportunities exist for our organization that we haven't yet thought about? What opportunities exist for your career that you haven't yet explored?"

>> "What changes could make a big impact on the organization? On your career?"

These questions show a leader's commitment to an employee who has successfully moved from being a bad apple to working his way up to the top of the tree. If the initial critical conversation did what it was supposed to do, the action plan will have created continued momentum toward getting the job done. With all the focus on an action plan, it can be refreshing to invite the employee to step back and see what's possible in the current role and in future roles, rather than jumping straight into action again and again.

Keeping It Close to the Chest: Confidentiality Is Critical

Confidentiality is an issue in almost every performance-focused critical conversation. This isn't just for legal reasons (although those are quite important too). Confidentiality during tough conversations helps create an environment of trust between the receiver of the information and the initiator. At the start of any conversation, especially those dealing with difficult behavior, discuss and agree on what is and isn't confidential. If you plan on sharing any of the information with your boss or the human resources department, make sure the employee knows (and agrees to) it before information is shared. That way the receiver of the discussion doesn't feel that you went behind his back.

Questions you may want to pose, especially if a performance issue is large or the work an individual is performing impacts multiple departments, include the following:

» **"What information stays within the walls of the conversation?"** Both sides should agree on what should remain confidential.

» **"What information needs to be shared with others, such as the human resources department?"** Part of this answer may be dictated by company policy. For example, if your company has a policy to let HR know every time someone needs to improve his performance, it would be good to make sure everyone knows that policy exists.

REMEMBER

Sure, employees need to let off steam sometimes. But, in the case of critical conversations, it's probably best not to have every detail divulged to other members of the company. Promote open communication, but tell employees that aspects of performance reviews or other important discussions should be kept confidential.

Chapter **2**

Hot Topics in Team Conversations

Y ou can use the critical conversation model in almost any situation. If you look at critical conversations as a method of collaborating and making agreements, then you can use the tools and techniques almost anytime, anywhere, and for any reason.

This chapter covers some hot topics at work where critical conversations can really shine. First off, you find out how to help teams exceed goals and expectations by making decisions with the critical conversation model. Next, you see how to facilitate group agreements that lead to action. And because critical conversations can happen to anyone, you get tips on what to do if someone is having a critical conversation with you.

Creating a Productive Team

Many organizations are leaning toward a dynamic way of working together: building teams. The thought of different minds collaborating on a common goal is enticing and seems like a perfect way to conduct business. But in reality, very few groups of people really operate as a well-run team. Usually, employees do their own tasks, give updates on projects, and often pull information and work together in the end to achieve a large goal. For example, a team of technology consultants may have individual responsibilities within a large project. Each consultant focuses on a task or a piece of the project, and when it's time for the new technology to go live, all the parts are pulled together.

Book 2, Chapter 3 walks through how to work through staff disputes, which occur within even the best of teams. Critical conversations can also help create an effective team by helping teams develop decisions and action plans everyone supports. To move from a group working on a bunch of stuff to individuals accomplishing something greater than the sum of their parts, the group needs to openly discuss ideas and decisions together.

Facilitating team conversations

If you're ready to get a team together to collaborate and build real consensus that leads to world peace (or something like that), it's worth discovering one more element of critical conversations: How to facilitate conversations. The goal of facilitating group conversations is to help groups become teams that work together to solve problems. That, as you can guess, isn't an easy task, but by using these techniques, you get one step closer to creating a capable and effective team.

A wonderful by-product of facilitating team conversation is the exponential growth a team experiences. Team relationships are often challenged because the pace of the team or project is moving so fast that the members have little time to sit back and agree on a balanced approach to decision-making. By slowing down to go through developing agreements, a team is more likely to collaborate than to have conflict. Most people know that conflict often results in lost time, extra work, back-and-forth agreements, weak commitment, and everything else that makes team members bang their heads against a very jaded wall.

The art and science of facilitating

You've probably heard that facilitators can help guide a meeting or decisions, or perhaps you've been asked to do so in the past. Being a facilitator is both an art and a science. The science comes from putting the critical conversation method to use. By following the basics, a facilitator can ramp up the power of the conversation. Make sure to:

>> Examine options, ideas, and opinions.

>> Acknowledge feelings.

>> Assist the team (or group) in making a decision.

>> Help the people in the room come up with next steps to get moving and evaluate results.

TIP

But the best facilitators know the art to the process as well. To be an effective facilitator, try putting some of the following artful concepts into action at your next meeting:

>> Discern the tone and feeling of the meeting and know when the participants need a bit more focus or when the group needs a break. Facilitators do this by reading the environment for body language, tone of voice, and language use (Book 1 covers both verbal and nonverbal communication).

>> Note whether people are crossing their arms, clenching their fists, and using a bunch of "they versus us" language. If they are, it probably means the group needs to work together a bit more to overcome emotions or differing views in the room.

>> Look for the group members nodding their heads, leaning in, and using language that focuses on "us" and "we." If you hear this language, the group is most likely working as a team and is ready to make decisions as a team.

Four vital facilitation factors

REMEMBER

Although artistry is best learned by practice, here are four areas to focus on as a facilitator of team decisions:

>> **Look out for group dynamics.** (You find out a little more about this topic later in this chapter.) Group dynamics include knowing the roles people play on teams, both formally and informally, and how individuals on the team interact with one another.

>> **Listen for the underlying meaning, both the spoken and unspoken, of conversations.** Facilitators listen and take note when individuals aren't being heard or are talking too much; they also can sense when participants say one thing but may mean another. No, facilitators don't have a crystal ball or an omnipotent force behind the curtain in a place called Oz; they just listen closely and observe reactions from others in the room.

>> **Provide feedback that has an impact.** It's one thing to observe a bully taking over the conversation, but it's quite another thing to be able to say, "Thanks, Bob, for that information. How about the rest of you? What are some of your views?" Giving feedback appropriately also means knowing when to intervene. Politely redirecting conversations may work, but facilitators also need to be prepared to talk to individuals who disrupt the group off-line about the consequences of their behavior.

>> **Know how to ask questions that drive a discussion.** Luckily, if you're an expert in critical conversations, you have a leg up on the types of questions that create discussion rather than shut it down. Consider these questions: "What could we do together?" "How do we work together?" "What problems are we trying to solve?" These questions are "we" questions that generate discussion and commitment to solutions.

Facilitation in action

Many people on teams and in groups come to meetings, think they come up with a great decision and action plan, and then come back to the next meeting to discover that absolutely nothing happened. Or worse, progress on the project or idea has backtracked. Developing agreements that lead to action takes a leader, team member, or even an outside party that's actively involved. Facilitating critical conversations within teams is a lot more involved than just writing what people say on flip charts.

Dialogue builds agreements and action. Here are some of the questions a facilitator would use to help the group decide together:

>> **Examine issues:** Ask, "Does everyone agree to work together to make a team decision?" People must be willing to work together before they can make any decisions. "What are the problems the team is facing?" A team facilitator shouldn't just assume that the organization needs to grow at a rate of 30 percent. Instead, the leader should first ask the team to identify the big changes or problems in the market that are putting pressure on profits and revenue. The series of questions would include: "What does the team think are the problems facing our financial performance, and why do we have these problems in the first place?" If the group seems to be conflicted about what the problem is, it may be useful to back up and ask, "What problem are we trying to solve?" In this example, the team may bring up anything from an old pricing strategy that caused margins to deteriorate or government regulations that opened the market to more competition. Whatever the answer, examining the issues as a team will launch a collaborative approach to finding a solution everyone can agree with.

>> **Acknowledge opinions and feelings:** Some people may have an emotional stake in the old way of doing business. Before a decision is made to find a solution, you may need to acknowledge areas of contention or where disagreement may still lie. It may be impossible to thrill everyone with the outcome, but it is possible to ask whether everyone can support it. In highly charged situations, it may be helpful to recognize that until the emotional feelings are dealt with, a good decision probably won't be made. You may sense that the team has hit an emotional barricade. In this case, state what

you're feeling and ask whether others feel the same. For example, you may say, "I feel like voices become a little tense when we talk about past solutions that didn't deliver expected results. Does anyone else feel this way?" Most likely, if you feel this, someone else feels it too.

>> **Decide how to move forward:** Now is the time for the fun part — or at least the part many teams (and groups) jump into quickly: finding solutions. After everyone agrees on the problems, ask the team members how they recommend solving the problem. After ideas are voiced, the team can agree on the value of the options and then choose which decision everyone can support in the future. A team facilitator may first ask, "What solutions can we agree will benefit the company?" After these solutions are identified, ask, "Which of these solutions can everyone support as we move forward?" The first question is a safe question for the team to answer because it isn't asking for commitment. Then, after the team narrows down the solutions to those that will solve the problem, they will be more comfortable with identifying the one or two that they're willing to support.

Facilitating after the conversation

As with all critical conversations, the discussion during the conversation is truly critical, but the measure of the success of the conversation is what happens after the talking stops.

REMEMBER

Create action plans to support decisions, and evaluate the success of those plans by identifying goals for each solution the team agreed on. Be sure to focus on SMART goal statements (goals that are specific, measurable, agreed-on and action-oriented, realistic, and time-bound). These statements help move a critical conversation from just talk to action. SMART goals and agreements are easy to understand, clear for all parties involved, and are able to be evaluated objectively. When an action plan is being created, take a minute to consider how SMART the agreement is:

>> **Specific:** Are the goals well defined to each party and clear to anyone who may read them?

>> **Measurable:** Will you know when your goal is achieved?

>> **Action-oriented and Agreed-on:** This A gets double duty. The goal of a critical conversation is to see a change in behavior or performance, and all parties need to agree on what will happen next. If all the parties don't agree to next steps, you're no better off than when the conversation started.

>> **Realistic (and Risk):** Is the goal realistic? If an employee is late to work, asking him to come in to work on time is realistic. If an employee isn't creating a positive team environment, expecting him to be seen as a superstar in 30 days isn't realistic, but asking him to use professional language in all his conversations is realistic. The R also stands for Risk, because the goal or change could be a challenge if the individual has to work outside of their comfort zone.

>> **Time bound:** When will the actions be accomplished? Have a clear deadline to make sure actions happen. A good rule of thumb when having a critical conversation is to have a 30-day timeline for the goal to be accomplished.

Here are examples of a not-so-smart and a SMART goal:

>> **Not-so-smart agreement:** Employees will be happy with their manager.

>> **SMART agreement:** The manager will ask human resources to complete a feedback survey (specific and action-oriented) to gather information on how the manager can specifically improve by September 30 (time bound and realistic). And this agreement is measurable, because the manager will do it or not.

Also take the time to determine who's responsible for each goal and any critical success factors. *Critical success factors* are often milestones or goals that have tremendous downstream impact on the overall time line of a project. Critical success factors may be the approval of a budget before any further work can continue or the support of an executive before communication on a project or decision can be completed.

TIP

Decisions are best made as a group, but action planning and taking action can be done in small groups and then presented to the team for final agreement.

Making team decisions

Different organizations and different situations use different approaches to making decisions that will affect the group. When you use critical conversation techniques during the decision-making process, you often have better follow-through because more than one person is involved in making the decision. Following is a list of four common approaches to decision-making:

>> **Decide and announce:** One person decides and announces the decision. When a leader controls the resources and output of the group (and therefore the group itself) she frequently tells people how to decide or makes the decision for them. In a critical conversation, a decision that will lead to change is a decision that's made together. If a leader makes decisions for the group, you can pretty much guarantee that the team is just a group of people who aren't really embracing change because they've had little or no input.

Suppose a company is rethinking its revenue streams because it wants to grow, and it needs to make a decision on what to do next. Using the decide-and-announce approach, the leader decides that all divisions in the company are required to make 30 percent more each year or their bonuses will be cut. This decision-making is most likely going to be met with rolled eyes, shaking heads, and individuals vying for their paychecks, even if that means people in the same company are competing against one another.

Sometimes decide-and-announce is necessary in business. If a CEO and CFO, and perhaps one other leader in the company, get together to decide something, it isn't a team decision — it's an executive decision.

>> **Individual input sought and leader decides:** Another approach is when a leader seeks input from individuals, but then makes the decision on what to do on her own. This type of decision-making is a telltale sign that people are working individually on results, with little collaboration. In this type of decision-making, the leader consults people one-on-one and then uses that information to make a decision. Although the decision-maker listens to the members in the group, the group doesn't listen to one another. Therefore the group isn't a team, but just a cluster of people working on a project or goal.

For example, the CEO of the company asks a few of the senior people in the firm what they would do to increase revenue, and then the CEO sends out a memo with his decision. What's the result? Because she uses some input but not other input, the decision may be met with a lack of buy-in because not everyone contributed.

>> **Team input sought and leader decides:** A leader may gather input from the team and then decide. Larger teams often operate quite well when their members are given the opportunity to examine options, acknowledge opinions and ideas, and then the leader or a subgroup of individuals on the team makes the decision. The key to the success in using this team decision-making approach is that the decision *reflects* the discussion. If a team works together as its members explore what's happening and possible solutions, and then the leaders who make the decision completely disregard the input, well, then this model is merely a façade and more of a decide-and-announce method. Additionally, after decisions are made, the leaders need to be present them back to the team. For example, a team may discuss the pros and cons of buying a new software system, and then a few people make the final decision. Before the decision is announced publicly, the decision is presented to the team.

This team decision-making model works well when a team frequently works together, has made decisions together in the past, and has a high level of trust within the team. Also, the teams need to be built of people that are trusted by employees who aren't part of the decision-making team. If the team members are just subsets of leaders, it isn't an improvement from decide-and-announce. During conversations that involve significant change, frontline councils and employee ambassadors are often ideal representatives to be involved in the discussion.

>> **Decide together:** Yes, collaboration takes time, but when a team is just forming or when the stakes are incredibly high or very personal, deciding together and agreeing to live with the decision is the best option. The goal of deciding together is to create a solution that the team can live with and support. When a team decides together, they also benefit from sharing information and ideas in real time.

Deciding together may take the most time, but when the team walks out the door after the decision has been made, you can pretty much guarantee that people will work together to accomplish the 30 percent increase in revenue target in the example from the first bullet point. You may have some compromise and some give-and-take, but if all the people on the team can live with and support the decision, they'll most likely do everything in their power to implement the decision.

Making decisions by using the critical conversation principles not only elicits feedback from employees, but also helps you gain clarity over specific next steps by building consensus on what the team is solving. After all, a team that decides together produces together. But the wonderful world of teams doesn't stop there — teams that work together to decide (rather than just work as individuals) are ready to identify the right steps to move forward.

WARNING

Group think is when a group takes on its own persona and individual opinions on the team are either ignored or disregarded. An experienced facilitator can help steer teams away from a one-mind philosophy. In the absence of an expert facilitator, before making decisions on the problem or solution, ask, "Have we talked about and looked at all possible solutions?" Teams reaching consensus is wonderful, as long as the consensus is reasonable. If a group doesn't take all ideas and opinions into consideration, sometimes groups can make worse decisions than individuals.

Improving Team Behavior

How a team behaves gives the facilitator a tremendous view into how the members will handle a critical conversation and how capable they are of moving forward. But you don't need to be a facilitator to recognize group and team behaviors — any team or meeting participant can start looking at the strengths and weaknesses of a team by examining how a team behaves. For starters, look at:

» **Roles, power, and influence:** As the conversation progresses, look for the different roles people play during the discussion. Does one person dominate discussions by talking too much or shutting down ideas before they have a chance to get up on a flip chart? Look out for individuals who take over meetings without letting all voices be heard. Additionally, are alliances being made during meetings? Minigroups can help direct teams toward making a decision, but they can also keep the participants not in the "in crowd" from voicing ideas and opinions.

» **Verbal and nonverbal cues:** A person who cuts off others in midsentence or speaks loudly may indicate an overly assertive individual. But also look for nonverbal cues to gauge how a team operates. Does everyone take the same seats, forming a visible pattern of who will talk when and who will lead the discussion? Do people start checking their phones and watches when a particular person starts talking? Watch for indicators of equality in the team. Not everyone has the same title, but in order for a team to use critical conversations to make decisions, every member of the team must have an equal opportunity to participate. (See Book 1 for details on verbal and nonverbal communication.)

» **Group silence:** The rule in movie theaters is just as powerful for appraising team dynamics: Silence can be golden. When you notice silence in a team, look for whether people are eagerly thinking or simply anxious. The ability to pause and consider options while in the heat of a meeting is a signal that the group is able to work as a team to make decisions rather than just jump to the easiest answer and get out of there quickly. On the other hand, too much silence can also create problems. For more on nonverbal skills like silence during a conversation, head to Chapter 2 in Book 1.

» **Conflict, consensus, and compromise:** Critical conversations can help overcome conflict, and often can create an even better relationship between parties than before the discussion began. As you observe group dynamics, look at how the team members work through conflict. Do they welcome it and use the exploring and acknowledging methods to build consensus in a decision? Or does the group compromise without any one person really feeling the team is better off than before the conversation began? Although compromise does happen on teams, highly functioning teams work to create a consensus on next steps during conflict rather than just giving in or finding the path of least resistance.

Observing how a team operates during the discussion provides insight into the areas the team can improve. The behaviors that occur during a conversation are often just as important as the decisions the team is making. For more on how to work through difficult behaviors that limit productivity, head to Book 2, Chapter 5.

POWER OF THE PRONOUN

A little word can hold a lot of impact. If team members are using *us* and *we*, they're probably conscious that collaboration is essential. Productive team participants ask others for information, opinions, and ideas. A good conversation starter is "How do we want to address the problem?" But sometimes individuals simply state what they think without soliciting input (for example, using *I, me, you* or *they* more than *us* and *we*), or they start conversations with a more accusatory "You need to do this" or "That wasn't my responsibility." In these cases, the group is probably operating more in solos than in concert. Flip to Chapter 1 in Book 1 for more about the use of pronouns.

WARNING

Don't jump into a team meeting and start making judgments about whether the team is operating well. It's much better to look at team patterns. Everyone and every team can have a bad day, but a true team continues to rally respectfully during tough discussions and decisions.

Chapter **3**

Staff Disputes

S taff disputes need extra care — and that's where critical conversations come to the rescue. Staff disputes can cover anything from different personalities having to work together to employees who think their co-workers talk too loudly or are just plain obnoxious, and everything in between. This chapter looks at how to use critical conversations to help employees solve their own problems and how and when a facilitator should step in when a resolution doesn't seem to be anywhere in sight. You also discover expert tactics for handling disagreements with the critical conversation model. And you find examples of how to use critical conversations to resolve five of the biggest workplace disputes.

Getting Results When Employees Aren't Getting Along

So you thought you dropped off your screaming kids at school this morning and would get to spend the rest of the day with adults, only to come into the office and find that your employees are having their own version of sibling rivalry. Different personalities at work will, at some time or another, lead to a staff dispute. Just like kids, sometimes employees need to work it out on their own. However, sometimes, a responsible adult needs to step in.

As the initiator of the conversation (also known as the responsible adult), your job is to know when to intervene and when to step aside. There isn't a perfect formula for when you should step in and help defuse — and perhaps even solve — the staff dispute and when you should let the employees work it out on their own. But if the arguments are escalating and getting in the way of productivity, initiate a critical conversation.

Knowing how to step aside

Before jumping in, taking time away from valuable work, and having to play referee, it may be a good idea to ask the employees to solve problems themselves.

Asking employees to identify the type of conflict they're having is a great way to help encourage them to begin to solve the issue on their own. With a little guidance, by helping the employee identify the real problem, you can help set the scene for how to defuse the issue.

Unnecessary conflicts

When an employee or co-worker starts complaining about another employee, use those active listening skills from Chapter 2 of Book 1, state your observation, and then ask the employee what she wants to do next. This is a good way to help coach the employee on how to solve the conflict.

Often mannerisms cause the most stress for people. For example, someone may not like the way another person dresses or talks, or even presents ideas in the meeting. Often this conflict is often unnecessary and a complete time drain (does it really matter that Mary happens to chew her gum a bit too loudly in the office?). However, this type of conflict is common and if it isn't handled directly, it will cause stress and productivity loss for those involved.

In each of these next examples, the manager takes two important steps by stating her observations and then asking the employee what she wants to do next:

> **Employee:** "Sally keeps talking too loudly on the phone."
>
> **Manager:** "Sounds like you and Sally may have different opinions about how to communicate. Why don't you talk with her and try to work something out?"
>
> **Employee:** "Billy is just so rude in meetings. He is just so annoying."
>
> **Manager:** "Sounds like you and Billy may have different ideas on how to work together in a meeting. Why don't you talk with him and try to work something out that you both agree with for next week's meeting?"

Employee: "Tommy can never keep his ideas to himself, can he? He's always jumping in and cutting off other people."

Manager: "Sounds like you and Tommy may have different ideas on how to present ideas to the team. Why don't you talk with him and try to work something out you both agree with for next week's meeting?"

Does this sound like a broken record? Yes. Why? Because the first step is asking employees to work it out themselves. The one thing that was common in all the reactions, and is sometimes overlooked, is stating what's happening. In each example, the manager states what she heard to be the problem and then proposed an action to encourage the employee to solve the problem directly with the individual they are having the conflict.

The response from the manager always examines what's happening by stating the fact, and then making a recommendation on what to do next. Although the manager responded with a simple sentence, she's using a light treatment of the EDGE model by examining and deciding.

REMEMBER

EDGE stands for:

>> **E**xamine data and perspectives and acknowledge other perceptions.

>> **D**ecide on options to move forward.

>> **G**ain commitment and get moving with a powerful action plan.

>> **E**valuate the impact of the discussion.

Necessary conflicts

In the previous section's examples, the staff disputes weren't about content. They were about the mannerisms of another employee, not what work is done. So what happens when people disagree on the work that needs to get done? Ah, that's the beauty of critical conversations. The same model can be applied again and again.

Note the manager's responses in the following two examples:

Employee: "Sally doesn't agree on the time line for the project."

Manager: "Sounds like you and Sally may have different opinions about what resources the project needs. Why don't you talk with her and try to map out the different resources you both think are needed for the project and collaborate on a project plan?"

Employee: "Tommy doesn't seem to agree on the problem statement."

Manager: "Sounds like you and Tommy may have different ideas on what you're trying to solve. Do you both agree there is a problem?"

Employee: "Yes, we do."

Manager: "Great. Why don't you try to agree on why the problem exists and then go back to working on the problem statement?"

You may notice that the manager seems a bit less like a recorder when the dispute focuses on content. Before stepping aside to let the parties resolve the situation on their own, you can help by pinpointing the source of the problem. Content disputes can often be resolved once the source of the problem is identified.

Realizing when to intervene

When your staff is in the midst of a dispute, intervene for any of these three reasons: when issues are being ignored, when working it out on their own doesn't solve the problem, and when you have a safety or danger concern.

Issues are being ignored

Sometimes, employees really don't feel comfortable addressing a staff dispute. You may sense this in their body language or tone of voice, or you may notice that they simply avoid at all costs the conversation that needs to happen. If you see this discomfort, offer to step in as a facilitator to get the discussion and agreements on the right track. If team members are so angry or upset that they can't focus on tasks, having a critical conversation will make great strides in getting a team back on track.

TIP

If you do agree to facilitate a discussion, let all the parties know that you're happy to fill this role to resolve an issue and that you'd also be happy to help teach each of the parties how do it on their own in the future.

REMEMBER

The goal of intervening when you see a problem is helping others to resolve the problem *and* helping others discover how to resolve their own issues in the future. Jumping in to help is fine, but being a permanent lifeboat isn't.

Working it out isn't working

If an issue has gotten so far out of control or if it's been there for so long, a facilitator can calm all the parties involved so the issue can be resolved once and for all. Whether the issue is focused on content or mannerisms, step in only when all parties have tried to work it out in the past and everyone understands your role is as a facilitator, rather than the person with the right answer. (Of course you can step in earlier if you're asked for help directly; see the previous section for details.)

TIP

While you can be both a facilitator and leader, the two roles are different. A facilitator is the process chauffeur, so to speak, the individual who protects ideas and helps steer the process. On the other hand, a leader is the individual who can direct the content within a conversation or discussion and make decisions about next steps. Be clear which role you're playing so all parties have clear expectations.

Safety is a concern

There are two types of safety concerns: one that is inherent to the job, like wearing safety goggles when working with chemicals or machinery, and one that stems from concerns about workplace violence. Workplace violence concerns need to immediately be raised to emergency professionals, no critical conversation needed. However, when someone is breaking a safety policy of the company, a critical conversation may help the individual understand the importance of following the rules. Two approaches to asking people to follow policy are to tell them they have to do it, which often lasts about one or two weeks until they go back to their old behaviors, or approach it as a critical conversation to make sure all parties understand the importance of the issue and how to resolve it in the future. The latter is recommended.

WARNING

If you have a safety concern or dangerous situation, follow your company policy on violence in the workplace or get emergency professionals involved right away. No critical conversation can or should resolve violent behavior or threats, period.

Considering Expert Tactics for Handling Staff Disputes

When you step in to help resolve a staff conflict, you have three goals for the process: resolve the conflict, make the conversation positive for all parties, and help teach all the parties how to resolve the conflict on their own in the future.

Yes, these are some pretty lofty goals, but consider for a minute the alternatives. If the conflict isn't resolved, the emotional drain will continue and the time spent trying to resolve the issue may be seen as wasted time. If all parties don't walk away from the conversation feeling positive about the result, one party may feel like they lost or both parties may feel like they compromised too much, and the conflict will start all over again. When people walk away from a critical conversation, they need to feel respected and valued. Finally, if you always solve employees' problems, you (or another responsible adult) may always need to spend time fixing their problems. With all those alternatives in mind, the three goals seem like pretty good options.

Using five steps to resolve conflict

Like any good critical conversation, this conversation should follow a common process: examine the issue, options, and ideas; decide on solutions; and then get moving and evaluate the results of the conversation. During staff disputes, the parties involved often need to spend more time appreciating others' points of view. Although appreciating others' feelings is part of other critical conversations, when you're dealing with conflict, this step can't be ignored or hidden within other agreements during conflict resolution. The five steps you need to follow are highlighted in Figure 3-1.

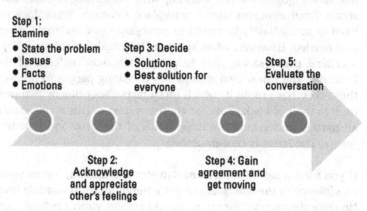

Step 1: Examine
- State the problem
- Issues
- Facts
- Emotions

Step 3: Decide
- Solutions
- Best solution for everyone

Step 5: Evaluate the conversation

Step 2: Acknowledge and appreciate other's feelings

Step 4: Gain agreement and get moving

FIGURE 3-1: Five steps to conflict resolution.

© John Wiley & Sons, Inc.

Here's how the five steps break down:

1. **Examine and identify the source or root cause of the conflict.**

    As the discussion begins, clearly state your reason for the meeting. Stating the purpose of the discussion helps set the tone for the rest of the conversation. Additionally, all the parties may be able to reduce some of the stress of the conversation by stating how they feel to one another. Just getting things off your chest can take away some of the pressure and stress, as long as it's done in a professional manner. Stating your own feeling is also a more neutral way to begin the conversation.

    During staff disputes, stating "I feel" in the beginning helps to frame the critical conversation in a constructive tone, instead of being accusatory. Right after stating your own feelings, use an objective, non-confrontational statement to state why you feel this way. Just as in other critical conversations, this links a fact (what the other person is doing or saying), to a consequence (how it is making you feel).

TIP

While you're clarifying how you feel and why you feel that way, keep the following tips in mind:

- Always use a friendly, polite tone. Even if there are waterworks in the room or someone is yelling or swearing like a sailor, stay professional.

- Keep your emotional statements short and to the point. Going on and on about how you're just so confused just muddies the water. Be clear and concise.

2. Appreciate and acknowledge the other person's point of view.

Often, conflict arises when people feel that their feelings and ideas aren't being heard. Whether you're the facilitator, initiator, or a party having the critical conversation, when parties disagree, that disagreement is often tied to another person's ego. If no one is acknowledging how other people feel during the conversation, the quality of the critical conversation and the results of the conversation most likely are going to be poor. By appreciating another person's point of view, you're legitimizing that what you see or hear has value. "I hear your complaint," or, "I can understand why you may feel betrayed," acknowledges that the individual's feeling is real. Note that appreciating another party's point of view and agreeing with it aren't the same.

TIP

Before moving on to the next step, ask whether everyone is willing to work together to resolve the issue. This question may seem obvious (who's going to say no?), but gaining this agreement before diving into solutions creates a mutual agreement in even the most hostile environments. Think of this mutual agreement as a baby step toward solving the problem.

3. Decide on possible solutions and then decide on the solution most acceptable to everyone.

If a staff dispute is out of control or if the parties have significant disagreements that may never be fully resolved, an alternative to 100 percent agreement is 100 percent acceptance. Although the conversation may not end with everyone going off into the sunset and working happily ever after together, the conflict can end with all parties being able to live with and support the decision and next steps. If the conversation is about an employee talking loudly on their cell phone (even for work purposes), the conversations may never stop, but all parties may agree to live with having cell phone conversations in a designated area.

4. **Gain commitment and get moving.**

When you're resolving conflict, especially staff conflict, action needs to be quick after the conversation ends. Because most staff conflicts are based on emotions, you want to see an immediate change (within 24 to 48 hours) in behavior. If you don't see change that quickly, the parties in the conversation may start wondering if change will ever happen, which can start an entirely new set of emotions and conflict in the workplace. If actions need to take place, put together an action plan to make sure the decisions made during the conversation happen.

5. **Evaluate results after the conversation.**

Evaluating the results of whether or not Sally and Jim like each other more or can agree to work together may not be as clear as asking an employee to improve sales performance or client retention, but it can and should be done. Simply say, "Let's check in next week and see how these decisions are working," and then check in a week later.

Turning a conflict into a positive experience

Making the critical conversation a positive experience for everyone involved makes great strides in keeping the team productive. Critical conversations are both an art and a science. The science is following the steps of the EDGE model: examining what's happening, deciding on the next steps, and then gaining commitment and getting moving and evaluating the success. The art is finding the most effective way to get information and using the information to make productive and positive change. The art of conversations during conflict takes time to perfect, but the benefits are tremendous.

REMEMBER

Here are some do's and don'ts when making the critical conversation a positive experience for everyone:

>> **Do** remain patient and relaxed. Be patient and try not to interrupt someone midsentence or midthought. Unless the other party is going on and on about information that isn't relevant, let everyone speak their minds. A facilitator can help make sure all ideas are heard; if you don't have a facilitator in the meeting, pause before stating a comment or asking a question.

>> **Don't** assume silence is a bad thing. Give the other parties in the conversation time to listen and respond to questions.

STARTING WITH FACTS AND FEELINGS

When you're describing personal feelings, always start with "I" to make it clear that you're describing your own perspective (as explained in Chapter 1 of Book 1). Try to avoid using a critical "you"; instead, ask a question or pose a statement that helps resolve how you're feeling.

Here are a few examples of how to express both fact and opinion when kicking off a critical conversation:

- When you feel frustrated when a discussion continues to go round and round without any resolution, you may say: "I feel frustrated. I understand that we've been talking about this issue for a few months now, but I'm still unclear about how we're solving the quality problem in the future."

- Emotions often focus on expressing personal opinions and ideas that aren't being heard. If this is the case, you may start with: "I feel undervalued when my opinions are not part of the discussion."

Of course there are wrong ways to express emotions during a critical conversation, so to avoid those, here are some ideas on how to revise what first comes into your head so you remain calm during the discussion:

Instead of saying: "I can't believe you need so much handholding!"

You may say: "I feel exhausted from having the same discussion about our project. It seems like we end up having two meetings to discuss ideas, one with the team during the weekly web meeting, and another face-to-face when we see one another the next day."

Instead of saying: "You are annoying."

You may say: "I feel anxious when we go into client meetings together. I think we have different communication styles. I have noticed you tend to talk loudly when you're passionate about a subject, and I think our client has a more reserved communication style."

Instead of saying: "You smell bad."

You may say: "I feel uncomfortable telling you this, but I think I may be a bit sensitive to your perfume or lotion."

>> **Do** use neutral questions and speak for yourself. Use "I" statements and facts to probe for the root of the problem. Say something like, "I feel you are ignoring my recommendations on the project. I have given a number of ideas on how to improve our quality, but none of them have been discussed at team meetings." (See the nearby sidebar "Starting with facts and feelings" for more information.)

>> **Do** give space to other parties when negative emotions arise during the conversation. If a person is angry or unresponsive, acknowledge the feelings in the room and either come back to the issue at another time or try to get all parties to agree to work together to resolve the issue. You may say, "I hear you're raising your voice when we talk about the issue. Do you want to take a break before we continue the conversation?" Or, "I hear you're raising your voice when we talk about the issue. Can you and I agree to work together before we try to solve the problem?"

>> **Do** acknowledge how the other parties may be feeling. But **don't** say you know how the other parties feel. Saying, "I can understand why you might be angry about the project being delayed," shows empathy. Saying, "I know you're upset about how the project is intruding on your other responsibilities," makes you seem like you know it all, which isn't a good position to be seen in during conflict.

>> **Don't** get angry, irritated, or annoyed. Even if the other individual is irate, try to remain neutral. If anger and other negative emotions aren't returned, the behavior tends to diffuse itself.

>> **Don't** give unsolicited advice. After reading this book, you may know exactly what the other party should be doing or needs to do. Even with the best of intentions, saying, "I can see you're ready to rip up my *For Dummies* book, but you really need to think about how to present facts and work on a mutually positive outcome," will most likely be met with negative feelings (and the book flying across the room). Instead, state how you feel and end it there. In this case, it may be better to say, "I see you're upset with my comments. Are you willing to work together to find a positive outcome?" You aren't in the conversation to solve the problem *by yourself*. All parties need to work together to resolve the issue at hand.

Talking today to solve tomorrow

REMEMBER

A critical conversation takes people through agreements to solve the current dispute; those same agreements can be a reboot button for how the parties work together in the future. Use the following four questions to gain agreement regarding how to fix the dispute, and then use them again to resolve any future obstacles:

>> **"What are the problems, and why do they exist?"** Solving a problem before the problem is defined is often quite hard. In the examination phase of a critical conversation, the parties discuss opinions, facts, and ideas. Approaching problems with the facts rather than accusatory opinion is a great way to kick off solving any problem in the future. *Use in step: Examine and identify the source or root cause of the conflict.*

>> **"Is everyone willing to work together?"** Before jumping into problems and solutions, everyone needs to agree to be in the same room and talk. During a staff conflict, this could be the first time the parties agree on anything; going forward, this agreement is a great way to unite everyone toward one goal. *Use in step: Appreciate and acknowledge the other person's point of view.*

>> **"What potential solutions will resolve the problem?"** During the deciding phase of a critical conversation, solutions are discussed and agreed on to fix the dispute. In future problem solving discussions on a team or one-on-one, use the same process to identify all possible solutions before deciding on which solution is the best. *Use in step: Decide on possible solutions and then decide on the solution most acceptable to everyone.*

>> **"Is everyone willing to support the decision?"** In a critical conversation, there may not be one solution that creates world peace. Because you need collaboration, ask the staff members whether they can support and live with the outcome. To use this to avoid conflict in the future, during future team discussions, rather than simply asking whether everyone agrees with a solution, ask whether everyone can (and will) support it. Agreement is easy to say and then ignore after the conversation is done; living with something and supporting it makes the solution more likely to stick in the long term. *Use in step: Gain commitment and get moving.*

Resolving the Five Biggest Staff Disputes

Because this book doesn't have enough pages to list every issue that has been seen, researched, or experienced, these five big disputes — and how to solve them — give you a well-rounded look at organizational dysfunction. Don't forget to check out other examples in this book as you tackle those critical conversations for performance management (see Book 2, Chapter 1), workforce complaints (see Book 2, Chapter 4), and difficult behaviors (see Book 2, Chapter 5).

FIGHT OR FLIGHT — OR A CRITICAL CONVERSATION

Conflict can make people feel anxious, stressed, and frustrated that the situation is out of their control. Biologists know a thing or two about stress, and it's not just because they're hanging out with rats and germs all day. Biologists have long known that organisms under stress will take actions to get out of the stressful situation. Many behavioral psychologists refer to the same fight-or-flight reaction when discussing how a lot of animals deal with stress; fight-or-flight reactions mean that under stress, animals either attack the source of stress or run away from it.

Employees and organizations react similarly. Although humans still have that fight-or-flight genetic makeup, as a species we have refined these responses to gossiping, ignoring, yelling, juvenile quarreling, sarcasm, bickering, and on and on. Critical conversations introduce new ways to eliminate stress in the workplace. You don't have to fight, and you don't have to run. Just share information and feelings and acknowledge how people feel.

Ending offensive comments from a co-worker

Even in the most professional workplaces, employees can tell jokes or make rude comments that cross the line from bad taste and poor judgment to offensive behavior that could be seen as harassment. Book 2, Chapter 4 talks about harassment claims in the workforce, but the goal is to stop the offensive behavior before it gets to the level of a legal complaint.

What is an offensive behavior? Offensive comments in the workplace include (but aren't limited to) name-calling, swearing, gossiping, and being argumentative with the sole intention of starting an argument.

Whatever the offensive comments, the tactics shown in the following example can help put an end to them.

Adam, the offensive employee: "Hey, Little Miss, how was that board meeting last week?"

"Little Miss" Linda: "Adam, I'm happy we're good colleagues and team members. However, referring to me as 'Little Miss' makes me feel like we don't have mutual respect for one another, and I feel it's condescending. I'd like to ask you to call me by my name so we can remain professional and respectful. Can you begin calling me by my first name?"

Adam: "I didn't realize you were offended by the comment. I thought I was being cute. I will use your name from now on."

Linda: "Thanks for understanding."

Linda followed the components of critical conversations perfectly. First, she examined the situation by starting with how she felt ("Referring to me as 'Little Miss' makes me feel like we don't have mutual respect"). Second, she helped direct a decision that could resolve the conflict ("I'd like to ask you to call me by my name so we can remain professional and respectful"). And third, she asked whether her colleague could support the recommendation she made as they gained agreement to move forward ("Can you begin calling me by my first name?").

Dealing with an obnoxious co-worker

Obnoxious co-workers somehow find their way into many workplaces. A co-worker blasting her music, slamming drawers or doors, never replacing supplies in the common area, talking loudly on the phone, "forgetting" to give credit to team members that do the work, or simply ignoring what other team members say . . . these are just a few of the obnoxious behaviors you may hear about before lunch today. These types of co-workers usually are behaving unattractively for one of two reasons. They may be completely oblivious to their own behavior. You may call these "blind spots," and even the best employees have them. Or they may not realize how their behavior impacts others. Regardless of why they act the way they do, a critical conversation can stop the behavior and perhaps stop other obnoxious behavior in the future.

Here is a positive and professional way to help resolve conflict with an obnoxious co-worker.

Jane: "George, I find your loud music is disruptive to my concentration. Are you willing to talk about how we both can be productive?"

Obnoxious co-worker George listening to his music on the highest setting: "That music must be in your imagination — my music is on my headphones. I would never think of being obnoxious."

Jane: "I understand you like your music at work, and I understand how you may think the music is at a low volume. Are you willing to work with me to find a volume that allows everyone to be productive at work?"

Now George has the option of saying yes or no. If he says no, Jane may have a valid workplace complaint that she needs to bring to a manager's attention. However, if George has any common sense, he will probably say yes, and then George and Jane can begin to brainstorm solutions and come to a mutual agreement.

Jane mastered the critical conversation elements in this discussion. First, she examined and presented the problem without threat or negative tone. George really may have a genuine lack of understanding of what makes a respectful workplace, and with Jane's help, he can see how a workplace needs to work for everyone. Second, Jane helped decide what to do next by making a recommendation to change behavior that would work for everyone. And third, she asked whether George would be willing to work together to create a solution (appreciate and acknowledge feelings) and get moving forward. This trifecta of critical conversation talking points avoids an autocrat "I'll tell you what to do . . ." and creates solutions everyone can live with and support in the future.

Putting away grudges

Putting away anger or pride is never easy, but settling a grudge, whether you have it or someone else has it against you, will make for a better workplace, even if it means putting ego aside. Of course, critical conversations can help (but you knew that already, right?).

REMEMBER

Simply examine and present the problem without threats or negativity, make a recommendation to help decide on next steps while acknowledging the other person's feelings, and gain agreement on how to get moving forward.

Suppose your boss decides to buy an island in the middle of nowhere. The $20 million price tag on the island is a bit of a hit to his checking account, so the boss decides to cut all bonuses for his employees for the next 100 years. Some of the employees (OK, all employees) are a bit mad and are holding on to some pretty strong grudges. If a critical conversation can solve this one, a critical conversation can probably solve just about anything.

> **Cameron, the employee, during a one-on-one meeting with the boss:** "Dennis, I'm still feeling angry about your decision last year to cut bonuses. I know we can't go back in time, but I'd like to be able to move on and make our relationship and company stronger."
>
> **The boss, Dennis:** "I had no idea you felt so strongly."
>
> **Cameron:** "I want to be up front about what I want from this conversation. It would be nice to find a way to reinstate the bonuses in the future. Are you willing to work together to find a solution?"
>
> **Dennis:** "Well, we just don't have the funds now."
>
> **Cameron:** "I understand that we're under financial pressure. Are you willing to work toward a solution all employees can live with?"
>
> **Dennis:** "Of course. I didn't realize this had such a negative impact on the company."

Now Dennis and Cameron can have a discussion about solutions to truly dropping the grudge and moving forward. Although it may be hard to put your feelings out there as honestly as Cameron does in this conversation, if you truly want to resolve the grudge, both parties have to be willing to put everything out on the table. Because grudges by definition have been going on for a while, coming to the conversation with a genuine desire to help make the situation better and being clear about intentions helps everyone to forgive and forget.

WARNING

If either party doesn't want to work together, the only option for resolution is for the initiator of the conversation to move on and let go of the grudge. No critical conversation can force another person to change — the conversation can only create an environment that makes change likely and possible.

Handling waterworks in the office

When an individual gets a bad review, is under stress, or is dealing with personal issues, one reaction may be crying in the workplace. Many people perceive crying as a weakness, when it's really just a reaction, much like anger, sarcasm, or silence. However, if you tend to react differently, seeing someone cry in the office may catch you off guard.

REMEMBER

What is an expert communicator to do? First and foremost, try to keep the crying in perspective, and don't judge the other person. Second, if the person isn't already in a private office when the crying starts, offer to go to one right away. The next step is to get the critical conversation going as soon as possible to help manage emotions. Many managers either quickly back down from a comment that made the other person cry or just do whatever it takes to make the crying stop. Neither of these options is a long-term solution. Use the critical conversation method to get to the real problem and allow everyone to maintain dignity.

During a critical conversation about poor performance, Alex starts to cry. Having just read this book, manager Maggie refocuses the conversation.

> **Maggie:** "I can see that you're upset about the feedback. I've found that everyone reacts differently to performance reviews. Would you like some time to yourself?"
>
> **Alex:** "No, just a tissue. I just can't believe I'm doing so poorly. I can't lose my job. My kids are in college, my mom is sick, and I have a mortgage."
>
> **Maggie (after a short pause):** "I can understand how you'd feel overwhelmed by everything going on in your life. My goal is to help you excel at your job, not to fire you. I've found that having a clear action plan makes doing a great job easier when you're trying to fulfill many responsibilities. Are you willing to continue the conversation now and find ways to boost your performance?"

At this time, Maggie and Alex can agree to continue the discussion, or, if needed, postpone it. Crying is no different from any other reaction employees may have during a critical conversation or leading up to one. State the problem or situation, acknowledge and appreciate other's feelings, and then decide what to do next (in this case, either work on the performance feedback or postpone the meeting).

Note that Maggie didn't apologize for Alex's feelings or back down from the issue they were originally discussing. And she kept the conversation going in a humane and respectful way. Critical conversations allow everyone to have feelings and express their feelings, but still get work done.

Discussing differing values and personal styles

It's a fairly well-accepted fact that people have different views on what is and isn't right. These views permeate through what you say, how you act, what you wear, and nearly everything else that happens from the time the alarm clock rings until bedtime. You and your staff are likely to have different opinions on what's right and what's wrong in the workplace. Luckily, company policies can help dictate appropriate behavior and dress code, but when the policy's line is blurry, a critical conversation can clear up the difference.

To help any workplace value diversity more effectively, teach employees to value differences and better understand their own communication, conflict, and leadership styles and the impact of their styles. Although leadership assessments and trainings that help to increase self-awareness and emotional intelligence are a great ways to make meaningful change, the conversation about these activities can start with a critical conversation.

Here's how the conversation may start:

> **Manager Max:** "I think diversity is the best way to generate new ideas. Over the past few months, I feel there have been a number of conflicts and differences in opinions within our team that seem to be inhibiting innovation rather than helping it. Do I have your commitment to work together to find out what's happening and then try to resolve it?"

Now Max can introduce training, assessments, or a group activity that can create a better understanding of differences with the team's support.

Chapter **4**

Workplace Complaints

Almost every manager has an employee who voices a concern about behaviors or actions in the workplace. These concerns aren't just personality differences or performance matters; these concerns are workplace complaints that could potentially lead to legal or ethical problems.

Don't take these concerns lightly. A critical conversation isn't the only tool you need to solve them, but the critical conversation approach can help you through these problems. If you hear about a workplace concern, or if you have one you need to voice to a leader in your company, the recommendations in this chapter can help.

This chapter defines what a workplace complaint is, and what to do when you hear or have one. It presents ideas on how to address the complaint and how (and when) to involve human resources or other outside professional mediators. Because workplace concerns aren't limited to the nonmanagement ranks, you also discover what to do when you have a legitimate complaint about a leader in the company. Although these kinds of workplace concerns are often considered from a legal point of view, they can be seen as ethical concerns as well. Ethics is a big topic in today's corporate culture, so ethical concerns are covered from two angles: cultural differences that can be perceived as ethical issues and the difference between ethical and legal concerns. Finally, you get the scoop on two important aspects of conversations that address workplace complaints: How to maintain confidentiality and how to move forward after the issue is resolved.

WARNING

This chapter doesn't replace the need for legal counsel, working with your internal human resources department, or involving government agencies that safeguard workers' rights. Using critical conversations can help focus the discussion, but they don't replace the need for legal expertise.

Addressing Workplace Complaints

REMEMBER

When considering whether to use a critical conversation to rectify a workplace complaint, there are three things to take into consideration:

>> First, for how long has the issue been present? If the issue has been going on for some time, even if it has just recently surfaced, heading to HR to help resolve the complaint may be a better option. However, if the workplace complaint is new, a critical conversation can help make the employee aware of the behavior and change it.

>> The second consideration is the severity and risk of the workplace complaint. If a workplace complaint is about an employee using foul language, a critical conversation can help turn the behavior around. However, if the employee is making employees feel threatened, unable to work, or putting them under extreme stress, the first step should be working with HR.

>> Finally, if an employee breaks the law, most organizations have steps in place to handle legal concerns, and a critical conversation should not take the place of a legal discussion. If a workplace complaint involves discrimination in the workplace or other violations of the law, work with your human resources team to keep things legal.

Defining a workplace complaint

A workplace complaint is a problem that disrupts the productivity of employees. Workplace complaints can range from the temperature of conference rooms or the noise level in an office, to harassment or legal concerns. The next two sections walk through some of the more common issues that need to go directly to the legal or HR team and other concerns that may be able to be resolved with a critical conversation.

Legal concerns shouldn't be taken lightly, but sometimes it's difficult to tell the difference between a legal concern and a staff dispute or personality difference. The steps during a critical conversation can help managers and employees, as well as HR teams and, if needed, legal or outside mediators, find out what's really happening.

Figuring out when critical conversations aren't enough

Critical conversations aren't the only tool you need to work through workplace concerns. A conversation isn't going to fix a legal issue. Verbal and nonverbal cues in a critical conversation can help steer discussions, but if someone is breaking the law, or potentially breaking the law, you can be charged with a violation if you do nothing or if you don't follow the appropriate regulation or law.

You shouldn't be scared into referring everything to the human resources or employee relations departments, but if you're unsure of or find yourself questioning what to do next, ask. That's always better than finding out later that you didn't do enough. Here are some of the most common workplace complaints that should not rely on a critical conversation:

>> **Breaking the law:** If the name "Enron" rings a bell, it should, because it sent an alarm through corporate America. Break the law, and the company could disappear almost overnight. Whether you have an employee stealing from the company, or an entire company being made up on a balance sheet, concerns about breaking the law should sound the alarms.

>> **Discrimination:** It's next to impossible for any professional outside of the legal profession to know every regulation that governs the workplace, but most boil down to not treating employees fairly. Treating employees equally — from the hiring process to the termination process — is covered by workplace regulations. If you don't follow those regulations properly, it could be considered illegal.

   It's good to handle an initial discrimination discussion with a critical conversation, but when someone says he feels that he's been discriminated against, convey this information to the legal or human resources department immediately to make sure you're doing what's legally required to find out the truth.

>> **Workers' compensation benefits:** In the United States, if an employee is hurt on the job, the specific states regulate what the company must do and what a company can't do. These regulations vary widely state by state, but if someone is hurt on the job and complains that he wasn't treated fairly, alert human resources immediately.

>> **Personal safety concerns:** Critical conversations also can't solve serious concerns of safety or a highly hostile environment. If the participants have restraining orders against each other, or feel their safety is at risk, a critical conversation isn't recommended without a mediator or another third party being involved (find out more on mediators later in this chapter). If there is any threat to or concern for safety, immediately bring in professional counsel to help keep the situation safe for all employees.

>> **Harassment:** Workplace harassment is a big concern in many organizations, and it should be. But because the name can make companies fear the worst (a lawsuit and horrible PR), it may be easy to overreact if an employment law specialist isn't involved. Employee relations professionals can help decipher what's harassment and what's just poor behavior. Critical conversations *can* help uncover some of the facts when a potential harassment issue is brought up and, if the issue is minor, can often be used to help stop the behavior. Critical conversations can help you understand what's happening, but if an employee feels that she's being harassed — or even says the word "harassment" — it's best to advise your human resources or employee relations department. If you don't have one of these departments, confidentially bring up the issue to your boss and document the critical conversations you already had. If you need it, seek out legal advice.

When dealing with any potential harassment issue, or any legal issue for that matter, document and raise the concern. The worst thing to do is to keep the information secret and do nothing.

>> **Ethical concerns that also break the law:** Laws governing ethics in business seem to change almost daily. In the past, it may have been unethical for a financial services company in the United States to give money to a political party and then bid on government work (with the same politicians the executives may have just given money to), but today the Dodd-Frank Act makes that explicitly illegal. However, some issues aren't that black and white. If an act is deemed unethical, but isn't illegal, what should you do?

If an ethical concern breaks the law, treat it as breaking the law (see the first bullet in this list). Corporations have created ethics hotlines, governance boards, codes of conduct, and social responsibility offices to lay the foundation for what the organization feels is ethically and morally right and to direct employees on how to respond when an unethical act is discovered.

These areas are by no means a complete list of when to use extra caution when considering a critical conversation. Anytime you're in doubt about what to do next, talk with an employment law expert or your human resources or employee relations department.

WARNING

This book isn't a replacement for legal counsel. If you find yourself wondering what's ethical or legal when a concern is voiced or you have such a concern yourself, corporate human resources departments, outside legal counsel, local business chambers, or even the United States Labor Department are resources that can help.

Looking at complaints that benefit from a critical conversation

After you know what you probably should not try to resolve with a critical conversation, you may be wondering whether a critical conversation can help rectify any workplace complaints at all. The answer is yes. Here are a few complaints you may hear that can benefit from a critical conversation:

>> **Employee morale issues:** Many employee morale issues may tie back to staff disputes (see Book 2, Chapter 3), but some may focus more on a larger group or team, or even the organization itself. Someone may complain that they don't feel valued, or are unhappy with co-workers' attitudes, or they are just plain old burnt out. A critical conversation can help get to the bottom of the complaint and resolve the issue.

>> **Issues that mask real concerns:** Some workplace concerns are not really concerns at all. They are personal grudges or cries of panic when the complaining employee knows they are underperforming. If an employee gets a poor performance rating, they may say they are being discriminated against. Of course, this could be true, but it also may be that the employee is blaming others for their poor performances.

>> **Some ethical concerns:** Most employers have rules in place that govern ethical issues, like surfing the Internet on a company computer and using a company-issued cell phone to make personal calls. Of course, you've probably heard of an employee checking his personal email or shopping for that last-minute birthday gift over his lunch hour. These ethical concerns can often be resolved by kicking off a critical conversation. Of course, if the behavior does not change with a conversation, then a manager may have to consider more severe options (like firing the employee or putting them on a performance plan).

>> **Off-the-wall inquiries:** Yes, there will be some complaints that may leave you speechless (at least until you kick off the critical conversation). These can include anything from the size of someone's office, when the trash is or is not picked up from the cubicles, and so on. While these issues may not seem like issues at all, the individual raising them could potentially be emotional about the outcome, and therefore a critical conversation could help.

The rest of this chapter focuses on what to do when these types of workplace complaints are raised and how to use critical conversations to help dig into these types of workplace concerns.

Using Critical Conversations When an Issue Is Raised

What do you do when an employee comes and lets you know that he has a concern that potentially can be resolved with a critical conversation? In most cases, you can follow the steps for handling a staff dispute (see Book 2, Chapter 3). But, as you're digging into what's really happening, the best thing to do is to listen before you act. Make sure you focus on finding out all the facts and maintaining a positive environment. Ask what happened, take notes, and then agree on what should happen next.

Here's an example of how to follow the critical conversation steps when an issue is raised. Suppose Sally comes into the office obviously distraught. She tells you that Frank, her co-worker, just commented on how cute she looks and makes inappropriate comments about other women in the workplace. As the receiver of this information, you should follow many of the main critical conversation elements of a staff dispute:

>> **Examine and acknowledge the other person's feelings.** Because these types of conversations usually aren't planned, take a minute to let the other party know that you're here to listen and to help resolve the issue. In this case, you may say, "Thanks, Sally, for coming to me. I want to help resolve this issue so we can all work together in a positive environment."

>> **Examine what happened.** Ask what specifically happened and whether the other person feels comfortable telling you more specifics. Often these conversations are emotional, so try to stick to the facts, but be sure to acknowledge feelings along the way. In this case, ask, "Can you give me a few examples of what happened so I can best understand the issue?"

Examining what's happening can help you uncover what the facts really are before you make a decision about what to do next. Try to avoid leading questions that sound like you're putting the spotlight on a person in an investigation room. For example, don't ask, "Since you didn't try to ask Mike to stop making comments, was there anything else you couldn't do?" A better option for uncovering the facts would be, "Did you think about talking to Mike about how his behavior made you feel?" Asking leading questions could lead to defensiveness and add to an already emotional situation.

» **Examine and acknowledge feelings and perspectives (once again).** Let the other person know she did the right thing by coming to you even if it may have been tough. This acknowledgment keeps the communication channel open for any future discussions. Say, "I can understand why you would be upset, and I appreciate your courage to come to me."

» **Decide what to do next.** If you recognize you're dealing with a potential legal workplace complaint or an ethical concern, bring in your human resources or employee relations resource to help with the process quickly. Balance this action with an agreement to do so, and with what you or the initiator of the conversation may or may not do in the interim. You may say, "This does sound like something we should involve HR in. Would you be comfortable talking with them, or would you like me to talk to them first?" Also ask the other party to do two things before the next step: first, maintain confidentiality (more on that later in this chapter), and second, come to you if the situation gets worse.

» **Gain commitment and get moving.** Now you do what you agreed to do and then work with the parties involved to solve the problem.

» **Evaluate the discussion.** After the issue is resolved, or in some cases passed on to the legal or HR department, follow up with the individual who voiced the complaint. You may say something along these lines: "Thanks for voicing your concern. Is there anything I could have done differently to help rectify the situation? I want to make sure you feel I have done my job well."

Digging into Workplace Complaints

An employee complaint can be resolved with a critical conversation, like those listed earlier in this chapter, and you can follow the critical conversations model (examine what is happening, decide on next steps, put the plan in motion to gain commitment and get moving, and evaluate results).

However, workplace complaints that can be resolved by (or at least started with) a critical conversation tend to have even higher emotions. Therefore it is a good idea to spend a decent amount of time repeating the steps of examining what is happening and acknowledging emotions before decisions on next steps are made. This might also involve bringing in other parties to find out a bit more about what is really happening. The bottom line: You will be doing a bit more analysis on what the real problem is before you can work with the other parties on ideas of how to fix it.

Let's say an employee comes to a senior manager soon after having a poor performance review with his manager and begins to complain that he feels discriminated against because the manager does not like him. The senior manager can effectively handle the situation by examining what is happening and acknowledging feelings, and then deciding what happens in the next phases of a critical conversation.

Employee Bob: "Terry is a horrible manager. He just does not like me and gave me a bad review."

Senior Manager Mike: "Thanks, Bob, for coming to me with your concern. Can you tell me a little more about the parts of your review that make you feel this way?"

Bob: "Well, he said I never contribute to the project. I work so hard. I am here every day and stay late. I work harder than any other person on that team. Terry just doesn't like me. He's just discriminating against me. I heard everyone else got great reviews and giant bonuses."

Mike: "I can understand how you might feel by putting in so many hours and not getting the review you expected. If we can try to keep the discussion focused on your performance and expectations, I would be happy to talk with Terry and get his perspective. Would you think that would help clarify parts of your review or would you like to recommend a different solution?"

Mike examined what was happening, acknowledged how Bob felt about what was happening, and then proposed one next step to continue identifying what is really happening. Now Bob has a choice of including his manager in the conversation or continuing to complain. If everyone agrees to talk about the review, they can follow the steps in Book 2, Chapter 1 on how to deliver a negative performance review and create next steps to resolve performance issues. (And, yes, Bob's manager, Terry, should have read Book 2, Chapter 1 before he gave a poor performance review in the first place.)

Of course, if Bob chooses to not involve his manager in a performance discussion, the conversation may continue like this:

Bob: "I really don't think that will work. He is discriminating against me every day because he does not like me."

Mike: "I hear your concerns and I know tough reviews are often difficult to give and hear. If you feel you are being discriminated against and it is not just a misunderstanding, you may want to talk with human resources about your complaint."

Mike diffused a potentially emotional situation by listening to Bob, and recommending approaches to moving forward to find out more facts. He did not place blame or disregard Bob's comments. Instead, he used empathy and honesty to help resolve the situation — the pillars of any critical conversation.

Outside of moving gracefully between examining what is happening, acknowledging the other's feelings, and involving others as needed, there are a few other expert tips to keep in mind while trying to identify why the complaint surfaced while maintaining confidentially and respect: maintaining confidentiality, not placing blame, and separating personal issues from real grievances.

Maintaining confidentiality during communications

REMEMBER

Whether the situation can be resolved with a conversation or series of conversations, or if the issue has to be referred to higher sources, confidentiality is key. Keeping conversations behind closed doors can be a legal requirement, but it also helps to maintain productivity and a positive work environment. If people are talking about the workplace issue around the water cooler, they probably aren't spending as much time doing their jobs.

Confidentiality is the responsibility of all parties. If you do have to escalate issues to a third party, be it HR or a more senior leader, make sure all the parties know how the issue will be handled so there are no surprises. Confidentiality also helps to maintain the dignity of everyone involved, regardless of the outcome. You can imagine how difficult it would be for the accused individual to regain credibility if the complaint turns out not to be accurate.

Not placing blame

It's hard not to have prejudged conclusions about people's behavior. If someone is in your office complaining about a potential law being broken by a colleague and you've always thought that colleague was a bit deceptive, do your best to maintain a clear head and not judge the colleague guilty before the facts are in. If you feel that you can't be objective, ask another manager or professional to work on finding the facts. That helps you maintain an innocent-until-proven-guilty perspective.

CLOSING THE RUMOR MILL

Sometimes a workplace issue is just blatantly obvious to anyone within a three-mile radius. People start asking questions and the rumor is at full speed. So how do you get the word out about the issue without discussing the issue? It is simply best not to say anything about the issue itself. Instead, focus on why confidentiality is important for everyone by saying, "I know there may be a desire to learn more about the issue, but for the sake of everyone involved, I ask that you respect my request for confidentiality." For more on how to use a critical conversation to quiet a gossiper, jump to Book 2, Chapter 5.

Your role is to gather information so you can help decide who needs to be involved. Your role is not to interrogate a suspect at a crime scene. Be careful not to turn into a special investigator, because holding something of a Spanish Inquisition could prevent the employee from feeling comfortable bringing any issues to you in the future. Instead, simply ask what happened and what he's comfortable telling you. If you need to involve anyone else, let the employee know what steps you think you should take as well.

Separating personal issues from valid grievances

Employees are smart — they read or listen to the news and may hear of harassment lawsuits that resulted in millions of dollars for some employee being unfairly treated. Laws are in place to protect employees, but not every workplace issue is a legal issue. Some people may cry wolf — either intentionally or not — when they feel they've been wronged.

You don't need to be an expert in employment law, but in many cases (with the exception of violence or gross misconduct), a critical conversation facilitated by a neutral party can help separate personal issues from potential legal concerns.

Bringing in a Mediator

Ideally, individual employees or groups of employees and managers will be able to resolve many complaints in an atmosphere of mutual respect by using the critical conversation fundamentals. People make mistakes, and sometimes they say things that they shouldn't say. And, in most cases, when these things are brought to their attention, the offending parties respond by changing their behavior. When that doesn't happen or when additional conversations aren't probable, you may choose to bring in a third party to facilitate the resolution.

What is a mediation expert?

Mediation is a process that allows individual opinions, emotions, and points of view to be heard when a direct conversation doesn't work. A mediator facilitates communication and negotiation between people experiencing conflict to assist them in reaching a voluntary agreement regarding their dispute. A representative from HR or the legal department may also act as a mediator.

REMEMBER

Although many good mediators are attorneys, a good mediator doesn't have to be an attorney. HR professionals, internal legal experts, or ombudsmen in the company are great resources to tap into when looking for help with the critical conversations.

TIP

Mediators may be internal or external to the organization. In any case, first determine whether the mediator has any conflicts of interest that would cause a participant or the mediator to feel that the mediator can't be impartial.

When to bring in a professional

Deciding when to work with a third party is often a judgment call based on the history of resolving issues between the parties and the state of the relationship before the issue happened. A mediator can make your job easier and prevent workplace concerns from turning into crises in situations like these:

>> **Emotions are at an all-time high.** High emotions are part of critical conversations, but if one person gets defensive or cries when the other speaks forcefully, and the parties can't move past this behavior, a mediator may be a good option. If emotions prevent either party from focusing on the real problems, a mediator may be a good option.

>> **The conversation is at an impasse.** You can use mediators not only for workplace or ethical concerns but also when a conversation is at an impasse, when multiple and complex issues continue to surface, or when multiple parties are involved in the conflict.

>> **The boss is in question.** A critical conversation with a boss who's behaving poorly may need to involve a third party to solve the issue. Critical conversations are tough enough when the concern *isn't* about your boss or another superior in the organization. If your boss is the one in question, a critical conversation isn't necessarily futile, but you may need to take a different approach. In some organizational cultures, questioning the boss and giving feedback is acceptable and encouraged. In these organizations, you may feel comfortable examining behaviors or actions with your boss. For example, you may mention that you didn't understand a certain accounting change or agreement with a customer. If you come to the table with a genuine desire to help and understand, the ethical or workplace issue may simply be a misunderstanding.

But not all cultures are this open, and it does take a tremendous amount of nerve and self-confidence to talk about workplace issues with leaders. Therefore, it may make sense to go to your human resources manager to talk through the issue. If you're still uncertain whether the issue can be resolved after speaking with HR, you may consider talking with a mediator to solve the problem.

In these situations, having a conversation mediated by a third party can help resolve a seemingly irresolvable issue.

REMEMBER

If no legal precedent is set, mediation is a cost-effective alternative to a lengthy lawsuit. Of course, if legal issues are at stake or one party is screaming "I want my lawyer," a mediator may need to step aside and allow for an even more formal legal process.

How a mediator can make your life easier

Because mediators are experts in conversation, your job in the conversation is to focus on what's happening instead of the process to resolve it. A skilled mediator can also help coach the participants about ways to improve their communication so that after the issue is resolved, all the parties can continue in civil working relationships.

If you're the boss facing a workplace or ethical concern, or if you feel the need to involve a third party, professional mediation can make the process easier. Mediation is simply a critical conversation with the added benefit of an expert in conversations and more formal documentation. If you find the conversation at an impasse, shifting to the mediation process should be relatively simple, albeit emotional, as it follows many of the same steps as a direct critical conversation.

Here are the steps involved in a professionally mediated conversation:

1. **Prepare.**

   Depending on the complexity of the issues and the number of participants, the mediator may request to review relevant documents, speak with participants individually, and ask that the participants sign a mediation agreement describing the role of the mediator, the process, and confidentiality.

2. **Set expectations and establish ground rules.**

   The mediator works with the parties to establish guidelines for respectful communication and confidentiality.

3. **Explore opinions, data, and feelings.**

   Just like in a critical conversation, the mediator asks participants to describe their perspectives of the events giving rise to the conflict. This step may also include identifying the underlying interests or unmet needs that are driving the conflict.

4. **Identify issues and set an agenda.**

   The mediator helps the participants identify the issues or problems they want to address during the course of the mediation.

5. Generate, evaluate, and choose options.

The mediator encourages the participants to brainstorm all possible options for resolutions and then guides the participants in choosing what to do next.

6. Develop final agreements.

The mediator usually prepares a formal document on what was agreed to and what should happen next.

Do these steps sound familiar? They should. The steps a mediator uses are almost identical to the steps of a critical conversation. The main difference is that someone else is in the room to keep emotions at bay and to help enable seemingly impossible conversations to occur.

Moving Forward after Tough Workplace Conversations

Workplace complaints and ethical issues can cause a tremendous amount of stress on the parties involved and in many cases on an entire organization or team. In order to move forward, it's helpful to have a critical conversation that conveys your interest in keeping open communication and getting everyone back on track — whether the issue was found to be invalid or valid.

WARNING

The alternative to having a direct yet critical conversation to close a workplace complaint is to say nothing. But by saying nothing, the void will be filled with rumor or assumptions. As with most critical conversations, be genuine, focus on the facts, and make sure you have a clear plan of action for what's happening next.

Keep in mind that confidentiality is not just a legal matter — when you're dealing with sensitive workplace complaints or ethical issues, it's essential to protect all parties and get employees back to work after the issue is resolved.

Part of moving forward after a complaint is resolved is to make sure that people feel they can get back to work. If the individuals in the conversation have maintained confidentiality throughout the process, even if the complaint was not valid, all parties may agree the issue was a misunderstanding and go on with work. This is the easiest solution and the reason that confidentiality is key.

However, if someone has said something to someone (and this does happen), the best way to handle invalid complaints is to ask the person wrongly accused how he wants to address the situation. Some may just want to move on, but others may want to bring closure to the event more publicly. Work with your employee relations or human resources expert to determine what is and isn't appropriate to say. You may even have another critical conversation to close out the complaint like this one:

>> First, *examine* what's happening and state the facts, keeping them short and simple. For example, you may say: "Over the past month, there have been concerns about our conflict of interest policy." Make sure all the parties know that you've been listening. You can do this by saying, "I know this process hasn't been easy for anyone, and I thank you for your patience and honest discussions."

>> Then, state that the issue was looked at, and that a *decision has been made.* Using the same example as in the previous bullet, this could be: "I've worked with all the parties involved, and I've found that the issue was a misunderstanding. We can support one another by getting back to focusing on what's most important: serving our customers."

>> Finally, allow others to provide confidential feedback (*a way of evaluating how the process was handled*). This will help everyone get back to work while helping all the parties involved maintain respect and dignity. A conclusion may be: "I also want to thank you again for feeling comfortable voicing concerns, and I'd like you to know that if you ever have concerns in the future, my door is always open."

TIP

If you find an issue is not valid, or not resolved the way an employee hoped, this is a good time to use those critical conversation skills again. If the employee is upset or angry, you may want to jump to Book 2, Chapter 5 to discover how to handle these situations.

Chapter **5**

Difficult Behaviors

Although it's tough to label anyone as difficult, almost everyone in an organization (or on Earth) can acknowledge that some personalities are just a little more challenging than others. A simple conversation won't solve the challenging behaviors — oh, if only it were that simple. But critical conversations can get the ball rolling in the right direction — right toward a productive working relationship.

Relationships based on trust and credibility take time to develop — there's no way to get around it. One of the best ways to develop these relationships is to give meaningful and timely feedback, with the intent of improving the situation for all parties involved. So if you want to just tell that annoying co-worker to take his loud gum snapping somewhere else, a critical conversation probably won't help. But if you're interested in building solid relationships, where you work though disagreements professionally, and everyone comes out ahead of the game, start working through these challenging behaviors with a critical conversation.

This chapter walks you through how to recognize the behaviors that push your buttons and how to separate these hot buttons from the person pushing them. Next, you load up your toolbox with different approaches to address the challenging behavior, using the critical conversation formula (examine, decide, gain commitment, and get moving, evaluate = successful conversations). Finally, you uncover some real-life examples of challenging workplace behaviors, and you get the exact script to start with as you take on any challenge outside of your cubicle.

Defining Difficult Behaviors

Some behaviors that may push your buttons include whining, pointing fingers, sarcasm, never picking up a phone call, always insisting on email, and on and on. Although hot buttons can create a tremendous amount of stress in the workplace, difficult behaviors are a little different. Difficult behaviors almost always stop or greatly impede performance in an organization.

Difficult behaviors, similar to staff disputes discussed in Book 2, Chapter 3, are issues that are negatively impacting the performance of a team or organization and will worsen over time if left alone.

What are difficult behaviors that some people display? Here are a few:

>> **Constant complainers:** These individuals think everything will fail and are constantly pointing out what is wrong to other employees or supervisors.

>> **Solo workers:** These individuals will often exclude certain people or groups from decisions or projects.

>> **Controllers:** Controllers may undermine others' abilities or just try to dominate or take charge of everyone's work.

>> **Know-it-alls:** They may use sarcasm to degrade other people's ideas and often must have the final say.

>> **Indecisive participants:** These types may just want everyone to like them, but are unable to manage making even seemingly easy decisions.

>> **Too busy for anything:** The types of behaviors are often driven by a mix of a number of difficult behaviors. They need to be involved or have some control in everything and have difficulty delegating or making decisions. They may want to take on all the work because they refuse to work with others. They are difficult because they cannot give the time needed to the work that matters, and therefore they often stall progress in an organization.

Difficult behaviors can also include blaming others for everything, frequent shouting or yelling, constant rudeness, or gossiping.

Difficult behaviors can, and often do, impact performance. These behaviors need attention with a critical conversation and plenty of critical follow-up.

TIP

Difficult behaviors are different from personal hot buttons or simple annoyances. Sure, it may annoy you that someone stands too close to you or chews her food with her mouth open in the cube next to you, but in the bigger scheme of things, these behaviors really shouldn't make or break the performance of an organization.

If you're faced with an annoying hot button that you just can't get over (why can't that person just close her lips when she eats!?!?!), having a critical conversation is perfectly fine. Start with how you're feeling and how it impacts your performance. Just don't be surprised if the other individual tells you that heating your food in the microwave has been annoying her for some time now, too. There's something annoying about everyone; your choice is whether you address the little things and knowing when to address big things (also known as difficult behaviors).

Keying in on Difficult Behaviors

As hard as it may be, when you're working with difficult behaviors, you need to separate the behavior from the person. Your observation of the behavior may differ from what the person's motivations actually are. Yes, you (and most likely many others) think the individual is incompetent, but she may actually think she's trying to help the situation.

Looking at intentions

In the workplace, some employees are persistently pessimistic. The difficult behavior is that the person in question complains about everything, but rarely offers ways to fix the situation. In her defense, the person may want to make sure all the risks are identified before moving forward with any decision, or she may just be fearful of doing anything different. The behavior may be difficult, but what the person is trying to achieve may be worthwhile (in this case, pointing out risks to avoid problems in the future).

When separating the behavior from the person, you can use either the gentle nudge approach or a more direct approach to examine what is happening:

>> **Gentle nudge:** A gentle nudge is just a subtle, yet genuine, way to state how you feel and what you observe, without the risk of creating too much conflict. If you're using this approach, you may say, "Hi, Julia. I noticed that you bring up many ideas about what could go wrong with the project during the meeting, but it does not seem like we have time to discuss any possible solutions before you bring up another potential problem. Are you willing to work together to find a way for us to talk about both the problems *and* possible solutions during the meeting with the group?" In this case, gently letting another employee see a different point of view can show how their way may have been counterproductive.

If the other individual is more direct in her own communication, you have a strong work relationship with the other individual, or if the behavior has been going on for a while, you may choose to use a more direct style of examining what is happening. Additionally, if you tried to use a gentle nudge and it did not work, you may need to use a more direct approach to separate the behavior from the person.

>> **Direct approach:** If you're using this approach, you may say, "Hi, Julia. I realize you have many ideas on what could go wrong with the project. I noticed that you bring up many problems during the meeting. Can we talk about what you would like to achieve in the meetings and then find a way to focus on solutions to these problems?" Directly asking the intent of actions may put the person on the spot if done in an accusing manner. Therefore, it's critical to follow golden rule #1: Come to the table with a genuine desire to help make the situation better (not a desire to tell someone she's an idiot and a time drain).

TIP

Be careful in your choice of words when using a more direct approach. When you're looking for the intent of the behavior, asking, "What are you trying to achieve?" can be perceived as a sign that the person is failing at what she wants to do. Asking "What would you like to achieve?" tends to be a bit more positive and goal oriented. A few words can make a world of difference.

If you find the intent or reason for a behavior, it will be much easier to find a resolution. In the case in the previous list, just telling Julia to stop discussing risks and problems could make Julia feel that her ideas are no longer valued. However, if you can find ways for Julia to voice her opinions during the meeting or even help put the agenda together, her desired goal may be achieved in a more productive way. Sometimes the simplest solutions, like making a point to ask for Julia's opinion, will resolve the problem. You might do this by being proactive and asking for her ideas and thoughts during the meeting.

TIP

A conversation with a gossiper isn't going to be the easiest conversation, but difficult behaviors call for strong leaders and team members to stand up and talk about what's happening. If the conversation seems a bit too hard to say for the first time, you can preface the statement with how you feel by saying, "I don't want to be too pushy, but can you tell me what you want to achieve by having conversations that counter the agreements we had just made?" To stay aware of your attitude and nonverbal communication during this conversation, check Chapters 1 and 2 in Book 1.

And sometimes the only way to find out the other person's intentions is to state the obvious problem in a non-accusatory voice, say how you feel, and ask what the purpose of the behavior is. Keep in mind that you may need to have these conversations more than once to resolve the issue. And of course, be sure to stay genuine.

REMEMBER

Difficult behavior may just be different perspectives and views on the world. A behavior you find odd or difficult may just be a person trying to do her job in the best way she sees appropriate.

Focusing on behaviors, not labels

As with all critical conversations, start with facts (I see), opinions (I think), or feelings (I feel). When working with difficult behaviors, it's more important than ever to base the conversation on what's really happening — not on the perception of the person or behavior or what you heard through the grapevine.

Asking for the meaning of the behavior is simply finding out the intention (like the example in the previous section). This approach not only takes the guesswork out of determining what's going on, but also helps to prevent labeling someone as a bad employee, an annoying boss, or a disruptive co-worker.

The easiest way to focus on behaviors rather than labels is to be as specific as possible, without feeling like you're nit-picking every little step.

You can imagine how differently these two conversations would be perceived by an employee who never answers her phone and only replies to anyone via email, even in highly charged discussions:

> **A labeling conversation (not a good approach):** "You have been so difficult to work with lately (labeling). You don't answer your phone at work; I have to email you to get any answer. And you're causing us to lose clients because I can't speak with you directly." Telling someone they are difficult, or any other label, can immediately put them on the defensive.

> **The behavior-focused critical conversation (a much better approach):** "I feel like I'm not communicating with you efficiently. Last week, I was working with a deadline on a client contract, and we weren't able to talk on the phone about a specific policy. I want to have a conversation about how we can avoid some of the back-and-forth clarifications over email in the future. Are you willing work on this with me?"

Staying away from labels isn't easy. People observe the actions of individuals and the interactions of individuals over time, and patterns of behavior start emerging. These patterns often prompt a critical conversation.

TIP

It's perfectly fine, and even preferable, to have two or three recent and specific examples of the behavior that's causing concern. When preparing for the conversation, list the most relevant examples of a behavior and share those observations. However, even if you think the person you're talking with is a horrible, difficult employee who yells, backstabs, and gossips, check your emotions at the door and be specific about the observed behaviors that are exhibited in the workplace.

If an employee comes to you and starts to label another employee, your job is to refocus the issue on the behavior (with a critical conversation) and then, when possible, ask the employees to resolve the issue on their own.

For example, suppose an employee comes into your office and says, "Boss, I'm totally fed up with Bill; he's such a slow worker!" You may refocus the conversation on behaviors (not labels) by saying, "Thanks, Jane, for coming to me with your concern. I know we are all working long hours these days. Have you had a chance to talk with Bob about your concern?"

If Jane says no, your response could be to examine what is happening by saying, "Well, it may make sense to try to talk with Bill. We are all part of the same team. Would it be helpful for us to talk about what you see as 'slow'? When you talk with Bill, it may be more productive to talk about specific actions rather than general descriptions."

If Jane says yes, and Bill is still slow, your response will be quite similar to the earlier one. "We do need to work as a team. If you are willing to try to talk with him one more time, I would be happy to help you better define what you see as 'slow.' When you talk with Bill, it may be more productive to talk about specific actions rather than general descriptions."

In both cases, you (the manager in this example) examined what is happening and acknowledged Jane's concerns and you have started to replace a label with behaviors. Now Jane can have a constructive critical conversation with her co-worker, all thanks to your brilliance. For more on dealing with staff disputes and how to earn a nice label of "Boss of the Year," head over to Book 2, Chapter 3.

Using a Critical Conversation to Turn Around Difficult Behaviors

If you know it is time to stop a difficult behavior that has a negative impact on productivity, and start finding better ways to work, it's time for a critical conversation.

The goals of a critical conversation, whether the discussion is delivering bad news or working through difficult behaviors, remain the same: use honesty and empathy to create a positive solution for everyone involved. When you are trying to create a more positive future when dealing with some pretty negative behaviors, you'll want to first pay special attention to your own emotions and perspectives. Then put the critical conversation into play by examining what is happening, deciding on next steps, and beginning to get moving on a more productive path.

Paying attention to your own opinions and perspectives

There are a few ways to get a grip on your emotions: stop assuming and start breathing. Here are a couple of ways to make sure your own emotions don't cloud the conversation.

Stop assuming

When trying to work with individuals who have more difficult personalities, it can be easy to jump to conclusions that their sole purpose is just to make your life more difficult. Even if it is not your immediate reaction, take the time to stop assuming the worst, and examine what is really happening without judgment. If you don't know what the other person is trying to achieve, ask and then find ways to create a resolution that will work for everyone (more on finding out about intentions earlier in this chapter).

Start breathing

Having any critical conversation is difficult enough, but when you add in even higher emotions and personal behaviors, it is easy to get overwhelmed and nervous.

TIP

The best way to control your emotions is to physically slow down your reaction. When a cell phone goes off during a meeting with some overplayed song from the 1980s and your blood pressure rises, you have two choices: You can stare at the phone, roll your eyes, and attack the other person with sarcasm, or you can count to five, smile, and ask for the behavior to stop in a calm and rational voice. The latter alternative is much more useful and productive, especially in a critical conversation. Practice controlling your behavior when hot button triggers arise in meetings and around the workplace to set you apart as a composed conversation leader.

Putting the critical conversation into play

Starting a critical conversation to change or modify difficult behaviors in the workplace is tough, but the ultimate goal is to make the workplace more productive for everyone. The following is what a critical conversation may sound like when working through difficult behaviors.

Examine what is happening

Honesty is the best policy when examining what is happening that leads up the conversation in the first place. When examining what is happening, it is often useful to make statements that balance facts and feelings. For example, say: "I feel our conversations end with arguments (fact), and this is preventing you and me from working together more effectively (feeling)."

Identifying feelings, even your own feelings, can be a challenge. If emotions are getting the best of you or the situation, say what behavior you see. With empathy you may say something like this: "I feel it is difficult for me to voice my opinion and be taken seriously in our discussions. When we talk, I often hear sarcasm. For example, when I recommended we hire an intern to help with our reports, you said, 'Is number crunching beneath Your Highness?'"

You may end this by acknowledging how the other individual feels, asking, "Do you understand my perspective?" You aren't asking the person with a difficult behavior to agree with you, you are just asking if they understand why you feel the way you do.

Decide what to do next

After calmly examining what is happening, find out whether the other person is willing to find a mutual solution. If someone has been using sarcasm to avoid talking directly with co-workers for their entire career, one conversation may not resolve the issue, but it can be a start. Ask, "Are you willing to work with me to try to find a solution to create a more productive workplace?" It may take time for someone to unlearn old, difficult behaviors, but that is where a plan of action can help.

Focusing on building relationships and creating an open environment to work together is the ultimate goal when deciding what to do next. This is much different than coming into the conversation saying someone needs to change his behavior. Of course, there still needs to be agreement on what is going to happen after the conversation ends, and that is where a plan of action comes into the conversation (see the next section).

Building a Toolbox: Action Plans for Difficult Behaviors

When you're moving through the critical conversation process (also known as the EDGE model — examining behaviors while acknowledging others' perspectives, deciding on actions, getting moving, and then evaluating performance), some actions to change behaviors may be incredibly obvious and others, well, not so much. If a person is losing it because she's working 24 hours a day, 7 days a week, and hasn't slept in about 3 months, find a way to give the person a break and get her help so that she can sleep and return to her normal self. But few difficult behaviors are caused by a lack of sleep; most run much deeper. You need an action plan to change difficult behaviors.

WARNING

Answers aren't always obvious. Some individuals don't realize that they actually need to change. If an individual doesn't acknowledge that her behavior has a negative impact on her career or on her team, action plans may scratch the surface, but in the end no real change in behavior will happen.

Before jumping into action planning, the individual needs to accept that she must change. The critical conversation brings awareness of a difficult style or behavior, and the next step is to gain acceptance of the consequences of the behavior. When you kick off the critical conversation about difficult behavior, you may ask what goal the behavior is going to accomplish. This question is a good first step in identifying the root cause of behaviors.

After you start the identifying process, dive into the following three areas to help change the behavior:

» Coaching and support

» Education and mentoring

» Rewarding

The following sections offer a how-to approach to each of these areas.

Coaching and support

Think about this unfortunately common workplace example: A manager never gives credit to employees for their work (behavior) because he wants to get more face time with the big boss (intention). Until the manager accepts how this behavior negatively impacts the team, he will always be looking for another way (potentially more damaging) to get the face time he craves.

REMEMBER

Coaching is providing ongoing support and guidance to employees and leaders faced with personal and professional challenges. Coaching a difficult behavior helps the individual see her current level of performance, style, and behaviors through another pair of eyes. Essentially, the coach is continuously providing critical conversations to explore what's happening and can help the employee work on new, more productive behaviors.

After the initial meetings and agreements, the coach begins the process of collecting objective data, reflection, experiences, and feelings from the individual, and sometimes from her peers. Then as the individual is made aware of her style and how it impacts others, she has a choice of becoming more proficient and competent in her role or continuing along her current path. Then the coach and individual work to create ways to communicate better, delegate more effectively, involve employees in decision making and problem solving, resolve conflicts, motivate employees, manage time, and the list goes on.

In addition to support and an outside perspective and feedback, coaching is about helping a person clarify what they want and guiding them to get there through powerful questions, active listening, and straight talk to help them align their thinking and behaviors to get what they want. During this process, the attitudes and behaviors that get in the way become undesirable and they want to change.

This coaching stuff sounds great, right? Yes, it can be — but it takes time, and a person has to want to be coached. Even the best coach cannot force someone to change, the individual needs to know and want to change. Accepting one's own behaviors and acknowledging that a change needs to happen may take time, but you can predict how successfully a person will be coached by how she answers these questions:

> "Imagine that this behavior we've been talking about is resolved. What would be possible?" "How will it feel when this outcome is achieved? How will it impact you and others?"

With these simple questions, you can find out whether the person is wants and desires to change. If the answer sounds something like, "Well, I'm not really sure I need to change anything. Everything will be the same," you probably can place a bet that no matter what you do, change is going to be a long, long process. In this situation, if the behavior is stalling progress, it may be best to think about whether the employee is a good fit for the organization.

WARNING

If a person is pushed into action planning before she accepts that her behavior is real, before she accepts its negative impact on others and on herself, and before she identifies what different goals she wants to achieve, the difficult behavior will surface again, and again, and again.

Education and mentoring

Changing behaviors means discovering a new way of working. If an individual has always pitted one employee against another to try to remain in power, that employee is going to have to learn that collaboration can generate much better results. Education can come in a number of ways.

Progress occurs when the difficult behavior is replaced with a positive behavior. After the conversation, one of the action items may be to attend a class on conflict styles or enrolling in How to Be a Decent Manager 101 so the individual learns about other ways to achieve her goals (ways that don't involve the difficult behavior). The training may also come from mentoring. A coach or mentor can help deliver personalized learning to a specific situation, the unique qualities of the leader, and the exact behavior that needs to change.

TIP

Although external coaches are often great, objective teachers, don't underestimate the power of role models and mentors in helping to change behavior. Encourage individuals to broaden their base of support by finding people who challenge them and provide constructive input on a regular basis. Mentors are people who have experience and knowledge to share that will help the individual do his job in a more effective and efficient manner. In other words, they have been down the same road and have firsthand experience.

Rewarding the right behaviors

So often, action plans focus on what was done wrong and what needs to be done to correct the situation. These steps are necessary, but don't forget the value of praise and rewarding the right behaviors. This isn't to suggest giving the difficult person a giant raise or a bonus because she stopped backstabbing people. Recognition can range from a simple "thanks" for a job well done to publicly recognizing the employee for high performance.

When an employee exhibits the desired behaviors, recognition should be:

>> **Timely:** Don't wait until the next team meeting or performance review to say thanks — just say it.

>> **Sincere and specific:** Be specific about what the reward is for, and make sure you're genuine in why you're recognizing the person in the first place.

>> **Positive:** When trying to change behavior, keep the message positive. Saying, "Congratulations, you didn't screw up that one," isn't a good recognition. Saying, "Congratulations, you really made the team come together to solve the problem," is a good recognition.

REMEMBER

Recognition is one of the simplest forms of performance feedback that behavior is changing. It delivers consistent messages about what's important, both to the recipient and to everyone on your team.

Difficult Behaviors

TIP

Some leaders love to talk about what the recognition is (cash, a team lunch, a pat on the back); try to focus more on why you're giving the recognition — to reinforce the behaviors you want to see continue.

TIP

Rewards are not the same for all individuals. It all depends on what motivates the individual. Some may prefer to be given a more flexible schedule, or a written note of appreciation, or public recognition. What motivates people? Money, respect, recognition, action, making a difference, building relationships . . . the list goes on and on. Sometimes it takes seconds to find out what motivates people; other times it can take years of working together to really find out what makes another person tick. Check out the list of common motivations in Table 5-1.

TABLE 5-1   **Motivations**

Motivation	Definition
Action	Getting things done is your first priority. Why handle it later when you can handle it now? You work quickly and take time lines and milestones seriously.
Money	Being paid fairly for the work done drives your work ethic.
Recognition	Being acknowledged for work done by your team and leadership is important to you. High praise and being admired as an expert drives work and actions.
Respect	You crave a professional work environment, where employees treat you (and one another) with genuine concern, listen to ideas with open ears, and value different opinions.
Teamwork	You value teams working together and can work quickly through conflict. You believe the whole team is much stronger than the sum of its parts.

Finding the Words for Special Circumstances

When you have all the tools in your toolbox and a solid understanding of how a critical conversation flows (covered earlier in this chapter), it's time to roll up your sleeves and have conversations! That cheer may not be as powerful as "One small step for man, one giant leap for mankind," but the result of the conversations can be just as powerful. If people can't work together, work can't get done. Not everyone on your team will want to be friends with one another, but by resolving difficult behaviors, teams can focus on what matters most: getting the work done right.

The following sections cover how to handle some of the more popular (er, not so popular) difficult behaviors. While the sections outline specific ways to work with each type of behavior, most of the approaches can be used with almost any difficult behavior you may face.

REMEMBER

None of the upcoming examples or critical conversation tactics is a quick fix that will turn a grumpy old gossiper into a star employee and team member. Reinforce the message through multiple conversations, and follow up to find out how the change is going. You may need to talk with a screamer, gossiper, or angry hostile type after seeing her in action and give critical and timely feedback on performance. Persistence and a genuine attitude does pay off with difficult behaviors, but the first step is having that first conversation.

Defusing a screamer

ARGH!!! SCREAMERS CAN NOW YELL OUT LOUD OR SIMPLY PUT EVERYTHING IN CAPTIAL LETTERS WHEN THEY RUTHLESSLY REPLY ALL (and then some) TO EMAILS.

Some screamers really scream; others choose to use technology to scream for them. You can address the problem behavior in the same way — just don't do it over email. Here's how:

» **Examine what's happening.** When the screamer is screaming, you can say, "I notice you're raising your voice when someone else presents their ideas. What is the goal of your communication?" That's a good way to present the facts and then ask why the behavior is happening. Or if you're talking with an employee after the meeting, say, "In last week's meeting, I noticed that you yelled at the team members when they didn't complete a task on time. What was the goal of your communication?" If you're dealing with an email screamer, pick up the phone or walk over to her office, and state the same thing, "I noticed that you tend to use capital letters in your responses. I feel that these capital letters are the same as screaming at another individual. What message do you want to send with the email?" This is the right place to acknowledge the other person's feelings and opinions. For example, "I understand you want people to know that this topic is important to you."

» **Decide on options.** Listen to the entire conversation before replying. Asking for clarification also helps in these circumstances. Say, "Are you willing to work together to find another way to let people know that you're passionate about a topic?" If necessary, you may need to take a break and specify the consequences of the behavior on the group. Say, "People stop listening to you when you scream" or "People delete your emails."

Very few people just yell for the sake of yelling. Find out what's driving the behavior and then focus on that intention.

Quieting the back-stabbing gossiper

Oh, if only high-school behavior ended in high school. But that little backstabbing gossiper somehow found her way into your company. What do you do? Just like in high school, the gossiper may feel that her opinions aren't being listened to, she may be insecure about her abilities, or she may just be looking for attention. Some things never change. But unlike high school, addressing this behavior by focusing on the intention is a much better option than writing something nasty on her locker.

The first step: *examine what is happening*. The challenge with gossipers is that they often don't have a specific action that you can observe (hence it's back-stabbing, not front-stabbing). They may sit quietly, smile, and just agree. Ten minutes after the meeting, they're telling anyone who will listen how horrible the meeting was, how dismal the project is, or how much they don't like their teammates (or you).

Here's how a team member may *examine what is happening* with the backstabbing gossiper:

> **Team member:** "I know we agreed in the meeting to all go back to our teams and ask for their input on the type of learning and development they want to see next year to help meet the company goals. I noticed that you told your employees that learning and development is unnecessary and an added cost to the company. Could I help clarify any of the agreements we made in the meeting?"

Next up: *deciding what to do next*. What happens next (the decision point) depends on how the information is received. If the recipient of the information replies with, "Oh, no, that isn't right. I would never say anything like that," your response could be, "Great. Do you want to schedule a meeting tomorrow to walk through the ideas the team may have?"

Of course, one day the backstabbing gossiper may say something like this:

> **Backstabbing gossiper:** "I don't agree. This whole project is nonsense."
>
> **Team member:** "Let's go back to last week's meeting. We agreed on the goal, the problem, and the time line. Did something happen to change that agreement?"

In both examples, the examining what is happening focuses on the facts and trying to find out why the backstabbing gossiper isn't voicing her concerns in front of other people. Of course, the gossiper may continue with the difficult behavior;

in that case, it is time to go back to examining what is happening by stating the problem and then asking for the intention:

> **Team member:** "We've been working through this project for six months, and I feel we've had some great success with our team discussions. I noticed that you voice your opinions to others after the meeting, and I feel this is going around the process we agreed on. What do you want to accomplish by having conversations that counter the agreements we had just made?"

Using the examine and decide steps should help the recipient of the information understand the impact of their behavior and provides a productive and positive way to help move forward.

Cooling down the angry hostile types

If you've ever been in a meeting with one of those angry hostile types, you know how difficult it can be to get any work done. These people are mad at the world, and they want you to know about it. Some angry hostile types start off as people with bad attitudes — they complain about everything, blame others, and never take responsibility for anything, ever. It's always someone else's fault. You may use some of the techniques described earlier in this chapter to have a conversation with an angry hostile type after the situation occurs, but here are a few ways to use critical conversation as the behavior is happening.

If you're in a meeting with an angry hostile type who has her arms crossed, taps her foot, and shoots down any possible positive comment before you can say "annoying," try this approach:

> **Examine what's happening.** Say, "I'm really confused by your behavior, John. I thought we agreed to talk about the possible solutions, not all the reasons the solutions won't work. Does the group want to talk about problems or solutions?"

In this example, the team member examines what's happening, states how she feels about the problem, and then proposes a way to go forward. The beauty of this approach in a meeting is that the group can help solve the problem — it's not up to just one person.

Another tried-and-true tactic for working with an angry hostile type is to state the behavior you see, validate it, and then either defer the problem to another meeting (perhaps a one-on-one critical conversation) or deal with it.

>> **Examine the situation by stating what you see.** Continue examining what is happening by saying what the person is doing as neutrally as possible.

If John is shooting down every idea in the book, you may say, "You don't think this solution will ever work, right?"

- » **Validate the comment.** After you state the problem, validate that whatever John is saying may be true. You may simply say, "You may be right. We're facing a really challenging issue."

- » **Decide what to do next by dealing with or deferring the comment.** Talk about the issue now or work it out later. If you choose to defer dealing with the behavior until later, you may say, "Would anybody disagree with brainstorming the possibilities that might work first? Then we can look at the risks and challenges." Use the group to help with this discussion. The other option is to deal with the problem right then and there. Be sure to stay genuine. You want to solve the problem instead of telling John that he's just the most negative person in the world and you wish he wasn't there. Say, "Thanks, John, for your comments. Does anyone else want to talk about the solutions?" If that doesn't work, you may want to take a break and confront the person with, "John, I feel that you're interrupting the discussion quite frequently. What would you like to achieve with this behavior?"

One of the big challenges when working with the angry hostile type is that often a number of other difficult behaviors are under that mean shell. These individuals may polarize teams or just argue with any new ideas for the fun of it. They may also be angry or moody by habit, even if they have nothing to argue about. They may also be critics, where nothing other than their own ideas is adequate.

WARNING

Although all these difficult behaviors may have an impact on performance, try not to overcommunicate during any conversation. Doing so can muddy the waters, detracting from the real behavior that needs to change. When preparing to have a critical conversation with the angry hostile type, or if you find yourself needing to deal with them at a moment's notice, be sure to have a core message. The core message addresses the single most important behavioral change you need this individual to address.

Stepping in When Bad Behavior Becomes a Pattern

Sometimes a behavior can work itself out. People have bad days and, rather than jump to conclusions, you may want to give them the benefit of the doubt. If an employee who otherwise is calm and collected becomes a monster during a meeting, it could be because of something completely unrelated. Exhibiting the behavior once or twice is just an incident — three times is a pattern. Having the empathy and trust to give a person the benefit of the doubt also helps to build relationships.

Although three times may not seem like enough to have a critical conversation, think of it this way: Because no one knows what the other person is trying to achieve with the difficult behavior, it can often just be ignored. Soon, the moderately annoying behavior becomes such a giant issue that no one wants to work with the individual anymore.

WARNING

In a genuine, otherwise healthy relationship, abrupt changes in behavior are a matter of concern. In this case, the conversation might be about the well-being of the person and have little to do with work.

Intervening when a pattern emerges doesn't need to be difficult. For example, you may have the following conversation:

> **Boss:** "Josh, I noticed you cut the discussion short when the team was brainstorming different solutions earlier today. It seems like the project setbacks are making this project frustrating."
>
> **Josh:** "No, the project isn't frustrating! It's been a long complex project with no breaks, team members keep being pulled off the project, the software has bugs, and I'm exhausted."

Now you have a reason for the behavior in the meeting, and you can start working on a solution. If you don't say something by using critical conversation principles, more people are likely to leave the team to avoid working with a monster for a project manager — barely recognizable as the composed employee he used to be. Letting some behaviors work themselves out is okay, but don't wait too long to explore what's happening.

Chapter **6**

Customer Conversations

"The customer is always right!" Or, so they say, but here is a different view: "The customer may not be exactly right, but the customer has a right to complain, go somewhere else for service, or accept the solution and continue being a loyal customer until the end of time." Yes, critical conversations can turn even the worst customer nightmare into a positive solution.

This chapter starts with uncovering what customers tend to want when they have a complaint. Then you get into applying critical conversation skills to start creating a solution everyone can agree to. You also find out how to let customers know they may be breaking the rules of professionalism — or that they're just plain being rude. Next, you get some advice on using critical conversation skills as a public relations tool. Keeping customers happy is always better than having to find new clients, so the chapter ends with ideas on how to open a discussion with customers when it's time to renegotiate the future of a business relationship.

Helping Customer Relationships

Unless your company is in a bubble with little or no contact with the outside world, at some point you need to talk with customers. Yes, really talk — and not just with some pretend agent wearing a headset on a customer service web page. It's nice to think that customers will just happily call you to say how great you are, but most likely these talks will be highly emotional because something has gone wrong. That's where critical conversations can help.

It would be generalizing to say that customer critical conversations can always help resolve complaints or concerns, but they can make a huge difference in maintaining a positive customer relationship. Here's an example to show you just how easy it is:

A customer storms into the store with a complaint about the new phone that he waited 26 weeks in line to get — he's probably still a little upset about not showering for half a year. Using critical conversation skills, the genius customer service agent says, "I can understand how you would be upset that the battery lasts only 12 minutes. There could be a few reasons why this problem may be happening." This statement examines what's happening by stating the problem and acknowledging feelings. "Would you be willing to let me take a look at it and we can try to solve the problem?" Asking whether the customer is willing to work together to decide how to solve the issue is a positive step.

And here's another example:

A client paid lots of money to a consulting firm to help the client solve all its problems. The problems still exist. Thank goodness the head of consulting read this book before the client called. He says, "Thanks for sharing your perspective with me. I've heard what you said about expectations and want to work with you to resolve the issue." This statement acknowledges how the customer feels and examines what just happened. "Are you willing to work together to make sure we're all in agreement with what happens next?" Deciding to agree on the next course of action is a step in the right direction.

These two examples are just the first few sentences of a bigger conversation, but it's clear that examining issues, acknowledging feelings, and getting that initial agreement to work together to solve the problem are much better than rolling your eyes behind the counter or just giving in and giving the customer everything. Giving the customer something to make him happy may seem easier, but taking the extra step to work with the customer to resolve a specific issue and to find out what the customer really wants and needs will set the stage for a long-term relationship with the customer.

WARNING

Giving in to anything the customer says may set a precedent that as long as the customer complains loudly enough, he gets anything and everything for free. This approach usually isn't a good business model.

Customer discussions that use the critical conversation format usually involve a type of customer service complaint, a customer who breaks the rules, a company giving bad news to a client, or a preemptive conversation on how the customer and company plan to work together in the future. Most of this chapter is devoted to these four main topics. But even if your conversation falls outside the lines of these topics, keep reading, because you can likely transfer these approaches to almost any customer interaction.

Providing Exceptional Customer Service

Businesses love customers. But loving your customers doesn't mean that the company has to bend over backward to fix any problem a customer may have and break the bank doing it. Customer service and customer satisfaction are two different things. Both need to be positive in order to avoid that horrible review on Google, Yelp, Twitter, or Facebook (or any one of the million other review sites out there).

>> *Customer service* is how the company reacts and what the company does when a customer has a problem.

>> *Customer satisfaction* is how the customer perceives the situation was resolved.

Critical conversations can help both customer service and customer satisfaction.

Suppose your flight was delayed for hours and eventually the flight was canceled. At this point in time, as a customer you are unsatisfied with the result (canceled flight) and probably think the service was pretty shabby, too (sitting through one delay after another, only then to have the flight canceled). Here is how a typical conversation may go in this situation:

Customer: "I can't believe I paid $500 for a ticket to see my friend's wedding and now I can't get there!"

Agent [typing about 20 letters a second]: "I can get you on a connecting flight tonight."

Customer: "I am so upset!"

Agent [still typing]: "Here is your new boarding pass."

With this situation, the customer is still upset with just being handed a new boarding pass, and who knows if they are satisfied or not since there was barely any interaction or acknowledgment from the customer service agent that there was even a problem. While even the best customer service agent can't control the planes or weather, a customer-focused critical conversation can turn a bad situation into a positive outcome. Here is how the previous example could create a better result using the critical conversation model:

Customer: "I can't believe I paid $500 for a ticket to see my friend's wedding and now I can't get there!"

Agent: "I understand how frustrated you must be. It is really hard to have no control over the delays in air travel, but a weather front over the region has made it unsafe to fly. Are you willing to give me a few minutes so I can try and find another option for you?"

Customer Conversations

Customer: "I guess I don't have any other option, do I?"

Agent (with empathy): "I would be happy to refund your ticket, but I bet you want to get to that wedding, right? Are you willing to give me a few minutes so I can try and find another option for you?"

Customer: "Sure, I guess that is fine."

Agent: "I have been able to find a connecting flight later tonight that gets you in at 8 a.m. tomorrow morning. Or, I can book you on the first direct flight out tomorrow morning. The flight in the morning can get you there by 10 a.m. tomorrow. Would either of these solutions work for you?"

Customer: "Well, the wedding isn't until 2 p.m., so the 10 a.m. flight is fine. Thank you."

This critical conversation delivered results by first acknowledging how the customer was feeling and then gaining commitment in regard to how to handle the situation. In the end, even the most irate customer would have to be satisfied with how the situation was resolved since the customer chose the outcome.

Critical conversations can help diffuse many of the situations that arise every day in every business around the globe. The following sections go through some examples, actions, and key phrases that can help you be a superhero when it comes to delivering exceptional customer service.

Using key elements to work through complaints

Using a critical conversation with a customer can help in any situation, regardless of the level of the complaint. If a customer simply needs a different size shoe shipped to him and that's what your company's promise says it will do, well, just ship it. Do what you promised and move on. If, however, the customer is ready to throw a shoe at you (whether the customer's complaint is valid or not), a critical conversation can help calm the situation. Critical conversations also work well if the issue is a little bigger than a pair of $100 shoes. Perhaps a consulting contract didn't meet expectations or you're having a business-to-business problem that can impact revenue targets of the customer.

In these situations, the best way to resolve a customer complaint is to solve it before it needs a referee to prevent it from getting out of control. Examining what is happening, acknowledging feelings, and then deciding together what the right solution may be gives you control of the situation quickly and efficiently so you can get moving to solve the problem and rebuild the relationship. Here's what to do:

>> **Examine what is happening.** Taking this step during a customer complaint may seem obvious, but when a customer complains, you need to examine what is happening. What you observe helps to make sure all parties understand the problem. Examining what's happening may be as simple as stating, "I can see that your computer is broken. Can you tell me a little more about when this problem started?" Or, "I understand that our billing process is incredibly stressful on your account payables department. Can you tell me about some of the information that seems incorrect from your perspective?" When you have multiple problems or when the problem isn't exactly clear, it may be helpful to ask, "Do you agree that this is the problem, or am I missing something?"

When you examine what's happening with a customer service complaint, always try to state what's happening or what you hear. Often, customer complaints, especially those in the service industry, result from the customer wanting to know that you're listening to his problem.

>> **Acknowledge what the customer is feeling.** A simple "I understand that you're upset about [having to wait on the phone/not getting the right shipment/missing a deadline]."

>> **Decide what to do next.** If a customer has a valid complaint and you have a no-questions-asked return policy or fix-it policy, the decision is pretty clear — follow the policy. But when the answer isn't black and white, a critical conversation looks at the problem from both the company's view and the customer's view. Usually the individual trying to resolve a customer's problem will make a recommendation.

Critical conversations take deciding what to do next to the next level — working together to come up with a solution. Here's how it works. The employee asks, "Are you willing to work with me to find a solution?" If the customer says yes, continue with, "I have an idea on how we can fix the problem. I can ask one of our service team members to fix the broken dishwasher today or tomorrow. Would that solution work for you?" And if the customer says no, he doesn't want to come up with a solution together (and yes, that does happen when customers are quite upset), then reply with, "How would you recommend we solve the problem?" Either way, the question and answer keep you in control of the situation and provide the opportunity for the customer to make the situation positive.

>> **Gain commitment and get moving.** If you say you're going to do something, do it. Did you agree to get a new team of engineers on a plane to fix the power system? Get them on the flight. Agree to fix an order that went terribly wrong? Fix it.

>> **Evaluate the results.** Almost every company — from a mom-and-pop flower shop to the Fortune 100, from government agencies to nonprofits — has online

customer service tools available to them, and following up with a customer complaint is easier than ever before. Ask for feedback, and if the problem isn't resolved, keep working at it until the customer and you agree that the solution has fixed the complaint. If you see a trend, make a plan of action to examine and decide how to fix the trend.

Noting the differences and similarities between internal and external issues

There are two big differences between dealing with issues of external customers compared to issues of internal employees. Take a look:

» **Most companies don't fire their customers for poor behavior.** Of course some companies don't do business with one another after a disagreement, and that guy who wears cut-up T-shirts and punches the bartender is no longer accepted in the local pub. For the most part, however, most companies want to keep customers coming back.

» **Business isn't Vegas.** What happens between a company and a customer doesn't stay between the company and customer. Whether you're an individual selling an old Star Wars set on eBay, or a giant corporation selling multimillion-dollar power generators, opinions on service and quality, and how complaints are managed, are somewhere out there on the Internet. Just search customer service complaints for any company you're thinking of using, and you'll find opinions, often lots of them. Of course, not all the opinions are fair, true, or even legible, but they're out there and can make or break a buying decision.

Although these two differences are important — some may even say critical — there are two similarities between customers and employees within a company that make using critical conversations a logical, and perhaps even easy, approach to problems. Here are the similarities:

» **Customers and employees both have personal opinions, perspectives, and ideas on how a problem should be solved.** If everyone is happy and in agreement, well, a critical conversation is probably overkill. When one person — a customer or an employee — is upset or has a disagreement on how to go forward, a critical conversation can help.

» **Just like it does with its employees, a company often has a long-term relationship with its customers.** (The business kind of "relationship" is discussed here, not an OMG high-school romance.) A critical conversation can preserve a relationship and even grow one in the face of conflict.

Knowing what upset customers want

When a customer is upset, he may tell you that he wants to talk to your manager, and your manager's manager. He may tell you that he wants to bring the company down or call his best friend who just happens to also be the CEO of the company (a bit of an exaggeration). But in the end, if a customer is upset, he wants to be heard, to be treated with respect, and to know that his problem is going to be resolved. Your job is to use a critical conversation to talk an upset customer down from calling the Supreme Allied Commander to fly the right shipment out the door within seconds to agreeing that a delivery person in a brown or blue suit can deliver a replacement in a more reasonable amount of time.

Although it may seem like Customer Service 101, finding out what the real problem is and then resolving it is the name of the game in customer service and customer satisfaction. A big problem companies make is to just hand over solutions or products for free anytime a customer gets mad. But customer satisfaction comes from a good relationship with the customer, and that's often best built with a critical conversation, not a 10-percent-off coupon on your next order.

If you can't find a mutually agreeable solution as you decide what to do next, use one of the most straightforward and often overlooked plans of action: go to the source (the customer, that is) and ask how he would solve the problem. Ask the customer what he thinks a fair solution is — it's one of those win-win solutions. A customer tells you a reasonable solution *and* you have the option of responding, "Yes, we can do that," or, "That's different from how we usually resolve these types of issues. Let's work together to see what's possible."

WARNING

Some people fall into the trap of asking, "What do you want to resolve this issue?" The problem with this question is that giving the customer anything other than what he says will result in poor customer satisfaction, even if customer service is exceptional.

Handling a Customer Who Crosses the Line

When leaders talk about customer service, there's an assumption that a customer is complaining about the service or performance. But what happens when a customer breaks the rules? If a customer lies, stretches the truth, or acts unethically, a company doesn't need to just accept that behavior.

Managing "I want to talk to the manager"

One of the most frequent unethical behaviors is when a customer treats an employee with disrespect by yelling, calling him names, or making threats to call

Customer Conversations

headquarters, the boss, or the President of the United States to complain. Some customer service courses tell you to smile and say okay or to ignore it. But here is another alternative: Create a conversation that not only finds a solution, but also creates a foundation for the customer–company relationship to continue in the future.

The following example shows you how a few simple sentences can take a customer interaction from producing a solution or finding a solution to creating a better relationship in the future.

> An irate customer is on the other line of the phone, threatening to call everyone he knows to 1) get the employee fired, and 2) put the company out of business. The customer service representative could say, "Yes, you can talk to my supervisor. I'm putting her on the phone now." Nothing is wrong with this statement, but you can guess that the customer now knows that if he starts complaining, he doesn't have to go through the process that everyone else has to go through; he can get to whoever is in charge if he yells loudly enough. Think of how this slightly modified reaction may work better:

> "I can understand how you'd be upset. If you want to talk to my manager, I can provide you with her email address or phone number. I suggest working through the returns process because that works for many of our customers. Would you like to continue our conversation about how I can help you, or would you like to talk to someone else?"

This critical conversation examines what's happening and acknowledges feelings by restating the customer's desire to talk to the boss and understanding how the customer could be upset. Then, the customer service agent (well versed in critical conversations, of course) gives options about how the customer could decide to move forward. Instead of just handing over the call to the boss (of course, the customer could still very well want to talk to the boss, and that's a perfectly acceptable option), asking the question helps the customer slow down and evaluate what the right decision may be and helps the customer save face if he realizes that he may have been a little over the top with his complaints and yelling.

Facing a hostile customer

Yelling customers making threats face customer service agents in almost every company on any given day. Sometimes customers break rules or cross the line from being upset and irate to being hostile to an employee or group of employees.

The following critical conversation sounds and feels like a critical conversation you'd have when an employee's behavior is disrupting work. In this case, a customer manager or leader in the company presents the facts, examines what's happening, and works with the customer to decide on what to do next.

Suppose an employee who works for one of your clients repeatedly ignores your emails and phone calls and frequently reschedules meetings at the last minute. When they do return calls or meet with you, it is often at the last minute and very rushed. This results in you having to stay until midnight to get work done on time, or not having sufficient time to incorporate their feedback when you have to deliver documents to their boss. The options are to ignore the behavior since the customer is, well, the customer, or to confront the problem in as positive a way as possible. As hard as it is, confronting a customer who breaks the rules is the right solution in the end, whether the customer is misrepresenting facts, not doing their job, or howling like a wolf under a full moon. How do you do it? The same way you do with any other critical conversation. Here's how:

Employee: "Mr. Customer, thanks for agreeing to meet with me. We appreciate your business and want to make sure we can give you the best customer service possible. Over the past year, I feel my ability to serve you has gone down because I don't have all the critical information I need to serve you in a timely manner. Before our meeting with the VP, you said you reviewed the presentation and had no comments, but then in the meeting, you said that you had never seen the presentation before. This also happened in our meeting with the directors last week, and with your team the week before. I know you're busy, and I'm hoping we can find a way to be more productive."

Customer: "Oh, no, that was just a mistake."

Employee: "I understand. Are you willing to work together to find a solution that helps us both be more productive?"

Customer: "Well, of course."

With this decision to work together in place, if the same behavior happens again, the employee can go back to this agreement to work together. The key to this discussion, as with all critical conversations, is to come to the discussion with a genuine desire to make things better. Luckily, most people are, well, human, and when kindly and honestly presented with facts, they eventually decide to at least look at ways to change the behavior causing the issue.

REMEMBER

You'll always have customers and employees who have no desire to change, let alone listen. But stay with it. Critical conversations in highly charged situations are rarely once-and-done discussions.

Delivering Bad News to Clients

If you've been around business for more than a few years or have read the news in the last 24 hours, you know that at some point in time businesses have less than fabulous news to give customers. This book isn't a public relations book, but public relations and critical conversations have much in common when it comes to talking to customers.

Public relations in companies, when done right and ethically, create an open and honest environment, and then present what's happening next, just like a critical conversation. The following recommendations are great tools to add to any public relations strategy.

Creating an open and honest environment

It's far better to say, "We're finding out what's happening and will tell you as soon as we do know," than to try to make up something that you may later need to alter.

As a customer, which statement would make you want to continue working with another company or individual?

>> **Initial statement:** "I didn't do it! We aren't wrong!" Two days later: "He was wrong." Four days later: "Well, maybe we were wrong." A week later: "Okay, I was wrong."

>> **Initial statement:** "Something went wrong. We don't know what it is, but we're working to find out what happened. We will do everything we can to fix the problem after we figure out what happened. I'll keep you informed every day to let you know what's happening." One day later: "This is what happened, and this is what we're going to do to fix it."

You're probably much more inclined to continue the relationship with the company in the second scenario. Trust and a genuine desire to make things better are not only at the center of a critical conversation, but also at the center of customer relationships.

Identifying solutions together

After examining the facts and sharing them, one of the immediate next steps is to identify alternatives or solutions to the problem. This is true with a critical conversation with an employee or a discussion with a customer after a PR disaster. And luckily, the same terminology can help you create an environment of trust and find a solution that helps to not only resolve the problem but also build the relationship.

Here's what a critical conversation may sound like when working through a PR issue with a client.

Examine the facts: "Our manufacturing line for trains and dolls broke down the last week in November, and our shipment to all the good little girls and boys is delayed."

Acknowledge feelings: "I can understand how you may be upset because of the timing of the breakdown. Are you willing to work with me to help find a solution as quickly as possible?"

Decide on next steps: "Our shipments will be ready the second to last week in December, and we can expedite the shipping with the help of little delivery trucks around the world, or I can help you partner with another supplier. Would any of these solutions work for you, or do you have another idea on how to fix the problem that we can agree to?"

The customer's response: "I think we can work with one of those solutions. Thanks for your honesty and quick work."

Not having the trucks, trains, and dolls for the children on the other side of the mountain in late December could potentially shut down this company. By being honest with the facts and working together to resolve the problem in everyone's interest, the solution can be resolved.

Keeping Your Customers

Everyone makes mistakes, but it's how you recover from those mistakes that can make or break a business. Keeping clients in the face of failure, whether it's a PR issue or simply a customer service problem, depends on what happens after the initial conversation occurs. Sound familiar? It should. The critical conversation model is only as good as what happens after the discussion ends; that's why getting moving and evaluating the results are a big part of the conversation process.

Checking it twice

The way to use critical conversations to keep customers is to get moving on what you promise, and check back with them to make sure the problem is solved. Almost anyone can pick up this book and repeat a few phrases to customers when the company is faced with a tough PR or relationship issue. But it takes patience, consistency, and action to see real results from any conversation. After the conversation happens with a customer, what happens next is what matters most.

Can you imagine how a customer could react if a company said all the right things and did nothing? "Mr. Customer, I understand you're upset about getting a purple tutu when you ordered a green one. We'll get a new one in the mail right away." But what if that never happened? The company would probably soon be out of business. If you say you'll let your customers know what's happening with a potential PR issue in the next day, make every effort to really do it, and if you don't, let the customers know exactly why you aren't delivering on what you promised.

Renegotiating the future

Critical conversations with customers aren't just for solving customer complaints. Many business-to-business companies find themselves renegotiating contracts as they expire, adding additional work to a current contract, or even having to alter what the current agreement is as products and services change. Whatever the reason, you probably know that a critical conversation can help.

Although it may be hard to come to a client with disappointing news, or when a problem has hampered the relationship, it's possible to grow a relationship in the face of these conflicts if you listen to your client's perspective and genuinely want to resolve the issue.

Here's an example of being willing to find a solution, even in the face of a potential relationship breaker:

> "I know you've been a loyal customer of our steam model train engines for 20 years. Next year we're changing our product line to more modern model trains. I'd love to talk with you about how we can still serve you and your clients. Would you like to recommend some initial ideas, or would you like me to talk about options we have thought through?"

What goes well in this conversation? First, the initiator of the conversation demonstrates a willingness to solve the problem but doesn't push a solution on the receiver of the information. The initiator examines what's happening and then asks for the client's perspective. So often sales teams come in and present the "right solution" and then ask for the client's opinions. The critical conversation model turns the discussion around, letting the client speak his mind first. After asking for your client's perspective, it's appropriate to state your own and decide what each of you can and can't support.

REMEMBER

Of course, in order for any conversation to work, the initiator has to be willing to listen and understand the client's point of view. Don't assume the client is wrong, but also don't assume that you know what's best for your customer. Ask for the customer's point of view and listen to what he has to say. This type of discussion opens up the opportunity for all ideas to be put on the table, and then both the initiator and the receiver can decide on the most favorable options for all parties.

3

Peace Talks: Having Influence When You're the One Involved in Conflict

Contents at a Glance

Chapter **1**

Identifying What Both Sides Want

You find yourself in a conflict that takes up way too much of your energy. People are starting to talk, the conflict is affecting work, and when you think about your long-term career goals, you know that maintaining the bad feelings and tension isn't a good idea, regardless of the other person's position in the company.

Whether you're a manager, a team member, or the head of an entire department, as a party to a current conflict, you may not know what to do. Perhaps you've tried a few tactics that you thought would fix the problem, like going over the other person's head, addressing the issue directly, or ignoring the conflict altogether. Yet the problem remains unresolved. You're now at a point where you want this whole thing behind you, and you need a plan.

But, if your plan involves living out a daydream in which you publically crush your opponent while Queen's rock anthem "We Are the Champions" blasts in the background, this chapter isn't for you. If, instead, you want to develop a strategy that uses a highly successful approach, read on. The information in this chapter helps you gain a better understanding of the real issues in a conflict and build a winning strategy to address the situation at hand, as well as conflicts in the future.

Asking Yourself What You Really Want

When thinking about addressing a conflict, ask yourself, "What's motivating me to have this conversation?" If resolution is your goal, then ask, "Am I emotionally and mentally ready to meet and talk with the other person?" If you're so angry that you can't stand to look at him, be real with yourself and don't schedule a discussion in the next five minutes.

Before you create a list of issues you want the other person to address, take a hard look at yourself and your motivation for staying in the conflict. When you figure out what you value and what you want to achieve from a meeting, you can shift your thinking to reflect on how you truly feel about the problem, and you may be surprised to find that the other person's past behavior affects you less. When you focus on what can be rather than what has been, you can think more creatively about solutions that meet your values.

In addition to helping you discover your values, the following sections help you identify your hot buttons, effectively listen to others, be humble, ask others for help, and recognize your strengths. Doing a little pre-meeting work in these areas helps you have a productive conversation when you do finally meet with the other person.

Figuring out your core values

Be aware: What you *think* you want and what you *really* want likely aren't the same — and to figure out the difference, you need to get in touch with your values. So, what are these values? Sometimes they're called interests or motivators, but basically, your *core values* drive you and influence the way you think and respond to different situations.

People often describe what they want as an action or an outcome instead of the larger value that inspires that desire. For example, if someone asks you what you want out of your retirement, you may respond that you want a million dollars in the bank. If you consider what that money allows you to do in retirement, you're getting closer to understanding values. You want to travel (freedom), you want a cottage on the beach (peace and quiet), and you want to care for your family (security). This example demonstrates how looking at desired outcomes helps you discover the underlying values you find most important.

Applying this process to a conflict allows you to state clearly what you want from the other person and work toward doing the same for him. Don't assume he knows what you're looking for — he can't know which values you find most important if you've only just found out yourself. A good way to start recognizing your values is to consider all the issues in a conflict and then ask yourself what's *most* important to you. Keep in mind that connecting the dots from a behavior to an emotion to a core value can sometimes be difficult and time-consuming.

WHAT DIRTY DISHES CAN TELL YOU ABOUT CORE VALUES

Values and interests can pop up in even the simplest situations. Consider the following example: Seven employees share a common kitchen area that often has cluttered counters and a sink full of dirty dishes. Employees frequently discuss the messy site at staff meetings. A few of the team members say they don't give it a second thought and wonder why it keeps getting brought up. One employee says it's embarrassing to bring clients past the area, another suggests a chore schedule, and yet another is irritated that grown adults have to be told to clean up after themselves.

The issue is the same for everyone — a dirty kitchen — but the values are different for everyone involved. Those who aren't bothered by it may feel that peaceful coexistence is more important than angry discussions about the dishes. Respect may be important to the individual who says he's embarrassed, cooperation may be an interest of the person requesting the chore schedule, and accountability is likely essential to the person who displays irritation. A manager in this situation may have the team brainstorm a solution that takes into consideration the stated values as a means to ending the conflict and getting on with other business.

TIP

Here's a useful exercise: Reflect on your current conflict, jot down a few words or phrases that explain what's happening, and see whether you can match them to one or two core values. This may take some practice before you find it effective, but it's worth the prep time.

For instance, if you say you're irritated by your boss's micromanagement, you may discover that one of your core values is autonomy, or maybe respect. Managerially, if you say you want error-free reports turned in on time, the value you're addressing is likely competence or responsibility. If your team works like a well-oiled machine except for one person who says his opinions don't matter, consider that he's looking for acceptance or recognition.

Identifying your hot buttons

During the meeting preparation phase, identify your *hot buttons*, or points that you're most sensitive about, and make a plan to address them when they come up (because they very well may come up). Identify the kind of statements (or actions) that can make you ready to scream or blow your top. Be aware of these sensitive areas, because other people often know what they are and how to take advantage of them. (Refer to the later section about hot buttons.)

Your hot buttons are closely tied to your values because anything that can make you that angry is probably something you care deeply about. If you get upset when a co-worker rolls his eyes or talks over you, respect is very important to you, and his behavior is counter to your definition of respect.

Knowing that you're likely to go off if a co-worker touches on one of your hot buttons allows you to prepare a response that doesn't include turning red and slamming your fist down on the table. Instead, you may answer, "You know, it may not really be control I'm after, but I can see where you might think that. I've discovered that respect is really important to me, and I can understand where trying to earn respect might come across as controlling." This kind of answer is sure to deflate *that* balloon!

WARNING

Preparing a response to hot buttons isn't the same thing as preparing a really good comeback to deflect responsibility, paint the other person in a negative light, or disempower him. A mechanical (or poor) response is one in which you seek to shut down or one-up the other person. You need not agree with his assessment; you only need to demonstrate that you've understood his perspective. Preparation is good and helps anticipate difficulties, but it's no substitute for being open to feedback. Mechanically reciting canned responses to anticipated attacks doesn't demonstrate good listening skills and may limit you when trying to create dialogue.

Considering your ability to listen

Determine how open you are to listening — really listening — to the other person's perspective. If you tend to think of his time to talk as a distraction or an interruption of the significant things you have to say, check that attitude at the door. If you haven't taken the time to show him that you're listening, then he likely won't bother listening to you. Before going into any conversation, be prepared to hear things you disagree with.

You may assume that because you're hearing the words another person is saying that you're actually listening to him, but what would happen if you were asked to summarize what he just said? Be sure you actively listen to his words, take them in, and then respond. (For tips on active listening, see Chapter 2 in Book 1.)

REMEMBER

Silence can be a powerful tool, and showing that you're taking time to consider what's been said can go a long way in demonstrating your willingness to resolve your issues. Prove to the other person that you're trying something new in an effort to change how the two of you may have approached problems in the past.

TIP

Think about how others show they're listening to you, and emulate that behavior when preparing to listen to others. This reflection helps you demonstrate that same level of attentiveness toward others. Start by trying the following:

>> Make eye contact.

>> Maintain open body language (see Chapters 3 and 6 in Book 1).

>> Nod once in a while (even if you disagree!).

>> Allow pauses between the other person's time to speak and your time to speak.

WARNING

If you jump in to respond to or correct the other person right off the bat, even with the intention of clarifying misinformation, you may be doing more harm than good. You want an open and honest dialogue, not a heated argument.

Taking notes may force you to listen, but don't bury your nose in the notes as a way to avoid eye contact. Bring a list of the key items you want to discuss, and set the list aside for when you need it. Let the other person know you'll be taking or reading from brief notes as a way to help you participate better in the conversation — not so you'll have evidence that can be used against the other person in the future. Add a comment about your willingness to shred the notes when the conversation is over.

Doing your best to be humble

Be ready to be humble. If you've had the same conversation over and over, maybe you're not taking ownership or responsibility for your share of the conflict. Even if the devil himself is working in the cubicle next to you and bullies you every minute of every day, you can probably think of at least one behavior you've exhibited that may have made the situation worse or kept it going. Being humble means owning up to your part of the conflict, even if your part was simply to ignore it for too long. And if you can't get yourself to say you've done anything wrong, just think of it as a strategic move that gets you what you want in the long run: A solution to the conflict that has eaten up way too much of your time.

WARNING

Being humble doesn't mean becoming a sponge for blame, however. If you feel you have some responsibility, by all means take it. But keep in mind the difference between being humble and taking a fall. Overstating your role in a conflict doesn't allow for an authentic conversation.

Consider this example: Diane was about to be called into the manager's office for a reprimand. In past conversations the manager would tell her everything she'd done wrong and Diane would spend too much time defending herself, leaving both parties frustrated. This time, Diane decided to try something different. She walked in, admitted the error, talked about her plan to avoid it in the future, and said, "Okay, now, let me have it!" Well, this response wasn't much fun for the boss, who was ready for a fight, not a mea culpa. Prepare to accept responsibility for your role right upfront instead of planning a defense.

Asking for help

If self-assessment isn't easy for you, ask for help. Invite a trustworthy person to be brutally honest with you — to give you unbiased information *and* keep your conversation confidential. If you and a colleague have been complaining about a conflict for some time, that confidante may not be a neutral person to approach for feedback, so choose someone else.

WARNING

Asking for help and gossiping aren't the same things. If you want someone to brainstorm an approach or help you identify interests and emotions, you're on the right track. If you're looking to trash the other person and just want a witness, reconsider. Gossip and trash talk are poison in a workplace.

When looking for advice, people often seek out others whom they know will give them the answers they want and support the positions they've taken. If you just want to vent and blow off steam, this approach is fine, but it doesn't do much to help you conduct an honest self-evaluation. Try to think of this person as someone who can help you prepare for the productive conversation you plan to have.

TIP

After you identify your sounding board, ask him the following questions:

>> What do you think I'm doing to keep this conflict going?

>> What am I not seeing on the other side?

>> How might others describe my values?

>> What do you think the other person might gain if I *do* take the time to listen and consider his ideas? What might I gain?

Be open to hearing what he has to say and then act on it. If he tells you that you don't respond well to other people's ideas, consider what impact that may have on others, and then figure out how that behavior lines up with a core value. If he describes you in a way that doesn't resonate, ask more questions. You may have to spend some time processing his observations to see the situation the way he does, but if you're asking him because you trust him, heed his advice.

Recognizing your strengths

Every core value has two sides. In one light, a value has the potential to get in the way of a cohesive team, and in another it can reveal itself as a great asset. If you value control, you may hear others complain about micromanagement, but that same value may be the very thing that gets you promoted! If you value independence, you may bristle at the idea of being paired with a co-worker on a project, but you may also be more likely to be viewed as a self-starter. And if one of your core values is accomplishment, your co-workers may have assigned you the unflattering title of "taskmaster," but your boss sees it as doing what it takes to get the job done right and on time.

Consider the upside and potential pitfalls of your values and recognize the positive aspects of each. Valuing respect allows you to treat others with dignity; regarding competence moves you to create reports your company can trust; and appreciating autonomy makes you a manager who knows how to encourage the people on your team to advance their careers.

REMEMBER

It's okay to honestly acknowledge your strengths and be proud of them. Just be sure to acknowledge and appreciate the strengths of the other person in the conflict as well (hard as that may be!). Recognizing and validating values gives you a great wealth of insight to pull from when assessing how to address a conflict. As you begin to pay more attention to values, you're able to view behavior, language, and activities that were confusing or frustrating for you through a whole new lens.

Thinking about What the Other Person Wants

The other person in the conflict also has core values that aren't being met, respected, or honored. He's probably ready for the problem to be resolved and is eager for someone to consider his perspective. The main difference between you and him is that you've had the luxury of thinking through a plan that meets *both* of your needs. Keep in mind that he may still be stuck on what he wants and unwilling to bend on certain issues, so you may need to include a strategy to help move him along in your plan for resolving the conflict.

REMEMBER

Before you ask to meet with the other person, take a minute and recognize that he isn't *against you*, he's merely *for himself*. As you prepare for a new conversation and begin to consider his point of view, you'll see him less as an enemy and more as a potential ally in solving the difficulty.

Identifying what you know

Consider what you know about your co-worker. Be honest, but be kind. What does his job demand of him? What stress could he be under? Think about what you've noticed when he's most upset. Be clear about what you really know, and separate out secondhand information you may have added to strengthen your initial point of view. Can you tie his words or actions to values? Take the time to jot down a few words that describe his needs from his perspective.

While you're talking to a trusted source about *your* strengths and areas for development (see the earlier section "Asking for help" for more information), be sure to ask him what he knows about the co-worker and why he may respond to you the way he does. This isn't the time to stir the pot, so be careful whom you chat with and when and where you chat. You want to get information that helps you present resolution ideas in an appealing way to your co-worker, not to dig up dirt on the fellow.

Run through a couple of ways to approach the situation. As you prepare, brainstorm some questions that may help you understand what your co-worker's values are. Some possibilities are as follows:

>> "What do you want to see happen here today?"

>> "What about 'x' is important to you?"

>> "I can tell it bothers you when I 'y'; help me understand your reaction."

REMEMBER

The most important thing is to be sincere and open with your questions when you meet with him. If your co-worker can tell you what he wants most, the two of you can look for solutions that fit.

Putting the drama aside

When trying to discover the other person's values and what he wants, you may fall into the trap of answering questions with dramatic responses like, "He wants to control everything and take my job, that's what he wants!" Instead, put the histrionics aside and follow these guidelines:

>> **Spend time putting yourself in his shoes.** If someone continues a conflict even after you've tried to address it, chances are his behavior is a symptom of his interests not being met. Thinking objectively about the other person's needs can be difficult, but if doing so can provide you with tools to manage future conflicts, then it's worth it.

>> **Stop thinking in terms of "always" and "never."** These definitive words tend to create more drama than they resolve. They cement you in place rather than help you look at the situation from a new perspective, so put them aside and use language that more clearly states the situation.

Check out this example: Rob and Karen have a pre-staff-meeting conversation where Rob talks about a project he's considering implementing. During the meeting, Karen mentions the idea, and it's well received by the boss. Rob feels as if Karen has hijacked his idea and his accolades. Rob thinks, "You know what? She *always* does that!" Rob calms down and decides to clarify the parts of the situation that bother him. Does he feel that he's not receiving credit for his ideas? Or does it bother him that Karen feels the need to speak for him? Or does he feel that Karen doesn't respect conversations held in confidence? When he figures out that he's most upset by Karen speaking for him, he talks with her and shares that he prefers to brainstorm ideas and present them together. Karen is receptive to his request, and Rob is thankful he didn't act on his first impulse, which was to storm into her office and let her know that she's *never* to do that again!

Considering what you don't know

It's impossible to know everything about everyone, so you have to do some guesswork about what the other person in the conflict values. You may be able to assume from someone's behavior and language that he values respect or autonomy, but many of his values remain a mystery to you. Not knowing everything that he values may work to your benefit, though. It may inspire your curiosity and reduce preconceived notions. Look to channel your curiosity about his values into creating a dialogue about understanding.

TIP

Start a list of what you think may be important to the other person, and have it with you when you meet. Let him know you've given his values some thought, and ask to hear from him to see whether your list is correct. (See Chapter 2 for more information on setting up a meeting.) Demonstrating curiosity shows a willingness to listen, creates the possibility for commonality, and can open doors that may surprise you.

REMEMBER

The other person may have personal, professional, or other difficulties going on in his life. Problems like these may have a significant impact on him and the conflict. Keep in mind that personal problems and pressures may be holding him back from being at his best, and give him the benefit of the doubt.

Taking a Look at Both Sides

Now it's time to get to work, take a broader perspective, and consider both sides of your conflict. Gather your lists, do a little considering, and put pencil to paper by filling out the worksheet in Figure 1-1. There's no right or wrong way to fill in the boxes. You can work your way down while only considering yourself before turning your attention to the other person, or you can answer each section for both of you as you consider each topic. The following sections help you get started by walking you through each topic.

	You	Them
Issues What are the surface issues?		
Values What are you really trying to satisfy?		
Hot Buttons What words, phrases, or references might cause an emotional response?		
Strengths What does each of you bring to the team?		
Common Ground Where do we agree?		
Proposals What solutions would work for both of us?		

FIGURE 1-1:
Use this worksheet to help you identify what you and your co-worker want.

© John Wiley & Sons, Inc.

Issues

Start by filling out the issues section of the worksheet for yourself. In the appropriate box, write down as many issues as you can think of that apply to the conflict from your perspective. Don't think too deeply at this point; just write what comes to mind. Keep asking yourself, "What about this is important to me?" The payoff is a discussion about the primary issues rather than the tangential ones. Having an authentic conversation keeps you from agreeing to solutions that sound good on the surface but don't actually line up with your values.

As an example, suppose you're having a conflict with a store employee about being late to meetings. Perhaps you make entries like these:

1. Shows up late.

2. Doesn't apologize.

3. Disrupts work flow.

4. Doesn't know what's going on.

5. Ignores requests to be on time.

Note every aspect of the conflict you can recall, and put your perspective in the column you've designated for yourself.

Complete the worksheet by filling in what you think the other person would write if he were completing the worksheet. Would he say that you spend too much time watching the clock, or that you micromanage group meetings?

Values

After you've had a chance to identify the issues, think about *why* those issues have impacted you. Take a look at what you've jotted down and spend some time evaluating the deeper reasons that these things have had an impact on you. Underneath the surface issues, what are you both trying to satisfy? Are you looking for respect, cooperation, autonomy, or teamwork? Really consider what may be most important to the other person, realizing that his values may differ from your own. After you've done some speculating and evaluating, jot down that information on both sides of the worksheet.

WARNING

Resist placing your own values on the other person. If you carry around the expectation that others should behave according to your value system, you'll be frustrated and disappointed. When you recognize that you may not share the same values as a colleague, you can go into future conversations without being let down by his behavior, making it easier to ask for what you need.

For example, if Cathy wants the corner office because she currently resides next to the copy machine, water cooler, and candy bowl where everyone meets to chat, one of her core values could be peace and quiet. Dave, who was promoted last year but stayed in the same cubicle, may want the corner office because he values recognition. If Cathy and Dave switch the conversation from who gets the office to how to create peace *and* get recognition, they'll end up with solutions they wouldn't have considered before.

Hot buttons

Move on to the hot buttons area and fill in the aspects of the conflict that bother you most. Here you should enter phrases like, "Thinks an apology isn't warranted," or, "Ignores me when I try to bring it up." Identify topics or conversations you've had in the past that have raised the tension in the room. Which specific words or phrases pushed you past a calm demeanor?

TIP

As you're creating your list and responses, include potential hot buttons you may inadvertently push with the other person. If you've been tiptoeing around subjects or certain phrases to avoid an emotional response on his part, those subjects or issues are his hot buttons. Complete both sides of the worksheet.

Strengths

Consider the strengths each of you brings to the workplace. The individual who has a difficult time focusing during staff meetings may be the most creative person on the team. The guy who points out the errors in his co-workers' daily receipts may be the person who catches disasters before they happen. Think about what each of you brings to the work group that's unique, valuable, and important. Be generous but realistic. Use the earlier section "Recognizing your strengths" to help fill out this portion of the worksheet for yourself.

Common ground

As you prepare to complete the common ground section of Figure 1-1, keep in mind that both of you would like improved working conditions and for the problem to go away. At least you agree on something! Beyond those things, you may both be interested in improving a process, fostering teamwork, or bringing success to the job site; you may just be working on these issues differently.

REMEMBER

Be open to the possibility that you may share goals with the other person, and make note of these goals on the worksheet. The goals are great starting points for ideas and for your conversation in general.

Proposals

When you have the bigger picture in mind, generate some proposals. Now that you have a better understanding of where the two of you stand, think about what you want to ask for and what you can offer the other person. Get creative!

REMEMBER

This is a time to be specific about what you'd like to see and what you want to stop. If the other person talks too much in meetings, rather than asking him not to talk, consider proposing he take notes, prioritize his top three issues prior to the meetings, or send suggested agenda items in advance. At this point in your preparation, think beyond fair trade negotiations and get creative about how you may solve the problem. Note that these are just proposals, and you can't know if they'll work until you have an open conversation with the other person. Give the ideas some thought, but don't get too emotionally attached to them until you know the other person is onboard.

Ask yourself:

>> What has already been tried?

>> What has worked in the past?

>> How can we be more creative?

>> What can we do differently?

>> What solutions or ideas work for both of us?

>> Who else might help us develop a solution?

>> What is within our power to change?

>> Are my proposals realistic and possible? Have I considered all the details?

>> Do I need all the answers right now?

>> What am I willing to give to resolve the conflict?

>> What are my intentions for proposing these ideas?

>> What would an ideal working relationship look like?

Chapter **2**

Asking for a Meeting to Talk about the Conflict

The steps laid out for you in Book 3, Chapter 1 lead you to a decision about meeting with the person you're in conflict with. (If you haven't read Book 3, Chapter 1, you may want to do that now.) You've considered what's most important to you, thought about what may be most important to her, and maybe even asked for a little help to make sure you're looking at the situation with an objective eye. Now it's time to ask for the meeting.

This chapter helps you to do just what the title says: ask for a meeting to talk about the conflict you're having with a co-worker. You get help with finding the best approach, preparing your responses to resistance and potential rough patches, and deciding on the time and place for the meeting.

Considering the Best Way to Approach the Other Person

Everyone has a different level of comfort with conflict. Some people don't worry about it, and some people obsess over the smallest upset. Keep this in mind as you prepare to approach the person with whom you're having a conflict. Be aware of her stress level, as well as your own. (Book 3, Chapter 1 can help you determine the underlying issue for both of you.)

If previous attempts at resolution haven't gone well, realize that the other person may see you and want to run the other way. Just because you've decided you'd like to give it another try doesn't mean she'll immediately embrace the idea. Be mindful in the way you introduce the request for a meeting so it will be easier for her to say yes to you. And keep this in mind: Conflict can be a good thing! Do a little self-talk to ready yourself for a good approach, and use this opportunity to enact meaningful change.

Recognizing that timing and location are everything

Before you attempt to resolve your conflict, consider when and where to approach the other person. Start by deciding what day of the week or time of day will get you the most receptive response. Before your co-worker has had her morning coffee or right at the busiest point in her workday aren't good options. Look for a moment of relative quiet, when the two of you have the ability to focus on your conversation. For example, early afternoon after lunch gives her some time to have settled into her routine while leaving enough time in the day to give you a few minutes to talk.

Additionally, pay attention to where you both are in the emotional cycle. If either of you is likely to raise your voice, completely shut down, or walk away, then by all means let the situation settle down a bit before asking for a meeting. Don't assume that if you're calm, everyone else involved will be calm as well. The best time to talk about a conflict is when both parties have had time to compose themselves.

Next, where should you approach the person? Where would she be most comfortable? Consider your location and what resources are available to you. Approaching the person in the hallway in front of someone else and telling her, "It's about time we figured this mess out" will certainly get her attention, but it probably won't set the tone for a productive meeting. It may catch her off guard, embarrass her, or instantly make her defensive. Instead, choose a private location or politely approach her in her own workspace.

The best option is to make a meeting request in person, but if logistics aren't in your favor and you have to make the request via phone or email, take care to choose your words carefully and speak in a sincere manner (see the later section "Selecting the best mode of communication").

Choosing your words wisely

REMEMBER

When you address the person to set up a meeting, use language that's respectful, hopeful, and genuine. It's important that your invitation actually be *inviting*. To demonstrate your desire to sincerely resolve the difficulties, what you say should communicate the following:

>> **Confidentiality:** Communicate that this request and any subsequent conversations will be kept in confidence, just between the two of you. Of course, you should also be open to your co-worker's request that another person be made aware of a meeting.

>> **Optimism:** Show that you're hopeful that the two of you can find a solution. It does no good to ask for a meeting if even you don't believe it will solve anything. Keep your language future-focused and constructive.

>> **Sincerity:** Make sure the person knows that you genuinely want to hear what she has to say. You already know you'd like this meeting to be a fresh approach, but she may not. Use language that demonstrates your interest in hearing her perspective as well as sharing your own.

>> **Safety:** Don't try to intimidate or bully the person. You may have the ability (or the desire) to force your co-worker into this discussion, but hostility or pushiness works against you in the end. Addressing your desire to see the situation resolved in a way that's mutually satisfying shows your co-worker that you don't want to corner or trap her but rather you want to have a real dialogue.

Here's an example of an optimistic and inviting verbal meeting invitation: "I'd like to meet with you to talk about the challenge we're having and to find a way to resolve it that would work for both of us. I think if we work together, we can find a solution. Are you willing?"

It's hard for someone to blurt out that she's *not* willing (who wants to be accused of not being willing to have a chance to find a solution?). This approach lets her know that you're thinking about all sides, not just your own. (Flip to Chapter 1 in Book 1 for an introduction to the importance of language.)

Selecting the best mode of communication

Think about what mode of communication will garner the best response. Communicating in person, on the phone, or in writing are all options. What method do you use most often with the other person? Is that method effective for both of you? Is there a benefit in trying something new? What approach would make the person most comfortable? What are your strengths in each area?

In person

Asking for a meeting in person is always your best chance for a positive response. Privately and politely letting the other person see the authenticity on your face, hear your friendly tone of voice, and witness your open body language speaks volumes about your sincere desire to work things out. It's difficult for a co-worker to rebuff your efforts at mending fences if you're on her turf and demonstrating how you'll behave in the discussion.

On the phone

If you're not able to approach your co-worker in person, or if it would be unsettling for you to show up in a workspace you never visit, the telephone can be an effective tool for requesting a meeting. Before you dial, take a deep breath, make a few notes about what you'd like to say, and above all else, speak with a friendly and approachable tone of voice. Make an effort to speak with the other person directly; leaving a voice mail should be a last resort.

In writing

If you think you may stumble over your words in person or forget what it is you want to suggest, a well-crafted email could be in order. Or if geography is preventing you from making your request in person and it's impossible to get your co-worker on the phone, spend some time writing an invitation that discusses your awareness of the difficulty and your interest in hearing her perspective, and ask if she's willing to chat with you in person so the two of you can find a solution that works for both of you.

REMEMBER

If you choose to send a note, be careful not to write more than is necessary. Keep it simple and honest, and include your intentions for a positive, productive meeting. Allow the other person enough time to respond before taking further action.

TIP

It can be helpful to craft a document, set it aside for a while, and then review it before you send it. Upon review, you may notice something that the other party could misconstrue. You certainly don't want to make matters worse by writing anything that may be misunderstood. It's also really easy to misinterpret tone and intent in written documents, so have a trusted friend look the note over before you send it.

Preparing for Resistance

In a perfect world, asking someone to meet to discuss a conflict is met with an enthusiastic, "Sure, yes, you betcha!" every time. But because workplace difficulties are often fraught with conflicting emotions and deep issues, a request to talk is usually unsuccessful. Therefore, think ahead to how you'll respond if the other person uses one of a handful of common refusals.

REMEMBER

The following sections tell you about some of the typical forms of resistance and give you strategies to work through them. But first, here are a few general guidelines to keep in mind:

>> Be specific and upfront about your intent for the meeting when you approach the person, and then tailor your reaction to her resistance as a way to let her know you're sincere in your attempt to resolve the conflict.

>> Identify a neutral third party that both of you trust (someone the other person respects who'd be willing to observe the conversations and who wouldn't hinder the flow in any way). You don't have to talk to this third party right now; just be prepared to suggest the idea to the person if she says that she's uncomfortable meeting with you alone.

>> Try to build trust steadily with the person by having discussions on topics other than the conflict, especially subjects in which you have a common interest. A quick conversation in the hallway in which you ask about her weekend activities, state your amazement at the last-minute three-pointer that won the game, or ask for her banana bread recipe is a great way for both of you to ease into bigger conversations.

>> Suggest a series of meetings as a means for the two of you to start building trust and to let her know that you're willing to try something completely new. If a conflict has been going on for quite some time, or if there are a number of issues involved, she may feel overwhelmed at a request to solve all the problems in one sitting. It may be more palatable to approach the subject of your meeting as addressing one issue at a time. Give your co-worker the option to choose the topic of discussion for the first meeting, and she'll be more apt to agree to (maybe even suggest!) a second one.

Responding to push-back tactics

Pushing back is the most aggressive of the reactions you may get from the other person. People who push back acknowledge the problem but often react defensively. They may see the responsibility for the problem falling predominantly on your shoulders, or they may throw out a variety of roadblocks or preconditions to a meeting.

Comments like the ones in this list are often indicators that you're dealing with push-back tactics:

>> You're the one who let this get out of hand; why should I help you fix it?

>> If we're going to meet, I think our direct supervisor should be there.

>> I don't want to meet with someone who's just going to yell at me.

>> I just don't want to. I don't have to tell you why.

>> You need to show some respect first.

>> If you have a problem with me, take it up with x.

>> I'm not meeting with you until you apologize.

>> We don't need to meet; it's not *my* problem.

>> You wanna talk? Okay, buster, you got it!

Be ready to let the person know that you understand how frustrating the situation has been for her. Try sharing some areas of common ground (go through the worksheet in Chapter 1 to help you discover these common ground points) such as, "It's clear we're both interested in the final outcome of the project, so I'd like us to find a way to work together that would work for both of us."

If she wants to escalate the conflict by bringing in a supervisor, the Human Resources department, or the union, show her that you see the benefits in trying to work it out on your own first. Provide examples such as the following:

>> Both of you having a stake in the process and ownership in the outcomes, as opposed to having a third party make a decision that perhaps neither of you will like.

>> The opportunity to build trust and a relationship that will see you through future disagreements so they don't turn into full-blown conflicts.

>> The chance to create a working relationship based on insight and understanding of the real issues and to grasp fully what each of you requires for a peaceful coexistence.

>> An opportunity to show others your problem solving capabilities and to avoid negative documentation.

Finally, if she wants an apology for the incident in the staff meeting, address that issue: "You're right; we should talk about that incident." If she insists on an immediate apology, you need to consider whether you're willing to give one. If not, make it a point for discussion: "I'm not saying I won't apologize. What I'm saying is that I'd like to hear how the incident affected you, and I'd like an opportunity to share with you my thoughts on the incident before considering an apology. Are you willing to have that conversation with me?"

TIP

Someone who pushes back may want to start the conversation right then and there. Be flexible but proactive, and explain that scheduling a private meeting for another time would be beneficial because it would give you both time to think of possible solutions.

Getting past denial

Some people may not admit that there's a problem. Either the conflict simply isn't a problem for them (they're fine with calling your ideas stupid in the middle of a staff meeting) or they're completely oblivious to what's happening around them. Or maybe they fit into the classic definition of *denial* — they don't want there to be a problem so they've convinced themselves that there isn't one.

Here are some examples of denial language:

>> I don't know what you're talking about.

>> Problem? What problem?

>> I don't even know what we'd talk about.

>> Your problem isn't with me; it's with someone else.

>> I know we had an issue in the past, but everything's okay now.

It may seem next to impossible to get someone to meet with you about a problem that she says doesn't exist. To combat denial, come prepared with responses to increase your odds of success. Gently point out inconsistencies — words versus actions. For instance, you can reply with, "I hear you saying that you don't think there's a problem, yet I've noticed that whenever I ask about the project, I see you roll your eyes. Help me understand." Replying in this way allows the person to respond to your observations and acknowledge that something may be going on.

REMEMBER

Be open to talking about anything, and be prepared to ask whether you can improve the situation by the two of you having a conversation.

You may also want to ask for the person's help as a means to keep the conversation going: "It sounds like you're hesitant to discuss *xyz*. Can you help me understand why?" Tell her that you're willing to listen to what she has to say, and describe the impact that the issue has had on you to see whether she's willing to provide some insight. A good response is, "I'm open to hearing your thoughts. Is there anything that you think would be beneficial for me to know? I'm willing to listen to whatever you have to say."

Addressing avoidance

Some people are masters at avoiding difficult situations. They'll often freely admit that there's a problem, but doing nothing about it feels better to them than having a conversation about it. They may also hope that the problem goes away on its own or think that it's not serious enough to deal with.

When you ask the person to talk, you may hear her say:

» Now's not a good time.

» I'm just too busy.

» Whatever you say — just tell me what you want [and then the person never follows through].

» Yes, let's talk. Have your people call my people.

» [Silence, crickets, dead air.]

» I'd really rather not.

» It's not a big deal; I'll get over it.

REMEMBER

The first step in a response strategy for avoiders is to create safety. Before you approach an avoider, have a plan that includes the possibility of adding a third party: "If you're uncomfortable meeting with me alone, would you like to bring someone else in to help us chat? I think maybe [name] is someone we both trust." This suggestion works well with peers but may be a little awkward if the other person is your boss or someone you manage. In those instances, the third party you suggest may be an ombudsman, someone in HR, an external consultant, or another employee who is your co-worker's equal (not yours).

Be flexible and focus on language that's open and inviting: "If now isn't a good time, I'll meet with you anytime, anywhere — you name the time and place." Concentrate on relationship-building and the employee's importance to the team: "It's important that we work well together and set a good example for the rest of the team." You can be honest about how the situation's affecting you: "Leaving this unsettled has left me feeling uncomfortable. I'd really like to resolve this so we can get back to working as a team. What would you need to make that happen?"

Acknowledge her excuse ("I understand that you're very busy"), find a benefit for her ("I think if we can work through this, it'll free up more of our time in the future"), and make sure she knows that she's being *invited* into a conversation, not ordered ("Are you willing to talk with me? Are you interested in resolving this?").

Finding hope in hopelessness

Some employees may have experienced disappointments that have led them to think there's no hope, the ship's sinking, and there's nothing but rough waters as far as they can see. Although you may come across folks who almost seem to thrive on conflict, at the other end of the spectrum are those who are nearly crippled by it and can't imagine ever finding a way out.

If you approach an employee who feels the situation is hopeless, you may hear the following:

>> What's the point? It isn't something we can resolve.

>> We've tried this before. You never listen.

>> Why bother? Nothing will change.

>> What's the use? It's not going to work.

>> What say do I have?

>> I don't trust you to have a different conversation than what we've already had.

>> How many times do we have to talk about this? I'm tired of rehashing.

TIP

These may be legitimate responses if this isn't the first time the two of you have tried to fix things. So acknowledge that and validate the response! Doing so demonstrates your willingness to see her perspective and empowers her to keep the conversation going.

If you've talked about your problems before and were unsuccessful, recognize where the missteps took place. Let the person know that you've given it a lot of thought, and point out a few areas you think could be different this time. Ask a lot of questions: "What would you need in order to feel as though a conversation about the issue might be a good use of our time?" "What would it take for you to feel I'm really listening to your perspective?" "How could we come up with some fresh ideas to approach this in a new way?"

Give the person hope and let her know that you're interested in change by saying, "I'm hoping we can have a new kind of conversation this time." Address additional concerns and confidentiality issues, and invite her to set the boundaries — time, place, length of meeting, topics to discuss, and potential participants — in hopes of making her more comfortable moving ahead with a meeting.

Setting a Time and a Place for a Productive Discussion

The devil is in the details when it comes to making sound agreements, and the same is true for choosing a time and place for a meeting. Spending time upfront to think through what will make both of you equally comfortable demonstrates your sincere desire to resolve this conflict.

Time considerations

Pick a time when both of you can focus on the conversation. Uninterrupted time is a key element to a successful conversation, so choosing to meet right before the staff meeting — when phones are ringing, last minute emails are coming in, and co-workers are knocking on the door — isn't the best move. Ten minutes isn't really enough time to discuss the issues and proposals for solutions, so schedule at least an hour, and make room in the calendar for the meeting to run over so that you don't end up cutting off the other person to get to your next appointment. Politely ask the other person to do the same.

Time of day may also bring food into the equation. Do you or the other person have problems with low blood sugar? Do you get really tired and lethargic late in the afternoon? Let her have a say in setting the time. You want her to know that working together is important to you, so use this as an example of your new perspective and get the meeting started on the right foot.

And while you're at it, give her the benefit of the doubt that she probably does want to meet with you — maybe just not right now. You don't know how much time she may need to prepare for a conversation, so be open to suggesting a compromise. You'll get better results if you can negotiate some middle ground between when *you* think the problem needs to be handled and when *she* may be willing to talk about it.

If you've calmed down and think you can handle the conversation, that's fine, but consider that the other person may not be emotionally ready. That doesn't mean you should let her off the hook and permit her to put the problem off indefinitely. You may have to press the matter later, but for now, be open to creating some space if needed.

REMEMBER

People at the height of emotion have the lowest ability to reason. Let yourself and others calm down before attempting to work through a problem.

Geography matters

Think about where to meet before you ask for a conversation. Be prepared to suggest a meeting place that demonstrates you've thought about privacy, safety, and the impact on the team. Impartiality is important to many people, so plan to meet in a space that screams neutral. Take into consideration titles, power, and the desire for a balanced conversation (Book 3, Chapter 4 tells you more about the importance of the organization chart when resolving conflict).

Here are a couple of things you can do to create a sense of safety and neutrality:

>> **Consider the location of the room itself.** Make sure the room you suggest doesn't hold more or less power for either party. Specifically, try not to schedule your meeting in any location that could be described as either employee's "turf." Work to balance the power early to avoid having to address a power struggle during the meeting.

>> **Suggest a meeting room that's as private as possible.** Meeting someplace where other employees are wandering in and out or lurking (and listening) won't create the kind of environment you want. So find a place where the curious eyes of others won't affect your discussion.

>> *Private* should also mean minimal distractions. A room with a telephone constantly ringing or computer beeps announcing the arrival of new email serves only to distract from the conversation. Listening well is hard when you have distractions competing for your attention.

WARNING

It's probably not a good idea to choose the glassed-in conference room that everyone refers to as the "fishbowl," or to choose your own office. More than likely, others know about the tension between the two of you, so pulling the other person into your office may make her feel as though she's being reprimanded in front of her peers, even if you have a positive conversation.

Approach the other person with a few options for locations in mind, but don't forget to ask her to provide input on a location that works for her. Asking her to suggest a setting shows that you're open to her opinions and that you won't be making all the decisions. Be prepared for her to suggest her own office or workspace. Consider whether you're comfortable meeting there, and have an alternative to suggest if you're not.

WARNING

If you think it may be better to meet away from work, like at a coffee shop or restaurant, consider whether the two of you will want to discuss emotional issues or stay as long as you'd like at a restaurant. Will she feel comfortable with interruptions from wait staff and strangers? Will you be able to stay as long as you like at an eatery, or do you run the risk of being herded out in the middle of an important point? You may decide that meeting off-site to have a surface conversation is a good first step in developing rapport between the two of you, but it may not be the most productive environment for a difficult conversation. Also think about how the two of you will get to the location (awkward car ride?) and whether the trip back to the office will be emotional for either of you.

TIP

A quiet, out-of-the-way conference room is a great place to set up camp and work through the issues. In large organizations with multiple buildings, you can arrange for a room in another location to ensure privacy. If you work at a location with just a few employees, or if the only conference room is also the communal lunch spot, consider asking for a private booth at a nearby restaurant and spend some time away from curious co-workers.

Chapter **3**

Sitting Down to Talk through the Issues

You've likely let a lot of little things go between you and the person with whom you're having a conflict. If left unchecked, little things can amount to a bigger problem. A better strategy is to sit down, discuss the situation, and clear the air. But initiating a productive conversation about difficult topics takes courage. Though it may feel uncomfortable and risky to talk about the situation, you can use the tools in this chapter to keep yourself calm and focused and to keep the conversation productive.

Prior to sitting down with the other person, identify both of your needs using the tips and tools in Chapter 1 of Book 3. Refer to Book 3, Chapter 2 for some details you need to consider when asking for a meeting, and, if necessary, tailor your approach to fit your audience by looking at how the organization chart may influence some of your decisions (see Book 3, Chapter 4).

This chapter walks you through how to mediate your own conflict, make your point, and consider the other person's perspective with an open mind. You get tips on how to keep things on track while the two of you discuss the issues, and you also get some ideas about what you can do next if you just can't seem to work it out.

Preparing to Mediate Your Own Conflict

You'll wear two hats in this meeting — that of mediator and that of contributor. Granted, you're not acting as an objective third party in this instance, but coming prepared with an understanding of the mediation process gives you an opportunity to step back a bit and make room for both perspectives while following a structured and proven method.

The following sections help you understand your two roles and give you an overview of how to adapt the mediation strategy to fit a one-on-one scenario.

Recognizing your dual role

Your task is complicated because you occupy two distinct roles at the same time, and one shouldn't overshadow the other. In mediation, all parties have the right to ask for what they want, and by keeping the focus of the meeting on both your needs, you reinforce that goal. In other words, by staying true to the role of the facilitator, you reinforce your role as a participant:

>> **Facilitator:** This chapter prepares you to bring a mediation skill set and process to the situation. Knowing this, your responsibility is to use the process for *both* your benefit and the other person's benefit, not just your own.

>> **Participant:** You have a right to speak your mind and ask that your needs be met, because this meeting is as much an opportunity for you to ask for what you want as it is for him. Use constructive language and make judicious use of the skills presented *while* striving for solutions that are meaningful and beneficial to you.

REMEMBER Be aware that the very fact that you asked for this meeting holds a certain power. *You* took the first step. *You* extended the olive branch. *You* took proactive measures to make sure that the conflict doesn't get any worse. And most important, *you* are the one who's coming to the table with a specific skill set and process to maximize returns on the conversation. That carries with it a lot of weight and responsibility. Researching mediation skills means you're coming to this meeting to resolve the issue, not outsmart an opponent.

Adapting a mediation process for a one-on-one meeting

Use your own words and be yourself during the meeting to discuss the conflict between you and your colleague. Have a plan, though, or the meeting probably won't result in the outcome you had hoped for.

Follow these steps for a productive conversation:

1. Sincerely greet the other person and briefly acknowledge the conflict and the impact it's had on you.

2. Explain that you'll be following a mediation process (because you think the method will help you both focus) but that you're just as much a participant as he is.

3. State your goal for a positive, respectful meeting, and that you both should consider this a time to confidentially present your views.

4. Ask the other person to share the events and the impact that the situation has had on him.

5. Reflect what you've heard, neutralize emotions, and spotlight values.

6. Share your perspective and ask your co-worker to reflect back to you what you've presented.

7. Build an agenda of topics for the ensuing conversation.

8. Collectively address any misunderstandings or assumptions.

9. Brainstorm solutions.

10. Filter through ideas to find those that best meet what's most important to both of you.

11. Finalize agreements, paying special attention to details and what to do if things don't work.

12. Share with others any details and results of your discussion *only* as necessary and appropriate.

The rest of the chapter covers these steps in more detail.

Getting the One-on-One Started

When you mediate, you should use a structured process (outlined in the preceding section) and briefly share the structure with the participants. This part of the meeting is called an opening statement. It should take no more than a few minutes.

Putting together a natural-sounding opening statement

Because the start to your meeting is so important, use language that feels natural and comfortable in your opening statement. Both of you will likely be a little anxious and concerned about how the meeting will go. That's normal, and it's okay to acknowledge your nerves at the start of the conversation. Prepare yourself by thinking about what you want to say, how you want to say it, and how it applies to your particular situation. Include all the points outlined for you in this chapter. Just make sure that what you say doesn't come across as rehearsed or phony. Your words should be authentic and come from a genuine desire to resolve your difficulties.

TIP

Have a cheat sheet in front of you to make sure to cover important points and to have an opportunity to practice a little beforehand. Use the rest of this chapter as a guide to what to include on your cheat sheet.

Here's an example of what your opening statement may look like. Note that this is only a sample, and you can tweak it to fit your particular situation.

> Reese, I want to thank you for being willing to take the time to sit down with me to talk about the challenges we've been having lately. This has been a tough couple of weeks for me, and I can imagine for you as well. I'm beginning to see and hear other people starting to talk about our conflict, and I think we have an opportunity to change that. So I'm grateful that we're taking this opportunity today. I've been thinking a lot about the situation, and I'm hopeful that we can put our heads together and have a respectful conversation so we can come up with some ideas on how we can solve things in a way that meets both of our needs. I think if we follow a structure, we should be able to get everything on the table and then work on how to solve our issues. I'd like to propose that we use the same process as mediators use — start by sharing our perspectives, listen to understand each other, build an agenda with the topics we'd like to cover, and then go into brainstorming. I also propose that our discussion be confidential and just between us. Does that sound like something that might work?

The next section gives you more information about the elements of an opening statement so you can craft your own.

Acknowledging the current challenge

Set the right tone for the conversation to come. Consider adding a few words to your opening statement that capture some or all of the following ideas:

>> **A sincere thank-you:** This conversation may be a long time coming, or an uncomfortable one for both of you. A quick (but authentic) thank-you to the other person for being willing to sit down and talk goes a long way toward kicking off your meeting with the right kind of attitude.

>> **A recognition that it has been difficult:** Feel free to share that the conflict has been tough on you. Saying that you've had enough is in no way a sign of weakness. In fact, it may be exactly what the other person needs to hear so he can acknowledge that he's been struggling, too.

>> **An awareness that others are watching:** If you've seen this conflict radiating outwards, say so. It's important to speak to what you see, and if you know that camps are forming or morale is dipping, share that you want to see the problem resolved before it goes any further.

WARNING

However, don't speak on behalf of others or attempt to interpret how the conflict is affecting them. Your colleague may disagree, so speak about this only in an objective manner:

- "I notice that there are whispers about how the two of us are interacting, and it would benefit both of us to work this out." (Good!)

- "The accounting department is having a hard time getting anything done, and they want this to stop." (Not so good!)

>> **Your desire to resolve the situation:** Let the other person know that you're committed to resolving the tension between you. Speak about how both of you will benefit from resolving your differences — you'll have less stress, you'll be more productive, and you'll have peace of mind.

>> **A new approach:** If you've tried to have this conversation before but the results have been unsatisfactory, share how this time will be different. What did (or didn't) you do last time that you won't (or will) do this time? Speak about the approach in a hopeful and positive way — a little optimism goes a long way.

Explaining the steps that the meeting will follow

When you mediate a conflict that you have a role in, you perform a number of steps in a certain order (see the earlier section "Adapting a mediation process for a one-on-one meeting"). At the start of your meeting, briefly go over what will happen when, sharing just enough about each step so your colleague isn't surprised when you call for a break or transition from one phase to another.

REMEMBER

You don't need to reveal specifically how each step contributes to your ability to bring parties to resolution in a neutral and transparent way. It's up to you how much of the process you want to share with the other party. But coming to the table and announcing, "So, I read this chapter in a book about conflict resolution at work, and I'm going to play mediator" may put off a co-worker who's already upset with you.

Conversely, your colleague may get frustrated if you are following guidelines he isn't privy to — if he's trying to tell you something, for instance, and you tell him that it's not his turn to talk. A brief explanation that you'd like the two of you to follow a proven mediation method in which you take turns speaking, listen to understand each other, and brainstorm solutions that benefit you both is likely to be viewed positively by the other person.

Committing to a productive meeting

After acknowledging the conflict, explain what you want to get out of the meeting, and what the other person can expect from you. Saying that this is a new and different approach isn't sufficient unless you describe *how* it will be different. Here are some talking points to cover:

>> **Looking for answers:** Emphasize that this conversation isn't meant to be a gripe session or a chance for the two of you to hammer away at each other's flaws and prove who's right or wrong. Unite yourselves around idea generation instead of being chained together by negativity.

>> **Being mindful of this opportunity:** Speak about this conversation as an opportunity to build the kind of relationship the two of you want to have and to paint the kind of picture you want to see in the workplace. Suggest that you'll do this by focusing on the things you *can* change rather than those you can't.

>> **Communicating respectfully:** Because this meeting is a step toward changing how you work together, it's important that you speak in a manner that's respectful, professional, and appropriate — and that goes for both of you, of course.

Sharing Perspectives

After your opening statement, answer any questions and then shift the meeting to the step in the process in which you both have an opportunity to speak about what you've been experiencing, to hear what each other has to say, and to understand how each other sees the issues at hand. This step is a very busy point in the process, but an important one, to say the least.

REMEMBER

So as you begin this sharing step, consider what you want to know and how you want to present your point of view. When speaking:

1. **Describe specific actions, statements, and events.**

2. **Then describe how they affected you.**

3. **Then make any requests you'd like regarding future incidents, keeping your language focused on what you want rather than what you don't want.**

At this point, don't spend too much time asking a lot of questions. When listening, make a mental note of, or jot down, any questions you'd like to ask in order to understand better. You'll have time to clarify and investigate later, when you get to the brainstorming part of the conversation, but here, all you want to do is be sure that each of you has heard and understood each other.

The following sections show you how to decide who gets to share his perspective first, how to listen for understanding, and how to explain your point of view constructively.

Deciding who will begin

Although each of you will get an opportunity to speak and respond to each other, you have to start *somewhere*. Your specific situation will help determine who goes first.

If both of you are fully aware of the reasons that you're having this meeting, it can benefit you to offer the other person the opportunity to begin. Doing so demonstrates openness and a willingness to hear what he has to say, and it allows you the opportunity to demonstrate how to summarize and highlight what he values before sharing your own point of view. Hopefully, when you reach the point in the process in which you reflect and reframe a party's perspective, you'll actually see a physical transformation from "ready to fight" to "ready to listen." This reaction is a testament to your ability to try something new.

REMEMBER

In a sense, you've *already* gone first. By setting up the meeting and creating an opening statement, you've already shared to some extent what you're hoping to accomplish and briefly touched on how the conflict has affected you. By giving the other person an opportunity to describe his own experience, you're modeling good behavior by sharing the spotlight with him.

WARNING

Your invitation for the other person to speak first must be open and genuine, however, and not a challenge or a threat. Nothing shuts down a conversation faster than hearing a disingenuous offer to start the ball rolling. For instance, mull over the following possible invitations:

> I'm going to let you start this off. I have my own ideas about this mess, but I'm sure you have your own take, too. So let's hear it — go.

Doesn't sound so good, right? Now try this on for size:

> I'd like us to get started, and I'm curious to hear how you see the situation, and what you think we need to do to resolve it. I want you to know that I won't be interrupting you, because I'm interested in your perspective. And when you're done, I'd like to have the opportunity to summarize what I heard so that I can be sure that I have a good understanding of your point of view.

WARNING

If the person is unaware of your reason for calling the meeting, asking him to start (even using the earlier good example) may be unproductive. Also, if you have some insight or information that may be helpful to the exchange, offering to begin isn't a bad thing. Bear in mind, though, that rumors, conjecture, and assumptions are *not* insights or new information. Be sure that the information is pertinent and helpful to your conversation.

Another time when you may offer to begin the sharing phase is when you sense that the other person is resistant or hesitant, and you believe his attitude is related to distrust — either of you or of the mediation meeting in general. Choose appropriate and constructive language that demonstrates your sincerity in resolving the problem and shows that this meeting will be different from what has happened before. Such an offer may sound like this:

> I'd like to take a moment, share my perspective, and tell you a little about how this situation has been affecting me. I want to stress, though, that you'll also have the same opportunity when I'm finished, because this conversation isn't just about me. I'm interested in hearing your thoughts as well, because I believe that if we each have better understanding, we'll reach a better solution.

Listening actively

As concerns about the conflict are shared, listen closely to how he describes the situation. How each of you interprets the events gives you insight into how the conflict developed, what's keeping it going, and what approaches you can collectively take that will lead you to solutions.

REMEMBER

Bear in mind that even though both of you likely experienced the same incidents, he'll probably describe the impact differently than you do. This isn't a time to question who's right and who's wrong, because both accounts are true. They're two different ways of viewing the same situation and are merely reflective of both of your experiences and perspectives. Keep in mind that you don't need to agree in order to understand.

Show the other person that you're listening by

>> **Presenting open body language:** Create an inviting space by assuming a comfortable posture with your arms at your sides or rested on the table. Lean forward a little, but be careful not to invade his personal space. (Flip to Chapters 2 and 3 in Book 1 for an introduction to nonverbal cues and body language.)

>> **Making and maintaining good eye contact:** Connect by looking him in the eye as appropriate (no need to freak him out or stare him down, though!). Checking your email or texting while he's talking may feel like constructive multi-tasking in the moment, but he'll certainly see such actions as a demonstration of your disinterest in his story. Put everything away and give him your full attention.

>> **Positively reacting to his statements:** A few well-placed nods and subtle verbal responses let him know you're hearing him.

Be careful not to react too much, though. You may hear some surprising things, but keep your poker face! A raised eyebrow, a rolled eye, or a dropped jaw can send a message that you think he's exaggerating, or that you believe he just doesn't know what he's talking about.

WARNING

>> **Waiting to correct or clarify:** Honor his time to talk. As tempting as it may be to set the record straight or to speak up when you feel you're being mischaracterized, *don't do it!* Even briefly clearing up minor misunderstandings undermines the integrity of the process, so be patient.

>> **Taking notes for the facts and more:** Getting the facts straight is important, because missing a date, stating an incorrect dollar amount, or getting a name wrong may give the impression that you're not listening or that you're not as interested in his perspective as you say you are.

TIP

As you take notes, make sure you also capture his emotions about the conflict and the values buried beneath his remarks so when it's time for you to reflect, you can speak to those things. A statement such as, "You're always looking over my shoulder at everything I do!" can give you some insight that he's looking for *autonomy* or *trust* in his relationship with you because he values those things in general.

>> **Looking for ways to neutralize strong language:** As the other person speaks, he may come out with some pretty strong opinions about the situation and anything else he thinks makes sense to throw in. Try to respond by confirming how upset he is but by using language that doesn't inflame him. For example, if he states, "Joe and everybody around him are idiots," you could mentally craft a neutralized response such as, "You're concerned about Joe's ability to get the job done."

REMEMBER

Don't expect your colleague to know what he's looking for when he first begins to tell you his point of view. He may say that he wants *x*, *y*, or *z*. He may say that he sees the problem in the simplest of terms and can't understand why you don't see it that way as well. Just let him talk. The more he shares, the more information you'll have when it's time to respond and you can demonstrate then that you understand where he's coming from.

Summarizing what you've heard

Before launching into a response to your colleague's initial remarks, take a moment and contemplate what to say and how to say it. You've been listening for the values and emotions that are important to him; now you want to reflect his emotions and reframe his statements into what he *does want* instead of what he *doesn't want*. Repeating "you want me to stop talking at staff meetings" gets the point across, but reframing the statement to "you'd like me to find a more effective way to communicate my ideas" gives the two of you something to work with when you get to the brainstorming phase. Plus, it frames the conflict as an opportunity to *do* something!

REMEMBER

You don't have to agree with the points you're summarizing — you just need to show that you understand what he said. Doing so may be more challenging when you're the subject of the conversation than when you're facilitating a discussion between other employees. Still, understanding the difference between reactive responses and meaningful summaries is the key to moving the conversation forward.

For example, two parties were being coached through a conversation when an employee informed his manager that he believed he played favorites when assigning shift assignments to the staff. The manager jumped in with:

> I never play favorites, Chris! I work really hard to make sure that the shifts are assigned in a fully transparent and fair way! In fact, I've documented everything and I can even show you how fair I've been.

When you boil it down, this reactive response was a fancy way of saying, "Nu-huh." And all it did was set up the employee quite nicely to answer with his own eloquent response of, "Ya-huh." Not a very useful approach. And the harder one tried to prove his point, the harder the other worked to do the opposite. Imagine instead if the response had been:

> Chris, it sounds as if you're concerned about the way in which the shifts are assigned. You want to make sure they're handed out in a way that's fair and equitable.

Can you imagine how Chris might have responded to this summary of his concern? He certainly couldn't say that his manager was arguing the point, or choosing not to see his perspective, which is how most conflict conversations end up going awry. Instead, the manager would have captured his interest and spoken to his concern without saying that he agreed or disagreed with him.

When you reflect and reframe a co-worker's point in neutral words, you re-inforce that you're open and receptive, but you don't sell short your own take. This technique buys you a lot of credibility as the process continues.

REMEMBER

Reflecting, reframing, and neutralizing take some practice. Take your time, be mindful of what you'd like to say, and don't worry if it doesn't come out exactly right. You'll see subtle clues that what you're saying resonates with your colleague. You know you're on the right track if you see his eyes light up, if his body language goes from crossed arms to an open posture, or if he's actively nodding. And if you notice that he has a quizzical look or furrowed brow, or that he's shaking his head, feel free to ask for an opportunity to try it again.

Speaking to be understood

When it comes time to chronicle your side of the story, speak in a way that's constructive and clear, modeling the kind of conversation you want to have.

Describe the incident and then the impact

If you have particular concerns, address them specifically. What was the event that you experienced, and how did it affect you? You can think of this in terms of the *incident* and the *impact*.

For instance, if you have a concern about an employee monopolizing the floor during staff meetings, you could say, "Don't monopolize the floor during staff meetings." But this example is non-specific, and it tends to place the other person on the defensive. He probably doesn't see his behavior as "monopolizing time," and he'll likely respond accordingly. Instead, present the incident and what its impact was, like this:

> At our last meeting, many of the other employees were unable to share their concerns. **(Incident)** It's important to me that all employees have time to talk about their programs. **(Impact)** I'd like us to look for ways to give all staff members the opportunity to voice their opinions.

This example differs from the first one in that it doesn't label behavior (or people), and it addresses in objective terms what you see as concerns. Additionally, it sets up the opportunity for you to turn your concerns into a proposal that's open and constructive and that invites cooperation.

Use "I" messages

When sharing your perspective, only speak to your own experience. Keep your comments focused on how you perceived an event and how it affected you. Use "I" language to take the sting out of a tough message. Talking about hurt feelings is better when you deliver the information by saying, "I felt confused and hurt when my phone calls weren't returned," even though you may want to say, "What's up with not returning my phone calls?"

Simply starting a sentence with "I" doesn't ensure a positive reaction. If you say, "I'm not the only one who thinks you should return phone calls!" the opportunity to state your perspective in such a way that your co-worker can understand your point of view and not react with defensiveness is lost.

Similarly, using "we" language to strengthen your perspective is intimidating and can make the listener feel like co-workers are joining forces against him, causing him to become defensive or shut down. Avoid speaking on behalf of the group, even if you're in alignment with others. (See Chapter 1 in Book 1 for more about the importance of pronouns in verbal communication.)

Avoid using language that places blame, points fingers, or affixes labels to people, because such language raises defensiveness in the other person and derails the conversation. For instance, steer clear of these phrases:

>> You always

>> You never

>> You should

>> You didn't

Imagine if you're the recipient of one of those phrases, like getting into an argument about the cleanliness of your office space when a co-worker says, "You never take out the trash!" The sting is the accusation that "you never." Meanwhile, all you can do is think about every time you've lugged a heavy, smelly bag of trash out to the container on the curb during a downpour, getting drenched in the process. And as you start recalling all your heroic efforts, you're probably thinking about how "no one ever" appreciates all the hard work you do. Think that conversation is going to go anywhere productive?

Be brief and clear

REMEMBER

Keep your message short and sweet. Get right to the point. Repeating the same information multiple times doesn't benefit anybody. Enough said.

Reaching across the divide when it feels as big as the Grand Canyon

After sharing your respective points of view, the two of you may feel that the perspectives couldn't be more opposite. Perhaps the talking has stopped, and all you hear are the crickets. That's okay. Try to keep the meeting going by

>> **Describing the stalemate:** Recap the positions in a way that shows you've heard the other person, and yet you still have hope you can come to an agreement. Say something like, "It appears we have very different perspectives. Your position is that you should take the lead on all the projects, and mine is that I should be the lead. Maybe we could each share why being the lead is important to us."

>> **Looking for common ground:** The two of you have at least one thing in common — you're experiencing a conflict. You probably both want to have it resolved, or you'd appreciate a little peace in the workplace. Say something to the effect of, "I can see right now that we have different points of view. Do you think there's any part of this we can agree on? Is it safe to assume that we probably share a desire to figure this out?"

>> **Talking about the future:** Just because you're stuck now doesn't mean you have to continue to be stuck. You could offer, "It looks like we have very different viewpoints on this. Maybe it would be more productive to talk about the future rather than what's happening now. How can we work together in a way that shines a positive light on us both?"

For more ideas on what to do if the conversation stalls, see the later section "Keeping the conversation on track."

Creating an Agenda

After you've each told your side of the story, create an agenda for the rest of the meeting. You may be wondering why you're being asked to create an agenda mid-way through the meeting. Well, an *agenda* in mediation is *not* a pre-generated list of issues, nor is it a schedule of events and activities for your dialogue. Instead, it's a list of topics the two of you want to talk about that you build together. By generating the list together, you're more likely to see each topic as belonging to both of you.

Use the agenda creation process to clarify and name issues. You can get formal and write them on a whiteboard or easel, or the two of you can create an informal document at the table. The agenda reminds you of the topics you want to discuss, and as you check items off the list, it becomes a visual indicator of your progress. The following sections have information on building neutral, effective agendas.

Transitioning from the past to the future

Use the agenda to make an important point: It's time to move from the past to the future. Set the stage for the conversation to come by saying, "As we begin to build an agenda, keep in mind that we'll discuss each of these items thoroughly, but we'll do so with a focus on the future rather than rehashing the past." Your statement should focus on moving away from where the problems have been and heading toward where the solutions are.

Demonstrating accessibility and flexibility

As you begin to create the agenda, make sure the list is visible to both of you. In effect, both of you should be working side by side. Also, make sure both of you know that you can add to the list at any time and that it's flexible. It should be seen as a living document rather than etched in stone.

Separating topics

It's possible that the other person will see all the difficulties the two of you are having as one big mess and lump everything into the same category on the agenda list. It's a lot like a big ball of holiday lights: It's hard to know how many and what color lights you have until you've pulled them apart, strand by strand. Unraveling the lights may take a little time and care, but it's worth it in the end. And conflict topics are no different.

Unravel complicated agenda suggestions by asking questions. Don't rush to write something down. Instead, take a few minutes to gently challenge the other person to give you more. For example, ask what he means when he says that he wants to talk about "the problem." How would he break that down into a small handful of specific topics?

Labeling and defining issues

The agenda list should be seen as belonging to both of you rather than having topics labeled as either "mine" or "not mine." So when possible, point out commonalities and reiterate that this is a collaborative agenda.

REMEMBER

Make sure all the topics you list are neutral and presented objectively. Creating neutral topics is an important part of generating buy-in to the process. How can you expect to keep the list civil? The truth is you may not be able to. What you can do, though, is reframe language to make it more palatable.

For example, the other person says she wants to talk about the fact that the staff meetings run way too long and end up in shouting matches. She wants to cut the meetings in half and has a pretty good plan to make it work. But you quickly respond that, in fact, the meetings are a necessary way of exchanging ideas and information, and it would be good to extend the time to make sure everyone is on the same page about projects.

If you list the topic as "Cut staff meetings in half," you've essentially recorded a position (or solution), which is only one person's way of resolving the issue. And if you list "Extend staff meetings," you've done the same thing in reverse. So what's really the topic here? The staff meeting is what's important, so list that. How the participants feel and what they think about the meeting remains intact, and neither of them is alienated by the topic as it appears on the agenda.

Make sure the agenda includes all the issues. You don't want to finish the meeting only to realize a key issue has gone unnoticed and unaddressed. After the list is made, ask whether there's anything else that needs to be discussed in order to find a resolution.

If both of you feel the list is complete, say again that items can be added or erased if one or both of you change your minds. It's a flexible list that belongs to the participants. Explain for now it's "a good place to start."

Considering common agenda topics

Although it's true that every facilitated conversation is different depending on the participants and their concerns, a few common themes tend to surface when dealing with work issues. Having some sample language at the ready helps you frame topics in an objective, constructive manner. The following agenda topics are common:

>> **Roles and responsibilities:** This topic can describe a number of situations in which employees see their job responsibilities differently. Put this on the board if you need to discuss disagreements about job descriptions and areas of influence.

>> **Respect:** Another common theme in workplace scenarios is the hard-to-define yet all-important concept of what respect means to employees. Although each party is likely to describe it differently, they get an opportunity to speak about how they want to be respected and what it means to show respect to others.

>> **Communication:** This agenda topic is a simple way to discuss differences in how employees speak to one another. Many workplace conflicts boil down to either a lack of communication or different approaches to communication. (Check out Chapter 4 in Book 1 for an introduction to communication styles.)

>> **Confidentiality:** Confidentiality is huge in mediation, so even if the other person doesn't bring it up, you should. This is a great topic that covers other employees' interest or curiosity in what's happening in the meeting or when to share details about the conflict.

Using the agenda for negotiations

The agenda helps you structure brainstorming, aids in problem solving, and creates an organized way to kick off negotiations (see the next section). Breaking the conflict into smaller pieces helps the participants feel that the situation is little more manageable.

The agenda is a tool you'll use throughout the negotiation and agreement phases, and it will serve you best in these areas if you

>> Choose one item at a time to discuss.

>> Be thorough with each item and do your best to work through one topic completely before moving on to another.

» Move on to another point if the two of you get stuck on something. You can always come back to the topic later.

» Talk about each and every concern on the list.

Looking for Win-Win Solutions

You've shared your perspectives and built an agenda. Now it's time to start capitalizing on all your hard work by proposing solutions based on the values you've identified and what you've learned from each other. The following sections can help you arrive at a solution.

TIP

Spend a few minutes considering (and explaining) that mediating a conflict between the two of you is different from other negotiations. This part of the meeting isn't about making sure you both get two scoops of ice cream, or bartering for the best price at the local flea market. It's about both of you walking away having addressed the values that matter the most. Dividing something in half only works if you both feel you've won because you moved beyond the surface issues and understood what's really behind your conflict.

Proposing positive alternatives

You may be really good at telling others what you *don't* like. But in telling your co-worker what you don't want, you haven't offered any alternatives. Alternatives help him understand what he could be doing. The foreman who tells a worker on a construction site, "Don't stand there," is letting the worker know that where he's standing isn't safe. But without further instruction, the laborer may just move to another spot that's just as dangerous.

The same is true in any work setting. Imagine telling a co-worker, "Stop being so negative, Bob! This project isn't getting any easier with all your doom and gloom. You're dragging us all down with you." The perceived problem is pretty clear, isn't it? But making a statement like this provides no framework for preferred behavior.

Imagine instead using the following language: "Bob, it's important to me that we all speak positively about this project. I recognize that the workload is a challenge, and I need us to stay focused to meet the deadline." This statement makes clear what you want without making a demand, challenging the other person, or putting him down. Instead of telling him to stop being negative, you've asked him to be positive and given him a concrete example of what you mean when you say "be positive." It's a subtle difference, but one that has a tremendous impact on conflict conversations.

TIP

Because your co-worker probably doesn't know how to frame his language to state clearly what he *does* want you to do, you'll have to do some of that for him until he catches on.

For instance, if you hear, "You always ask Darren for his opinions first!" don't jump in with a defensive response. Instead, try to help him by summarizing the intentions of his statement to include what you think he would like you to do: "You feel you have valuable contributions that you'd like to share, and you'd appreciate it if I asked for your opinions first."

You've effectively helped him craft a proposal out of what would otherwise be seen as an attack. And you can't do that if you're quick to react, become defensive, or try to prove that he's wrong. Patience and grace go a long way toward helping you get through this part of the meeting. If you feel you're backing down too much or giving in to his demands, think of the situation in terms of applying a strategy that in the end gets you *both* what you want.

REMEMBER

While you're speaking about alternatives, give a nod to the values that are inherent in both of your requests. This helps you identify what motivates each of you to find a solution to the problem. For example, consider these contrasting statements:

>> "You're always late to meetings" versus "It's important to me that you arrive at our meetings on time because I want to make sure there's enough time for everyone to provide updates on their projects."

>> "You never bother to proofread your reports" versus "I need to make sure that your reports are accurate and error-free because I take a lot of pride in the team's reputation with other departments."

>> "Your workspace is a disaster!" versus "I'd like our workspace to be organized and tidy so I can find things quickly when asked."

You may already know what you'd like to see based on filling out the worksheet in Book 3, Chapter 1, or you may need to tailor your request based on what you discover in this meeting. Either way, speak to what each of you wants in order to prevent confusion and increase the likelihood that you'll both follow through with requests.

Keeping the conversation on track

Even in the most structured of conversations, sometimes things start to go haywire. Work through the tough spots first by using the agenda and choosing another item that may be easier to discuss. Then be sure to

>> **Spotlight shared interests:** Look for things that unite you. For instance, although you may not agree on the best way to build morale on a team, you both recognize that it's important to have a satisfied staff. When you can validate that you're operating with the same goals in mind, you may be able to find ways to meet those goals that satisfy both of you.

>> **Underscore progress:** Stay positive. It may be a challenge to look for the silver lining when the two of you seem to be at each other's throat, but keep in mind that changing relationships and building trust takes time. Build on the small victories — they add up in the end.

>> **Focus on what you *can* control:** You can acknowledge if much of the conflict is out of your hands, but don't dwell on it. You won't be able to change some things, but you *can* change plenty of other things. Although you may not be able to control gossip in the workplace, for instance, you can certainly control whether you participate in it.

>> **Get creative:** Some of the best solutions come when you least expect it. Don't put any limits on your brainstorming or you'll focus all your energy on what *won't* work instead of what *may* work. Sometimes the wackiest ideas lead to the most effective outcomes.

>> **Remain future-oriented:** After you both share the events that led to the conflict, you gain very little by revisiting and staying invested in the past. Your answers and solutions will come from a more future-focused conversation about what's possible instead of what didn't work.

WARNING

>> **Allow for saving face:** This conversation may create vulnerabilities in your co-worker; *never* take advantage of that fact. Don't hold him hostage to the process or use information he shares against him. Instead, allow him the opportunity to test and explore ideas in a safe place. You can point out inconsistencies you hear, but do so from a position of curiosity and inquiry rather than as a means to rub it in his face.

>> **Take breaks:** Exhaustion is the enemy of constructive dialogue. Take a few minutes to stretch and refocus. And, reaching a satisfying outcome may take multiple sessions, so allow some time between meetings to gather information, test proposals, or just to see how things go.

Making decisions

Look at the proposals you have on the table, and turn them into specific actions that will give you the best outcomes and will likely hold up over time. Consider

Sitting Down to Talk through the Issues

asking some of the following questions as you both test the boundaries of the proposals:

>> **Does this solution fully address the problem?** Make sure that your agreement speaks to the root of the conflict. If it doesn't, you increase your chances of ending up right back in the same situation that led you to this meeting in the first place.

REMEMBER

All the work you do to uncover values in the course of the conversation is for naught if your solutions don't meet those needs. Values should be your primary consideration when filtering through proposals.

>> **Are these agreements realistic?** It does you no good to craft an agreement that the two of you are happy with if it violates company policy, doesn't account for time restrictions, costs more money than is available, or (gasp!) is illegal. Be sure that agreements fit within the scope of reality.

>> **Can we both support the decisions?** In other words, is your agreement likely to hold up because both of you can get behind the outcome? If your decisions are imbalanced or unsatisfying, one party may end up feeling short-changed and abandoning the agreement.

>> **Are our agreements specific?** Make sure that both of you are clear about expectations and the terms of your agreements. You won't do yourselves any favors by ending your conversation with different interpretations of what you intend to do. That's just a new problem in the making.

>> **Do our agreements have the potential to improve our working relationship?** By having this conversation, you've been able to address and validate each other's emotions and values. If your agreements are designed with these things in mind, your relationship with your co-worker is much more likely to improve over the long term.

Concluding the Discussion

At the end of your discussion, summarize what you've accomplished and what you intend to do next. If you've reached agreements, be specific about follow-through. If you're at an impasse, consider what both of you can do before coming back together. Either way, end your meeting highlighting the progress the two of you made, and be open to continuing the dialogue if necessary. At a minimum, keep in mind that the fact that you both were willing to talk is progress. Good for you!

The following sections help you move beyond the conflict if you and your co-worker have reached a solution. If you're still at an impasse, the final section offers ideas for what to do next.

Capturing the intent

You may want to include a statement about your collective intentions, followed by specific details, such as one of the following:

>> We agree that we want our communication to be respectful and courteous. (Details follow.)

>> Our goal is to leave the past behind and work together to create a positive work environment. (Details follow.)

>> Our desire is to create a safe and comfortable workplace. (Details follow.)

REMEMBER

Focusing on a goal (or intention) can change the way you interact. You may find as time goes by that the details of your agreement are unrealistic, yet both of you are still focused on resolving issues because you have a greater goal in mind and are therefore more apt to come together to work on answers.

Fine-tuning the details

Be specific about what actions are necessary to accomplish the goals you've set. Who will do what? By when? And for how long? Be sure to consider the following:

>> **Third parties:** Your solutions may involve other people. Take into consideration the time required for one or both of you to seek permissions or get buy-in from someone else. If that's the case, have a few alternatives at your disposal rather than relying on a single strategy. If your plan is completely dependent on whether Misha in accounting will allow expense reports to be turned in on the 15th rather than the 10th, you may run into trouble.

>> **Possible conflicts:** Pull out the calendar and look at a significant period of time to determine whether agreements about dates will work. If you agree to meet on the fourth Thursday of every month, what will you do on Thanksgiving? It's better to plan than find yourselves in another disagreement.

>> **Vague language:** Saying, "Oh, we know what that means" may work in the moment, but avoid unnecessary problems by explaining what each other means when you use phrases such as "when time allows" or "as soon as possible."

>> **Attempts versus commitments:** It can be beyond frustrating to hear from a colleague that he'll "try" to make it on time to meetings. Either he's committing to make it on time or he isn't. If he's concerned about traffic, or other projects getting in the way of the meetings, make sure that the agreement contains a contingency plan for such "what if" situations.

>> **Written versus verbal agreements:** Are your agreements straightforward enough to be remembered verbally? Or would it be helpful to jot down the details? Put it in writing as a way to memorialize the spirit and the details. The two of you may think you have an understanding at the time, but memories can (and often do) change over time. A simple email that you write together and send to yourselves may suffice.

Ending without agreements

As hard as you try, you simply may not be able to reach any agreements. Perhaps it's because the dispute is so complex that keeping track of where you are is difficult. Or maybe you've recognized that the two of you are just so far apart in your positions and expectations that you can't see the light at the end of the tunnel.

Whatever the cause, you can do some things to end on a constructive note:

>> **Summarize where you are.** Have a quick discussion about your attempt to resolve the situation. Acknowledge that you've hit a rough spot but that you need to discuss what your next steps are.

>> **Agree to return to the conversation after a period of time.** Though you may not have been successful in this conversation, don't close the door on the possibility of another. After some time has passed and each of you has had a chance to reconsider the situation, you may both find some benefit in returning to the discussion for another shot at it.

>> **Bring in a professional.** You may need some assistance in having this discussion. A neutral third party may be able to shed new light on the situation. For more information on bringing in a professional, see Chapter 4 in Book 2.

REMEMBER

Whatever decisions you end up making about your future, be sure to take a moment and acknowledge each other's efforts. Maybe the two of you haven't seen eye to eye, but at the very least you can thank each other for devoting the time and energy to finding a solution. Doing so also sets the right tone for returning to the work environment while you begin looking forward to whatever next steps you decide to take.

Chapter **4**

Tailoring Your Approach to the Organizational Chart

Finally resolving a conflict in which you're one of the players may be at the top of your to-do list, but having to actually sit down and address it is probably causing a certain amount of anxiety, especially if the person you're in conflict with is a peer on equal footing or an individual higher up than you on the corporate ladder.

After you decide to tackle a one-on-one conversation using the skills in Book 3, Chapters 1 through 3, give some thought to how you'll tailor your approach based upon your audience. Before you jump in with both feet, you need to take into consideration who the other person is in the organization, what title she holds, and what power she has to affect your future. (*Hint:* Everyone has power!)

Who hasn't heard the nightmare story about an employee who treats his co-worker badly only to face her a few years down the road in an interview for his dream job at another company. Ouch! So take care to treat everyone with the same level of professionalism.

This chapter covers the nuances you need to know so you can effectively conduct yourself in a conflict meeting when your role changes from that of manager to peer to subordinate. You find out how to acknowledge hierarchies and still have productive conversations about conflict. You also break down the possible scenarios into altering your style when you have the power and when you may feel a colleague's title trumps yours.

Resolving Issues with Someone You Supervise

You've probably seen the Hollywood images of the dastardly boss who relishes any chance to destroy his underling. That scene can make for good entertainment, but the truth of the matter is that confronting someone you supervise because the two of you are butting heads is never fun. Yet it's a necessary part of being a manager — and when the subordinate is causing more grief than good, you have no other choice. (For even more information on handling complaints and difficult behavior, see Chapters 4 and 5 in Book 2.)

Creating a dialogue

If the employee you're approaching has admitted to a grievous action and you're bound by law or company policy to act according to the letter, then do that. But in other cases, you can turn the need for a disciplinary conversation into an opportunity for a new working relationship.

Punitive meetings are usually a *monologue* in which there's no room to negotiate — the boss talks and the employee listens. Facilitating your own conflict discussion should be a *dialogue* in which you and the employee *both* talk and listen to understand the issues and then work to bring about change — together. Being part of a productive dialogue gives your staff member the opportunity to rise to the occasion, maybe even beyond your expectations, instead of operating out of fear or anger.

TIP

Keep the employee focused on what you'd like her to do instead of allowing her to be interested only in what she needs to *stop* doing to get out of trouble.

To expand a corrective discussion from monologue to dialogue, try the following:

>> **Have a discussion about how long the difficulty has been happening, and express your regret at not having contended with the issues earlier.** This approach gives you the opportunity to demonstrate your desire for

something different moving forward and sends the message that just because you didn't address the issue doesn't mean the actions or behaviors are okay with you. It also sets your expectations for what the two of you will do when other issues arise. Don't fall on your sword if you don't feel you've done anything wrong. Merely saying, "The strain between us has been evident for some time and I should have addressed it sooner" is enough.

>> **Tell your employee that the meeting is a chance for the two of you to come to agreement without having to go through a formal process and without placing documents in his personnel file.** Find language that allows for the spirit of the statement instead of sounding threatening or foreboding. For example, you may say, "I'd really like the two of us to figure this out without having to involve other departments or get formal with anything. I know we have it in us to come up with something that works for everyone."

>> **Communicate that this is an opening for her to create something new and play a part in her own destiny.** The employee doesn't get to call the shots, but you can open the window for her to undo some wrongs, fix sticky situations, and develop as an employee. In essence, if she has the opportunity for a do-over, is she going to take it or continue on the same path? Allow for a choice.

Understanding what the conflicts are usually about

Most conflict conversations with subordinates are usually about interpersonal relationships, work styles, or behaviors. Here's a sampling of common points of contention:

>> **Communication:** An employee's perception of what information should be shared, and when, as well as the way she addresses you can get in the way of healthy supervisor/employee relationship. Tone and body language speak volumes! (Flip to Chapters 2 and 3 in Book 1 for an introduction to these topics.)

>> **Work habits:** Being out of sync with a subordinate's daily work routine — and she with yours — can create a negative environment pretty quickly.

>> **Treatment:** Poor conduct in the workplace mimics life on the outside and runs the gamut from bullies to passive-aggressive manipulators. Just because you're the boss doesn't mean you're immune from becoming an employee's target.

>> **Attitude:** The *way* an employee approaches her work can sometimes be more important than *how* she performs it. And when she snarls, gripes, and blames you for everything that goes wrong, her attitude can be distracting at best and easily lead to damaging consequences.

>> **Gossip:** Your staff talks about you — you know that. But having an employee who spreads rumors, keeps the gossip mill running at full speed, and speaks on your behalf creates a difficult situation. You have to walk a fine line between giving her comments credence and allowing gossip to spread out of control.

>> **Honesty:** Realizing that there's a good chance that the conflict you're having with a subordinate boils down to honesty can be devastating and maybe even a little surreal. Addressing someone's truthfulness can be tricky, complex, and daunting. Giving her a chance to come clean is an important step in getting the relationship back on track.

>> **Insubordination:** Completing disregarding you as a manager, refusing to acknowledge the authority your title holds, or fighting you at every turn may feel like a personal attack — and be one of your greatest challenges as a boss.

Proactively adapting your approach

When you're having a meeting about a conflict you're directly involved in, and that meeting is with one of your subordinates, you need to adapt your approach. Here's how:

>> **Keep in mind that, even though the person you're addressing is below you on the organizational chart and you may not want to give her concerns credence, the two of you are in this conflict together.** Only you, as a duo, can choose to resolve the conflict in a positive way — a way that reflects well in the eyes of other team members and upper management. It takes two to tango and two to untangle; you need each other.

TIP

>> **Put yourself in your employee's shoes and think about how you'd want your boss to approach you about your communication style or your integrity.** Especially if you were in conflict with your boss and had your own opinions about *her* ability to treat others well or *her* attitude toward staff. You'd probably want to speak in private, in a neutral place, with enough time to allow each of you an opportunity to share your concerns and desires about these touchy subjects. You'd probably also want her to have done a little contemplating before she even asked you for a meeting. You'd want her to consider the situation from your point of view, and figure out exactly what she wants so she doesn't "um" and "er" her way through the discussion. Then you'd want her to be prepared to propose solutions that meet both your needs, not just hers. In essence, you would want her to get familiar with Book 3, Chapter 1 so she could be ready for a positive, productive meeting with you and listen to your side of the story.

>> **Set a goal for the discussion that allows the employee to get back on track and motivated to reach team goals.** Keep her focused on what's going well and what needs to be improved. Then be open to hearing what she has to say. If her ideas don't lead to the outcomes you want, you can always be more direct later in the conversation, but initially see whether she has any ideas about resolving whatever problems the two of you are having. Let her be a part of the solution so she has more buy-in and follows through with whatever pledges you make to each other.

>> **Think about your part in the trouble.** Being at odds with a subordinate is frustrating. Oftentimes, putting the entire onus for the problem on the employee is easier than taking personal responsibility — especially if you're genuinely unaware of the negative impact that particular words or actions may have on him.

REMEMBER

Being open to addressing your own behavior helps you create a management style that brings out the best in your employee, instead of resorting to playing the power card and insisting that she do everything your way "because you said so." Don't, however, own up to anything if you don't know what you're supposed to own up to.

FOCUS ON THE TASK, NOT PERSONAL SHORTCOMINGS

Having a discussion in which you have to mesh attitude with tasks, mesh behaviors with team goals, or tie an employee's communication style to end results can get complicated. In one mediation case, a manager was disappointed in his employee's performance and attitude on the job. He had repeatedly told her she wasn't doing her job, to no avail. Each time the employee was asked to perform a task, she would look to her job description and snap back that it wasn't her job, causing the two of them to clash on a daily basis.

During the mediation, the manager listened to the employee's point of view and came to understand how important continuity and security were to her. He realized that she wasn't using the official job description as a way to get out of work — she was using it as something she could count on in an otherwise ever-changing work environment.

When the manager commended her for her performance on the tasks she did well and spoke in terms of the position and its requirements and not her personally, the air in the room changed, the body language between the two became more relaxed, and they jumped into solving problems. Both saw how they could use the document in a positive way, and the manager approached future requests by saying, "This position requires these tasks" rather than saying, "You're not performing up to par."

Establishing a positive environment

Because you're the boss, you have to be a little more mindful of the environment you ask a subordinate into — especially given that the topic of conversation is about the conflict between the two of you. Work to put her at ease. Follow the general process for a one-on-one conflict meeting (refer to Book 3, Chapters 1 through 3), and weave these suggestions in as you go:

>> **Open the meeting by acknowledging the tension or difficulties between the two of you.** She may be expecting you to say something akin to "You need to straighten up, buddy." If, instead, she hears you say, "Donna, the last few weeks haven't been easy for either of us and I'm sure it comes as no surprise that we're having some difficulties," she'll appreciate that you're setting the tone for a positive discussion.

>> **Explain, if relevant, where your work responsibilities may be getting in the way of the relationship.** For example, have you been too busy on a large project to really work with her on addressing smaller conflicts that have now escalated? Have outside factors distracted you from your usual management role?

>> **Own up to your share of the frustrating dynamics in your work relationship.** Perhaps you've played favorites or not given her the same respect you give her co-workers. Or perhaps you've been aware of the problems and let them grow while you considered your next move.

>> **Commit to a new approach.** Tell her you're willing to create a different working relationship that you'd like her to help build. Express what you'll be doing to change it from its current status.

REMEMBER

>> **Be open to her suggestions for a different relationship.** This may be a tough spot in the conversation, but see it through. It's likely your employee sees you differently than you see yourself, so it may be difficult to listen as she ticks off your shortcomings. Resist being defensive and using your position to justify your actions. You may find a nugget of truth in what she's telling you that'll allow you to expand on some of your managerial strategies and help you build your career. Just because the information is coming from an underling doesn't mean it's of no value to you.

>> **Apologize when and if necessary.** Don't say you're sorry for something you didn't do, don't offer a blanket apology with no meaning, and don't think you have to apologize because it's part of the recommended process. But if during your conversation your employee tells you that she feels personally slighted by your behaviors, a sincere apology starts to repair past misgivings and affirms your commitment to building trust. Just keep it simple without adding in complicated excuses. Include a description of what you're sorry for, an assurance that it won't happen again, and a request for an opportunity to make it up to the injured party.

>> **Ask for the changes you'd like to see between the two of you.** Clearly, honestly, and respectfully describe what you'd like to see from her that will change the relationship for the better. Phrase your requests with what you want her to do instead of what you want her to *stop* doing. For example, say, "I'd like you to return from lunch by 1:15 every day" instead of "Stop being late all the time."

TIP

If you think a conflict conversation with a subordinate may be especially difficult because of the nature of the tension or the fact that it's been going on for quite some time, prepare for the meeting by talking it through with a trusted source, such as a supportive supervisor or a human resources representative. Use brainstorming meetings not as a way to strengthen your position but as a way to prepare for the best possible outcome and plan how to track your success. Plus, if you discuss the situation confidentially with HR, you can ask about any boundary issues and get coaching on how to comply with company policies and employment laws.

REMEMBER

You're the one applying a mediation process to the conversation. Your subordinate may not have as much tact or skill when it's time for her to communicate her concerns. Help her by

>> **Modeling as best you can the way you'd like her to speak to you.** In this conversation, lead by example and create a framework for future dialogue.

>> **Reminding her of the meeting's goal.** Do this by refocusing the conversation and her comments toward future actions that you both can control and build on versus staying stuck in the past.

>> **Being mindful of your responses.** How you respond to poor communication on her part can mean the difference between a successful outcome and a firestorm rolling down the hallway. Your ability to defuse aggressive approaches without aggravating the situation allows more information to be shared and will lead to better working agreements. Decide not to react defensively. Think about how she may represent the discussion to others, and create the opportunity for her to speak highly of you and the process.

Keeping your power in check

A smart manager once said that those with real power don't need to remind others. Because you're in a position of power over your employee, you have the muscle to intimidate, push, and demand that she do what you say. You also have the ability to frame your conversation as a productive learning experience for both of you.

Power starts with location. If you're sitting behind your big desk, which sits a good foot above the little chair you've placed her in, you're already setting the tone for a disciplinary meeting even before you utter a word. Your subordinate will appreciate your efforts to level the playing field a bit, so move to a table where the two of you can see eye to eye (literally and figuratively!) or sit on the couches at the café down the street. Create a comfortable environment for both yourself and your employee by applying the tips in Book 3, Chapter 2. Taking responsibility for your actions or admitting that you were affected by her actions is easier in a comfortable, private setting in which phones aren't ringing and other staff aren't knocking on the door with "just a quick question."

Create the emotional space for your employee to be forthcoming about what she's willing to do to repair your relationship. A subordinate commonly acquiesces to her manager's position out of fear. Be sure she's not agreeing just to agree and get it over with. That sort of caving feels good in the moment but has the real probability of enraging you down the line when she doesn't follow through with something she agreed to do. Help her feel comfortable about sharing her point of view by letting her know that you're in this together (at least for now) and you're open to finding a long-term solution. Tell her that the best way to achieve that goal is for the two of you to put an equal amount of input, perspective, and ideas on the table. If appropriate, suggest that there will be no negative consequences when you both come clean about the situation.

REMEMBER

Switch up how you think about power when it comes to subordinates. Start by erasing the idea that power is self-serving. Your power isn't only for your own betterment or just to prove that you're in charge. True, sometimes you have to exert strength in decision-making or perform triage when emergencies arise. But applying your power to a conflict discussion with an employee by exhibiting a "just do it and shut up" stance may cause you to lose her respect and diminish your ability to influence her as time goes by (or when it really counts). Your power is expanded, not eroded, when you make room for her perspective. Using "my way or the highway" as your only approach focuses on the fight for power rather than the problem. Instead, open the floor to your employee and hear her out; it takes a certain level of command to step back and let an employee come up with answers.

Considering nerves

It should come as no surprise to you that, when you call a meeting, your employee will experience some level of worry or stress because she's not sure what to expect, what topics will be covered, or what approach you'll take. And with all the planning and prepping you're doing, you're likely to feel a little nervous yourself!

REMEMBER

Your employee may be a little jumpy, her ability to process information may be slowed, and you can probably expect her to be overly defensive. Her emotions may even take over, which means her ability to reason will be low.

TIP

Try the following tips to keep you both cool, calm, and collected:

» **Slow down the conversation.** Neither of you needs to get every detail of every event that has taken place between the two of you out in the first five minutes of the meeting. Let her know you have as much time as it takes.

» **Ask her to take a deep breath with you.** Taking a moment to breathe and focus at any point in the conflict discussion — as many times as is needed — is a way for you to acknowledge the nerves in the room, and it allows you the chance to calm any anxiousness you may be experiencing yourself.

» **Ask questions to understand her point of view.** If she doesn't seem to be making sense or is putting multiple thoughts together that appear unrelated, ask some open-ended questions so she has an opportunity to clarify her position. Help her focus on one thought at a time without making comments on her scattered approach.

» **Be aware of your own defensiveness.** If your employee's voice is cracking and her hands are shaking to the point where she'd never pass the final exam with the bomb squad, and yet she's able to blurt out her dissatisfaction with the way you organize the schedule, now's not the best time to tell her you think she's dumber than a stump (actually, there's probably never a good time to tell her that!). Instead, go back to the tactic of asking open-ended questions to pinpoint what *about* the scheduling process doesn't work for her.

» **Use language to focus on the goal of the meeting.** Reduce butterflies for your subordinate by being clear about what you want to accomplish and using *we* and *us* language to indicate you're in this together and she doesn't have to come up with all the answers. (See Chapter 1 in Book 1 for more about the importance of pronouns in verbal communication.)

Used correctly, word choices that denote collaboration are far more inviting and allow you to reach the same goal: to improve performance and outcomes. You'll still discuss what she needs to do to accomplish the goals, but the conversation can now be focused on future requirements that she can control. Here are a few examples to get you started:

- Instead of stating, "I wanted to call this meeting so we can discuss how to improve your performance," say, "I'd like us to discuss what's happening with the project and share ideas for reaching the projected goals."

- Instead of saying, "We need to talk about your attitude," say, "I've noticed some tension between us and I'd like to talk about how we can improve our working relationship."

There's a difference, though, between setting the stage that you're working on the conflict together and using *we* in the royal sense of the word, which is condescending. For example, you wouldn't want to say, "We seem nervous" when you really mean "You seem nervous."

Tailoring Your Approach to the Organizational Chart

Addressing Conflict with a Peer

On the surface, it may seem easy enough to treat an equal like an equal, but when you're angry or frustrated, not building armies or creating competitive situations around personal conflicts with another manager can be tough. For the good of your own career aspirations, resist the urge to one-up a peer or compete for the limelight; instead, work to keep a level playing field as much as possible.

How you approach a colleague about an ongoing conflict depends on a number of factors. Take into consideration how well you know her, how often you interact, and how important the working relationship is to you. Use the steps for a one-on-one conflict discussion in Book 3, Chapters 1 through 3, and then adapt your conversation with the following information.

Respecting a peer's position

When you think about all the managers in your organization and what each of you brings to the table, a diverse set of talents and capabilities probably comes to mind. Companies benefit from having dissimilar managers who bring with them a multitude of work and life experiences, varying lengths of service, different educational backgrounds, and a variety of communication styles. Even establishments that are strictly regimented in the way they do business don't have cloned, robotic employees running each of their departments in the exact same way. So when you approach another colleague about a conflict the two of you share, first take into account how the top brass may value her unique skill set — even if her talent isn't quite evident in your eyes!

Consider that you may not truly understand what it takes for her to work with her unique staff and manage the intricacies of her programs, just as she most likely doesn't know what it takes to walk in your shoes. Focusing on your own team's goals and, in the process, inadvertently affecting another team is common. Give her a little latitude by going into a one-on-one conflict discussion with an open mind about her actions and the motivations behind them. She may be protecting her flock just as you're safeguarding yours. Respect her priorities, the pressures of her job, and any deadlines she may have looming, and carve out an adequate amount of time to address fully whatever problems you're having.

REMEMBER

Even though you're a manager, you're not *her* manager. Be mindful of the tone you take, and err on the side of using the same decorum you would use with a superior. If she's in management now, there's always the chance she'll one day manage you, so think beyond your current problems and consider who or where she'll be tomorrow.

Being sensitive to location

Both you and your peer want to retain the respect of your respective staffs and the company at large, so meet in a private place, especially if your disagreements have been public up to this point. Even if you think she's 100 percent wrong, allowing for some dignity and the opportunity to save face demonstrates to the higher-ups that you're capable of having a focused, productive conversation without creating fallout that disrupts others. For general information about choosing a good location for a conflict conversation, see Book 3, Chapter 2.

Preserving the working relationship

If you share the same grade level or sit on the same dotted line on the organizational chart but don't know the other manager well enough to talk with her on an ongoing basis, or if you merely think of her as someone you have to tolerate once or twice a year, you may choose not to bother approaching her with a formal mediation process over a minor disconnect. However, if the two of you getting along matters to those above you (and it probably does), take the time to resolve the conflict in order to eliminate the possibility of any negative talk about you to superiors. Keep your reputation intact.

If you know your peer well, the issues may be easy to address and the two of you can get back on track, keeping your professional relationship undamaged before anyone is the wiser. Having a discussion with someone you consider a friend may actually be tougher — but rest assured that addressing conflict and keeping friendships aren't mutually exclusive. The level of respect you're willing to give her, the amount of interest you show in her proposed solutions, and your combined abilities to tackle the problem without personally destroying each other will serve as an excellent example for your respective teams.

WARNING

A good motivation for addressing difficulties with a peer is to consider who else is talking about your problems. Think about the effect this conflict can have on your career and your reputation, and work to resolve the issue as soon as you can. Don't let the rumor mill take on a life of its own. Gossiping and speculating about dueling managers can be great sport! If the conflict between you and your colleague is affecting even one person in the workplace, you run the risk of the impact being discussed not just horizontally but vertically as well.

You may need to consider whether the topics at hand are ones your peer can even affect. If the two of you decide it's really out of your hands, at the very least express your interest in keeping — and growing — a working relationship with her. That way, when a problem arises that you *do* have some control over, you've set the groundwork to address it with each other without letting it escalate. Similarly, if she can control something and chooses not to (even after your openness to partner with her on solutions), *you* may need to change the way you interact with her instead of asking *her* to change her behavior. Your reputation will be better for it.

Having One-on-One Conversations with Your Boss

You may have heard the story about the employee who tells his buddies that he's going to discuss concerns *about* his boss *with* his boss. The colleagues respond by asking whether his résumé is current and hope he has at least eight months of savings in the bank. In essence, they're saying, "Are you kidding? You can't talk to your manager about his performance issues — it's easier to quit than it is to have *that* kind of conversation!"

REMEMBER

How you attempt to resolve a conflict with your manager may depend on both short-term and long-term goals, though you're encouraged to think more long term than short. Even if you know in your heart of hearts you're just here for the short term, burning a bridge with your boss is never a good idea. Leaving with dignity and knowing that you gave it your best shot will keep you from being an outsider if you ever cross paths again.

Weighing the pros and cons of asking for a meeting

You may want to know the hard and fast rules about when (or when not) to open yourself up to possible repercussions with someone who has the power to end your career with the organization. You have to decide for yourself what you're willing to do. To help you weigh your options, though, here are some points to consider that have been gathered through various mediation cases.

When it may be a good idea to meet

A productive meeting with your boss can be a relief and can motivate you to be the best you can be. But if you're not sure you're ready to tackle a discussion about the conflict between the two of you, here are some motivations for a meeting you may want to consider:

>> **You're determined to stay with the organization.** If you want to establish yourself as an integral part of the management team, your boss can help you do that, so work with her, not against her. If you're so frustrated that you can't imagine respecting her anytime soon, try respecting the position instead.

>> **One or both of you are relatively new to the position, and you got off to a bad start.** Building trust and taking time to share and relate to a new boss while you work through minor conflicts is important. Set the stage for an ongoing relationship by asking her opinion, valuing her input, and offering your insights as well. Show her that you're capable of having honest and respectful conversations when needed. Going to a superior with a concern or complaint is much easier when you've already laid the groundwork.

>> **You're concerned about your reputation.** You may not continue your employment under this manager, but slinking away without making an effort to repair a damaged reputation may not be in your best interest. At the very least, try to clarify your actions and work to clear the air.

>> **Values such as respect and dignity have been violated.** If you're at a point in your life in which you'd like to get more out of your job than just the paycheck and want to focus on what you value — respect, trust, cooperation, and the like — having a conversation may be worth your time. Be genuine in your approach and provide specific examples of how her actions have affected you. Merely saying, "I value respect and I don't feel respected" may leave her a little bewildered and thinking you're just there to complain.

>> **The situation is impossible to overlook and can no longer be ignored.** If this conflict is negatively affecting your quality-of-life and has started to seriously impact personal relationships or is robbing you from sleep, and if you're willing to address it at any cost, then by all means go for it. However, don't ignore the process in Book 3, Chapters 1 through 3, and make sure to be mindful of your approach, tone, and willingness to listen.

When you should consider holding off

Here are some examples of times when you may consider waiting to ask for a meeting to talk about your difficulties:

>> **Tempers are ratcheted up.** When emotions are high, reasoning is low. If you want the best possible outcome, consider your timing. Trying to paint your boss into a corner isn't a good idea — and doing it when steam is pouring out of her ears is a really bad idea.

>> **All the relevant issues and players have yet to be revealed.** If there's a chance the story is still unfolding, hold off a bit until you feel more comfortable with the facts and figures involved.

>> **You're showboating.** Be careful not to fight battles on behalf of others just for the sheer experience. Yes, you want to represent your team or your subordinates as best you can, but having co-workers put you up as the

sacrificial lamb isn't in your best interest. Decide for yourself whether the conflict is really yours and whether you would feel as compelled to take it on if no one else was urging you to do so.

>> **The situation is in flux.** If there's a chance your manager (or you) may be reorganized into a different department or is leaving the company, or if the very issue you're in conflict over may be solved without the two of you, hang tight for a while. Meanwhile, conduct yourself professionally and keep your reputation intact.

>> **You want to deliver a diatribe and aren't ready to hear her out.** Showing up to a meeting to discuss your problems with nothing more than a laminated list of complaints will only frustrate her, especially if you're complaining about things outside of her control. Even if she does have the power to change things and you rush in with directives about what she ought to do, you run the risk of her not being able to see any perspective but her own and, subsequently, asking you to move on. Consider a venting session with a trusted confidante instead.

CHANGING THE STATUS QUO

A new manager was told by his colleagues that a particular vice president was impossible to work with and to avoid her at all cost. All her co-workers had a story about a bad experience they'd had with her, and they did everything they could to steer the new manager away from working with the top brass.

Instead of accepting that his future would be the same as his co-workers' experience, the new manager tried creating respectful working relationships with everyone he met. He went out of his way to greet and smile at those in upper management. Over time, the VP started asking him questions about his projects, and he gave a brief description about a new product or development that his team was focusing on. During a meeting a few months into the job, the VP turned to the manager and asked his opinion of an idea that others were discussing. She had begun to trust him, his ideas, and his insight. The two developed a mutually beneficial working relationship.

Years later, the VP unknowingly made an offhand remark about the manager's team. Because of the existing relationship, the manager didn't feel forced to accept the slight without an explanation. He was able to call a meeting with the executive in which he shared with her how her comment had affected him. She was genuinely surprised and apologized for speaking without thinking. Their relationship was stronger for it, and when the VP left the company a few years later, the manager remained with the knowledge that creating his own lasting relationships was not only a possibility but also a smart move.

Redefining your concept of power

You are not powerless — ever. You may not like some (or any) of your options, but you always have a choice, even with a superior. Here are just a few ways in which you have power in what may seem like an otherwise powerless situation:

» **You have the power to expand your boss's perspective.** When you approach a conversation with your manager believing that you have some knowledge that's beneficial to resolving a conflict, you'll have a more productive discussion than you would if you went in asking what the heck your boss was thinking. Knowledge is power, and there's no way your manager can have a 360-degree view without you. She can benefit from your perspective, so at the very least you have the power to share what you know. And, at a minimum, what you know is how her actions, attitudes, or behaviors have affected you.

» **You have the power not to act like a victim.** If you go into a discussion already defeated and acting the victim of your manager's power, you're essentially creating your own reality. Not acting the victim, though, doesn't mean being arrogant and disrespectful — it means giving some thought to the areas of the conflict you can control and working to improve them.

» **You have the power to tread lightly.** Keep the raging to yourself and, instead, channel your energy and power into doing what's right for you. If after sincere attempts to resolve a conflict with your manager you conclude that the two of you just don't mesh, you may have to rethink the traditional concept of power (refer to the earlier section "Keeping your power in check" for some insight). If letting her think she has won or choosing to defer to her experience and decisions will calm things down, do so in a respectful way. Going over her head or behind her back, or attempting to sabotage her in any way, erodes your integrity. Use your power to control your attitude, your work product, and your destiny.

Making the most of your time

Like you, your boss is busy, so use the time you have with her wisely by following these tips:

» **Let her calendar trump yours, and ask for a block of time that will allow for an in-depth conversation with few distractions.**

» **Have a specific goal in mind for the meeting.** Do you want to address a particular incident, or are you more interested in speaking in general terms about your working relationship? Either way, come prepared with specific examples.

>> **Write down and prioritize what you want your boss to know before you start the meeting.** If you're especially anxious about the conversation, you could forget and miss a great opportunity to talk about what's most important to you.

>> **For every complaint or issue you bring up, suggest at least three (yes, three) solutions.** Coming in with nothing makes you sound like a whiner, coming in with only one solution may be misinterpreted as an all-or-nothing ultimatum, and having only two solutions doesn't show the range of your capabilities. Presenting three solutions opens the door for her to add more, and then the two of you can work together to refine the proposals.

>> **Be the first to apologize if you've erred.** Get your mistakes out in the open, on the table, and out of the way.

>> **Strategically admit your limitations so she can no longer use them against you.** If you're constantly defending yourself, you miss the opportunity to look at a behavior and choose whether to change it. You also miss the chance to build your résumé with educational opportunities.

>> **Graciously accept any apology she makes, and don't hold her to an impossible standard.** She may be above you in rank, but she's still human, and admitting mistakes is tough. Give her some credit if she's able to say she's sorry.

4

Go, Team! Building Influence across Teams and Functions

Contents at a Glance

Chapter **1**

Driving Engagement through Team Development

One of the most important things a successful leader does to foster engagement, particularly in the early stages of a team's development, is to build
trust and relationships. In this case, *trust* is the confidence among team
members that their peers' intentions are good and, consequently, that it's unnecessary to be defensive or wary within the group.

Building trust doesn't just happen. It requires shared experiences over time, evidence of credibility and follow-through, and an in-depth understanding of the
unique attributes of each team member. Ultimately, the team leader and team
members must become comfortable with each other and get to know each other
beyond a purely work-related context.

A great team environment can engage a person as much as a great job can. For
the details on how team dynamics can act as a significant engagement driver (or
a big-time driver of disengagement), read on.

Yay, Team: Identifying Characteristics of an Engaged Team

Most people already know the characteristics of an engaged team. After all, everyone's been on a sports team, a dance team, in Boy Scouts or Girl Scouts, on church committees, or in a playgroup, and has seen what works and what doesn't. In fact, you're probably already so familiar with the characteristics of an engaged team that you may be tempted to just move on to the next section. But in the interest of being thorough, this section spells out the basics.

REMEMBER

Engaged teams demonstrate the following:

>> Accountability

>> Authority

>> Clarity of roles

>> Decisiveness

>> Direction

>> Mutual commitment

>> Open communication

>> Performance

>> Productivity

>> Respect

>> Selflessness

>> Transparency

>> Trust

>> Vision

REMEMBER

But that's not all. For a team to be *truly* engaged, focused, and motivated, it must also demonstrate the following:

>> Accessibility

>> Agility

» Appreciation

» Balance

» Celebration

» Collaboration

» Complementary skills

» Diversity

» Drive

» Empowerment

» External focus

» Flexibility

» Fun

» Morale

» Ownership

» Pride

» Recognition

» Sense of purpose

» Visibility

Unfortunately, many teams don't demonstrate these characteristics. In other words, these words describe what characteristics teams *should* have, not what they *do* have. Why? For one, people get busy, and they don't always feel they have the time to exhibit these ideal behaviors. Additionally, some people are just mistrusting, cynical, or skeptical by their very nature. They're not bad people — these traits are just part of their DNA.

For many, the default is to assume the worst of people, or that people have bad intentions. But perhaps the most significant hallmark of a successful team is that members assume good intentions. In addition, people on successful teams hold each other accountable when they see their teammates demonstrating less-than-ideal characteristics.

Stormin' and Normin': Exploring Tuckman's Stages

In 1965, psychologist Dr. Bruce Tuckman proposed a model of group development that he called "Tuckman's Stages." This model included four stages:

>> **Stage 1:** Forming

>> **Stage 2:** Storming

>> **Stage 3:** Norming

>> **Stage 4:** Performing

To understand this model, consider an example: Suppose you and your partner decide to have a child. Fast-forward nine months, and — boom! — you bring the baby home. You're crazy excited. You're *forming* a family!

Soon, the reality of parenting sets in. The baby won't sleep through the night. He cries all the time. You and your partner are exhausted and increasingly irritated with each other. You haven't had an evening out together, just the two of you, in months. Welcome to the *storming* stage of your new family, or team.

Eventually, the baby starts to sleep. He figures out how to soothe himself, so there's not so much crying. You've found a few babysitters to step in so you and your partner can have some time alone. You settle into a routine. This is your team's *norming* stage.

Before you know it, your baby is 2 years old. Although some challenges remain (they don't call them the "terrible twos" for nothing), things have settled down. Your "team" is *performing* quite well! In fact, having forgotten how painful the storming stage was, you're even thinking of having another child. When you do, you'll be right back at the forming stage, and the cycle will start again.

Of course, growing families aren't the only "teams" that follow Tuckman's Stages. These stages also apply to work teams and to the lifecycle of companies. And although this example showcases what happens to a "team" when new people are added, the same cycle occurs any time a significant event occurs, such as an acquisition, starting a new project, converting to a new system, organizational changes, changes to company leadership, or the departure of team members. (Just ask any parent whose child goes off to college about how their "team" has changed!) These days, the one thing you can count on is that change is a constant. Understanding Tuckman's Stages can help leaders ensure that team members stay engaged amidst change.

REMEMBER

All teams must go through the forming, storming, and norming stages to get to the performing stage. If you think you've skipped a stage, look a little more closely. Teams rarely skip stages. The speed at which a team progresses through these stages will depend on the size of the change, the experience of the team members, the experience of the leader, and how engaged the team is as a whole. Strong, engaged teams will find ways to accelerate through the stages.

This simple but powerful team-development model has stood the test of time, and continues to be used even today by academics and consultants in classrooms and workshops across the world. The key points to keep in mind about Tuckman's Stages are that they're a natural aspect of team development, they should be anticipated, and in many ways they're part of a virtuous cycle.

The forming stage

Teams, whether at work or at home, always begin in this stage, and will return to this stage whenever a significant change occurs — for example, when people are added to the team, when members of the team leave, or when a new project starts.

In the forming stage, particularly on new teams, team members tend to exhibit the following behaviors:

>> **They're fired up to be part of the team, and they're eager for work ahead.**

>> **They have some anxiety and uncertainty.** They're wondering things like, "What's expected of me?", "How will I fit in?", or "How will my performance measure up to others?"

>> **They may be reticent to ask questions and share ideas.** During this stage, politeness often prevails. On the surface, team members will appear cooperative, and there will be lots of face-to-face agreement. Often, however, there are unspoken opinions and silent disagreements.

>> **They may test the situation and each other.**

>> **Their commitment and motivation levels are high.** Productivity levels, however, are merely moderate, as people are still learning the goals, the roles, and what's expected.

TIP

To expedite the forming stage, the team leader must focus on providing direction and structure and building relationships and trust. This kickoff process involves the following:

>> Defining and clarifying team and individual goals, roles, expectations, and practices.

>> Discussing past practices to determine what worked and what didn't.

>> Building relationships and rapport by ensuring that the team spends time together and engaging in team-building activities.

>> Establishing team norms (that is, the "rules of the tavern" and best practices for communicating, making decisions, and so on).

>> Assessing strengths and weaknesses of team members and identifying ways they can help each other improve.

>> Articulating your management philosophy, your strengths, and your weaknesses, and asking the team to provide ongoing feedback.

For maximum engagement, team leaders must help team members understand and manage transition and change. That includes familiarizing team members with the four stages of team development (forming, storming, norming, and performing). This will help team members prepare for what's coming and deal with the inevitable highs and lows. Team leaders must also teach and model the skills and behaviors they want to see on their teams, and recognize those skills and behaviors when they see them.

REMEMBER

Whether you're the leader of a new group, your existing team has "inherited" new members due to an organizational restructuring, or you've just joined the company in a supervisory position, the members of your team are depending on you to provide direction, structure, and support. They'll be watching you closely and taking their cues from your leadership. Certainly, you want your new group to become a cohesive team — to perform at high levels and be highly engaged from the start. The trick to achieving this is to take charge with a strong kickoff process early on.

The storming stage

Over time, teams will move from the forming stage to the storming stage. Why? Because as team members become more familiar with each other, they become comfortable enough to state their true feelings and beliefs, which inevitably leads to disagreements.

During this stage, conflict is the watchword. Think: *Hell's Kitchen* with Gordon Ramsay. Team members may experience some of the following:

>> They may discover that the team doesn't live up to early expectations.

>> They may feel frustrated, confused, or angry about the team's progress or process (or lack thereof).

>> They may react negatively to the team leader and to other members of the team. Power struggles may ensue.

>> They may have conflicts and disagreements about goals, roles, and responsibilities, expressed openly or behind the scenes.

>> Commitment, morale, and productivity may take a downturn.

TIP

As frustrating as this stage may be for team members and leaders alike, keep in mind that it's OK to storm. In fact, it's healthy! What's *not* healthy is to remain in this stage indefinitely. To accelerate movement from the storming stage to the norming stage, leaders should legitimize the conflict to ensure that it's constructive. That means doing the following:

>> Bringing conflict out into the open.

>> Acknowledging with the team that storming is natural, inevitable, and essential to the growth of the team.

>> Creating forums and encouraging open discussion of issues, even if it's directed at you as the leader.

>> Establishing norms for constructive discussion and debate.

>> Reinforcing positive conflict-resolution efforts.

>> Balancing individual needs with team needs.

For more on resolving conflict, see Books 2 and 3.

In addition, team leaders should revisit and clarify goals, roles, and expectations. (Note that teams may move more quickly through storming if the tasks in the forming stage were done well.)

The norming stage

In the norming stage, things begin to smooth out. Turbulence subsides, a sense of calm prevails, and commitment and productivity take a turn for the better.

For team members, this stage is characterized by the following:

>> They begin to resolve the discrepancies between their expectations and the reality of the team experience.

>> They have an increased understanding of accountabilities and expectations.

>> They develop self-esteem, as well as trust and confidence in the team.

>> They become more comfortable expressing their "real" ideas and feelings.

>> They start using "team language" — that is, saying "we" rather than "I."

TIP

The danger inherent in this stage is complacency. Teams become so comfortable that they just stay here. To nudge team members to the next stage (performing), leaders must focus on encouraging participation, the development of norms, and continuous improvement. That means doing the following:

>> Being less directive and more participatory.

>> Collectively reviewing team norms, processes, and practices and adjusting them based on what's working and what isn't working.

>> Encouraging and giving recognition for taking initiative, taking risks, creative problem solving, and seeking and acting on feedback.

In addition, the team leader should continue to build trust and relationships through personal interactions and team building.

The performing stage

Ah, the performing stage . . . the sweet spot of group development. In this stage, life is good. Members feel excited to be part of the engaged, high-performing team. That's not to say there's no conflict or disruption, just that the team has set rules for handling it.

During this stage, team members

>> Are focused on team versus individual results.

>> Understand and take advantage of team members' strengths, valuing their differences.

>> Exhibit high levels of confidence.

>> Demonstrate a sense of true collaboration and shared team leadership.

>> Demonstrate high levels of commitment, morale, and productivity.

>> Can function at a high level, even absent of the team leader.

Not surprisingly, people on teams in this stage are hesitant to introduce change, thereby reverting to the forming stage. After all, if it ain't broke, don't fix it, right? Besides, moving through all those stages can be painful! But introducing change is a must. Otherwise, the team risks becoming complacent, stale, or overconfident.

THIS IS THE END: WHAT TO DO WHEN A TEAM ENDS

Some teams will dissolve after a period of time — for example, when their work is completed (such as a project team or task team, which is typically temporary) or when the organization's needs change (such as in the case of a reorganization or integration). When this happens, you may find that team members have various feelings about the team's impending dissolution. They may also exhibit varied emotions and behaviors, such as anxiety (due to uncertainty about their new role or future responsibilities), sadness or a sense of loss, or satisfaction about the team's accomplishments. Some may lose focus, causing productivity to drop. Others may find focusing on tasks at hand to be an effective response to their sadness or sense of loss.

To help usher team members through the termination of a team, team leaders should

- Acknowledge team members' feelings and address their concerns ("What's going to happen to me?") in a straightforward and caring way.

- Complete any deliverables and achieve closure on remaining team work.

- Capture "lessons learned" as a team and pass them on to a new team leader or sponsor for future use.

- Have some kind of closing activity or event that acknowledges and celebrates the contributions and accomplishments of individuals on the team, as well as the team as a whole.

REMEMBER

It's far better to spur change voluntarily than to be put in the position of having to react to an unplanned alteration in course. If you don't believe this, take a moment to ponder successful sports franchises. These organizations recognize that they must continually cycle back to the forming stage by bringing in new players, coaches, and/or systems, even when they're winning. The same goes for companies. Kodak and Polaroid may have owned the print film business while in the performing stage, but they were ultimately toppled by competitors who smartly re-formed around digital photography.

TIP

Clearly, a key task for team leaders in this stage is to be on the lookout for new challenges, and to guard against complacency and groupthink. At the same time, they must work to enhance the skills of team members, and inspire more interdependence, shared ownership, and accountability for results. That means doing the following:

>> Giving people more responsibility and delegating some of your tasks to develop team members' technical, business, and leadership skills.

>> Providing more feedback and additional "big picture" information to help team members make links to the larger organization.

>> Injecting new perspectives into the team via transfers in or out, promotions, new hires, external expertise, market intelligence, and benchmarking.

>> Continuing to celebrate individual and team successes.

Putting it all together

Need a little assistance assimilating all that information about Tuckman's Stages? Table 1-1 should help.

TABLE 1-1 **Characteristics of Tuckman's Stages**

Element of the Team	Forming	Storming	Norming	Performing
Member behavior	Anxiety Search for structure Silence Being reactive to the leader Superficiality Being overly polite	Increased testing of norms Fight-or-flight behavior Attacks on the leader Polarization of the team Power struggles Hostility or silence Failure to commit to action plans	Effort to get along Constructive conflict Realistic norms and guidelines Functional relationships Acceptance of each other and of the leader Caring, trust, and enjoyment	Cohesiveness Conflict management Active listening Shared leadership Creative problem solving A focus on the here and now
Attitude about leadership	Being accepted or tested by members Tentativeness	Power struggles Jockeying for position or control	General support Acknowledging differences	Distributing leadership among members by expertise
Decision making	Domination by active members	Fragmentation Deadlocks Team leader or the most powerful or loudest team member making decisions	Decisions being made based on individual expertise Decisions often being made by the leader in consultation with team members	Decisions being made by consensus Teams doing whatever it takes collectively or individually to make decisions

Element of the Team	Forming	Storming	Norming	Performing
Climate	Caution Feelings of suppression Low conflict Few outbursts	Subgrouping Overt or covert criticism Disagreements between subgroups	Teams dealing with differences Members opening up and sharing true feelings Straight confrontation	Shared responsibility Open expression Prompt resolution of disagreements
Task functions and major issues	Getting the team started, establishing identity Developing common purpose Orientation Providing structure Building trust Managing transitions	Questioning identity Managing increased conflict Openly confronting issues Increased participation Testing of group norms Increased independence from leader	Establishing realistic guidelines and standards Team responsibility Cooperation and participation Decision making Confronting problems Shared leadership Quality and excellence Team assessments	Progress toward goal True collaboration Monitoring of accomplishment Critiquing of process Assessment of interactions Avoidance of "groupthink" Satisfaction of members' personal needs
Leadership roles	Reduction of uncertainty Setting of goals Clarification of purpose Drawing out questions Letting members get to know each other Modeling expected behavior	Legitimizing conflict Examining own response to conflict Reinforcing positive conflict-resolution efforts Acknowledging conflict as essential for change Not becoming more authoritarian	Encouraging norm development Developing goals Using consensus Redirecting questions Developing positive listening skills	Maintaining team skills Maintaining technical and interpersonal skills Providing feedback on group's effectiveness Assisting in gaining more meaning from meetings

From a Distance: Leading Teams from Afar

If you're charged with leading a team from afar, you'll need some special competencies. Most notably, you'll need the ability to manage boundaries and barriers. Staff members in remote locations face significant obstacles — logistical and otherwise — which impede and even prevent success. You have to be prepared to help your team navigate those obstacles. In addition, you'll need to master technology for communication and collaboration, such as Microsoft SharePoint, Skype, extranets, and of course, email. (Note that this includes understanding email etiquette.) Finally, particularly if your staff members are located in other regions or countries, you'll need a strong dose of cultural awareness.

TIP

Here are a few tricks to keep up your sleeve:

>> **Focus on relationships first, and cultural and language differences second.** Get to know your employees. Do you know their family situations? Do you know the names of each employee's spouse and kids? Do your remote employees feel you care about them as people? *Note:* You can't be an empathetic boss without knowing your employees personally.

>> **Develop a way to share information.** When managing remote or virtual employees, technology is the great equalizer. Make sure remote employees have an opportunity to share their information with the team via SharePoint, Skype, webinars, and so on. The idea is that they should feel like they're in the room with you.

>> **Consider time zones and share the associated sacrifices equally.** If you're leading people in a different region or country, be sensitive to their time zone. Shift calls so they aren't always the one whose phone rings at 11 p.m. Rotating time-zone hardships is a simple way to reinforce that you're sensitive to the work–life balance.

>> **Identify communication preferences for team and individuals.** Some individuals and/or teams may be more visual by nature, so using tools to share documents may be better than describing them over a conference call.

>> **Create a team-level communication protocol and stick to it.** This protocol might outline how communication will be handled, when team members can expect communications, and what to expect on an ongoing basis.

>> **Be accessible.** Although you do need to set some boundaries if there are time-zone differences, you have to make yourself more available than you

might if you were right down the hall. Remote employees are prone to feeling isolated. If, when they reach out, they get the "I'm too busy right now" treatment, their sense of isolation will increase exponentially.

>> **Develop ways for your remote employees to virtually "stop by."** Have a virtual open-door policy and encourage your remote employees to "swing by" when they need to chat, have a question, want to check in, and so on. Confirming that it's okay to text or instant-message you whenever and wherever will minimize their loneliness. Texting is often a great "check-in" communication tool because it's quick and informal and happens in real-time.

>> **Make sure remote employees have the opportunity to participate in company initiatives.** These include surveys, task teams, meetings, socials, holiday parties, and so on. Be aware of the "out of sight, out of mind" phe-nomenon that exists with remote employees. Camaraderie is a significant engagement driver — and even more so with remote employees, who don't get the benefit of the "water cooler" companionship that in-house workers experience. Effective remote managers go out of their way to include their remote employees on intradepartmental initiatives and special projects.

>> **Communicate more often, and in different modes.** Send frequent informational emails, and regularly keep in touch with remote team members with phone calls or other forms of communication.

Hit Me with Your Best Shot: Conducting a High-Impact Team Workshop

Picture this: You've just been asked to lead a major, high-profile, long-term proj-ect that requires your staff to work closely with employees from other departments and outside consultants. Of course, you could try to engage these myriad dynamic forces via email and teleconferences, but there's a better way: a high-impact team (HIT) workshop.

A HIT workshop is designed to align and engage your employees to work toward a common goal. It involves bringing together all the key players, face-to-face if possible, for a one-and-a-half-day gathering. This highly interactive and engaging workshop mixes team dynamics analysis, process improvement, com-munication networks, group problem solving, action planning, and of course, fun!

To conduct a HIT workshop, follow these steps:

1. **Clarify the current state of the business and/or project (that is, "Where we are now?").**

   This step involves a thorough discussion of the key metrics of the business and/or project.

2. **Have breakout discussions on where the business or project should go (that is, "Where are we going?").**

   This phase should weave in discussion of current impediments and strengths.

3. **Construct a high-performing action plan (that is, "How we will get there?").**

   This action plan, along with an implementation strategy, should be created and agreed to by participants in the workshop.

TECHNICAL STUFF

Experience shows that an individual or team that develops its own action plan is overwhelmingly more likely to follow through on the actions than when the action plan is assigned.

Throughout the workshop, apply team-building activities liberally. Opt for activities that are focused on building the competencies required of engaged teams.

A well-structured process like the one in a HIT workshop pays countless dividends, including the following:

>> Improved communications, which expedites work and work processes.

>> A common sense of direction, established through mutual goals and expectations.

>> The ability to hit the ground running and avoid costly startup mistakes.

>> Practice working together in a controlled setting.

>> Group interaction, and getting to know one another.

>> A level of comfort and joint ownership of solving a common problem.

IN THIS CHAPTER

» Identifying the "great communication fissure"

» Establishing two-way communication and a protocol

» Maximizing communication tools

» Communicating change and engagement efforts

» Being aware of some communication don'ts

Chapter **2**

Improving Organizational Communication

S aying communication is "important to engagement" is a little like saying Mardi Gras is "kind of exciting." It's an understatement. There's no doubt about it: Communication helps drive most successful new company initiatives, ideas, and ventures. Unfortunately, it's also at the root of many organizational failures, boss–employee issues, and problems with disengagement.

This chapter focuses on the importance of communication both generally and in your engagement efforts, and the obstacles to achieving excellent communication. It also provides simple, practical methods for cascading the company message from upper management down through the ranks in ways that are clear, concise, and compelling — and that will result in higher engagement, and therefore higher discretionary effort, on the part of staff.

Mind the Gap: The Great Organizational Communication Fissure

In many organizations, there is a disconnect between leaders and employees. This fissure is at the root of many communication problems in organizations today. For management, the disconnect centers around the question "Why aren't employees onboard?" For employees, the question is, "What are those idiots doing now?" This disconnect is often a key factor in disengagement.

A 5K running race may remind you a lot of how information is communicated in some organizations. The CEO and other executives hear the starting gun — or, in many cases, are the ones firing it. Just like the elite runners at the front of the pack, leadership is at the front of the communication pipeline. When an important change is communicated, leadership has time to weigh alternatives, debate options, and digest the decision.

The rank and file employees, relegated to the back of the field, are not afforded the same depth of background, and may be unaware of how much time leadership has invested in the decision. When communication about a decision or change finally reaches them, employees inevitably wonder, "What are they thinking?!" They don't hit the ground running; they merely shuffle forward. Then, when employees are hesitant to jump onboard, leaders lose patience. They ask, "Why don't they get it?!"

Unfortunately, this communication pattern results in a lack of alignment. After all, if a company neglects to articulate a clear vision, it can hardly expect its employees to invest more than the bare minimum. In one oft-quoted study, conducted by Robert S. Kaplan and David P. Norton in 2001, a mere 7 percent of employees reported that they fully understood their company's business strategies and what was expected of them in order to help achieve the company's goals.

REMEMBER

Companies that successfully engage their employees don't allow this to happen. Employers or leaders who articulate a clear vision and strategy will find that employees will help them reach their goals quickly and efficiently. Indeed, according to research by Dale Carnegie Training, employees indicated that working in a company that encourages open communication with senior leadership has a significant impact on their level of engagement. To cultivate an engaged culture, open and consistent communication must become part of the air your employees breathe.

"THE MATRIX IS EVERYWHERE": COMMUNICATING IN A MATRIX WORLD

Does this sound familiar? "I have one boss who tells me one thing, and another boss who tells me something else!" Or, "Who reports to whom around here?" Or, "How do I get anything done when my team members all report to different people?" Or, "No one knows who is responsible anymore!" If so, you're likely living in the matrix. No, not the one in the movie. Instead, you're dealing with a matrix organization, in which employees may report to two or more bosses. For example, say you work as a cost accountant. You may report to a member of your regional leadership team, but also to someone in the corporate finance department.

How effectively a matrix organization functions often depends on how healthy the communication channels are between the key players. To ensure clear communication in a matrix organization, keep these points in mind:

- Establish the "rules of communication" when the matrix is first established or when a new participant enters the matrix.

- Establish a schedule in which the three parties will meet to discuss goals, objectives, and so on.

- Everyone involved should make it a habit to copy all other parties on messages to ensure everyone is in the loop.

- Decide early on which boss will communicate key organizational changes. This person should also take the lead in performance appraisals.

Establishing Two-Way Communication

Communication starts at the top, with the CEO, president, or other appropriate executive. But in order for clear communication to become part of your corporate culture — and make no mistake, this is absolutely critical for engagement to take hold — there must be a process by which the message is cascaded down and reinforced by every level of management. The goal is to align what the CEO or other executives say with what line managers tell their direct reports. This takes time, repetition, and leveraging of available communication options.

In a *cascade communications strategy* (sometimes known as a *waterfall communications strategy*), the buck stops (or, more precisely, the message starts) with upper management. But the responsibility for communication is shared across every level, from the region to the district to the office to the line manager. No one individual, committee, or department should be placed in charge of disseminating information throughout the company (although there are many professionals who are highly skilled at greasing the gears of communication and finding creative ways to broadcast and publicize individual messages). The key is to make every leader a message ambassador, and every management level responsible for informing the next.

Eventually, this will happen as effortlessly as water pouring over a waterfall. But it will require some initial effort on your part, and ongoing vigilance. Keep these points in mind:

>> **Identify your communications ambassadors.** Your initial recruits will be employees with management responsibility, and their duties will include transmitting company messages. Let them know that their performance in this arena will be evaluated — and follow up on that promise.

>> **Enlist other engaged employees.** Provide a forum for their input and give them well-defined communications tasks within their peer groups (and beyond, if appropriate).

>> **Supply direct channels and appropriate tools.** Every important message from the top should be accompanied, at minimum, by general talking points for managers at all levels, an (anticipated) FAQ, and a means by which unanticipated questions will be answered and publicized.

>> **Scale your tools to fit the task at hand.** If a large-scale announcement or rollout needs to be communicated, look closely at the available vehicles and explore new options if necessary. Engage your communications ambassadors to find the most appropriate communication methods for your staff. And don't overlook the need to customize your communication approach depending on the audience. Your Millennial staff members require a very different communication approach than your Boomers. (See Book 5 for more information on working with different generations.)

If you're worried that communication will add to the workload of already-harried line managers, the answer is to communicate effectively with *them*. Equip them with the information and tools they need to be effective message ambassadors, and let them know precisely what is expected: alignment with, and wide and frequent distribution of, the top-line message.

The bottom line? According to research by Dale Carnegie Training, employees are more highly engaged when their immediate manager communicates openly with them, recognizes their contribution, and gives feedback and encouragement that enhance their job performance.

IMPLEMENTING INNOVATION BOXES

Here's one great idea that, by itself, will make your read of this book worthwhile: Eliminate suggestion boxes. See, suggestion boxes often lead to complaints. In other words, people don't use them to suggest ways to improve your business; instead, they use them to carp about receiving too many emails, criticize the cafeteria fare, or grumble about having too many layers of management. Instead, provide innovation boxes. You'll quickly find that instead of receiving complaints, you'll wind up with innovative ideas and suggestions for improving processes.

To close the loop, assemble a cross-sectional group of junior-level to midlevel employees to evaluate ideas from the innovation box and send the best ones up the ladder. Assuming the organization's leadership actually listens to these ideas and implements them when possible, this can be a great engagement driver! And in time, membership on the committee will be seen as a great honor.

In addition to communication waterfalls for top-down communication, you also need *communication fountains* — that is, vehicles to propel communication from the bottom up. For engagement to truly take hold, employees must feel comfortable communicating upward.

Generally, this type of communication will come in one of two forms:

>> **Questions:** Managers at all levels must answer questions in such a way that the overarching message is reinforced. If the answer is beyond a manager's knowledge, he must push the question to the next level while assuring the questioner that an answer is forthcoming. (Of course, it's important to deliver on this promise. The responsibility lies with the manager who has posed the question to his superiors.)

>> **Feedback:** Whether it's positive or negative, managers must be provided a means by which to funnel employee input to the people responsible for processing and, if warranted, incorporating it. Employee engagement surveys, conducted biannually, with a pulse survey in the alternative years, are one mechanism to ensure that this happens. Communicating those results back is the way to complete the loop. Companies that establish a continuous feedback loop between themselves and their employees virtually guarantee alignment. (Chapter 3 in Book 5 has more about feedback.)

REMEMBER

Communication cannot be one way, and calls for feedback must be genuine. A company where employees feel comfortable participating in a dialogue with anyone, anytime, however senior, is a company well on its way to an engaged culture. If individuals are afraid to approach higher-ups with questions or feedback, or if they sense that their questions and feedback are not being addressed at the appropriate level, engagement will suffer. Moreover, having good feedback mechanisms in place is the only way to ensure that any engagement initiatives you've undertaken are the right ones, are progressing, and are embraced and supported by management and staff.

Building a Communication Protocol

There isn't a manager around who says they shouldn't communicate openly and frequently with their employees — but often they don't. See, for many managers, communication falls in the category of "should do" rather than "must do." And when we're busy, "must do" trumps "should do" every time.

That's where a communication protocol comes in. A *communication protocol* is a formal process that outlines the types of information to be communicated to an organization, as well as identifying the person(s) responsible for communicating particular topics. The protocol also outlines the audience, frequency, and suggested communication vehicles.

A communication protocol, which should be displayed in all common areas such as lobbies and conference rooms and distributed to all new hires, ensures that communications align with the company's key strategic priorities, whether they be related to engagement or some other initiative. As importantly, the protocol represents a set of company commitments to employees. These include the following:

>> Leaders will be held accountable for fulfilling their communication responsibilities, and will be assessed on the effectiveness and timeliness of their communication.

>> Employees will receive regular updates about the progress, initiatives, and changes that affect them.

>> Most important from an engagement perspective, each communication milestone provides opportunities for employees to ask questions, contribute ideas, and give or receive feedback.

In turn, the expectations for employees are clear. All employees are responsible for sharing information and giving feedback to help the company reach its goals, thereby reinforcing the desire for employees to communicate "up" and bolstering the mutual commitment shared by employer and employee.

There are several benefits to implementing a communication protocol. A communication protocol does all the following:

>> Defines communication expectations for both employees and leaders.

>> Builds consistency in communicating the firm's mission, vision, values, and strategy.

>> Creates alignment with employees at all levels.

>> Builds in circular communication. Circular communication includes communication between those in a traditional hierarchy, such as the boss and subordinate, as well as communication between business units and departments and communication that leverages task teams and focus groups. In a healthy circular communication culture, you're also including 360 feedback assessments (which combines self-review by an employee with anonymous feedback from those surrounding the individual, including peers, supervisors, direct reports, and even clients), customer feedback, and feedback within the matrix relationship.

>> Ensures shared accountability, from top to bottom.

>> Helps ensure that messages are communicated 13 times, which is the number of times some experts believe an employee needs to hear something to absorb it.

>> Helps to leverage different communication venues and tools — for example, town hall meetings, emails, vlogs (video blogs), department meetings, and so on. (You can find out more about these venues and tools later in this chapter.)

>> Helps connect all levels of your organization with your brand.

To build a communication protocol, you need a cross-sectional team of executives (preferably including the "top dog") along with a cross-sectional group of key influencers, or *connectors*. The first thing this team should do is assemble a draft of the communication protocol. (This will take the group anywhere from two to eight hours.) Figure 2-1 shows a template for teams in this phase to help guide them in their efforts.

TIP

When drafting the protocol, the team should consider the following:

>> How can we build in the communication of metrics that are key to our strategic plan (for example, growth, profit, employee engagement, customer service, quality, and so on)?

>> How can we ensure that staff are given an opportunity to communicate up?

>> How can we build in redundancy in messaging between each level?

Message	Communicator	Audience	Frequency

FIGURE 2-1:
A communication protocol template.

© John Wiley & Sons, Inc.

When the draft is complete, it should be sent to those who report up through the CEO (and perhaps their direct reports as well) to obtain additional input. This key step will also help you get buy-in. Once the input has been received and appropriated, the protocol can be finalized (see Figure 2-2).

	Message	Communicator	Audience	Frequency
Day-to-Day Operations	Strategic plan Regular business reporting	CEO	All	Monthly Quarterly Annually
	Strategic plan Strategic activities Regional news Performance to date	Regional manager	Regional staff	Monthly Semi-annually
	Strategic activities Office news Performance to date Information sharing	Office managers and managing directors	Office/department staff	Quarterly
	Strategic activities Department news Performance to date Information sharing	Department manager/ team leader	Department staff	Weekly
	Project news and updates Technology and innovation sharing	Project managers	Project team	Weekly
Corporate/ Strategic Direction	Strategic plan	CEO	Executive committee	Bi-monthly
	Strategic plan Market updates	CSO	All	Semi-annually
	Market updates Strategic actions Information sharing	Market/service leaders	Market/service practitioners	Quarterly
	Strategic plan Senior strategic direction Business health	CEO/operations group chair Corporate leaders (finance, legal, HR, IT, marketing, facilities)	Operations group	Quarterly
Governance	Governance issues	Board of directors	Stockholders	Annually

FIGURE 2-2:
Sample communication protocol.

© John Wiley & Sons, Inc.

A WORD ON CHARISMA

Of course, some people are just naturally better at communicating than others. For every charismatic Steve Jobs at the helm, there may be ten more introverted Bill Gateses. This is not to say that charisma is the be-all and end-all of great leadership. Indeed, there are plenty of examples in every field — even politics — where quiet brilliance and a keen business sense has served better than any amount of charm or eloquence. Still, in successful enterprises of all sizes, more often than not, leaders who know communication is not their strong suit still find ways to leverage their talent to disseminate big messages at all levels.

Smart leaders know that what they themselves may not be able to articulate in the most compelling way can gain power as it filters through the ranks of the passionate. All that being said, while certain people are better communicators than others, this does not diminish anyone's responsibility to communicate. Those for whom consistent, frequent, and genuine communication do not come easily must be given the tools to succeed — and held accountable regardless of their personal preferences or comfort zones.

WARNING

With a finalized protocol in hand, the team's next move is to build a plan to roll out the protocol. This rollout should involve significant fanfare to generate excitement. The launch of a communication protocol is great news, and will be embraced by employees as, to quote Martha Stewart, "a good thing." That being said, you'll likely meet resistance from middle management, who will likely view the protocol as "one more thing to do that takes time." To overcome this roadblock, educate them on the protocol's benefits as well as on how to be an engaged participant in the protocol. Over time, they'll see that the administrative effort involved in maintaining a robust communication protocol will be offset by the gain in their employees' alignment and engagement.

Maximizing the Various Communication Tools

Never before in the course of human history have we had more communication tools available to us. Where before we were limited to grunting and sharing our thoughts via cave paintings, now we have any number of ways to express ourselves. This section covers the myriad communication vehicles available to you, and helps you determine which vehicle is most likely to engage your employees.

Face to face

At the end of the day, nothing beats good, old-fashioned, face-to-face communication. Why? Because face time eliminates assumptions, allows for body language (see Chapters 2 and 3 in Book 1 for an introduction), and enables real-time give and take.

This medium is almost always the most effective way to communicate. It's especially important for receiving feedback, performing annual employee reviews, and resolving conflicts. And it's the *only* way to communicate when delivering bad news. (There are plenty of horror stories out there of managers firing employees via a voice mail or e-mail. Ouch!) Face-to-face communication is also a wonderful way to share good news. One person received a bonus check accompanied only by a yellow sticky note on the envelope with the word *Thanks* on it. Talk about an opportunity lost!

Engaged managers can leverage face-to-face communication by implementing an open-door policy, engaging in drop-bys, having face-to-face meetings with direct reports, and planning periodic face-to-face meetings with remote or telecommuting employees. Face-to-face meetings can be one-on-one, with the entire team, or in a town-hall format, and can be ad hoc, formal, scheduled, and/or unscheduled.

One-on-one meetings

One-on-one meetings are a time for you to focus on an employee and his or her needs. As such, you should follow the 80/20 rule: Listen 80 percent of the time, and talk 20 percent of the time. To ensure the employee doesn't feel she's being given short shrift, schedule more time than expected. For example, if you think the meeting will take 30 minutes, put 45 minutes on your calendar. And of course, make sure there are no distractions. Meet in a private room (an office or a meeting room with a door), and turn off your phone and computer. If time and logistics allow, perhaps meet for lunch off-site. (Check out Book 2 for the full scoop on conducting important conversations.)

TIP

For best results, prepare an agenda beforehand, with objectives for the meeting. Key topics may include the employee's roles and responsibilities on the team, performance goals, strengths and challenges, concerns and issues, and professional development and opportunities.

Team and department meetings

For many organizations, weekly or biweekly team and department meetings are the communication bloodline for employees. They help establish department expectations and goals, and provide an opportunity to celebrate good news and recognize staff. (See the nearby sidebar plus Chapter 2 in Book 2 for more information.)

If possible, these meetings should be face to face. If you have remote employees, make sure they participate, even if only virtually. If possible, schedule time for remote employees to occasionally attend in person.

REMEMBER

On the topic of virtual meetings, be aware that these lack the visual cues found in face-to-face meetings, even when conducted using such visual services as Skype. (Sure, people may be able to see your face, but your body language may be hidden.) As such, they require more concentration when listening, more care when speaking, and more rules for structure.

TIP

A great way to boost engagement at department meetings is to rotate the meeting "chair" among department employees. The meeting chair establishes the agenda (with guidelines from the boss, of course), runs the meeting, and captures minutes and actions. In addition to boosting engagement, this is a great way to evaluate the leadership capabilities of staff and to foster innovation.

MEET MARKET: TIPS FOR RUNNING A GREAT MEETING

Do you feel like your organization holds too many meetings? Perhaps. But maybe it's not the *quantity*, but the *quality* of these meetings that's suspect. To ensure your meetings are productive and engaging, keep these points in mind:

- **Stick to the schedule.** Start and end meetings on time, and make sure they don't last more than two hours — but preferably one hour. To stay on track, use meeting time for discussions, not presentations. In addition, keep conversations concise and quick.

- **Prepare for the meeting.** Create and distribute an agenda 24 to 48 hours in advance. Identify participants, but don't invite more than you need. Assign roles to participants, such as facilitator (usually the team leader), note taker (to jot down meeting minutes), timekeeper (to keep things moving), and assessor (to provide feedback on the meeting's effectiveness). If you're rotating the leadership of the meeting between team members, this week's chair will assume most of these duties.

- **Develop a solid agenda.** This may include a discussion of general "housekeeping" issues, actions taken since the last meeting, ongoing reminders and updates, and a list of key topics in order of priority. Consider involving your team in this process, as a team-building activity.

(continued)

(continued)

- **Set up the room.** Ideally, arrange to meet in a private meeting room. Arrive early enough to rearrange the seating, if needed. Also, be sure you have all the necessary equipment — phone, projector, flip chart, markers, and so on.

- **Set the ground rules.** These may include no multitasking, no smartphones, limitations on speaking times, and expectations of confidentiality.

- **Stay neutral.** As the leader, your opinion can sway the discussion and decisions made. Don't show your hand until you've heard all members' thoughts. Leaders should consider speaking last when seeking feedback from others.

- **Listen actively.** Listen for words and emotions; then paraphrase what you hear back to the group to clarify your, and their, understanding. Also, ask questions. Push the group to clarify positions and react to challenges.

- **Manage digression.** Make sure the discussion remains focused on the agenda items. If it starts to stray, rein it in with a simple "I'm not sure this applies to the topic. Let's go back to. . ."

- **Assess the meeting's effectiveness.** Did you meet your objectives and desired outcomes? Did you achieve the desired level of participation? Did the technology add value? Did you manage your time well? Did participants demonstrate confidence and trust in the process and results? Will participants look forward to attending another one of your meetings, given the choice?

- **Follow up.** After the meeting, send out the meeting minutes, along with a summary of decisions made and subsequent task assignments. Also, survey meeting participants to gauge their impressions of the value of the meeting.

Town hall meetings

Whenever a manager needs to deliver a consistent message to a large number of employees, town hall meetings are a great way to go. That being said, the town hall format often discourages employees from participating in any sort of Q&A. Indeed, in large town hall–type settings, you may be hard-pressed to think of a circumstance in which honest, insightful questions are likely to result.

TIP

To avoid hearing crickets when you open up the floor for questions, try soliciting questions in advance. That way, if they aren't brought up during the course of the meeting, you can address them anyway. Also, before you show up, do what you can to learn about the specific concerns of your audience.

One more thing: Consider leaving your executive entourage behind. A CEO by herself in a folksy town hall venue can more effectively convey to staff that she's "one of us," and thereby increase their engagement.

TECHNOLOGY-AIDED MEETINGS

There was once a FedEx commercial in which a boss is talking via videoconference to his project team, who appear to be back at the office. To the project team's horror, the "office" is revealed to be a backdrop, which tips over to reveal their true location: a beautiful golf course.

Humor (and scheming employees) aside, only managers stuck in the Dark Ages fail to leverage technology as a meeting tool, whether said technology is inexpensive (read: free), such as FaceTime or Skype, or an elaborate enterprise-wide solutions, such as TelePresence from Cisco Systems. For sharing and viewing information across geographies with many meeting attendees, technology tools such as GoToMeeting (www. gotomeeting.com) are a great resource.

Phone

If meeting face to face is not an option, and a video service such as Skype is not available, then a phone is the way to go. Communicating via phone is also great for answering questions, gathering information, and having discussions not involving the whole team.

REMEMBER

When using the phone, be sure to turn your entire attention to the caller. Don't multitask! Also, answer the phone only if you have time to talk. Otherwise, let calls go to voicemail.

Speaking of voicemail, be sure you check yours regularly, and return calls promptly. If you're going to be out, consider recording an outgoing message to communicate this. And when it comes to leaving messages on other people's voicemail, keep things brief.

Email

Although Millennials may insist that "Email is so yesterday," it remains the communication form of choice for many businesses today. Email is particularly well suited for information-only communication that must be conveyed to a group — for example, to schedule meetings and phone calls, to distribute materials for meetings, and to gather input between meetings. Email is also a great tool for maintaining a written record of key points.

Email is not great for everything, however. For example, you should never use email to communicate bad news or to relay sensitive or confidential information. It leaves too much unsaid. Also, never send an email when your emotions are running high. The 24-hour rule is a great check and balance; save the email as a draft and wait 24 hours before you send it.

WARNING

If you wouldn't want an email message to be posted on a public bulletin board, don't send it. Moreover, *never* make any libelous, sexist, or racially discriminating comments in emails, even if meant as a joke.

Social media

With the assimilation of Millennials (also known as Generation Y) into the workplace, adding social media to your communication toolkit is moving from a "nice to have" to a "must have." This generation — which will soon be the dominant generation at work (if it isn't already), and which by 2025 will comprise half the workforce — depends heavily on technology to communicate. It's incumbent upon you to "speak their language," so to speak. That means getting hip to such communication platforms as Facebook, Twitter, YouTube, and blogs.

CHANNELING EMILY POST: A WORD ON EMAIL ETIQUETTE

Here are a few tips to ensure you don't accidentally annoy anyone over email:

- **Include a subject line.** Try to use one that will be meaningful to the recipient as well as to you. That way, the recipient will have some idea what your message is about even before he reads it. In addition, including subject lines makes it easier to find emails later.

- **Be concise.** Don't make an email longer than it needs to be. No one wants to read a message that rivals *War and Peace* in its length.

- **Use proper spelling, grammar, and punctuation.** Yes, sending an email riddled with errors in spelling, grammar, and punctuation makes you look like an idiot. Worse, messages with these types of errors can be easily misinterpreted. Grammatical rules exist for a reason: To ensure clear communication. Follow them, and you'll minimize misunderstandings! Also, avoid the use of abbreviations (think "BTW" for "by the way," and so on).

- **Reply swiftly.** Try to reply to all emails within 24 hours, and preferably on the same working day. If you aren't able to provide the necessary information within that time frame, then drop the sender a line to let her know you're working on it.

- **Don't write in ALL CAPS.** IF YOU WRITE IN ALL CAPS, IT SEEMS AS IF YOU ARE SHOUTING. THIS IS VERY ANNOYING.

REMEMBER

Baby Boomers, Generation Xers, and Millennials communicate very differently. To engage Millennials, leaders must communicate using their tools: tweets, blogs, vlogs, and related social and mobile tools, such as texting. A message that you text or tweet to one of your Millennial employees will almost certainly be read right away. But a message sent via email? Maybe, maybe not. (Flip to Chapter 1 of Book 5 for more about engagement across generations.)

WARNING

Don't commit to maintaining a blog, a YouTube channel, or a Twitter feed and then fail to follow up. You must have the staff and resources to handle any new communications program. The popularity or "sexiness" of a new vehicle is not, in and of itself, sufficient justification for utilizing it.

Putting it all together

Not sure what communication format to use when? Table 2-1 should help. It contains at-a-glance info on each form of communication.

CONSIDERING CORPORATE BLOGGING

In recent years, many companies have begun publishing blogs authored by their CEOs, presidents, or other top-level executives. This idea has considerable merit if the executive in question is truly committed to the idea and the process, and if the communication strategy incorporates checks and balances to ensure that both entries and comments are communicating productive things.

If, however, an executive is *not* committed to blogging, or expects his or her entries to be ghostwritten or excessively vetted, then a blog is ultimately of negative value. A disconnect will result between what the blog is saying and what the executive "knows." Once this is discovered, the credibility of the project — and of corporate communications as a whole — will be undermined.

If a senior-level employee doesn't have the time or motivation to blog, consider spreading the responsibility among several midlevel employees who have a passion for it. Ideally, this will include a roster of bloggers who are representative of your firm's diversity in terms of discipline and cultural background, but first and foremost, you should recruit on the basis of passion and commitment. For some companies, blogging is a perfect vessel for discretionary effort by midlevel or junior-level staff for whom self-expression and new technologies are motivators.

TABLE 2-1   Forms of Communication

Form of Communication	Best Used For	Tips for Success
Face to face: The best communication tool available	Team meetings (discussions, decision making, problem solving) One-on-ones between managers and supervisors Conflict resolution Annual employee reviews Feedback	Look the person or people you're talking to in the eye. Listen to words and tone of voice, and observe body language. Listen more than you talk (observe the 80/20 rule). Paraphrase what you hear to clarify your understanding.
Telephone: The best communication tool to use when face-to-face communication isn't available	Answering questions Gathering information Discussions not involving the whole team	Answer the phone only if you're willing to talk. Give all your attention to the caller. Don't multitask. Set your outgoing message to notify callers if you're out for the day. Check your voicemail often and return calls promptly.
Email: Great for group communications that are simply informative in nature	Messages for more than one person Distribution of materials for team meetings Scheduling meetings and phone calls Gathering input between meetings Messages that need a thread or record	Don't send an email when your emotions are running high. Use descriptive subject headings. Be brief. Use good grammar, punctuation, and spelling. Reply swiftly. Use a mixture of uppercase and lowercase letters. DO NOT USE ALL CAPS.
Smartphones, mobile applications, and social media: Excellent for communicating with younger employees	Younger employees Quick communication (texting) Communication that you aren't worried about going public	Leverage your junior-level employees' knowledge and social media expertise. Establish baseline rules and guidelines of what is and is not appropriate. Link to both your marketing and employer branding (HR) efforts.

Form of Communication	Best Used For	Tips for Success
Videoconferencing	Conference calls with remote employees or communicating with telecommuting employees Sharing documents	Learn how the technology works. Nothing is more painful for meeting attendees than having to sit around for 15 minutes while the meeting organizer fiddles with the technology, trying to get it to work.

Communicating Change

As you're no doubt aware, people resist change. Why? Lots of reasons. Often, it's simply fear of the unknown. Sometimes, it has to do with lack of trust. On occasion, it may simply be due to bad timing. In a work setting, people resist change because they're afraid of losing job security or control. And some people don't like change "just because" — even when it's a change for the better.

And yet, change is everywhere — and with good reason. If we didn't undergo change, we'd be at a considerable disadvantage. After all, "changing" often translates to "keeping up with the times." We've all survived significant change in the past, and we'll survive it in the future as well.

Communication is never more important than during a period of change. That's because people tend to assume the worst during a change event. During times of change, employees tend to be less trusting and less direct. They're more careful when choosing their words. Often, they're fearful of disagreeing with management, whether said management is old or new. Fear also causes them to expend more energy looking after their own self-interests, and to be more open to messages that reach them via the rumor mill — especially in the absence of actual information.

To stave off anxiety among the troops, leaders must increase the level of communication during a change event such as a merger, reduction in force, reorganization, change in strategic direction, or change to the leadership team.

TIP

If you're facing a change event in your organization, keep these points in mind:

>> **As a leader, you go first!** Make sure you fully embrace the change initiative and its implications before attempting to persuade others. Be cognizant of the influence you have on those around you.

>> **Talk the talk, and walk the walk.** Be a positive role model and an ambassador for the change. Support it both publicly and privately, and demonstrate the behaviors that you expect from others in the face of change.

>> **Overcommunicate.** Whether good news or bad, sharing information as often as you can and being forthright with the truth are critical. Communicating is the number-one way to maintain trust and employee engagement. As you do, assess your employees' understanding of the change initiative. Do they grasp the change initiative's goals and pertinent details? If not, provide any missing information and clear up any misconceptions.

>> **Check in with your staff and encourage candid feedback.** In your role as leader, you must check in with your people to see how they're doing — especially during times of change. Allow and encourage employees to candidly express their feelings. Get any resistance to change out in the open so it can be dealt with.

>> **Establish crystal-clear priorities.** Going through change can be confusing and stressful. Be ultra-specific with regard to team priorities and staff expectations throughout the change initiative.

>> **Delegate.** Move less important tasks off your plate so you can focus on leading through the change. When possible, delegate tasks to staff members to further their skills, knowledge, and abilities.

>> **Be there.** Make yourself available to your people. You're undoubtedly busy, but don't close your door and stay in your office all day. *Remember:* These are the times when your staff needs you the most.

>> **Make your employees feel valued and give positive reinforcement.** During times of change, motivating your employees and making them feel appreciated are especially important. Reward positive behaviors as often as possible, and celebrate accomplishments whenever you can. Pay extra attention to your top performers!

>> **Re-skill your employees (and yourself) as needed.** Determine what competencies will be required to work in the "new world" and provide relevant training and development opportunities for your team.

>> **Pass information up as well as down.** Be sure to pass questions, issues, and feedback up to your manager or leadership team in addition to conveying information down to your team.

>> **Stay sharp!** Leading change is hard work. Keep your change leadership skills finely tuned. Take advantage of the resources at your disposal to build your knowledge and abilities in this important competency.

>> **Get help.** Don't underestimate your own need for assistance during change. Reach out to a peer or seek advice from your boss on how best to handle your own situation during change.

TIP

To help your employees through the change, advise them to keep the following points in mind:

>> **Adopt a proactive mind-set.** You make things happen; things don't happen *to you*. Don't assume a victim mentality, in which you perceive your life to be controlled by others. Yes, some things will be out of your control during change. But your attitude is always entirely within your control.

>> **Think evolution, not revolution.** It may not always feel like it, but change is never a conscious attempt to make our lives more hectic! Change is rarely introduced to tear everything down. Most changes are initiated to improve and build on results.

>> **Focus on what is *not* changing.** Few change initiatives change *everything*. Let the stable aspects of the situation give you a sense of security as you adjust to what *is* changing.

>> **Ask questions.** Get the facts about the change. Speak up and find out more about the things that aren't clear to you. Try not to fill in your own blanks; often, you'll be wrong.

>> **Keep doing your work.** Chances are that many aspects of your job are not changing. Keep doing what you do best. Onward and upward!

>> **Use the change as a development opportunity.** Change often brings new opportunities and prospects. Leverage the change to your advantage by identifying ways to improve your skills, knowledge, and abilities to help you meet your career goals.

>> **Be prepared for mental fatigue.** Change can be challenging, unsettling, and exhausting, even for the most experienced employees. Don't be surprised if mental fatigue sets in — especially during larger change initiatives. Expect it, normalize it, and find ways to deal with it.

>> **Be forgiving and tolerant.** Change is difficult, and people are bound to make mistakes. Be forgiving and lenient with others (and yourself) during times of change.

>> **Ask for help when needed.** Nobody can read your mind. Be vocal about your needs and about how the company, your manager, and your co-workers can support you.

Improving Organizational Communication

Communicating Your Engagement Efforts

There once was a company whose management decided it wanted to be an "employer of choice," which would naturally involve improving employee engagement. Like many organizations, they knew they had a lot of work to do to get there.

A chief concern was how employees would react to this goal. The leadership worried that cynicism might trump their efforts. In fact, they were so concerned about this that they considered not even telling employees about their aspirations.

Thankfully, they came to their senses. They realized that they were embarking on a multi-year journey, and that if they were *truly* committed to being successful, they were going to have to communicate exactly what they were trying to do and why. They were going to have to report on milestones, regardless of whether they were proud of the results. In addition, they were going to have to make themselves accountable. That was the only way they could command the respect and trust of the very people they needed to make the culture shift a success.

Yes, employees *were* skeptical. But this didn't take the leaders by surprise or dampen their resolve. They stuck to the plan. The CEO made employee engagement one of the eight key elements of his strategic plan and issued monthly progress reports. In addition, all ten members of the leadership team spoke continually about employee engagement. They became true ambassadors of an employee-focused culture.

REMEMBER

Your senior leaders — up to and including the president, CEO, COO, and/or CFO — must communicate the business strategy every month, especially with regard to how engagement fits in. This communication can be via newsletter, email, report, video, or presentation — just don't let it fall by the wayside. The communication protocol discussed earlier in this chapter (in the section "Building a Communication Protocol") is a great first step.

Welcome criticism and deal with it transparently. This in and of itself helps to defuse the more vocal skeptics. It's hard to maintain a sour outlook when you're clearly being heard and when management is openly fessing up to missteps and seeking ways to correct the course. Even the most ardent skeptics will have to acknowledge the evident effort on the part of management. They won't be able to deny when gains, however small, are made. Again, the key is communication. Skeptics who continue to grumble in the face of clear progress will quickly find themselves without an audience.

How did the story end? Well, engagement became the foundation of the company's business culture, ultimately leading to best-in-class performance in profit, growth, client service, and yes, employee engagement survey scores. The company even promoted the head of engagement, proof of the pudding that engagement drives business results.

Looking at a Few Communication Don'ts

Throughout this chapter, you get the scoop on communication "do's" — establishing two-way communication, developing a communication protocol, maximizing communication tools, communicating change, and broadcasting your engagement efforts.

WARNING

To ensure you don't put your foot in it, here are some communication don'ts:

>> **Don't underestimate the importance of communication.** Communication is the cornerstone of employee engagement. Communication should never be viewed as anything but essential in engaging your employees.

>> **Don't be afraid to overcommunicate.** "Gee, I left that company because management just communicated *too much*," said no one ever. Simply put, your employees want to know what is going on, and proactive communication is your way of keeping them in the loop. Key messages, especially those pertaining to progress or success, must be queued up and pushed out with the highest possible frequency using a variety of communication tools.

>> **Don't focus on the negative.** The vast majority of the time, your employees are doing something right. But too many managers focus the majority of *their* time discussing the few times employees did something wrong. (And more often than not, the "something wrong" wasn't really "wrong" at all. It was just "different.") Although it's certainly important to let employees know when they've made a mistake, you'll find that focusing on the positive will pay long-term engagement dividends.

>> **Don't be afraid to communicate setbacks or losses.** Yes, you just read that focusing on the positive will pay long-term engagement dividends. But that doesn't mean you should refrain from sharing bad news. Many managers are hesitant to communicate news of setbacks or losses, fearing employees will grow demoralized. But for employees to feel invested in their work, they must know how the business is doing with respect to its goals. Simply put, you can't improve if you don't know you're underperforming.

One regional manager of a company shielded employees from negative news about their performance in an effort to maintain morale. But by doing so, he failed to create any impetus for change or any channel for constructive input from the ranks. Fortunately, the company replaced this manager. The new boss kicked off his tenure with a frank conversation with his staff about their performance (or lack thereof). In doing so, he tapped into the staff's innate urge to be competitive and to excel. As a result, engagement scores, revenue growth, and profitability all improved. Indeed, the region went from *losing* $1 million per year to *making* $1 million per year — a $2 million swing.

>> **Don't shoot the messenger.** Too often, top-level executives become angry in the face of unflattering feedback. This attitude, especially when displayed in a public forum, will effectively stifle any benefits that may arise from the sharing of employees' opinions. In other words, if executives get mad at people who tell them things they don't want to hear, people will stop telling them things, period. When you create feedback mechanisms, you must accept the bad news with the good. That means creating an environment in which people are comfortable speaking truth to power. Otherwise, all you're doing is creating a culture in which people tell you what you want to hear — which is *not* a model for business excellence.

Chapter **3**

Strengthening Team Performance with Mindfulness

The old adage "many minds are better than one" is true. Working as part of a great team is usually better than struggling alone in isolation. Teamwork can increase creativity as members share knowledge and build on each other's ideas. It can provide a great opportunity for members to develop and acquire new skills. It can get things done more quickly and, when it works well, increase employee satisfaction. But as any leader knows, teamwork can also be one of the most challenging aspects of the job. In this chapter you explore team dynamics and discover how mindfulness can help you make teams work together more effectively.

Identifying and Harnessing Team Dynamics

As a leader, you already know the impact that team dynamics can have on your team. As a team member, you'll have observed its impact also. You can see team or group dynamics at play in a variety of situations: The family gathering for a holiday or a wedding, friends socializing at a restaurant, or a group of people meeting for the first time.

Although you may have seen many complex theories on team dynamics in management textbooks and academic journals, understanding team dynamics is really quite straightforward.

Understanding team dynamics

Few humans exist in isolation. As a human, in common with many other animals, your behavior is likely to be based largely on habit, adapted and influenced by your social networks. These social networks include family, friends, and work colleagues. Your behavior is also likely to be influenced by social and cultural norms.

TECHNICAL STUFF

The modern workplace is rarely set up to accommodate the human need to connect, understand, and work with each other. Neuroscience research into areas such as how the brain enables you to undertake tasks such as decision-making and prioritizing (cognitive neuroscience), the way the brain processes social interactions (social neuroscience), and how the brain deals with emotions (affective neuroscience) is beginning to identify the drivers of human social behavior.

The evolutionary principle is what your brain seeks to minimize danger and maximize reward. This fact often motivates humans to spend more energy avoiding things they think may be risky or non-beneficial than approaching and exploring new possibilities. Many aspects of work can be seen as threatening or rewarding, including the following:

>> **Job role or position within the organization:** Your position in the organizational hierarchy is likely to shape your social relationships at work — that is, those with whom you feel relaxed or those with whom you have much or little in common.

>> **Extent to which you can control your working environment:** In a senior or specialist role you may have a high degree of control over your work, but in administration or a manual laboring role you may have little. Research suggests that staff members with low job control are more prone to stress and four times more likely to die of a heart attack than those with high job control.

>> **Sense of equality:** Lots of research demonstrates that humans are drawn to fairness and dislike unfairness. If you feel unfairly treated, or see others unfairly treated, you're likely to experience a strong threat response.

So what does all this have to do with mindfulness? Mindfulness can help both leaders and employees become more aware of these social dynamics as they arise and change in the present moment. This awareness is key if you're to be successful in identifying team dynamics at play and harnessing them for the good of all concerned.

Before you look at specific ways that mindfulness can be used to assist with team dynamics at work, you need to look how social dynamics work. Here's an example: Peter worked for a major rail maintenance operator in the United Kingdom and managed large teams that are responsible for repair and maintenance of the railway tracks and buildings. Peter knew that in a few weeks' time he would be managing a major renewal project that involved coordinating a team of signal engineers (who maintain the signals) and Pway engineers (who maintain the track). The team of signal engineers had a different working culture to that of the Pway engineers. Although all are dedicated to keeping the trains running safely, communication problems are evident between the teams and all sorts of other frictions existed.

With help, Peter identified some of the social dynamics at play in his work. The signal engineers regarded their *job role* as being more skilled and of higher status than the Pway engineers. As highly trained and qualified engineers, the team had considerable *control* to decide on the right course of action, and how the job would best be carried out. They felt a strong sense of social cohesion with other signal engineers, and those on the railway who had similar technical jobs. They had little in common with the Pway staff, who mainly did routine, manual, heavy work.

The Pway staff regarded the signal engineers as "geeks." They argued that, without the tracks themselves, electric masts, points, bridges, and other railway infrastructure, no need for signals would exist. Their work was thus, in their eyes, of equal importance. They felt that their *job role* as Pway workers should be equal to that of the signal engineers, and resented the *inequality* evident in the signal engineers being treated with more respect by those in charge. On top of these issues, they had less control over their work, which was often dictated by factors beyond their *control*. If new track was late being delivered, they could not lay it. If the signal engineers were at work on one area, they had to work somewhere else. They regarded the signal engineers with mistrust, as several years before a signal engineer had reported a Pway engineer for larking about on the job. They saw *inequality* in the situation whereby signal engineers always seemed to spend the last hour of work "doing nothing" while they bust a gut to get the job finished in time.

Peter recognized that the Pway staff worked in a much more uncertain environment, and had much less control — both factors that humans can find highly threatening. He also recognized that the roles of the two teams were different so they were unlikely to feel part of the same social group as they had little in common. Peter saw that the Pway staff members were feeling threatened by the apparent preferential treatment they felt the signal staff received. Peter started to understand how these factors may be making the Pway staff feel unconsciously threatened, and that this situation explained why they sometimes appeared to be arguing over trivial points or being difficult. It was just their brains trying to look out for them, trying to keep them safe and well.

Although Peter could see the problems, and why the friction was occurring, he was not sure how to deal with it. This situation is where mindfulness would have come in.

Managing team dynamics mindfully

If you look at Peter's dilemma from a mindful perspective, you discover the following:

>> Consciously or unconsciously the Pway staff were feeling threatened by the working methods and attitudes of the signal staff. This threat was likely to release powerful hormones into their bodies, and to some extent diminish their capacity for rational behavior.

>> Over time, both the signal and Pway staff had created their own mental record or story of what was going on. It was highly likely that they then treated this story as reality — a solid fact — and based their behavior to each other on this story rather than what was actually happening. Believing their story to be reality, it was likely that their brains were actively seeking evidence to reinforce this picture of what was going on.

>> Peter needed to find a way to get his teams to start work with a clean slate, working together in the present moment rather than defaulting to auto-pilot reactions.

Peter's tasks were to

>> Try to get staff to work from a present-moment perspective, working on present-moment facts and setting aside past working relationships.

>> Try to get both groups to feel that they were equally valued on this job (similar status).

>> Help increase certainty as far as practical for the Pway staff.

>> Provide some more autonomy if possible for the Pway staff.

>> Try to engender a feeling of "all working together to make this project happen on time and to maintain line safety" (a feeling of all being related or belonging to the same group).

>> Offer a reward for all staff if the project was completed on time to the required standard (fairness and valuing all).

So how could Peter have applied this knowledge to his work challenge? It might have gone something like this . . .

At the planning meeting Peter gathered together team leaders from the Pway and signal teams. He ran through the tasks, describing what needed to be done and when, and outlined the fines that would be incurred if they overran and trains were stopped or delayed as a result.

Peter explained his findings, and asked for ideas about how they could start this job with a clean slate. He encouraged the staff to look at what was happening in the here and now. Together, they made plans to address the six points that Peter had identified. It was agreed that some Pway staff and signal staff should swap places so that they could gain a greater appreciation of each other's roles, and also increase certainty and relatedness for both groups. They agreed on the joint reward of a free breakfast for all if things went according to plan.

Peter started the project by bringing the staff together and emphasizing that everyone was responsible for getting the job completed, to the required standard, on time. He explained that the company would get fined for lateness and delays caused, and that would impact on each and every one of them. He emphasized the importance of all the workers playing their part, with no job being any more or less important than another.

The team leaders worked hard to nip things in the bud when staff reverted to old thought patterns and behaviors. They brought team members back to the present moment if they started to spiral into anger or frustration in anticipation of what would happen next, based on past experiences. They reinforced Peter's messages and changed the subject if anyone started to moan about other teams working on the project.

Peter's project finished early, leaving time for an additional quality check at the end, resolving some last minute issues. Everyone enjoyed breakfast, and Peter gained a sense that this shared experience was the start of better working relationships within his teams.

TIP

Here are some tips for mindfully creating better team dynamics:

>> Use up-to-date models to identify things that may detract from good working relationships within your team.

>> Lead your team with fresh eyes every day. Focus on what's happening in the here and now, rather than what you think is happening based on past experiences.

>> Keep in mind that, although your team members are there to do a job of work, they're human beings, not human doings!

>> Be constantly aware of the huge impact that emotions and physiology have on thoughts. If your team members are worried, angry, or uncertain, their work suffers. Help your team create as much certainty as possible and stay focused on the present moment.

>> Give your team a break — literally and emotionally:

- Encourage staff to take a few moments to refocus their efforts by taking a three-step focus break (see the later section "Becoming mindfully ready for anything" for more information).

- Encourage team members to celebrate success and achievement, ticking off each little job as another task done.

- Encourage self-kindness. As a leader you probably want all your team members to strive to be the best they can, but working harder and harder and later and later results in less performance. Encourage staff to take some time out and come back to the task with fresh eyes and renewed attention.

REMEMBER

Walk the talk! Demonstrate a mindful approach to your work and the way you lead. Doing so encourages your team members to adopt new, healthier, more productive working habits.

REMEMBER

Remind your team members that the problem isn't the problem! Your interpretation and response is what can cause the problem. You may not be able to make the problem go away, but you can alter the way you think about it and respond.

Improving Team Performance by Staying Focused on the Important Stuff

As a leader, your primary role is to motivate and lead team(s) to achieve desired organizational outcomes. A key aspect of this leadership role is identifying team dynamics at play (as explained earlier in this chapter), and encouraging good working relationships and understanding between different teams and team members.

When trying to improve team performance, leaders often lose sight of what's really important. Mindfulness is a great way to bring yourself back to the present moment, see what's really important, and refocus your efforts.

As more neuroscience research into mindfulness emerges, leaders are adopting more mindfulness techniques to help them lead effectively in times of constant change, pressure, and uncertainty. Wise leaders are introducing mindfulness within their teams, helping their staff get more from their job role and to find a new way to relate to their work.

Lastly, as a leader, keeping your eye on the goal is vital. What is it that your team is supposed to be doing for your organization? What is the greatest contribution you can make?

Recognizing what's important

You may have chosen to work for your company based on a mental picture of it formed from your perceptions of its products, services, mission, and vision or what you have read. You may have been lucky enough to have insider knowledge gained from friends and family. When you started to work for your company, you may have found that your perception of what it was like to work for it was different from the reality — for better or worse!

In much the same way, when you applied for the job role you now hold you formed a mental picture of what the job role was all about, the difference you could make, and probably things you could improve or introduce. Again, you may have found the reality somewhat different from your perception of how it would be. Why is this?

Humans tend to dislike uncertainty. Thus, when you don't know what the future holds, your brain tries to anticipate what will happen in the future based on past experience. Your brain then treats this mental picture of the future as a fact until something happens to make you alter or replace this representation of reality.

Being conned into thinking that how you see the world is the same as how others see it is all too easy. The same applies to what you think is important. In order to be effective as a leader, you need to take a step back now and again to see what's really important for yourself, your team, and the organization as a whole.

HOW PEOPLE MAKE SENSE OF THE WORLD

Schema theory is an attempt to make sense of how humans organize knowledge and form pictures of the world. The theory states that all knowledge is organized into units. These units are called *schemata*. Schemata represent knowledge about concepts: objects and the relationship they have with other things.

As a simple example if you think about a cat, you'll have knowledge of cats in general (four legs, long tail, ears, teeth, whiskers). You're likely to have knowledge of a specific cat (black, long whiskers, loud meow, loves food, called Bramble). You may also think about cats in the wider context (pet, living being, furry, hunter). Your knowledge may include that they're warm-blooded mammals. Depending on your personal experience, you may add in "bite, scratch, and hiss" if you've had a negative experience of cats. If you're very concerned about hygiene, you may add "shed hair everywhere, dirty paws, carry fleas." If you're a cat lover, you may add "purr, rub against my legs, sit with me, and keep me company."

All this information combined creates your picture of the world. This picture remains in place until you encounter new information; you then decide whether you should alter your picture of the world to accommodate the new information or dismiss it and keep your picture of the world exactly the same.

The preceding explains why different people can have a different picture of the same thing — and thus react to the same thing differently. Practicing mindfulness helps you to see the bigger picture. By recognizing that your mind "edits out" things it thinks are irrelevant, you can train your brain to consciously observe more details when you need them to gain a more balanced view.

Mindfully seeing what's important

Here's a 15-minute exercise to help you identify important issues at work. Follow these steps:

1. **Settle yourself into a dignified upright position in a chair or on the floor.**

   Make sure that you're in a place where you feel comfortable and where you won't be disturbed for a short while. Put a pen and notepad nearby.

2. **Spend around three minutes focusing on the sensation of breathing.**

   Feel the breath coming in and the breath going out. Experience your breathing in the present moment, as it is right here, right now. You've nothing else to do in this moment except experience breathing. Nothing else matters.

If your attention wanders, congratulate yourself on recognizing that it has done so and then gently escort your attention back to your breath.

3. **Spend around three minutes focusing on how your body feels at this moment in time.**

   Start at your feet and work up to your head:

   - Look for sensations such as stiffness or tingling. In some areas, you will feel sensations and in others nothing.

   - Let go of any expectations regarding how your body should feel; just see what's there at this moment in time.

   - Gently escort your attention back to your body if your attention wanders.

4. **Spend two minutes focusing on what you currently do for your organization.**

   See what arises. Observe your thoughts impartially, with kindness and curiosity. Avoid the temptation to think about what's arising and to get involved or judge it — just observe.

5. **Spend two minutes focusing on what your team could do to add most value to your organization.**

   See what arises. Again, just observe and avoid the temptation to think about it.

6. **Spend two minutes focusing on how you could be leading your team in this present moment.**

   See what arises. Again, just observe and avoid the temptation to think about it.

7. **Return your attention to your breath.**

   Focus on your breathing for the remaining two minutes.

8. **Open your eyes and spend a moment gathering yourself together.**

9. **Write on the pad the thoughts that emerged in steps 4, 5, and 6.**

   Consider whether

   - Any disparities exist between your job role to date and what you should be doing in the future.

   - Your team's efforts are focused in the right direction.

   - Anything needs to be done differently in the future.

Taking five minutes to refocus your work efforts

TIP

If you've been practicing mindfulness for some time, you may want to try a shortened 5 minute version of the exercise in the previous section. Follow these steps:

1. **Settle yourself into a dignified upright position in a chair or on the floor.**

   Make sure that you're in a place where you feel comfortable and where you won't be disturbed for a short while. Put a pen and notepad nearby.

2. **Spend two minutes focusing on the sensation of breathing.**

3. **Bring your focus to your job role and spend two minutes asking yourself:**

   - "What do I currently do for my organization?"

   - "How should I be leading my team in this present moment?"

   See what thoughts emerge.

4. **Bring your attention back to your breath.**

   Focus your attention on your breath for the remaining minute.

5. **Open your eyes and spend a moment gathering yourself together.**

6. **Write on the pad the thoughts that emerged in step 2.**

   Consider whether

   - Any disparities exist between your job role to date and what you should be doing in the future.

   - Your team's efforts are focused in the right direction.

   - Anything needs to be done differently in the future.

Introducing mindfulness to your team

Mindfulness is increasingly being offered to employees as a development option. More research into the impact of mindfulness in the workplace is needed, but data suggests that it can help you

- » Function better when under pressure.
- » Focus your attention better on the task in hand.
- » Improve the way you manage strong feelings and emotions.
- » Respond differently to challenges and difficulties at work.
- » Improve relationships with colleagues.
- » Look after yourself better at work.

If doing more of the same isn't producing the results you desire, why not try a different approach? Why not offer staff mindfulness lessons in work time? Mindfulness equips staff with the tools and techniques that can help them work with their brain rather than against it, and gain new perspectives and ways of working.

Keeping your eye on the goal

As a leader, keeping your eye on the goal is crucial. From time to time, you need to check and, if necessary, redefine your team's purpose and goals. Peter (who you met earlier in this chapter) redefined his team's purpose using the exercise in the earlier section "Mindfully seeing what's important."

Peter identified the following:

>> His job title is senior infrastructure project manager.

>> His role is to ensure that projects are delivered on time, to budget, and matching specifications.

>> He currently spends 60 percent of his time documenting, agreeing, monitoring, and refining project plans; 20 percent on reporting to stakeholders and documenting items; 10 percent directly supervising work teams to ensure project delivery to the required standards; and 10 percent on routine administration and attending organizational planning and strategy meetings.

>> He is finding it more difficult to deliver projects on time and to budget despite being confident that his skills as a project manager are still effective and have improved over time.

>> He is spending an increasing amount of time managing team dynamics and adverse reactions to organizational change.

Peter concluded that, at the present moment and for the foreseeable future, the important things he needs to do are:

>> Manage projects on time and to budget.

>> Provide more support to his direct reports to help them cope with the organizational changes and uncertainty they are facing.

Peter reorganized his schedule to allow more time to lead and support his team, which led to improved teamwork and projects being completed faster and to a higher standard. He identified those aspects of his project management role that required the most skill and those that were more administrative. He started developing a member of his team as a project management assistant, supporting her to take on some of the more routine aspects of his work. He made more of an effort to identify the impact that planned changes were likely to have on his direct and indirect teams, and actively involved them in deciding the way forward.

As you can see, by taking time out to clear his mind using mindfulness, Peter was able to identify what was important in the present moment and to take steps to restructure his work and the work of his team to ensure that organisational goals continued to be met.

TIP

To mindfully keep your eye on the end goal, bear these tips in mind:

>> Set aside regular time to practice mindfulness. Doing so reduces your tendency to work on auto-pilot and helps you see things more clearly.

>> Every three months or at the end of your mindfulness practice, ask yourself, "What's important in my work at this present moment?" Restructure your work if necessary.

>> Every six months or so, test your understanding of where the organization is heading. Try to

- Arrange to meet with a few carefully selected senior managers to identify the organization's key priorities at this moment in time and how your team can best contribute.

- Prepare for each meeting by practicing mindfulness for five to ten minutes, ideally just before walking into the meeting.

- In the meeting really focus on what's being said, avoiding the temptation to jump to conclusions.

- After the meeting identify four or five key things you've discovered, and decide whether any of your work goals need to change.

Enhancing Internal and External Business Relationships

Whatever your role within an organization, actively cultivating good business relationships with colleagues and external contacts and clients is important.

Most relationships at work develop and are maintained with little effort. Some, however, require a lot of input. In the busy world of work, you need to make time to be really present when you're involved in one to one or group interactions with others. Many people say, "Of course I'm fully present when I meet with people;

I'm in the same room at the same time." Although you can't argue with this statement, many people are rarely present. Their body may be there but their brain is juggling multiple things, retrieving related past experiences, and trying to anticipate what will happen next. Mindfulness can help you quiet the mind, reduce your "mental noise," and return to the present moment. In the present moment, you can see more clearly what is going on in full Technicolor glory — body language, facial expressions, tone, and intonation, all which add to the message but are often unnoticed. (See Chapters 2 and 3 in Book 1 for an introduction to these topics.)

The following sections show you how to be ready for anything in meetings and get the most from your face-to-face interactions.

Becoming mindfully ready for anything

Managers and staff spend a huge amount of time in meetings. Research suggests that many managers regard much of this time as unproductive. With a little mindful preparation, this need not be the case. Most meetings are arranged with one or more goals in mind; indeed, many start with a set agenda. "Without a reason to meet, why meet?" you may be asking. While establishing the issues to be discussed is a good idea, retaining some flexibility to deal with equally or even more important things that arise unexpectedly in the moment is useful.

Are you one of those people who are too busy to prepare for meetings, arriving just in time and winging it? You're not alone! However, taking a little time out to prepare leads to better meetings in which you get more done. Consider the following:

>> Why the meeting has been arranged.

>> The organizational benefits that may be achieved.

>> What you can contribute to the meeting and gain from it.

>> Who will be there and why.

REMEMBER

Bear in mind that all the preceding points may or may not be true and accurate; they may just be mental constructs you've put in place to make sense of the world. Your thoughts here are only a starting point — be open to the meeting taking a new direction if beneficial.

TIP

When preparing for meetings, use a three-minute focus break to calm your brain chatter and return to the present moment. This simple technique consists of doing three things for one minute each: acknowledging your thoughts, focusing on the present moment sensation of breathing, and acknowledging your bodily sensations. It can be compressed or extended and can be used anywhere at any time.

Creating a short break helps you return to the present moment. Returning to the present moment enables you to put things into perspective, see the bigger picture, and make wiser choices and decide how to get the most from the rest of the day. The phases are as follows:

>> Settle yourself into a comfortable, upright position with your feet firmly on the floor — avoid slouching if you can. Although you can do this exercise with your eyes open, most people find it easier with closed eyes. By closing your eyes, your brain has one less stimulus to deal with. Spend one minute recognizing and acknowledging all the thoughts going round in your head. As thoughts arise, acknowledge them, and then let them go.

>> Now narrow your attention to focus on the present moment sensation of breathing — feeling the breath coming in and the breath going out. If you mind wanders, it's fine — that's just what minds do. Just kindly, gently escort your attention back to where it needs to be. Note that there is no need to control your breathing or alter it in any way. It's fine if all you are doing is using it as a kind or anchor to direct your attention to.

>> Spend one minute recognizing and acknowledging how your body feels, right here and now. Become aware of the actual physical sensations in your body, including both the pleasant and unpleasant feelings. If you do encounter any unpleasant sensations, try if you can to just accept that they are there without trying to make them go away and without judging them. Doing so will evoke an emotion that will increase your tension and make things worse. Accepting that the sensations as they are in the present moment adds no further fuel to the fire, and as a result the sensations may diminish or change.

Being in the meeting

When you enter the meeting room, try to ensure that you're fully present. The same applies if you're holding a one-to-one meeting in your office. Make an effort to be aware of any preconceived ideas you bring into the room with you, and try to set them aside as they may be inaccurate or unhelpful. If you've been practicing mindfulness for a little while, you should find it easier to quiet your brain chatter and accurately identify these ideas, realizing that they're only mental constructs and that they should be treated as such.

If, as the meeting starts, you find that lots of thoughts are going around in your head, try grounding yourself in the present moment.

Grounding yourself in the present moment

TIP

You can use this simple technique when you enter a meeting as a participant or as the chair. Perform the following:

>> Observe your thoughts as mental processes that come and go. No need to fix them or do anything with them, simply focus on observing them.

>> Experience how

- Your feet feel in contact with the floor.
- Your bottom feels in contact with the chair.
- Your neck, shoulders, and jaw feel in this moment in time.

>> Observe any sounds in the room or outside the room. Observe which are constant, which change, and notice any impact the sounds have on you.

>> Return your focus to the meeting.

>> Check every now and again that you're still in the meeting in the present moment and that your thoughts have not hijacked you and taken you elsewhere.

TIP

If you're chairing the meeting, you may want to start with a mindful minute for everyone to center themselves in preparation for the meeting. Although the exercise is called the *mindful minute,* you can extend it if time permits. This exercise is designed to be done anywhere, anytime, seated or standing. Using this exercise before mindful communications isn't essential, but many people find that it helps by creating a short space between the busyness of their working mind and the present moment state that's ideal for mindful communications. Follow these steps:

1. **Center yourself (about 20 seconds).**

   Feel your feet feel in contact with the ground. Imagine that your feet are rooted to the ground and that your legs are like tree trunks, firmly supporting you in place. Use your feet as an anchor for your attention.

2. **Acknowledge what's going on (about 20 seconds).**

   Now focus your attention on everything that's going on — the thoughts entering your mind, sounds, smells, and bodily sensations. Acknowledge your experiences and let them go without judging or getting involved, just noticing the present moment.

3. **Take a mindful pause (about 20 seconds).**

Now focus your attention on nothing but your breath. Feel the breath coming in, and the breath going out. If thoughts arise, kindly acknowledge them and let them go.

As the meeting continues, try really focusing on each agenda item, seeing it with fresh eyes, and contributing to the discussion when appropriate. When you're more present in meetings, you may notice a host of other things going on that others may miss as their minds take them in different directions.

You may notice positive or negative body language, weariness, or subjects that keep arising that aren't on the agenda, are dismissed, and then pop up again. These subjects may need to be discussed and resolved in order to make the remainder of the meeting more productive. If appropriate, try to get these hidden issues on to the table and discussed. If doing so is wholly inappropriate, publically acknowledge that you've noticed them, and propose another time to discuss and resolve them. While this approach may seem counter-intuitive because you're adding more items to an already packed agenda, if people are distracted by a burning issue the meeting is likely to be unproductive or take longer. Surfacing, acknowledging, and setting aside time to discuss important hidden issues saves you time in the long run.

Always ensure that meetings end with a thank you — so few meetings do! If you're the chair, propose a mindful minute to end the meeting. Next, sincerely thank attendees for their time and attention, and acknowledge what's been achieved. This simple act pays dividends. If done correctly, it has the power to activate people's parasympathetic nervous system (associated with rest and relaxation), resulting in them leaving the meeting feeling good. In addition, it recognizes and rewards the efforts people have made to make the meeting a success and engenders a sense of completion and accomplishment.

Following up mindfully

Always make sure that you follow up promptly on the promises you made in the meeting. These promises may include both major actions and more informal promises such as getting data for someone or even a favor that someone asked of you in a coffee break.

Always make a note of these promises before you leave the meeting room. Your mind may easily be hijacked when you leave the meeting room, and as your working memory becomes overwhelmed, it may drop these promises and you may forget them. Noting the promises down means that you can delete them from your working memory, which frees it up to do other things.

Deliver on your promises as promptly as you can — especially the informal ones. Sometimes the more you think about doing something, the more of a story you create in your mind about it. This self-created story (based on your past experience and anticipation of the future) is treated by your brain as reality. It may procrastinate or try to avoid doing the task. Diving in and getting a task done without over-thinking it probably leads to its faster completion and stops you wasting time and distracting yourself from other tasks by over-analyzing it.

Boosting Team Morale and Effort

Mindfulness can benefit individuals and teams in many ways, but isn't a magic solution or cure all. Being more mindful as you carry out your work can help you improve relationships with those you work with, and become more aware of what's happening, both of which are important when trying to boost team morale.

Morale is all about the team's capacity to consistently pull together in pursuit of a common purpose. Organizations with high morale tend to experience higher productivity and staff engagement. They have lower employee turnover and absenteeism, and a happier workforce.

Team morale may suffer as a result of change and restructuring, poor communication, or a lack of control over work. Often managers are so busy with their inner story that they fail to realize what's happening right before their eyes. Increased complaints about work or team members, greater workplace conflict, more absenteeism, and higher staff turnover are all indications that morale may be low.

The leader's morale can also have a profound impact on the morale of the team. Maybe you've been lucky enough to have worked for an energized, enthusiastic, positive boss. You may also have worked with a negative or disenchanted manager and noticed that this experience is a very different one. Team morale often starts with the leader, so leaders need to be good role models.

Improving morale with mindfulness

TIP

Here are a few tips for boosting morale:

>> **Set a good example.** Whether you're the boss or the most junior member of staff, you can still set a good example at work. Mindfulness shows you that you may not be able to control everything that life throws at you, but you can choose your response. Your behavior has an impact on how others think and behave, so make sure that you set a good example.

>> **Look for signs of poor morale and nip them in the bud.** The sooner you notice that morale is taking a turn for the worse, the easier it is to do something about it. Always be mindful of the signs of low morale, such as increased absenteeism, work conflict, and complaints. Look for the causes, and take steps to bring things back on track. If you're a leader, try to discuss the issue with the team in an open and honest way and really listen, without judgment, to people's responses. (Book 2 provides more guidance on these types of important conversations.)

>> **Bring in the good.** When you become particularly busy, you may find it yourself stopping doing the things that nourish you (such as meeting friends for coffee or playing a musical instrument) and to focus more on the things you think are important, such as work deadlines and projects. This focusing more on work is a mistake. When you're busy you need more of the things that nourish you, not less! Make sure that you pencil time into your schedule to do the little things in your life that feel really good. If you're a leader, try to encourage your team members to make time to do what they enjoy too. Discourage routine late working, and encourage staff to have a more appropriate life/work balance.

>> **Celebrate success and gain a sense of completion.** Do you find yourself complaining that you've got nothing done today? In reality, you've probably got lots done, but you just haven't acknowledged it. When you're busy you may find that one job tends to merge into another and another, giving you little sense of completion. Mindfulness shows you the need for a sense of completion — the need to be kind to yourself and acknowledge that you have completed one task, before you start the next. Each time you complete a task, congratulate yourself on a job well done, however small: "another email responded to — yes!", "another meeting concluded — yes!", "another customer order completed — yes!" Congratulating yourself helps you recognize just how much you've achieved and allow you to end the day with a sense of achievement.

>> **Create certainty and avoid threat.** Mindfulness shows you how your brain craves certainty and tries to avoid things that may be threatening. If little certainty exists at work, most people try to create some by anticipating what will happen next. This self-created story may be accurate or inaccurate, and yet you're likely to respond to it as if it is real and really happening. If things are uncertain at work, try to find out as many facts as you can, and be aware of when your mind is trying to fill in the gaps. Try to respond only to present-moment facts rather than worrying about things that haven't happened, and may never happen. As a leader, be mindful of the negative impact of uncertainty on team morale. Try to create as much certainty as possible. Be open and honest and take steps to actively involve staff in what's going on. Doing so gives staff a greater sense of control and certainty, reducing stress and improving morale.

>> **Encourage staff to get in the happy habit.** Happiness is a state of mind. Try to encourage happiness in the workplace. The Action for Happiness (www. actionforhappiness.org) website offers lots of free resources including posters for the workplace.

Focusing team effort with mindfulness

Mindfully refocus your team's efforts on what was important in this moment in time — just like Peter did earlier in this chapter.

Mindfulness is all about being able to switch your attention to the present moment, seeing things as they really are rather than how you perceive them to be. Even if your team has little knowledge of mindfulness, you can still use mindful techniques to focus on what's important in the here and now.

Try to make time to prioritize prioritizing. Individually or as part of a team, make time to regularly reassess what's important. Try to do this reassessment early on in the workday, when your mind is fresh. If possible, use the mindfulness technique described in the earlier section "Mindfully seeing what's important."

Recognize the power of habits. The more often you perform a task in a certain way, the more likely you are to do it in the same way in future. Each time you repeat a behavior or set of actions, you strengthen the connections in your brain associated with those activities. Routine tasks you do regularly become habits and get stored in a primitive part of your brain as a "habit." Research suggests that you cannot erase a habit when it has been formed, but you can, over time, replace it with another set of behaviors and thoughts. Use this knowledge to help yourself and others change habits so that they can do things differently at work.

Improving team relationships with mindfulness

TIP

Sometimes conflict may occur between members of your team. Maybe an actual incident has created problems or possibly team members simply don't get on. Whatever the cause, your team is less effective if it doesn't pull together. As the leader, you need to resolve such situations. Follow this three-step guide (and find additional tips in Chapters 2 and 3 of Book 2):

1. **Diagnose problems.**

   At the first signs of poor relationships within your team, using the diagnostic methods used by Peter (detailed earlier in this chapter), or another method of your choice, to bring the issues to the surface.

2. **Bring the problems into the open.**

While problems remain beneath the surface and not discussed, there's little you can do about them. Bringing them to the table in a supportive non-judgmental environment allows them to be explored and resolved. To ensure that the meeting is as productive as possible, do the following:

- Prepare yourself for it by practicing mindfulness for a short while to center yourself and help you approach the meeting in a supportive, non-judgmental, less reactive manner.

- Create a calm space for the discussion to take place.

- Explain to the people involved that you think there may be some tension and you'd like to help all of them discuss it, air their views, and collectively agree a way forward. Avoid telling them what you think is going on — let things unfold in the moment.

- Allow all sides equal time to state their case, without interruption. Be mindful to ensure that everyone sticks to present-moment facts rather than judgements and "their own story" of what's going on.

- Allow the team members to decide a way forward for themselves. Only intervene or mediate if absolutely essential.

3. **Observe the unfolding situation and support all concerned as they make the changes needed.**

Reward and encourage improved behavior.

TIP

Be mindful that, however hard you try, some people are never going to get on. In this case, encourage people to "sit with the difficulty" and find a way to acknowledge the discomfort and accept the impact that the person has on them without causing themselves any more unnecessary pain. Encountering difficult people at work is probably a universal experience. The following activity can prepare you (and others) for the next challenging encounter:

1. **Spend a few moments thinking about an encounter with a difficult colleague, client, or customer, and briefly summarize it on a sheet of paper.**

2. **Sit comfortably in a chair, with your feet on the ground, in a comfortable upright dignified position.**

Focus your attention on your breathing — feeling the breath coming in and the breath going out. Count six breaths (one inhalation and one exhalation equal one breath). If your mind wanders, don't worry. Just congratulate yourself on recognizing that your mind has wandered and begin counting again at 1.

3. **Now bring to mind the difficult encounter. Approach it with openness. Focus on it fully.**

   Observe your thoughts, emotions, and any sensations in your body.

4. **Approach and explore this difficult encounter with kindness and curiosity.**

   Stay in being mode — being with the memory of the difficult encounter. If you find yourself trying to find solutions to problems or alternative ways to behave, you've slipped into doing mode. Kindly escort yourself back to the present-moment experience of observing what's going on. If things feel too difficult, remember that you can let it go, and return back to your breathing at any time.

5. **Shift your attention to focus on observing how the difficult person is behaving.**

   How are they behaving? Can you notice anything about their body — for example, is it stiff or relaxed?

6. **Wish the person you've been thinking of well in his or her life and career.**

   Wish them happiness and good health. If you're uncomfortable doing so, that's fine; this step of the exercise can be challenging. Don't get annoyed, just acknowledge that at this moment in time you find it hard, and skip to the final step of the exercise.

7. **Let the memory of the difficult encounter go and focus on your breathing again until you reach a count of six in- and out-breaths.**

   Open your eyes and return to your day.

IN THIS CHAPTER

» **Dealing with HR tasks mindfully**

» **Tackling staff health**

» **Helping the trainers**

» **Improving customer service**

» **Making marketing and PR more switched on**

Chapter **4**

Using Mindfulness to Assist Different Business Functions

C ultivating mindfulness is a valuable skill for staff working at all levels of an organization, in all business functions, in all industries. Mindfulness won't diminish your drive for excellence and attention to what's important. It won't make you weak or ineffective, or brainwash you into donating all your worldly goods to a worthwhile cause in a far-flung corner of the world. Also, despite media portrayal of mindfulness, you do not have to sit cross-legged on a cushion, light incense, or become religious!

To get the most from mindfulness, you really need to attend a course and practice mindfulness each day, but the hints and tips in this chapter should prove valuable to specific business functions. Many of the tips and techniques provided are equally applicable to multiple job roles.

Mindfulness for Human Resources

What's in a name? "HR" (human resources), "personnel," or even "human capital management" are all names for the business function responsible for recruitment and selection of staff, defining job roles, and setting pay structures. HR teams may also develop policies on how staff should behave and be treated, including equal opportunities and employee assistance programs. Where the learning and development function sits under HR, the department is also responsible for developing staff at all levels. Although some aspects of HR such as telling someone they got the job or have been promoted are satisfying, other parts can be highly stressful. Potentially stressful parts of the job include dealing with grievances and dismissals. This sometimes earns the HR function the nickname of "the personnel police" or "policy pushers." This section includes suggestions on how mindfulness can help you mindfully manage three key functions of most HR departments.

Managing downsizing and dismissals mindfully

The economic downturn has led to cost-cutting initiatives in both the public and private sectors. In many organizations, these initiatives have led to downsizing and dismissals year on year.

While you may not be able to halt the tide of downsizing and dismissals, you can undertake the process in a manner that's kinder to yourself and those people at risk. You can start by focusing on the impact that managing downsizing and dismissals has on you.

WARNING

Although managing downsizing and dismissals is likely to be a key element of your work that you've probably studied and practiced over the years, this doesn't necessarily make it any easier. Even the most cold hearted of HR professionals are likely to experience a form of negative response to the task. Everything that you do or think has an impact on your thoughts, emotions, and physiology, but in most cases you're unaware of the impact. This lack of awareness can be a good thing because it frees up your brain to work on other things. It can also be bad news if you start to unwittingly activate your sympathetic nervous system, flooding your body with powerful hormones that can be damaging. You may also unwittingly carry around tension in your body, which can have a profound impact on your decision-making. So although you may think that you're giving your best at all times, your actions and responses may be being governed by a host of things you're completely unaware of.

This is where mindfulness comes in. Mindfulness training progressively trains you to direct your full attention to where you want it to be. It allows you to passively observe the interplay between your thoughts, emotions, and physiology, and make conscious choices about how to best respond, rather than being governed by your unconscious mental programming.

Another factor to consider is the potential impact of mirror neurons. Mirror neurons (described in the nearby sidebar) may cause you to experience the emotions of the people surrounding you, which may impact on your decisions and behavior. Mindfulness helps you focus attention on the present-moment experience, allowing you to notice when your emotions are being influenced by mirror neurons, and decide on a wise course of action.

While you cannot necessarily "manage" the emotions of others, you can take steps to avoid any negative emotions you are harboring from spiraling out of control. By being fully present in meetings with others, you can observe if and when emotions start to spiral and take steps to avoid things escalating.

TIP

Here are a few mindful ways in which you can keep your meetings on track when strong emotions arise in others:

>> **Take a few moments out.** Change the course of the conversation or just pause for a few moments to avoid adding more fuel to the fire.

>> **Acknowledge the emotions, and try to help the person identify the thoughts driving them.** You can ask them, for example, "I can see you're really upset. Would you like to share with me what's going through your mind?"

>> **Demonstrate empathy.** Although you have a job to do, the world may be falling apart for the employee in front of you. Be as kind and compassionate as you can be while still ensuring that you deliver the organizational messages you need to.

>> **Cultivate empathy.** If you find yourself suffering from compassion fatigue (common in the caring professions) and becoming immune to the suffering of others, make it a personal priority to cultivate empathy. Mindfulness can help you do so. You need to care about the people you are dealing with professionally while at the same time ensuring that you do the right thing for your organization.

Dealing with discipline and grievances mindfully

As with downsizing and dismissals, dealing with discipline and grievances involves both care and doing the right thing (legally and ethically) for your organization.

MIRROR NEURONS

According to researchers, a mirror neuron is a neuron that fires in the brain both when you act and when you observe the same action performed by someone else. So, in effect, mirror neurons "mirror" the behavior of others. In humans, mirror neuron activity has been found in the premotor cortex, the supplementary motor area, the primary somatosensory cortex, and the inferior parietal cortex.

The exact function of the mirror system is still subject to speculation, but scientists believe that mirror neurons help people understand the intentions of others, their mental state, and to pick up new skills by imitation.

Neuroscientist Marco Lacoboni argues that mirror neurons are the neural basis of the human capacity for emotions such as empathy. He believes that, when observing the physical or mental experiences of others, mirror neurons make people experience similar feelings or sensations. This may explain why, if you're surrounded by angry people, you become angry, or if you observe people eating, you start to feel hungry.

Mirror neuron theory has important implications for the world of work. It impacts on the leader–follower relationship and for those, such as HR staff, who routinely have to manage highly charged emotional situations.

Preparing well for these sorts of meetings is crucial. Most HR people are fully aware of the need to check the facts from all concerned, company policy, and the law. What you may fail to do is check that you're mentally prepared for the meeting. In other words, you need to ensure that you enter the meeting in the present moment rather than your body being there but your attention continually being hijacked by thoughts about other jobs you have to do or what you'll be doing when you get home. You also need to try to ensure that your thinking isn't overly influenced by past experiences or by what people *may* be saying or how they *may* be behaving.

Only through practicing mindfulness regularly do you gain an appreciation of the elaborate stories that your brain creates when trying to anticipate the future. The problem with these stories is that your brain can treat them as reality, and you can start to experience emotions in response. For example, if you're entering a grievance session and you think that the manager concerned will become angry and the employee tearful, you may unconsciously interact with the manager in an assertive or even aggressive manner and treat the employee with patience and concern.

By being in the present moment and following an appropriate meeting structure, allowing each part to unfold moment by moment and responding to present moment facts, your meeting is likely to run more smoothly for all concerned. (Check out Book 2 for details on handling all types of important conversations.)

Increasing resilience and relationship quality

Several research studies suggest that training staff in mindfulness can increase employee engagement. In addition, mindfulness has been shown to improve interpersonal relations, help employees improve the quality of relationships, increase resilience, and improve task performance and decision-making. Mindfulness training can improve your ability to cope effectively with your own and other's daily stresses, thus improving the quality of your relationships.

The following techniques have been developed for HR staff, but may be equally applicable and useful for other business functions.

Dropping into the present moment

When dealing with difficult issues, maintaining your balance and well-being by dropping into the present moment every now and then is important. Doing so helps you

>> Observe what's grabbing your attention and regain control when your thoughts are spiraling.

>> Release any tension you're experiencing and reduce the risk of your physiological responses impacting on your decisions.

>> Shift yourself from avoidance mode (when people are motivated by the desire to avoid something happening) to an approach state of mind (when people are able to explore new possibilities and opportunities with an open mind). This shift helps you become more productive.

TIP

This exercise can take as little as three minutes or be extended to take up to ten minutes. Sit yourself in a comfortable upright position. Close your eyes or hold them in soft focus. Regain your equilibrium using the **NOW** technique:

1. **Notice (but don't judge or start to interact with) the following:**

   - The sounds in the room and nearby.

   - How your body is feeling — any tensions or sensations.

   - Any emotions you may be feeling.

2. **Observe the impact (if any) that the points under 'Notice' in Step 1 are having on one another.**

   For example, does a certain sound make your body tense? Are your emotions having any impact on your thoughts? Is a trend or theme emerging as you observe your thoughts? Again, you don't need to do anything or solve anything; just observe what's happening in the present moment.

3. **Wait.**

Resist the temptation to jump into action based on what you've noticed and observed. Just let everything go and give your brain a break by focusing on nothing but your breath for a short while. Fully experience the present sensation as the breath enters your body and leaves your body; do so playfully, as if for the first time.

Open your eyes and make a decision on what's the best use of your time **NOW**, in this moment.

Mindfully managing difficult meetings

TIP

When planning difficult meetings such as discussing job losses, being in the present moment is important so that you can judge the situation as it unfolds based on present-moment facts rather than mental projections about what may happen in the future or did happen in the past. Doing so can make the meetings less stressful for all concerned. Follow these steps:

1. **Ensure that you've all the relevant documents ready and are fully acquainted with all the facts and people involved.**

   Be as well prepared as you possibly can be.

2. **Practice mindfulness for a short period.**

   Try the three-minute focus break or a mindful minute (see Book 4, Chapter 3 for details).

3. **Start the meeting by stating its purpose and what you are going to cover and specify when people will have the opportunity for questions.**

   This last point may sound obvious, but it's amazing how often this detail is missed when emotions are running high.

4. **Check in with yourself regularly to check that you are operating in approach mode in the present moment.**

   Periodically observe your thoughts or tune in to how a specific area of your body feels.

5. **Try to see things through the eyes of your audience.**

   They're likely to be feeling threatened, which will influence their thoughts and behavior. When in the grip of strong emotions, they're unlikely to be fully aware of their words and actions. This situation is natural; try not to take people's responses personally. Try to remain kind and considerate, bearing in mind the situation these people find themselves in. Keep in mind that while managing meetings like this may be a regular occurrence for you, being threatened with a job loss may be new to them.

6. **Be kind to yourself!**

   Meetings about downsizing or grievances, for example, can be unpleasant and emotions can run high. You are a human being and not a machine, and as such you're entitled to feel emotional (angry, sad, or even anxious). The important thing to remember is that the emotion is transient — it will come and go — it won't last forever.

Mindfully supporting staff

TIP

In your role you're likely to have many one-to-one informal and formal meetings with staff who may be worried about a variety of work-related issues. Your role isn't only to provide them with sources of information and support, but also to tap into how you can best help them in this specific moment in time. Unfortunately, if you've been involved in many meetings with staff over the years, acting on auto-pilot is all too easy. You need to remember that each meeting is unique and should be approached with a beginner's mind — as if you're experiencing it for the first time. Although approaching meetings this way may require a little more effort, the outcomes make it worthwhile. Follow these guidelines:

>> **Jump into the present moment by setting aside thoughts of what you were doing before the person walked in or what you need to do later on.** If you've time before the person arrives, practice a short mindfulness technique.

>> **Closely observe what's unfolding in the present moment.** Rather than responding in a routine manner to what you think the person's needs are at this stage of the process, really listen to what is being said and how it's being said.

>> **Respond based on what's being asked for in the present moment rather than on what you think you should be hearing.** Be honest, open, and authentic.

>> **Recap and summarize at key points in the meeting to clarify understanding and reassure the other person that you've heard and understood what they're saying.** A quick overview gives the other person the chance to correct your understanding if necessary.

>> **Provide a quick summary at the end of the meeting and agree on what should happen next.**

>> **Check in with yourself.** After the other person has left, let go of any tension or negative emotions you may be harboring so that you're ready to tackle the next part of your day. A three-minute focus break (see Book 4, Chapter 3) should help you do this.

Mindfulness for Occupational Health

A great deal of research has concluded that mindfulness is great for well-being. Hundreds of research studies over the last 40 years have demonstrated the effectiveness of mindfulness in reducing anxiety, stress, and depression. Mindfulness has also been proven to help people with chronic pain, such as back pain, and even to boost immunity. Several workplace studies have demonstrated its effectiveness in reducing sickness absence.

Improving staff well-being with mindfulness

Taking proactive steps to improve staff well-being is now more important than ever. Ongoing restructures and downsizing are taking their toll on those who are "lucky enough" to still have a job. Research has identified that not only do these people frequently feel guilty, but continued uncertainty also can have a huge impact on people's health and increase long-term sickness absence. A constant sense of uncertainty can cause excessive stress, which can also lead to increased occupational accidents and serious illness such as heart disease, high blood pressure or diabetes.

Organizations can work to improve the well-being of their staff in many ways. Offering mindfulness courses to staff is a good way to improve not only well-being but also productivity and interpersonal skills. Some organizations offer staff mindfulness courses in work time and some outside working hours; some make attendance on mindfulness courses compulsory for certain staff, while others prefer it to be optional. While some organizations prefer to stick to the most widely researched method of teaching mindfulness (an eight-week Mindfulness Based Stress Reduction or Mindfulness Based Cognitive Therapy course), others integrate aspects of mindfulness training with other well-being initiatives.

Tackling stress with mindfulness

It should come as no surprise that stress has become one of the greatest causes of long-term sickness absence from work. Mindfulness has been used to treat stress since the 1970s. Mindfulness Based Stress Reduction (MBSR) was developed specifically to deal with mental distress such as stress, and thousands of research studies demonstrate its effectiveness in doing so.

As with all mindfulness at work interventions, evaluating staff both before and after taking part in a mindfulness course using well-recognized measures is important. If you wish to reduce stress specifically, you first need to measure individuals' current levels of stress. Consider getting staff to complete the DASS 21, a shortened version of the DASS (Depression Anxiety Stress Scales), developed by the University of New South Wales in Australia. The DASS 21 measures the severity of a range of symptoms common to depression, anxiety, and stress. This measure can then be used as a benchmark pre- and post-mindfulness training.

WARNING

A word of caution — mindfulness isn't a silver bullet. Simply attending a mindfulness course won't reduce stress. Reducing stress takes effort and commitment on the part of the stressed participant, who needs to practice what they're taught for a short time every day for the entire duration of the eight-week course. Research suggests a direct correlation exists between time spent practicing mindfulness and the benefits experienced. In general, the more time spent practicing, the more benefit is derived. Note also that, if a staff member is *very severely* stressed, a mindfulness course may prove unsuitable as the staff member may not be in a fit state of mind to work with the techniques they're taught. In this instance, seeking clinical help would be wise.

Reducing sickness and absence with mindfulness

Well people who are well managed result in a well organization. Well-being at work isn't the sole responsibility of the occupational health team but the responsibility of the whole organization. Policies and working practices can have a huge impact on staff well-being, and are worth reviewing if staff absence and sickness are on the increase.

Mindfulness can equip staff with the tools to deal with life's challenges more effectively, which can reduce stress and anxiety. Mindfulness can also help people stop small things escalating out of control and causing unnecessary stress. Mindfulness can help people live with long-term health conditions, including back problems and even cancer, by giving them new ways of dealing with their mental and physical pain.

TIP

Offer staff a place they can go to practice mindfulness in work time when the need arises. Just knowing that there's somewhere quiet that they're allowed to go to center themselves and regain a more positive frame of mind can make a massive difference. Organizations offering this facility to staff report that the facility is rarely abused and is highly valued. Allowing staff to leave their desk for 10 minutes every now and then can save hours of unproductive time in the office and weeks off sick.

Mindfulness for Learning and Organizational Development

In order to serve your organization well as a member of the learning and development team or organizational development team, you need to be able to see the bigger picture and think creatively. You may also at times have to focus your attention on statistics and diverse organizational performance data. A major part of mindfulness is all about training your brain to focus your attention where you want it to be. You won't be surprised to discover that research demonstrates that mindfulness does indeed improve your ability to focus on the task at hand. Evidence also exists that mindfulness training can increase your creativity and ability to step back and see the bigger picture.

Improving learning with mindfulness

Mindfulness can help improve learning within your organization in two key ways:

» First, practicing mindfulness can improve your capacity to learn. It does so in several ways. Research studies have shown that mindfulness can improve your working memory. (Working memory gives you the ability to hold and use a limited amount of information in your brain for a short time; you couldn't perform mental arithmetic or follow a set of directions without it.) Working memory is essential for learning and development. Research has shown that practicing mindfulness can result in positive changes in the brain areas associated with learning and memory processes, among other things.

» Second, elements of mindfulness can be incorporated into many development programs to make them more effective. A few are described in the following sections.

Using mindful minutes at various points during a training day

You can use mindful minutes at the start, after lunch, or as a break between two different topics.

Mindful minutes help participants quiet their mental chatter and put them in a more receptive frame of mind for learning. It helps them release any tension and makes it easier to absorb what is being taught. (See Book 4, Chapter 3 for more about mindful minutes).

Explaining that thoughts are simply a mental process that you have created

Use this knowledge to help people be more open when exploring new ideas or when challenging old, ineffective ways of working.

Many people have a tendency to react to thoughts as if they were facts, especially when busy or under pressure. As an example, say that your boss likes you and is impressed by your work, but you think that your boss dislikes you. You start building up a story in your head about your working relationship. You may worry about being treated unfairly, overlooked for promotion, or picked on. Your brain is then likely to treat these thoughts as facts, which in turn have a negative impact on your interactions with your boss.

REMEMBER

Making mental constructs of the world as you see it is normal and helpful. However, if these mental constructs are different to present-moment reality they're not helpful.

Distinguishing approach and avoidance modes of mind

Explain the motivations underpinning both modes of mind and how cultivating an approach mode of mind is more productive. Staff can use this knowledge when trying to generate new ideas or new ways of thinking about things. Understanding the modes of mind is also useful for exploring things that underpin resistance to change.

Many people live their lives in avoidance mode of mind, their actions and thoughts motivated by the desire to avoid something happening. Living in this way closes your mind to new ways of doing things and new opportunities.

Describing the human threat response

Explaining the human threat response can help people understand why people find it difficult to focus or think straight at certain times. This understanding can also help them recognize when they're feeling under excess pressure, thus allowing them to take steps to return to peak productivity and put them back in control.

Modern-day stressors can lead you to a high state of arousal, triggering a surge of strong hormones through your body that are intended to keep you safe from mortal danger. In this state your brain is focusing on keeping you alive, so your capacity for higher-brain functions (which are unnecessary for survival) are diminished. These higher-brain functions include decision-making, strategic planning, and big picture thinking.

Improving strategic thinking

In order to offer maximum value to an organization, learning and development initiatives need to be linked to organizational strategy. Organizational development teams work to improve organizational performance, and need a good grasp of strategy and the bigger picture.

Many mindfulness techniques help you develop the capability to think out of the box. Research demonstrates that practicing mindfulness helps you see the bigger picture. Other research studies suggest that practicing mindfulness can help you let go of your personal agenda. It can also help to increase creativity.

TIP

When undertaking complex planning and strategy work, you can easily get bogged down in details. Juggling stakeholder wants and needs with financial targets is never easy. When you can't see the forest for the trees, try this mindfulness technique. It helps you step back and view things with a fresh mind, and encourages creativity. This exercise takes about 25 minutes, which may seem like a long time, especially when you're really busy. However, you can easily waste 25 minutes getting nowhere if you just continue working as you are. The act of focusing on your breath and body brings you back to the present moment (even if your mind does keep wandering!) and encourages an approach mode rather than an avoidance mode of mind.

1. **Find a room where you won't be disturbed for the next 25 minutes.**

2. **Write down the questions you're struggling to resolve.**

    Identify a maximum of three key questions and write each on one sheet of A4 paper.

3. **Settle yourself into your chair, sitting in a comfortable, upright position.**
    Close your eyes or hold them in soft focus.

4. **Focus your attention on the present-moment experience of breathing.**

    If thoughts arise, that's fine; just part of the process. Just acknowledge them, let them go and refocus on your breath.

5. **Spend five minutes seeing how your body feels in this present moment.**

    Start at the feet and work slowly upwards to your head. Notice any sensations, and how they differ. If you notice any pain or discomfort, try breathing into it on the in-breath, and letting it go on the out-breath.

6. **Open your eyes and concentrate your attention on the questions.**

    Restrict yourself to a maximum of two minutes to answer each question. Write down whatever pops into your head, however random, without judging or trying to make sense of it.

7. **Close your eyes or hold them in soft focus.**

Spend around five minutes focusing your full attention on your breath.

8. **Look at what you've written on your A4 pad.**

Identify any key themes or things that leap out at you.

TIP

If you're really pushed for time, follow only steps 1 to 6, or better still, just focus on one key question.

Introducing mindful practices into the workplace

Unlike many other development techniques, mindfulness isn't a concept that you can grasp intellectually and then instantly benefit from. Most benefit is derived from practice. Practicing mindfulness helps you, over time, change the way you think and behave. This means that in order to introduce mindfulness into your organization, you need to find an external mindfulness teacher (unless you're lucky enough to have a qualified one working for you already!). As a long-term goal, developing internal capacity to deliver mindfulness programs is desirable, but this is likely to take a minimum of 24 months from start to qualified teacher status. This time can be reduced if you develop a member of staff who has already been practicing mindfulness for some time.

TIP

You can cultivate and encourage mindfulness in the workplace by starting meetings with a mindful minute or using the three-minute focus break technique when things are going round in circles or getting stuck (see Book 4, Chapter 3 for details). You may also wish to provide a quiet room where staff can go to spend a few quiet moments practicing mindfulness to recharge their batteries and regain clarity of mind. No special equipment is needed — just comfortable, upright chairs and maybe a few large cushions for people who like to sit on the floor. Decorate the room with calming colors and install a blind at the window that staff can adjust to their liking.

Mindfulness for Customer Service

Customer service and customer-facing staff are among the most important personnel in an organization nowadays. They're the face of the company, interacting with customers on a day-to-day basis. Top companies appreciate the need for excellence in customer service, and the importance of achieving customer loyalty.

In order to be fully effective in these roles, you need to be fully in the present moment and avoid auto-pilot responses. This can be easier said than done, especially when you're dealing with customers face to face or on the phone all day long, many with similar questions and issues that need addressing. This section provides some mindful strategies for maintaining customer focus, communicating with clients, and dealing with customer feedback.

Maintaining customer focus

Maybe you think that you know what your customers want and need, but are you sure? When was the last time you really listened and fully focused your attention on the customer? Many companies focus intensively on customer needs and desires when they're bringing a new product to market, but fail to keep their finger on the customer's pulse as soon as sales targets are being met. Wise companies dig beneath online reviews and recommendations, regularly making opportunities to hear what the customer has to say and act on it to ensure that their products and services continue to meet or exceed customer needs. When interacting with customers (one to one as a customer service representative or when running a focus group), mindfulness can be highly beneficial.

TIP

Take a few moments before talking to customers to observe your mental chatter, acknowledging whatever arises, and letting it go kindly without judgement or any further action. (See Chapter 6 in Book 2 for more about customer conversations.)

1. **Center yourself for a few moments by focusing on your breath.**

2. **Focus your attention for the duration of your meeting or phone call entirely on the present-moment experience of assisting, advising, or listening to your customer.**

3. **Start with initial questions, but if unexpected things arise, go with them, really listen, and reflect on what's said.**

   This approach is particularly useful if you're running a focus group.

4. **Make sure that the customer feels heard and that their input is valued.**

   Reflect back and summarize to confirm understanding, especially if the conversation is lengthy or complex.

5. **Check in with yourself regularly to check that you're 100 percent focused on what's unfolding in the present moment, and that your mind has not wandered to the past or the future.**

   If your mind has strayed, be kind to yourself — you're only human! Kindly and gently escort your attention back to the present-moment discussion or conversation.

6. **Summarize after the call or meeting what you've gained from your interaction with the customer, and ensure that trends and new ideas are reported back to other areas of the business.**

Identify whether you felt any strong emotions during the discussion. Take a moment to explore the impact these had on your thoughts and body.

Dealing with customer feedback mindfully

While most companies have some form of procedure for dealing with complaints, few have a process for dealing with positive feedback!

Dealing with criticism and hostility can be particularly challenging. When people are critical or hostile, feeling threatened is natural, even when you know that it isn't personal, and the customer is far away at the end of the phone line. Most customer service staff have been trained to deal with situations like this in a manner that's professional, polite and that, hopefully, leads to a happy customer. Unfortunately, dealing with difficult customers can take a toll on the staff member, as customer service training rarely shows you how to manage your mind and the importance of self-kindness.

TIP

The next time you have to work with a customer who is distressed or angry, try this:

>> **Be as fully present as you can during the conversation.** Keep in mind that, while your product or service may have been the catalyst for their anger or distress, there may be hidden factors driving the intensity of their reaction that may have nothing to do with you, your company, or your products.

>> **Be compassionate toward them — think of them as a human in distress.** Adopting this attitude does two things. First, it can help diffuse a volatile situation. Second, it reduces your threat response, reducing the pressure you put on yourself. By reducing your threat response, your hormones return to normal and you can think more clearly and act more calmly.

>> **Give yourself a few moments to check in with yourself after the call or meeting to make sure that you're in the right mental and physical shape to deal with the next customer.** Sitting at your desk, starting with your toes and working toward your head, see whether you're holding any tension anywhere. If you find any tension or discomfort, breathe into it on the in-breath, and release it on the out-breath. This small act of self-kindness does two things.

- First, it allows you to fully release any tension you may still be unconsciously holding (bodily tension can have a major impact on thoughts and mood).

- Second, it puts you into a more receptive, open, present moment state for dealing with your next customer interaction, free from the baggage of your last meeting.

TIP

If you work in a call center or in an environment in which you don't have full control of your time, try to use your breaks to recharge your batteries and check in with yourself using the final guideline in the preceding list. Taking a few minutes out a few times a day is good for you and good for business. When in a state of (often unconscious) stress, your ability to provide an excellent service to customers is reduced, and you are much more likely to pick up bugs and viruses as your auto-immune system is diminished. Maintain your peak performance with these mini mindfulness exercises.

Communicating mindfully with customers

Mindfulness can be powerful in your communications with customers, whether face to face or via the phone, email or letter.

TIP

When you've just written a letter or email, pause and take a few full breaths before you send it. As you do so, try forgetting the email and everything else and just focusing on your breathing. Then read the letter or email from your customer's perspective. According to Mirabai Bush, who taught mindfulness to staff at Google, doing so helps clear up potential misinterpretations.

Mindfulness for Marketing and PR

In 2013 the job-finding website CareerCast listed public relations manager as the fifth most stressful job in the United States. Stress can be helpful, motivating you to strive and achieve more. But it can also cloud your judgment, have a negative impact on your mood, reduce your ability to make good decisions, and cause serious illnesses.

In some organizational cultures, stress can be worn as a badge of honor; if you're not seen to be openly stressed, you're judged to be not working hard enough. Similarly, some organizations may encourage a culture of working long hours. Both stress and a poor life/work balance are bad for business. The statistics and research backing this up are hard to ignore.

When you're really busy, stopping and "doing nothing" — even for five minutes — may seem counter-intuitive. Spending five minutes practicing mindfulness can sometimes feel like doing nothing, but in fact you are working hard to develop the neural pathways in your brain associated with directing your attention to where you want it to be, and switching yourself into a more helpful mode of mind. You may want to direct your full attention to communication, consumer trends, culture, or your own working methods, for example.

Communicating powerfully

The foundation that underpins powerful communication is a deep understanding of yourself: your beliefs, perceptions, judgment, and intentions.

Humans are strongly motivated by their beliefs. These beliefs are often unconscious, but can override or impede what you consciously intend to do or say. Remaining fully present is impossible unless you understand what's motivating your feelings and behavior in the moment. Practicing mindfulness can help you develop a conscious understanding of your beliefs. This conscious understanding allows you to decide the extent to which your beliefs shape and influence your work.

Although you may think that you see the whole picture, your brain just picks out what it feels is most relevant at any given time and you make up the rest based on past experience and knowledge. If you accept that your perceptions of any given situation are likely to be limited, you can use mindfulness to help train yourself to see more and guess less.

Your judgment also plays a role in how you communicate. Again, this may be unconscious and can be highly damaging, both to yourself and others. When you feel judged harshly by others, your threat system motivates you to take defensive action. Practicing mindfulness helps you recognize this response and minimize its harmful impact.

Lastly, but most importantly, you need to ensure that outcomes you desire from your communication are linked to your intentions. Make sure that you are fully aware of your intentions before you start to communicate, as these intentions gently steer you through your meeting or presentation. Try to remain open to what others are trying to communicate, and what a positive outcome looks like from their perspective.

Keeping in tune with consumer and cultural trends

However much time you spend reading trade journals and industry reports, try to accept that you'll never be 100 percent in tune with consumer and cultural trends.

A better starting point is accepting a 50–70 percent level of understanding, and using your eyes and ears to fill in the gaps when working with consumers or conducting market research. Don't forget that, while you only have one mouth, you have two ears and two eyes — use them wisely to see what's unfolding in front of you in the present moment.

TIP

When analyzing consumer research and sales data, quickly note your top three observations immediately after reading. Take a mindful minute. This mindful pause can take the form of focusing your attention on taking 10 full breaths, or mindfully drinking a hot drink, focusing on nothing but the present moment sensations, smells, and tastes. What you do doesn't matter; the important thing is to quiet your mind, jump fully into the present moment, and reduce your state of arousal so that you can view things with a clear, open mind.

Following the mindful minute, revisit the documents and look for any alternative trends or key facts you may have missed. Bear in mind that the researchers or authors of the documents will have interpreted the facts they were presented with according to their own judgment. They may have missed or discarded something that you think is important. Looking at the documents with a beginner's eyes can yield surprising results and eureka moments.

Improving responsiveness

When you practice mindfulness, you discover that a distinct difference exists between "reacting" and "responding."

» Reacting is seen as defensive, often based on auto-pilot reactions stored in the fast to react primitive areas of your brain. Reactions are often fueled by emotions, rather than rational, higher-brain thoughts.

» Responding is altogether more thoughtful. By pausing before acting, you allow yourself time to apply your more powerful higher brain. Responses contain reasoning, and are guided less by emotion and more by logic.

Although responding may seem more passive, a response is more active and can change the direction of an interaction. Practicing mindfulness helps you become more centered and aware of others. By embracing mindful prevention of reacting, you can focus on more beneficial responses that improve your interaction with clients and colleagues alike.

5

Boomers and Beyond: Influencing across Generations

Contents at a Glance

Chapter 1

Driving Engagement across Generations

D o you have teenagers or kids in their 20s? If so, have you ever tried leaving them a voicemail? They probably texted you back with a one-word response: "What?" Don't bother asking if they listened to the message — they didn't. See, young people today communicate differently than, say, Baby Boomers.

People of different generations don't just communicate differently. They also have different motivational drivers. Smart managers adjust their communication, leadership, oversight, recognition, and patience levels when leading a department populated by people of different generations.

Just who comprises each of these generations? And what do they want? For a run down, read on. This chapter focuses on the unique differences between the three generations that dominate today's workplace — Baby Boomers, Generation X, and Millennials (also known as Generation Y) — and how you can best drive engagement with each group.

REMEMBER

The descriptions that follow are merely generational generalizations. Expect some exceptions to the rule. That said, most employers (and employees) will recognize the truths in the traits associated with each generation.

Boom Baby: Working with Baby Boomers

Generally identified as being born between the years of 1945 and 1964, Baby Boomers are idealistic and have a tendency toward personal and social expression. The first generation to earn and possess more than their parents, Baby Boomers are typically ambitious, materialistic, and prone to being workaholics.

Questioning authority — a tenet for masses of young people in the 1960s and 1970s — is still very much a part of the Boomer approach to life and to work. Boomers are far more apt to challenge leadership than those who came before them, and also to embrace change. Boomers also remember when getting email was a good thing and not overwhelming.

Unlike their predecessors, Baby Boomers have largely opted against retiring at age 65. Why? For one thing, they like their jobs. Sure, if they'd worked in a coal mine or an assembly line for the last 30 years, they may feel differently. But many Baby Boomers work in knowledge-based positions, which are often quite engaging. Besides, with the demise of traditional pension plans — plus the fact that people are, on average, living longer — many Boomers have found that retirement at 65 is not financially feasible.

TRADITIONALISTS (AKA "THE SILENT GENERATION")

Don't assume that Baby Boomers comprise the oldest members of your employee roster. There may remain a few "Traditionalists," or workers born between 1925 and 1944 (though not many, given their age). Traditionalist workers are motivated by conformity, stability, security, and upward mobility. They tend to pledge allegiance to the company that employs them. They identify with the statement "I will give my all to my company" with nearly the same fervor they may once have felt for "I will fight for my country." This theme was popularized in Tom Brokaw's book *The Greatest Generation* (Random House). This generation is also characterized by a respect for authority. As such, their fidelity to the company often blends seamlessly with their loyalty to superiors and co-workers.

Traditionalists take pride in doing their work consistently, dependably, and well, but they likely aren't interested in the latest technological tools or the hottest trends in management. With retirement looming, many Traditionalists are motivated by the desire to leave the workforce in security and comfort, and pleased that they fulfilled their employment obligations to their companies. Due to today's difficult economic conditions, however, some Traditionalists, like many Boomers, have postponed retirement until their savings recover. This can lead to tensions with the younger staff who are looking to move up.

Attracting and hirin[...]

Boomers are ambitious — always h[...]
ing trend is Boomers' increasing i[...]
Having successfully climbed the c[...]
parents couldn't afford, Baby Bo[...]
concern about social and enviro[...]
the importance of CSR among [...]
younger generation seems to [...]
associate with their youth.

TIP

Smart organizations includ[...]
Many older workers who vi[...]
careers are more inclined than ever to [...]
sure) to take on a job with a more altruistic th[...]
this generation include job variety, travel, opportunities [...]
opportunities to teach and mentor younger workers.

Training Boomers

Everyone knows the saying "You can't teach an old dog new tricks." But the thing about that saying is that it's wrong. You *can* teach an old dog new tricks. You just have to know what training method to use!

When it comes to training Boomers, you'll want to keep these points in mind:

>> **Include team activities.** Yes, everyone says they hate team activities, role playing, and experiential exercises. But in course evaluations, team activities almost always get the highest marks. See, people *say* they don't like these activities, but they dislike sitting in a chair for hours, being lectured to, and looking at PowerPoint slides even more. If done well, team activities can be incredibly effective ways to teach and engage Boomers (as well as other generations). In fact, based on research by the National Training Laboratories in Arlington, Virginia, hands-on training is effective with 75 percent of people, second only to teaching others.

>> **Let participants experience different team roles.** Job rotation, even on a temporary basis, is a great way to reinforce learning with Baby Boomers. It will also build greater understanding of and appreciation for others' jobs — the "walk a mile in her shoes" thing.

training with the company's strategic plan. Boomers are goal driven. The more a company can link learning with organizational goals, the better. If employee engagement is a strategic goal of the company, Boomers are far more likely to embrace engagement-training initiatives. Training "stickiness" is greatly enhanced when the engagement workshop is connected to the organizational goals. Decoupling from organizational goals turns the learning opportunity into a "flavor of the month."

>> **Allow time after training for participants to evaluate.** The best evaluations to weigh the effectiveness of training occur 60 to 90 days *after* the learning event. Waiting two or three months provides you with feedback on whether the participants are applying the learning in their jobs.

Engaging Boomers

To engage Baby Boomers on your staff, consider the following:

>> **Foster a non-authoritarian work environment.** Boomers don't like being told what to do. An authoritarian culture will meet resistance at best, and disengagement at worst. At this stage of their careers, Boomers are set in their ways. They have — or believe they have — accomplished a lot. Not surprisingly, a democratic leadership style goes a long way toward engaging Boomers.

>> **Tap into their experience.** Ask questions like the following:

- "So, what do you suggest?"

- "How have you done this in the past?"

- "What has worked best when you've tried to do this?"

- "How would you recommend we proceed?"

Asking these and related questions will engage Boomers. It shows respect for their years in the trenches.

>> **Offer fresh assignments and other development opportunities.** After years of climbing the corporate ladder, Boomers may be interested in lateral or even lower-level positions — *if* the positions will allow them to do new jobs or learn new skills. Shifting assignments will also boost innovation, because it invites new and different perspectives.

>> **Be aware of the challenges they face.** Many Boomers wrestle with various personal challenges, such as paying college tuition for their children, subsidizing older children, and/or taking care of aging parents. In addition, some Boomers may be experiencing their own medical issues for the first time. Managers who are empathetic about all the things Boomers must juggle in their complex lives will be rewarded over time with above-and-beyond effort.

>> **Foster collaboration.** The idealism that encouraged many of this generation to boycott the Vietnam War still kindles a desire to be part of "something bigger." As such, Boomers tend to be highly engaged by working in partnership or as part of a team.

>> **Encourage expression.** Boomers enjoy opportunities for expression. They're among the ranks of workers who are truly engaged by meetings — especially when said meetings involve the exchange of ideas that intrigue them.

>> **Engage in CSR.** To engage Boomers, encourage social activism, volunteerism, and CSR activities. Boomers are looking for ways to give back.

Rewarding Boomers

Boomers respond well to the following types of rewards:

>> **Key assignments:** Although people tend to associate the term *reward* with something monetary, that's not always the case. Why not reward a Boomer with an international assignment, a transfer, or a key slot on the company's five-year strategic planning committee? Leveraging and acknowledging Boomers' experience is a benefit to both the company *and* the deserving Boomer!

>> **Acknowledgment of their accomplishments and their years of service:** Public recognition, handwritten notes, saying "Job well done!", and similar acknowledgments of an employee's accomplishments and/or tenure are important engagement drivers for all generations, including Boomers.

>> **Promotional opportunities:** Baby Boomers are the wealthiest generation ever, and they didn't build that wealth by accident. They are, and remain, quite ambitious. Many organizations fail to understand that ambition is a competency that must be leveraged among employees who demonstrate it. In this world of work–life balance, organizations often struggle to find the employee who is willing to take on a key position that requires above-and-beyond effort. Thankfully, Boomers have a history of climbing the next rung of the ladder, and many continue to be motivated by that next great promotion.

>> **CSR activities:** Rewarding Boomers by enabling them to give back is a great engagement driver. For example, many Boomers would respond very positively to a paid week to build homes for the homeless with an organization such as Habitat for Humanity.

X Marks the Spot: Working with Generation X

The first generation to insist on work-life balance, this group, born between 1965 and 1980, includes more women, as well as men who have assumed more home and family responsibilities. Not surprisingly, Generation X was also the generation that pushed for paternity benefits and support for stay-at-home dads. This generation was the first to rely heavily on technology.

After watching their parents and older siblings get laid off or fired by an increasingly un-loyal corporate America, Generation X brought free agency to the workplace. What does "free agency" mean? Consider a sports analogy. It used to be that a top-level athlete would play his whole career for a single team. Magic Johnson and Dan Marino are but a couple of examples. These days, however, these athletes are in the minority. More and more athletes follow the money. At the same time, the franchises they play for are quick to trade or cut players. Loyalty is dead in sports, and in many ways, it's dead in business as well. Cradle-to-grave employment has been replaced by business free agency. Employers no longer offer the same long-term benefits and security to their employees, and employees are quick to quit a job to follow a boss, to pursue a new opportunity, or to stay home to raise their children.

Caught between Baby Boomers and Millennials, Gen X workers are experiencing growing unrest. Because their Baby Boomer predecessors have delayed retirement (or opted out altogether), members of Generation X have been denied opportunities to advance. The Great Recession of 2008–2009, which resulted in fewer growth opportunities, worsened their situation. And of course, there are the Millennials — soon to be the largest demographic in the workforce — breathing down Generation X's neck. It's no wonder many Gen Xers, who often view their younger cohorts as spoiled, lazy, and the recipients of way too much attention, feel stuck with no place to go! Nonetheless, they do represent the next generation of senior leaders. Figuring out how to attract, develop, and engage Generation X will be key to any organization's success.

Attracting and hiring Generation X

Members of Generation X have been frustrated by their career progression — or lack thereof. Having been pummeled by a deep and painful recession, Gen X is waiting for its next big opportunity.

In the years ahead, money will be more of a driver for Generation X than for its Boomer and Millennial counterparts. More than any other generation, Gen X has borne the brunt of the collapse in the mortgage industry, and many still owe more on their homes than those homes are worth.

Fairness is also important to Gen X. Many Gen Xers feel that the cards have been stacked against them, and they're looking for an opportunity that evens the score — at least financially. (The perception of unfairness is a major *dis*engagement driver.) Other recruitment hooks for this group include technology, benefits (after all, they're the ones now having babies), and development opportunities.

Training Generation X

Training is important to Generation X. They're all about development opportunities. When training members of this generation, consider the following:

>> **Include lots of activities and individual report-backs.** As with Boomers, building experiential exercises and activities into training opportunities is important. However, unlike their Boomer predecessors, Gen Xers are still looking to prove themselves and itching to show their stuff. It's a good idea to give members of Gen X opportunities to co-lead the training, take the lead on report-backs, and otherwise shine in front of their peers. "Teaching others" is the top way in which people learn; Gen Xers are primed to take the lead in teaching others while boosting their own learning during training events.

>> **Have more than one solution to case studies.** Now more than ever, Gen X wants to be heard, seen, and given an opportunity to make its own footprint. Pressed between two sizable generations, Gen X has ideas and wants to share them. If you expect Gen Xers to follow suit or go along with the tried and true, you risk disengaging them and losing out on a significant learning opportunity. Best-in-class organizations bring together their high potentials (often disproportionately made up of Gen X) and invite them to tackle organizational challenges, explore new markets, or evaluate the business case to expand their product offerings.

>> **Align training with the company's mission.** Members of Generation X are similar to members of other generations in that their training time can best be leveraged if they see a "line of sight" between the time necessary to train and the relationship of the training with the company's overall mission.

TIP

>> **Allow participants to provide feedback during the training session.** Whereas Boomers are often more comfortable providing feedback after a training event, members of Generation X are more "instant" in their willingness (and desire) to provide feedback on the training they're receiving. Consider it "real-time" quality improvement for your training program.

Engaging Generation X

If you're tasked with engaging Gen Xers, consider these points:

>> **Don't pile it on.** Boomers may be motivated by a heavy workload, but the opposite is often true of Generation X. Instead, *independence* and *free agency* are watchwords for Gen X. If they sense that these values aren't being honored, they'll likely become cynical about their jobs.

>> **Avoid meetings.** Generation X was the first generation to grow up with technology. As a result, members of this group often prefer to communicate via email rather than attending meetings.

>> **Flexibility is key.** Despite a perception on the part of some of their elders that they work less, Gen Xers usually make up for the time they've taken to attend a child's play or soccer game by working nights or weekends.

>> **Offer training and development opportunities.** Right now, members of this generation are quite career oriented. They see themselves as next in line to take the reins. But as older workers stay on in the workplace, Gen Xers may grow impatient. To keep them engaged, you need to make them feel that they're learning and growing. Thus, training and development are huge engagement drivers for this group.

TIP

Looking to attract and engage more Gen Xers (and Millennials) to your firm? Use the sheet in Figure 1-1 to note what you do now in terms of CSR, workforce flexibility, innovation, rotation of assignments, and branding, and what you *could* do in each of those categories.

Attracting Gen X and Gen Y

What do you or could you do right now to be more attractive to engaged Gen X and Gen Y employees?

	What do you do now?	What could you do?
Corporate Social Responsibility		
Workforce Flexibility		
Innovation		
Rotation of Assignments		
Branding – "We're great!"		

FIGURE 1-1: Attract and engage Gen X and Gen Y (Millennials).

© John Wiley & Sons, Inc.

Rewarding Generation X

Here are some rewards that can help motivate members of Generation X:

>> **Time off:** Gen X brought the concept of work-life balance to the workplace, and today they're at the age where they're working parents with dual responsibilities. Companies should occasionally offer the option of a financial reward or an enhanced vacation or time-off benefit.

>> **Professional development opportunities:** Gen Xers see themselves as next in line and are often hungry for the necessary stretch assignment, executive education course, job transfer, or other opportunity to enhance their personal and professional development.

>> **Accelerated promotions:** Early in their careers, it was common for Boomers to wait their turn for a promotional opportunity. For example, at one engineering company, project managers were required to have ten years' experience. Generation X — and Millennials, for that matter — won't and shouldn't wait a certain number of years for a promotion. Instead of "putting in their time," they'll simply quit and go elsewhere. Accelerating Gen X into stretch assignments will go a long way toward engaging this generation.

WARNING

>> **Technology upgrades:** Generation X grew up with technology and is tech savvy. If you saddle a Gen Xer with yesterday's technology, it will become an irritant. Giving a Gen Xer a laptop (instead of a desktop) may not, in and of itself, make her feel satisfied, but if you *don't* provide it, she'll feel unhappy. In other words, technology may not be critical to Gen Xers' overall engagement, but not having it may lead to their *dis*engagement.

>> **Participation on a prestigious committee:** If Gen X represents the next generation to lead your firm, why not ask those employees to lead the next strategic planning committee or other high-profile organizational subcommittee? Not only will this help engage them, but you'll also benefit because their insights are different from those of their Boomer predecessors.

>> **Opportunities to present to the senior leadership team:** Want to engage a high-potential Gen Xer? Ask him to attend — or better yet, present at — the next board meeting, senior management off-site, or executive leadership team monthly meeting. Presenting to the bosses will be highly engaging to your high-potential Gen Xers.

Working with Millennials

Born between 1981 and 2002, this highly computer-oriented group is characterized by hope about the future, social activism, family-centricity, and the desire for diversity. Before the recession of 2008–2009, the average tenure of Millennial, or Generation Y, workers at any given job was a mere 20 months — significantly shorter than their older cohorts. Experts predict this behavior will likely recur as the economy picks back up.

Millennial workers — which will soon be the largest workforce demographic (if they aren't already) — require a continuous flow of positive feedback. Keep in mind that members of this generation were somewhat pampered by their Baby

Boomer parents. For this generation, trophies were awarded to both winning *and* losing teams; seat belts and car seats were *required* car accessories; and in some cases, the traditional A through F school grades were replaced by the gentler "below/meeting/exceeding expectations" metric.

Attracting and hiring Millennials

Gen Y in particular wants to work for a "company that cares" — one that donates to charity, is concerned about the environment, and supports volunteerism. That means that if you're looking to recruit the best of the best among Millennials, you really need to crystallize your company's "why" as part of your company's employee value proposition (EVP).

Your company's EVP is who you are and why people should work for you. Think of this as your "employment brand." An EVP consists of a clear and compelling story that describes, among other things, why people want to work for your firm, key points that differentiate your firm from its competitors, and a message that resonates with and engages staff. If your firm has an engaging, healthy culture, developing an enticing EVP is a breeze.

TIP

Every firm should crystallize and document its EVP. An effective EVP includes the following:

>> A clear and compelling story that describes why people want to work for you.

>> Key points that differentiate your firm from its competitors.

>> A theme that prompts candidates to self-select in or out. (A strong EVP helps to ensure the "right" people seek out your firm and helps to discourage those who simply aren't a fit from applying. Let's face it, the Marines aren't for everyone — which is why their EVP is all about being one of "the few.")

>> A message that resonates with and engages existing staff.

That last point is key. It's how you know your EVP is accurate. That said, the EVP doesn't have to be based strictly in reality. It can be equal parts reality, aspiration, and inspiration.

Millennials are also quite receptive to branding, and they're willing to work for a cool brand for lower pay. If you don't believe this, walk into any Apple Store. You'll see the highest engagement with the lowest pay anywhere. These store associates are willing to accept low wages for an opportunity to work for one of the coolest brands and cultures around.

Training Millennials

As the youngest members of the workforce, Generation Y is perhaps most in need of training. When training Millennials, keep these points in mind (and check out Book 5, Chapter 2):

>> **Use technology and lots of variety in teaching methods.** If you're speaking to Millennials in a class setting, don't even think about using bulleted PowerPoint slides as your mode of delivery. Today's training professionals understand the importance of incorporating videos, movie clips, video blogs (*vlogs* for short), music, and other media into their presentations. For example, when training on team development and cohesion, you may show the movie *Miracle,* about the U.S. men's hockey team, which won the gold medal in the 1980 Olympics, followed by a highly interactive debrief. Your Millennial attendees will respond far more favorably than the standard (and oh-so-Boomer) data-intensive PowerPoint slides.

>> **Don't have just one solution to case studies.** Millennials, like their Gen X predecessors, feel they have lots to offer (no doubt due in part to the fact that their parents have been telling them how wonderful they are since birth). And in reality, they do. They'll push you to include in your case studies solutions that are rich in technology, mobile applications, cloud computing, social media, gamification (the use of game mechanics and rewards in a non-game setting to increase user engagement and drive desired user behaviors), and other key trends that Boomers may just be reading about.

>> **Align training with the company's values and positive image.** Millennials want to work for a purpose-driven organization. Linking training to your firm's values and brand will have longer-term leverage.

>> **Allow participants to provide feedback during the training session.** Be aware that participants will expect praise for providing this feedback. Consider leveraging the many real-time feedback tools available to enable your employees to be active participants in the training event.

Engaging Millennials

Are you tasked with engaging Millennials? If so, here are a few ideas:

>> **Harness technology for communication.** Where Gen Xers are technologically *savvy,* Millennials are technologically *dependent.* Having grown up well after the advent of computers, the Internet, and mobile phones, Gen Y is accustomed to enjoying instant communication and having information at their fingertips. Note, however, that they increasingly eschew both phones and email in favor of text messaging — important to consider if your company's communication protocol involves lengthy missives from the CEO.

» **Allow for mobility and flexibility.** Millennials are attracted to new technologies, especially those that grant them increased mobility. If your Gen X workers looked at the desktop computer as a dinosaur, preferring a laptop computer in its stead, don't be surprised to see your Millennial employees take things a step further and request tablets to get their jobs done. You'll recoup the cost by capturing their discretionary effort during non-work hours. And if telecommuting and/or flextime is an option, all the better.

» **Allow for job rotation.** Earlier generations saw job rotation as nice to have. For Millennials, however, job rotation is a must. Unlike some older employees, Millennials aren't particularly concerned with permanence or security. Instead, many view abruptly changing career directions to be perfectly acceptable solutions if they're dissatisfied with their jobs. If you want your Millennials to stick around, you must allow them to take on different jobs or do the same jobs differently.

» **Give frequent feedback.** Boomers may happily go years between performance appraisals. But recognition, praise, and constructive criticism are not only welcomed by both younger groups, but are means to motivate them. Gen Xers require a little more attention in this area, but will likely be satisfied with mid-year performance feedback in addition to their annual performance review. Millennials, however, are likely to ask, "How am I doing *today?*" When you have Millennials on staff, be prepared to offer constant feedback! (Find out more about feedback in Book 5, Chapter 3.)

» **Don't restrict Internet or social media use.** Many organizations restrict employees' use of the Internet and social media, citing employees who "waste time" using these technologies. But if your employees are downloading the latest video off YouTube or socializing on Facebook four hours a day, you have a *performance* problem, not an Internet or social media problem. Too many IT departments look at the Internet and social media as a hardware issue ("They'll shut down our server!") and block the use of these invaluable communications tools. The Internet, along with social media, can be amazing research, communication, branding, and engagement enablers. Plus, if you restrict their use, employees — particularly Millennials — will simply obtain access via their own mobile devices during work hours. Trust your employees to do the right thing, and more often than not, they will!

» **Invite Millennials to serve on social committees.** If Gen X brought work-life balance to the workplace, Gen Y is bringing work-life *blending*. Millennials are a social and networked generation, accustomed to connecting with a wide universe. For them, the walls between work and play are porous. They're hungry to bring their work colleagues into their social sphere. Engage them to participate and perhaps even lead your social committees, CSR initiatives, and so on. They're a ready and able committee waiting to be asked to help socialize your business.

ENGAGEMENT AND GLOBALIZATION

Experts predict that in the United States and other parts of the Western world, Millennials will be the first generation that *won't* make as much money as their parents did. For developing nations, however, it's a different story. Young workers elsewhere around the world — for example, in India and China — will likely see opportunities that their parents were never offered. It's no surprise, then, that these workers behave more like Baby Boomers than their Millennial counterparts. Many are even Traditionalist in nature, feeling nearly as committed to their companies as they are to their families. Less important is work–life balance, which is such a priority among younger generations in the United States. The point here? If you work for a global organization, you'll need to be aware that the "regular" generation-based engagement drivers may not apply.

TIP

Looking to attract and engage more Millennials to your firm? Refer to the sheet in Figure 1-1 and note what you do now in terms of CSR, workforce flexibility, innovation, rotation of assignments, and branding, and what you *could* do in each of those categories.

Rewarding Millennials

The following serve as excellent rewards for Millennials (see Book 5, Chapter 4 for more info):

>> **Professional development opportunities:** According to a 2011 PricewaterhouseCooper study, training and development is the most highly valued employee benefit among Millennials. In fact, the number of Millennials who cited this as their most prized benefit was *three* times higher than those who chose cash bonuses.

TIP

>> **Regular feedback:** As far as Gen Y is concerned, your annual performance appraisal process is, like, so yesterday. Instead, they need — indeed, they *require* — frequent feedback. They expect to be told they've done a terrific job, time and time again. In fact, some experts say that to truly engage members of this generation, they need to be recognized eight times a day. (Book 5, Chapter 3 has more information about feedback.)

NEXT UP: PREPARING FOR THE NEXT GENERATION

So far, not much is known about the next generation — the "Net Generation," "Generation Z," "Generation Edge," or whatever else society decides to call the generation that follows Gen Y. All that is known is they *will* be different from all generations that preceded them. Born after 2002, the next generation will primarily be children of Gen X parents and will be the most connected generation ever. These kids, some of whom played with iPads as babies, believe having access to all things electronic is a way of life. They don't view technology as a tool or a device; instead, they view everything in instant and connected terms.

Putting It All Together

As you develop your organization's engagement plan, you'll want to take all these generational differences into consideration. First, however, you should get a sense of how many Millennials, Gen Xers, Boomers, and even Traditionalists you have in your firm. Use a form like the one in Figure 1-2 to write down your numbers.

	Traditionalist	Boomer	Gen X	Gen Y
National average	4.7%	38.6%	32.2%	24.7%
Total				
By location				
Location #1				
Location #2				
Location #3				

FIGURE 1-2: Track your generational demographics.

© John Wiley & Sons, Inc.

For help juggling the various priorities of each generation, see Table 1-1.

TABLE 1-1 **Generations at Work**

	Baby Boomers (Born 1946–1964)	Generation X (Born 1965–1980)	Generation Y (Born 1981–2002)
Values	Workaholic	Work-life balance	Team player
	Competitive	Global thinking	Enthusiasm for change
	Innovative	Diversity	Respect for authority
	Questions authority	Unimpressed by authority	Tempered hopefulness
	Materialism	Fun	Sociability
	Personal/social expression	Self-reliance	Optimism
	Skepticism	Cynicism/pessimism	
Work is	An exciting adventure	A difficult challenge	A means to an end
Leadership style	Consensual	Challenges others	To be determined
	Collegial		
Communication	In person	Direct	Text message
	In meetings	Immediate	Direct message
		Email	Twitter
		Voicemail	Instagram
			YouTube
Feedback	Doesn't appreciate it	Asks, "How am I doing?"	At the push of a button
Rewards	Money	Freedom	Meaningful work
	Title	Independence	
	Recognition		
Motivation	The need to feel valued and needed	Do it "my way"	Work with bright staff
		Work-life balance	Work-life balance
			Social interaction through technology

Engagement strategies	Baby Boomers (Born 1946–1964)	Generation X (Born 1965–1980)	Generation Y (Born 1981–2002)
	Establish non-authoritarian environment	Allow time for questions	Provide interaction with colleagues
	Offer fresh assignments	Provide references	Bring up to speed quickly
	Provide developmental experiences	Use time-efficient approaches	Encourage mentoring
	Tap into their expertise	Keep up a quick pace	Use technology
	Ease pressure of complex life	Be specific about growth	Nonparental approach
		Allow time to earn their respect	

TIP

Knowing the traits commonly found among members of a particular generation can help you pinpoint what drives the individuals in your firm. One Millennial woman was incredibly driven by recognition. Money was practically irrelevant to her. So, she had plenty of face time with executives whenever the opportunity arose. On the opposite end of the spectrum was a Boomer in his early 60s, who showed signs of becoming disengaged during a period when layoffs were necessary. Because this man's various financial responsibilities likely made security a key driver, he was frequently reassured that his job was safe.

REMEMBER

The generations do have very different views on authority, teamwork, development, and work–life balance, but everyone — regardless of age — wants the following:

>> **Achievement:** Taking pride in one's work.

>> **Camaraderie:** Having positive, inclusive, and productive relationships.

>> **Equality:** Being treated fairly in matters such as pay, benefits, and developmental opportunities.

Smart bosses know that to boost engagement, they must build cultures with these three values in mind.

Chapter **2**

Encouraging and Facilitating Collaboration among Generations

One thing that's hard to dispute about the Millennial generation is that they're a collaborative bunch. Of course, individual preferences can dictate the level of collaboration they enjoy, but as a whole, Millennials take workplace collaboration to a whole new level. They gravitate to whiteboards like moths to a flame. If a new idea is on the table, their first inclination is to flesh it out as a group, right then and there. For them, working together trumps working alone — teamwork makes the dream work.

As a manager, you may be thinking, "Okay, a naturally collaborative group is the stuff that managerial dreams are made of, but I also need my employees to be capable of independent work." And you may be wondering whether Millennials' desire to work with each other extends to working with other generations too.

Over the course of this chapter, you'll discover how to wield the Millennial penchant for collaboration as the mighty tool that it is. You walk through one of the biggest generational workplace clash points — the independent Gen Xers' work flow bumping up against the highly collaborative Millennials' — and you get tools for alleviating tension and encouraging comfortable collaboration. This chapter explores onboarding and training techniques that appeal to this Millennial collaborative tendency and reviews best practices for building a collaborative mentorship model. Lastly, you discover what it means to have a truly open and collaborative work infrastructure, from the physical space to the virtual tools you use to making remote employees feel they are truly a part of the team (as a heads-up, "collaborative space" isn't synonymous with open square footage occupied by beanbag chairs and ping-pong tables).

Shifting Your Perspective on Collaboration

First things first: Millennials and collaboration aren't like Prometheus gifting fire to the human race. Millennials didn't invent collaboration and bring it to the working world as their unique contribution to workplace functionality. Every generation wants to collaborate and sees the immense value in it, but there are two key things to keep in mind.

>> First, each generation has a different perception of what collaborative work looks like.

>> Second, that perception is influenced by how that generation grew up, how they were taught to work together in school, and what was drilled into them during their first few years in the working world.

Boomers: Come together, right now

The Baby Boomer experience and resulting perception on collaboration is defined by a couple of significant conditions from their past. The first? The many human rights movements of the '60s. Through these movements, the earlier Boomers saw the great power their generation could effect as a group. They learned the power of the collective and brought that with them into the workplace. They believe that if everyone collectively moves toward a shared mission, they'll accomplish great things.

On the other hand, later Boomers grew up in a time when the Baby Boom effectively overwhelmed the country's infrastructure. They saw scarcity in the classrooms (desks, books, teachers), scarcity of jobs, and scarcity of opportunity. Their takeaway from this condition of fighting for resources is that to succeed, you need to have a competitive edge. Collaboration is well and good for these late Boomers, but in the back of their minds, whether working alone or in groups, they know they need to stand out from the crowd.

REMEMBER

The resulting Boomer perception of collaboration is that teamwork coupled with independent work is best, but individual recognition is most motivating. Collaboration should be structured.

Gen Xers: Stop, collaborate, and listen

When Xers were growing up, the world looked very different than it did for Boomers. It was during their formative years that the divorce rate tripled and more women entered the workforce. Consequently, the term "latchkey kid" came to describe children who let themselves into their homes after school, zapped a Hot Pocket for dinner, devoured the latest music videos on MTV, and took care of themselves while their parents wrapped up the workday. This generation learned, from early on, how to take care of themselves. TV was their favorite babysitter, and even their video games — Pac-Man, Tetris, Frogger — reinforced the idea that it was just fine to do things solo.

REMEMBER

To be clear, this does not mean that Gen Xers are a bunch of recluses who don't like interacting with other human beings. They can collaborate when needed, but they're a generation that really subscribes to the idea that if you want something done right, you'd better do it yourself. And when they do collaborate, they want to do it in a hyper-efficient way. The Gen X perception of collaboration is individual work first, teamwork only if necessary and truly beneficial.

Millennials: We belong together

Millennials, who grew up during the self-esteem movement, were bombarded with messages like "two heads are better than one," "there is no 'I' in team," and "you're better together than you are alone." Group projects were the norm and a frequent feature of their education. At home their parents encouraged a more democratic and collaborative family structure. Parents frequently solicited opinions and advice from their kids on all sorts of decisions, from small matters (like "What movie should we see this weekend?") to big ones ("What car should we buy?"). On top of that, technology created yet another way for Millennials to collaborate, whether that meant working together on homework over AIM or — especially for the next generation — FaceTiming to practice a group presentation. With the ultimate collaboration tool in their pockets, their phones, Millennials expect to be able to connect and collaborate whenever and wherever.

REMEMBER

Millennials' perception of collaboration is team first, solo work later. To them, group wins feel just as good as, if not better than, individual wins. Collaboration should be informal.

Reconciling Differences: Independent Xers versus Collaborative Millennials

When you say "let's collaborate" and every generation comes to the table with a different idea of what that means, it's easy to see how things can get confusing — and frustrating — fast. Each generational combo can yield its own specific frustration. Boomers' proclivity for more meetings can bother Xers' need for fewer. While Millennials and Boomers have their own unique challenges around the formality factor of collaborative work, when it comes to working together (or alone), one clash comes up as almost iconic in its intensity: Xers versus Millennials, with the former strongly favoring solo work and the latter showing a stalwart preference for collaboration.

This Xer-versus-Millennial dynamic, and the reason it causes so much frustration, can be boiled down to one fine point: Millennials lead with their collaborative foot, and Gen Xers lead with their independent foot. Someone is bound to get stepped on. Add to that the managerial dynamic, often that of the Xer managing the Millennial, and you've got quite a puzzle on your hands.

Both sides have good intentions. You've heard the concept of the golden rule — "Treat others the way you want to be treated" — likely as early as pre-K, when teachers were trying to stop you from swiping your fellow student's snack pack. While this saying imparts great wisdom in principle, especially for a group of mischievous toddlers, in the workplace the value of that golden rule crumbles when you're trying to manage or work with others. Xers assume that Millennials want to be managed the way that they, the Xers, like being managed. Millennials assume Xers want to collaborate the way they, the Millennials, like to collaborate. Good intentions, bad results. So as you attempt to take off your own generational lens and put on that of another, check out the following sections to view collaboration from both an Xer and Millennial standpoint.

Looking through Gen Xers' eyes

Independent Xers are fully of the mindset that if you want something to be done right, you need to be the one who does it. They're the kind of employees who, when given a project, say, "Tell me what you want, when you want it, and how you want it. I'll take it back with me, work on it alone for a while, and bring it back to you later." In a nutshell, "Back off — I got this."

To Gen Xers, micromanaging is borderline insulting, because it suggests they're incapable of carrying out a project to completion independently. They prefer to create their own structure, because at the end of the day, they are the ones who understand their work flow best.

In Xers' minds, solo work is by far the most efficient way to complete a project, and check-ins along the way, while sometimes needed, are not integral to getting their work done on time and getting it done well. Teamwork and collaboration have their uses, but like a fine seasoning, they should be used sparingly.

Seeing Millennials' viewpoint

On the other hand, for Millennials, collaborative work is the quickest way to develop the best and most innovative work. Working with their peers and managers is a way to pull winning ideas from the collective. For them, it's almost presumptuous to believe that their own individual ideas are the best ones.

Millennials tackle projects with the belief that working collectively is a quick way to reveal inefficiencies and weaknesses — more eyes on a certain project means more varied perspectives and more ways of testing as you're creating. Why would you wait until something is fully baked to present it to others? Odds are good that you'll have missed something, and it seems like such a huge waste of time to backtrack and fix the problem after the fact. That's why they gravitate toward collaborative work, with many eyes on any given project, lots of clear structure, and multiple opportunities for feedback along the way. These constant check-ins during a project are one of the most obvious showcases of Millennials' collaborative nature.

Finding the right ways to manage collaboration

TIP

Here are some tips for managing the Millennial collaborative spirit:

>> **Don't get frustrated.** This may seem like a silly tip, but many an Xer manager can hardly mask the annoyance in his voice when talking about a super-collaborative Millennial employee. "Are they even capable of thinking for themselves?!" The answer is, of course, yes. They may just need a little help along the way — at least at first. Don't lead with frustration. Start by understanding the Millennial's perspective and go from there.

>> **Explain the why.** Often the best strategy to encourage a Millennial to do anything is to explain the why. There will be moments when independent work is clearly the best way to approach a task. When that's the case, take a few extra minutes to explain that's the case.

>> **Encourage independent work, even if it's not great at first.** Understand that odds are good that working independently is not a comfortable thought for your Millennial employees. They will fumble during their first try, fear failure that can lead to losing their reputation or job, and look to you as a guide. Help them through the process, gently pointing out where they can improve while simultaneously encouraging their wins.

>> **Offer yourself as a resource.** What? Doesn't this negate the whole "work independently" thing? It's true that offering yourself as a resource makes you and your Millennial a mini team of two. But, especially during the first few projects, Millennials are going to feel like they're on an island. Let them know you're available as a resource and for support, within reason, as they work through their first few solo projects.

>> **Preemptively schedule check-ins.** Many Millennials are intuitive enough to know when they're pestering instead of questioning. If you are one who's prone to a "less is more" mentality when it comes to the project touch-base and smile to mask clenched teeth when a Millennial knocks on your door, articulate your needs early and let them know the most appropriate time to check-in. Take it upon yourself to create the check-in schedule. It will save you and that Millennial from playing the "I wonder if they're annoyed with me yet" game.

>> **Decide where and when collaboration would be most useful.** All independent work makes a Millennial a dull boy (or girl). Sometimes team-work is a good approach to a project or assignment. Find those opportunities to vary the work your Millennial reports are involved in. Note that if all your Millennials' work is independent, they'll find it draining and demotivating.

Understanding what Millennials really want when they ask to collaborate

When you think about Millennials and their desire to collaborate, what comes to mind? There are definitely those who paint quite the picture in their head. Xers may think that Millennials just want to sit around a campfire and hold hands, singing in unison and swaying back and forth. Others envision a room of Millennials sipping on IPAs and shouting out ideas during a brainstorm, with those thoughts all written in colorful dry-erase pens on a massive whiteboard. Yes, Millennials are a hyper-collaborative generation, but that has been a part of their cultural upbringing.

OLD MILLENNIALS AREN'T LIKE THE OTHER YOUNGLINGS

Chances are high that if you ask a Millennial to describe herself, she won't use the word "collaborative." In the eyes of many, the meaning of the word has become synonymous with "too dependent on group-think to function." While this entire chapter digs into the collaborative mindset of Millennials, research shows that some specific nuances exist when comparing Old Millennials to the next generation of Young Millennials and Generation Edgers. In brief, here's what you need to know:

Encouraging and Facilitating
Collaboration among Generations

- **Old Millennials are more collaborative.** On the scale of who's collaborative, this segment is the most group-oriented of the generational cohort. In a BridgeWorks survey conducted in 2016, they were also the most likely to describe themselves as collaborative. They will be more likely to have the open brainstorm sessions.

- **Young Millennials are less collaborative.** This group knows the power of collaboration and seeks it out, but not as often as Old Millennials. Rather than desiring the opportunity to chat as a group, they want to sit together in a room with their peers, working silently.

- **Generation Edgers are also less collaborative.** Many of this generation have Gen X parents, and they've adopted their independent nature. They're more likely to see collaboration as a waste of time if it brings the focus too far from the goal. Their priority is to get the job done with as few check-ins as needed. Though this is a great shift in working style, there are concerns that they may not check in as often as needed as new hires. Keep your manager eyes peeled for this scenario and adjust as needed.

Once you deconstruct the pieces of the collaborative workplace pie, you'll find that, ultimately, all Millennials want is to work together on a project to reach a goal. Working collaboratively is not limited to having a brainstorm session with a huge team of their peers. Collaboration can be seen when they get feedback from a manager or a peer. It's a natural part of their mentor–mentee relationships. It occurs in-person and virtually.

Instead of writing them off as a needy, pack-minded bunch, think about what Millennials are really asking for when they ask to collaborate:

> » **Millennials want the best idea to come to the fore — even if it's not their own.** As much as this generation gets the title of "narcissist" slapped on their persona, they can be incredibly humble when it comes to the workplace. That love of the group brainstorm? It's because they know that the collective will almost always produce a better idea than the individual. They can bounce thoughts off one another, using one thought as a jumping-off point for another. Millennials truly want the best idea to win out, even if it's not one that they dreamed up.

» **Millennials want constant feedback to know they're on the right track.**
The whole "Millennials love feedback" thing is not because they're needy, but
because they want to know that they're on the right path. It's a "Millennials
love efficiency" thing. If you give them feedback, or if they solicit feedback
from their coworkers or their team, they can then course-correct before it
becomes a bigger problem. (Flip to Book 5, Chapter 3 for more about
feedback.)

» **Millennials don't want a babysitter; they want a coach.** When they look
for guidance and collaboration from their managers and leaders, they want a
relationship that's more coach and less babysitter. A babysitter hovers and
watches your every move, may talk down to you, and knows he is in charge.
A coach, instead, grooms you. He doesn't scold you when you make a mistake
but rather builds a path to refine your skills. It's about bettering your
Millennial employees rather than punishing them or hawking over them.

TIP

» **Millennials don't need to collaborate with you, but they want to collaborate with someone.** The onus doesn't always lie with you to be the one to
work with them. You're busy; they get that. The pressure on you to be the
collaborator can be easily alleviated by giving them a chance to collaborate
with one other. Team up people who complement each other. Assign work in
team-based projects when possible. Or simply assign Millennials a buddy they
can check-in with if they need to run something by someone.

Helping Millennials do independent work

Millennials don't need help when it comes to collaboration. That piece they've
got down pat. The struggle that many managers wring their hands over is getting
their Millennial employees to do more independent work.

REMEMBER

It's not that Millennials are incapable of solo work, or even that they don't enjoy
it. They're just used to a collaborative work style. The key is to support them in
their independent endeavors, not get frustrated at their attempts to collaborate.

TIP

When encouraging Millennial independent work, be incredibly explicit about the
first independent project you assign them. No detail is too small. A foolproof way
to help Millennials as they embark on independent projects is to schedule a kickoff meeting with them to explain the assignment. Lay it all out. Assure them that
you'll be there along the way to help them with any snags they may encounter.

Before those meetings, refer to this checklist. If you want Millennials to do their
best independent work, you should be able to confidently say you have done each
of the following bolded statements. A good way to test if you have, in fact, done all
you need to do is that you should have provided clear direction on each question
following those statements as well before sending them on their way:

» **I set crystal-clear expectations.**

- What is the desired outcome of the project?

- What should the final deliverable look like in terms of length, form, tone, font, style, production, and so forth?

» **I provided a road map of the project.**

- What is the deadline?

- What milestones need to be checked off in the process?

- If the schedule gets derailed, how should it be readjusted?

» **I described the frequency of check-ins and what a typical check-in meeting might look like.**

- Are you meeting once a week? Twice a month? Every other hour?

- How long do your check-ins last?

- Who puts them in the calendar and schedules follow-ups?

- Do you want the employee to prepare questions ahead of time?

- Did you include a directory of all the resources that may be needed?

- Are there online tools the employee can use to answer questions?

- What can you provide the employee with in advance to help with the project?

- Who is held accountable for note-taking, and how will those notes be captured?

» **I told the employee who he can collaborate with besides me.**

- Is there another teammate the employee can turn to for support?

- Who in the workplace is best to turn to for what kinds of questions?

- Does the employee feel comfortable taking charge independently?

- Does he have a good idea of when to seek someone else's opinion instead of relying on his own?

The skeptical reader may be thinking this checklist seems like massive overkill and way too much work. Just keep in mind that you won't be doing this every single time. You're getting the Millennial primed to succeed at independent projects and laying the groundwork for successful solo work in the future. Though it may represent a heavy time investment upfront, you'll see major payoffs later on. And eventually, the Millennial may even run these project kickoff meetings with other Millennials for you.

Onboarding Millennials

When new employees join your ranks, getting them up to speed and ready for the task is a huge part of their manager's job. This process, known as *onboarding*, isn't a one-day or even a one-week task. Often, it can take several months before a new hire is fully onboarded, and collaboration can be key to a manager's success. Knowing that collaboration is a core part of the Millennial personality, you'd be wise to find ways to incorporate more team-based activities into your onboarding and training. Not only will Millennials like it more but it will also spread the responsibility around so it doesn't all land on you. First impressions go a long way, but you don't need to roll out the red carpet and crown them next generation all-stars to make them happy. Stick to these strategies of onboarding, and you'll appeal to the next generation's collaborative nature:

>> **Connect the dots to the bigger picture.** Take time during their first week to show Millennials how even when it seems like they're doing independent (and sometimes even menial) work, their efforts weave into the company's goals and benefit the team at large.

>> **Involve people from all levels and layers.** The more, the merrier. Though in many cases it's impossible to involve everyone in your company in the onboarding process, the more you involve (within reason), the better. Don't just introduce new hires to their managers, but also to colleagues from different departments, to the custodian, to accounting. They want to meet their team.

>> **Introduce them to the higher-ups/leadership.** Introductions and, even better, conversations with leadership are more than what they seem. They are a way to show new hires that they matter, they have access to leadership, and that collaboration of some kind is possible with people at all levels.

>> **Connect them to their peers.** Where is their team? Where are the people they'll be working with from day to day? With whom will they be able to collaborate? Show them. Make sure you introduce Millennials to the peers and potential collaborators they'll be working with on a regular basis.

>> **Do something fun.** Millennials are embracing the idea of a #workfamily, integrating work with home, and bringing their authentic selves to the workplace. Do something outside of the ordinary lunch with colleagues on the first week. Do something fun that can spark friendships and bonds with their colleagues and provide a foundation of trust and understanding, which serves as a springboard for collaborative work. Activities can range from a friendly competition of office Olympics to happy hour at the local haunt to a scavenger hunt around the city.

» **Find out about their individual goals.** They want to know that, as their manager, you're not just treating them as employee #329, but as Rebecca. Get to know Rebecca: her goals, what she's interested in, what her passions are outside of work. Invest in her as a person and show that you're interested in working with her to build her career and help her become an important and contributing member of the company.

» **Set expectations about feedback.** Millennials want feedback from you — probably more often than you're used to or even comfortable with. Be clear about expectations of feedback. Ask them what their ideal would be and build a structure around what works for the two of you. (See Book 5, Chapter 3 for more about feedback.)

AN ONBOARDING ADVENTURE: A CASE STUDY

While there are numerous creative ways to onboard Millennials in a fun way, one great example included a scavenger hunt around the city, complete with cupcakes, selfies, conversations with leadership, and the element of surprise.

- **The scenario:** A group of 20 next-generation hires all began at the same time. They received their onboarding agenda and thought they were heading to a compliance presentation. Yawn. (No offense if you're fond of compliance.)

- **The surprise:** They sat down to listen to compliance, mentally trying to remember the lyrics to the new Rihanna song they just heard on the radio while maintaining composure in what was meant to be a very serious presentation. After the first ubiquitous company slide came a colorful one proclaiming, "Scavenger Hunt!"

- **The scavenging:** Millennials were put into teams with their peers and given their first clue. Solving riddle after riddle, they were sent around the city to their managers' favorite cupcake shop, the local hotel where they had to take a selfie with the doorman, and a trendy café where senior leadership sipped lattes and awaited their questions. The first team who made it back won a group prize. All were treated to a nice evening meal.

- **The reaction:** Not to blow it out of proportion, but one Millennial said, "This is why I chose to work here and why I'll stay. I love that there's such a focus on company bonding and fun, even in the onboarding process, here."

Training Millennials

How do you train a generation that wants to do almost everything as a group? Obviously all-group all-the-time isn't feasible. In many cases, employees are not hired together like a graduating team of first-years, but individually. The following strategies of training appeal to that desire to collaborate with those around them and render your training more effective:

» **Mix the formal with the informal.** Classroom-style training and/or clicking through e-Learning program after program isn't going to do the trick. Mix this type of training with more informal styles — say, a lunch and learn — with other employees in the same role or the role above theirs, who can fill them in on the organization's unwritten rules. Bonus: Cater in unique food from a local favorite restaurant.

» **Keep training interactive and experiential.** Ditch the traditional training manual. Millennials will no doubt assign it the TL;DR (too long; didn't read) acronym. Build real-time, live practice training whenever possible. Contrary to popular belief, Millennials — and especially the next generation — actually favor in-person training. They live most of their lives in a virtual world and savor the opportunities to step outside of it where everyone can learn at a similar place and experience the edutainment together.

» **Use team-based learning when possible.** Some organizations put groups of hires through Training 101 courses, where they "graduate" together as a team or present at milestones after a job rotation. This is a great way to build connections among new hires. Again, this won't always be possible — but when you can use team-based programs, you start building those invisible bonds that become natural venues for the Millennial collaboration that is so sought after.

» **Keep *tweet-sized* top of mind.** Don't overload your new Millennial hire with all the information he could ever need on that first day or week. Space it out. Keep in mind that Millennials are a generation used to consuming bits of information. When you make it bite-sized, they'll share the best of the information with their peers. Great training deserves to be discussed, even if it's in a list of "the ten things I learned in my training."

» **Teach the basics.** Don't assume that the new hire will know all the professional ins and outs on day 1 — or day 500. Topics like formality of dress, how to write an email, and when it's okay to reach out to leadership (and when it's definitely not) should all be covered in your training. The written and unwritten rules change over time, and you have the opportunity to create a safe zone of honest conversation in trainings. Maybe something will come up that they can even work through together! (Subdue the "Kumbaya" groan if you feel it coming on.)

>> **Assign them a training buddy.** You're not going to want to be the one answering all the questions that will undoubtedly bubble up to the surface as they learn the details of their job. Give them a buddy to lean on who can help them along the way or serve as an extra support as they both navigate your training program together.

>> **Give them training options.** Most learning and development departments have a library of training they roll out to their workforces. This element of customization is especially appealing to the generation that masterfully filters through information. Much like choosing courses in college, Millennials will turn to each other to see who is going to what and when — get ready to see increased attendance and chatter if there's a fun list of trainings to choose from and attend.

REMEMBER

Effective training is about more than just teaching skills. It's teaching your employees the tools they need to succeed in your organization. Some of those are very concrete and tactical, like understanding who to call for purchase orders or how to use the printer. Others are more intangible and strategic, like building lines of communication among employees who want so badly to connect and collaborate with one another.

Mentoring Millennials and Vice Versa

It's no coincidence that there's been a renewed interest in mentorship programs right as Millennials have become a major presence in the working world. Why is that the case?

>> Firstly, technology has changed the game, in more ways than one. It used to be that mentoring wasn't a collaborative sport, or at least not nearly as much as it is today. Your mentor was a wise sage: think Obi-Wan to Skywalker. The mentee soaked up all the information from the wise mentor. Nowadays, young employees, many with less than a decade of work experience, are bringing digital expertise that make them valuable mentors to more senior employees (enter the era of reverse-mentorship).

>> Secondly, Millennials are pretty savvy about where they could use some extra help. They're used to collaborating with people in positions of authority and know this access is the best (and maybe only) way to get the 411 on institutional knowledge and other must-know info that you just can't Google.

Millennials are clamoring for mentorship programs, and leaders are taking note. After all, these programs are a win-win. Not only do Millennials get more opportunities to make valuable contributions to the company, but they get access to someone who'll invest in their future and help them level-up their skills. This allows Millennials to have their voices heard, grow their range of proficiencies, and collaborate with high-level employees, all of which are key to Millennial retention. Mentorship programs touch so much more than Millennial collaboration. They have become essential to keeping attrition rate low and Millennials engaged.

Checking out the Millennial mentor and mentee roles

Millennials and the generation after them are entering the workplace with a wealth of knowledge about how to use technology and the Internet. Because they've grown up with this tech, they have a level of comfort exploring new systems and tech tools that is unparalleled, earning them the title of "digital natives." Though their love of technology can also lead to Millennial scorn, this skill isn't something to be scoffed at. They're frequently looked to for advice and sometimes even IT help from the older generations. Millennials' comfort and knowledge around technology is a real value add and something they bring to any mentor-mentee relationship. That one-way has quickly widened into a two-way street. Beyond technology, they may have innovative perspectives on processes or systems that could change. They may be eager to apply the latest technique they learned in school to their current role. At the right times, these perspectives can be powerful.

On the other hand, Millennials often get a bad rap as know-it-alls who are so used to Googling everything that they feel they don't need to rely on anyone's wisdom or expertise, because the answer to any question lies at their fingertips. The good news? This is absolutely false. Millennials are only too aware of the limitations of their good friends Google and the Internet. The practical and real-world experience of other generations is a wealth of knowledge that they are incredibly eager to tap into. Millennials want to be mentored; they want access to authority; they are thirsty for knowledge.

Establishing effective mentorship guidelines

As you're reading this, you may be thinking to yourself, "Awesome — check! We totally have a mentorship program. It says so on our website. Done and done." Wait a second, though. It's one thing to say you have a mentoring program, but another thing entirely to *actually* have one that people use and appreciate. Though leadership may think a mentorship program is in place, there are so few guidelines or such slight assistance in developing those mentorship relationships that employees don't even try. They have no idea how or where to start. If you want to create a productive and celebrated mentorship program, you have it in you!

WARNING

Without easily accessible guidelines and training, your mentorship program is in all likelihood lacking. It doesn't matter what your website copy says or what you say to new employees. A handful of examples of successful mentor-mentee relationships does not a successful program make. Having some sort of structure is crucial, and for Millennials, the more prescriptive, the better. Your mentors may want more freedom to define the relationship, because they'll likely be the ones with the fuller plates, so it's not a bad idea to allow them to have some level of autonomy in setting the specifications for what that relationship looks like.

To ensure that the right people are matched up and that both are getting what they want out of the pairing, ask potential mentors and mentees to answer these questions:

>> What is your desired outcome?

>> What type of skills are you trying to improve?

>> Do you have a personality or gender preference?

>> What is the weekly or monthly time commitment you are willing to put in?

>> How often do you want to meet?

>> How often do you have access to the other? (For example, are Fridays the only good day? Do you never work in the office at the same time?)

>> What is the preferred structure of the meeting (agenda-driven and formal, free-flow and informal, themed each time, long- or short-term goals, and so on)?

>> Is there a company-prescribed model that each mentor/mentee can follow or use as a jumping-off point?

>> When will you know that the learning has been accomplished and that it's time to move on to another mentor/mentee?

Use the information gathered to be sure the right mentors are paired with the right mentees and to create guidelines that will work for everyone involved.

REMEMBER

Be as unambiguous as possible about the time allowance and access that Millennials will have to their mentor. Think about the kind of access they've had with their parents. It was basically all the time and any time. In the workplace, this type of access is improbable if not impossible. By setting clear expectations at the top of each relationship, and then later at the top of each meeting, you avoid overloading your mentor with the eager, info-hungry, and sometimes overbearing Millennial mentee.

TIP

As nice as it would be for mentors and mentees to naturally gravitate toward you, don't hold your breath waiting for this to happen. A best practice is to inquire of every new hire whether she's interested in a mentor and then utilize a member of the HR team to actively place this new hire with the appropriate mentor.

Harnessing the power of reverse mentorship

When pairing your mentors with mentees, be sure to consider what each party would like to learn more about. Use that information to build successful partnerships that even Sherlock and Watson would be proud of. There is much to be gained by opening the relationship to a two-way model of learning, rather than the more authoritarian "I'll-tell-you-what's-what" style of the past:

>> **Learning-hungry older gens will add to their skills repertoire and feel quite valued in the process.** Just because an employee has been around for years and years, has a wall of career accolades, and is incredibly proficient in his role doesn't mean he has bid adieu to learning anything new. Too often, companies stop investing in these types of employees because they incorrectly assume that they've learned everything they want to learn. Cue the disengagement. In fact, older Millennials usually are the most eager to learn new skills and will seek roles outside of the company to get the education if they aren't offered the opportunity at work. (See Book 5, Chapter 1 for an introduction to engaging Millennials and other generations.)

>> **Millennials will feel empowered and less likely to seek a new environment to work in.** Millennials may be known as the generation with the shortest work tenures, but that doesn't mean they'll necessarily be that way. Many Millennials choose to stay in an organization when they know the impact they have and when their voices are being heard by their peers and leadership. When they join a symbiotic mentor-mentee relationship, they witness firsthand the impact they're having on an individual and, consequently, the organization as a whole. This could be the magic tonic to retaining Millennial employees.

Building a Collaborative Infrastructure

When thinking about building a collaborative workplace, you can consider interpersonal relationships and communication styles between managers and employees. Next are the Workplace 2.0 considerations: physical working space, tech tools that encourage collaborative work, and managing to balance collaboration with remote learning.

Considering the changing physical office space

In response to this hyper-collaborative new generation of employees, the physical working space has shifted as well. Office cubicles have been replaced by open rooms with pods, lounge areas, and plants. Whiteboards have been painted onto large walls, affording Millennials spaces to brainstorm at will. Rooms with plush couches and mood lighting invite employees to come in, sit down, get comfortable, and innovate or meditate. In some extreme cases, treehouses have actually been designed for the office (you may think that one's a bit excessive).

The light side of these developments and changes is revolutionary and positive. Millennials see closed doors and corner offices as an extra barrier they need to break down to pursue their goal of collaboration. Many prefer the access and opportunities for impromptu collaboration that open workspaces afford them.

The dark side of these developments is how unproductive and unwelcome some feel in these environments. Baby Boomers may bristle at an email announcement that they're going to lose the four walls they worked 30 years to achieve. Gen Xers could run in the other direction once they find out that they're losing the solace of a private space. All that darkness aside, many can see the benefits of open space for its encouragement of conversation and transparency.

Building your dream space

TIP

To build the best environment of flexibility for your office, take appropriate steps to make sure that the space matches trends for your workforce. When in doubt about what to do, ask your staff! They'll like the ability to contribute to a dream and feel a sense of pride when they see their ideas materialized in a new space.

Defeating the nightmares to achieve your dream

There are numerous constraints to building the dream. If you confront any of the following, don't fret! There are some simple solutions:

> **Conundrum: What if I can't knock down walls?**
>
> If you have offices that aren't going anywhere anytime soon, leave doors open as much as possible to promote that feeling of collaboration. Open windows and shades to allow for as much natural light as possible. Don't underestimate the power of greenery — it gives the vibe of open, natural environments. Or consider turning one of those walled rooms into a meditation room or a lounge area to serve as an alternate room for working with a quality vibe. Don't worry, people who want to make that change will eagerly assign themselves to the task force to get it done well and get it done cheaply. (Hello, IKEA!)

>> Conundrum: If I have a collaborative work space, how do I signal that I need to work without interruption?

- Use headphones as a sign that you're busy (headphones on means "I'm not available").

- Adopt the stoplight method. Create red-yellow-green signs for employee desks that signify their availability. Red means "no distractions at all, please," yellow means "you can interrupt only if necessary," and green means "I'm available for any and all inquiries!"

- Give everyone a chalkboard and chalk. Then, people can write their own modern version of an AOL "away message." Depending on their current working state, they can indicate whether they want to be bothered or not. For example, the chalkboard could read, "Acceptable interruptions today are client questions. Tomorrow, I'll accept cat video interruptions."

- Appoint flex offices as refuge rooms. Many companies are taking to the idea of a "refuge room" where people can find an environment they need to get work done. This way, it's like a haven.

WARNING

Don't alienate generations that don't want a collaborative workspace. You may have heard the horror stories about companies that completely did away with all walls and corner offices in a misguided attempt to appeal to next-generation hires. Guess what happened? Those Boomers and even Xers who worked so hard to get to the corner office . . . well, that tangible reward and acknowledgment of their hard work was all ripped away, somewhat brusquely, from them to make room for the next generation. Don't fall into that trap or you'll see a mass exodus of the older generations that have been so loyal and fought so hard to get where they are in the organization today. Find a way to meet in the middle. Offer some open collaborative spaces but leave room for closed-door offices as well. Exactly where you land on the spectrum from traditional closed-door offices to completely open-office spaces filled with beanbag chairs will depend entirely on your company culture, but the important thing is to keep all generations in mind when deciding where you stand.

Using instant messaging as a key workplace tool

Technology offers a wealth of tools to help expand upon and improve how your employees collaborate. Email changed the game when it entered the scene, and it cut down on unnecessary meetings. A new method of collaboration was introduced — the virtual way. Millennials, perhaps infamous for their love of email (over phone anyway), are embracing another way to collaborate in the workplace — instant messaging (IM).

THE EXCEPTION TO THE RULE: THE CASE FOR THE ANTI-COLLABORATIVE MILLENNIAL

The unspoken elephant in the collaboration room is the debate of: "Isn't this just the difference between extroverts and introverts?" That question is a valid one, because while this entire chapter digs into the collaborative mindset of Millennials, research shows some specific circumstances where collaboration nation is just not where Millennials want to live. Some exceptions to the rule include the following:

- **Extrovert versus introvert:** Many introverts need their quiet space at work more than extroverts. They'll wear their headphones as part of their work uniform and sign up to use flex spaces more often than their peers.

- **The "engineer's focus":** Engineering is not the only career that requires extreme focus, but engineers, and people who think similarly, are sometimes the most averse to an open work environment. If you have a staff that values focus and grows irritated by distractions, they're not going to thrive in an open room of desks.

- **The multi-generational office:** Do not, repeat, *do not* change your environment for one generation. It will likely backfire, and then your staff won't carry the same respect they once had for their environment or their job. Millennials are sensitive to changes made for them; don't let them bear the brunt of shame for a changed environment that works for the minority.

Say "IM" to some managers, and you might induce some eye-rolling. *Childish. Frivolous. Unnecessary. Silly. Inefficient.* These are just a few of the many words that bubble up when managers are asked to describe instant messaging within their workforce. Instead of seeing the value that instant messaging can bring to day-to-day tasks, this platform is written off as a Millennial tool for chatting or sending memes to one another in the office.

While, yes, instant-messaging tools are used for strengthening interpersonal relationships at work, the effect also extends far beyond that. Millennials use IM platforms as a way to quickly and efficiently communicate ideas. Much like Xers saw email as a desperately needed and blessed way to cut down on meetings, Millennials view IM as a desperately needed and blessed way to cut down on emails. They use it as a way to improve the work flow of the day, and, in many cases, it works.

The problem seen is managers rebelling against the idea of these IM platforms and laying judgment on Millennials who choose to use them as a main communication tool. The frustration around this topic is understandable. Managers can barely keep from coming unhinged when they tell the typical "Millennial-on-IM" story that goes something like this:

> "We all sit in pods in our office, and Ron was at his desk while I was sitting right across from him. He had a question about a project, and instead of just taking off his headphones and asking me directly — thus saving time — he IM'd me. It was the simplest of messages. Why, I mean *why* couldn't he just stop what he was doing and take two seconds to ask me directly? He does this all the time, and so do his peers. For the life of me . . . I just don't get it."

At face value, it does seem like Ron was being lazy (and maybe averting yet another face-to-face encounter that he's not super fond of). But if you look at this through Ron's eyes (and those of many Millennials), it's likely he was just trying to be polite and respectful of her time. He'd probably be the first to agree that he'd pinged his manager with a simple, straightforward message. The reason he didn't just get up and go talk to her in person is that he didn't want to interrupt her work flow. To him, it might have seemed presumptuous to interject with such a small query. In his mind, sending her an IM was a way for him to ask his question without demanding an immediate response (or clogging up her email inbox). It was a way to be conscientious of her time. She could finish up the task at hand, and get to his IM when she'd wrapped up her email, thought, project, or whatever it was she was working on. It was a move made out of consideration, not out of laziness or a lack of respect.

TIP

Despite the frustrations of other generations, IM can be the most efficient and effective way to have quick conversations at work. Recently, there has been much research published about how interruptions, however small, can be incredibly disruptive to the workday. Some suggest that it can take upwards of 20 minutes to regain focus. IMs are a way to skirt the issue, to ask without disrupting workflow or burying a co-worker in unnecessary emails. If you have an IM system, embrace it! Refrain from monitoring it so closely that everyone feels like they're being watched for response time and content. Millennials use IM tools to increase productivity and to communicate in a smart, thoughtful way. And yes, it is possible that Millennials will also turn to IMing as a fun outlet to communicate with their peers, and that's a really beautiful thing because they'll be building relationships that are critical to a happy workplace.

Collaborating from afar

Remote workers are becoming more commonplace as technological advances make it easy to work from home, or anywhere really. Whether they're working from home or from a coffee shop or wherever the case might be, they're still a part of your team and they still want to feel like they're a piece of the overall pie.

You've probably heard the phrase "out of sight, out of mind." When your employees aren't showing up at the office day after day, this becomes a very real danger. The onus falls on the manager to implement guidelines that ensure remote Millennial employees feel as if they matter, they're being invested in, and that even though they're not in the office, their contributions are still an important point of collaboration for the team.

TIP

Think about what you do for the Millennials who are in the office. How often do you meet with them? Look at everything from the casual morning hello to the feedback you may give them after a presentation or a project. Try to mimic this behavior with your remote worker, plus an extra 20 percent to make up for what's lost in translation. Try to check in with them every morning for a quick hello. Solicit their ideas and opinions about meetings they dial in for. If at all possible, create opportunities for them to come into the office and interact with their peers and managers.

IN THIS CHAPTER

» **Delivering feedback in an instant age**

» **Revising your review strategy**

» **Managing feedback up and down the ladder**

» **Being more of a coach than a boss**

» **Troubleshooting the most common feedback challenges**

Chapter **3**

Supercharging Your Feedback Loop

No matter your level of leadership, if you're not able to deliver meaningful and constructive feedback to your employees, you're simply not doing your job. Deft delivery of feedback is arguably among the top most important managerial skills to have. It's how you refine your employees, giving them the input they need to accomplish their goals and meet the organization's expectations. Without a proper feedback loop, you're at risk of company stagnation and employee disengagement. At its worst, infrequent feedback or poor delivery can lead to employees running for the exit sign. At its best, a manager who can curate feedback for employees is grooming skills, improving morale, positively affecting the bottom line, and building a pipeline of next-generation talent.

Back in the day, feedback was boiled down to a "no news is good news" mantra, and an annual review was your one chance to get development insight. Nowadays, with new generations in the workplace bringing different expectations and perceptions, that model has become woefully outdated. Now leaders, managers, and employees are required to give feedback regularly, in formal and informal environments, and in a way that caters to each employee's unique individual needs.

This chapter shows you how to present good and bad news to next-generation employees in a way that resonates. You also discover how every element matters: the time, place, frequency, style, written delivery, and verbal delivery.

Giving Feedback in the Instantaneous Age

Instant gratification nation: That's a term that's been used to describe the Millennials and the generation after them. Growing up in a world where technology peeled open the world, Millennials were raised with unprecedented access to information at ever-quickening speeds. Slow dial-up Internet transformed into super-fast, fiber-optic web surfing. Anyone can download or stream a song on a whim, Amazon Prime delivers goods faster than ever before, and Google is always around to answer any and every question that pops into your head. So, how will Millennials expect to receive feedback?

While you chew on the preceding question, it should become clear that your method and style of delivering feedback to Millennials should undergo some substantial customization. The once-a-year thing just isn't going to cut it, nor will the super-formal, boss to employee "let-*me*-tell-you-what-*you*-did-wrong" approach of the past. The instantaneous age has groomed Millennials to expect the feedback they receive to have some form of these three pieces: speed, frequency, and transparency.

Speed: I can't wait a year for feedback

Technology has given the workplace many gifts, and a prominent one, perhaps above all, is speed. For Millennials who were raised on rapidly changing technology — so rapid that their emotional intelligence can barely keep up with it — quick-fire communication is a necessity. If it takes under five minutes to read through three lists of the best Bluetooth headphones, and another minute and a half to post your own review, why can't in-person reviews be just as fast? While annual feedback used to make employees thrive, the world has become too fast for that process to be as effective.

Luckily, a solution lies in the midst. Some managers employ a daily three-minute one-on-one. Others deliver feedback via text or IM. Still others use what kayak. com has dubbed the five-word performance review. Whatever your method, when possible, deliver feedback as soon as you can (ASAYC). No matter what. ASAYC likely has varied specs in the fine-print for every leader, so expectations need to be set earlier rather than later.

Frequency: I want to be kept in the loop

It's not just about how quickly you deliver information, but also how often. Regular feedback, whether good or bad, lets your Millennial employees know whether they are on the right track. If yes, awesome. They can keep soldiering on without having that pesky voice in the back of their heads, questioning whether they're doing things correctly. If not, they have the opportunity to ask some questions and change their approach before investing too much time. Either way it's a win-win. With frequent micro check-ins, you have a constant pulse about where your employees are at and how they're feeling, and they get the benefit of knowing exactly where they stand and how they're doing. Exactly how often is often enough will depend on your organization and, frankly, your Millennial. But simple things like checking in every morning or sending a weekly email can go a long way.

Transparency: I want the whole truth

Managers often have to learn the art of delivering feedback that couches, cushions, structures, and/or positions criticism. While this attention to feedback detail makes a nice written paragraph on a page, it does little to tell a Millennial that you're giving them constructive feedback they need to hear. Growing up in an instant era made them accustomed to instant feedback, and one of the gifts of instant is the lack of time to finesse your words. Adopting speedy and frequent feedback methods will naturally lend itself to a transparent dialogue that communicates trust. When you provide a mostly unfiltered piece of feedback, you're saying to a Millennial: "I'm telling it like it is because that's all that I have time for!" This transparency (as long as it isn't clear to the point of rude) delivers an authentic message that Millennials need, and want, to hear.

Avoiding potential drawbacks of the instant feedback style

Too much of a good thing is always possible. When adopting this new style of feedback, you may all of a sudden find yourself sucked into the vortex of an inescapable feedback loop with your Millennial employees that keeps you from getting anything done. Setting clear expectations about when, how often, and how long your check-ins may be is crucial to keeping your resources from being drained and your Millennials happy. Additionally, there *will* be times when pausing to let the dust settle before launching into a critique will be the smartest approach.

As you embrace the instantaneous feedback method, keep in mind that

>> **Millennials are humans, not robots.** Speedy delivery of feedback doesn't mean blunt delivery of feedback. If they just gave a bad presentation, don't catch them on the way out the door with ideas for doing better next time. They're probably feeling the sting, and it's probably a case of "too soon." Be sure to consider when instant is a good thing and when letting the clock tick for a bit is best.

>> **Time to reflect is still important, especially for younger employees.** Millennials love all things instant, and they may struggle to realize that reflection is crucial to having a productive feedback session. Encourage them to take some time, write a handful of reflections on the project/meeting/task, and then come back together for a quick debrief.

>> **Documentation may be needed.** No one likes it, but it's necessary in today's work environment. It can serve as a great record of celebration and also the necessary steps to take if you have to let someone go. Try to keep some of your check-ins informal, but make sure to take some notes afterwards so that you have documentation for your files.

TIP

Take a "celebrate, then deliberate" approach with Millennials. *Celebrate* wins in the moment (with messaging customized for the length, size, and breadth of the project or task), and then *deliberate* — meet with necessary people one-on-one and give direct feedback, negative and positive. If you don't take enough time to celebrate wins with Millennials (not just point out the shortcomings), you'll sow resentment and they'll become more and more likely to leave your organization.

REMEMBER

It's not all about the Millennial. You need to take care of yourself and your work flow too. Try to find a speed and frequency of delivering feedback that takes care of your Millennials without sacrificing your work or well-being.

Rethinking the Review Session

When Baby Boomers entered the workforce, they entered into stiff competition with millions of peers to try and get ahead. In order to better understand how they stacked up with others, Boomers collectively created the annual feedback process. At the time, this yearly review was considered revolutionary.

Fast forward 20 years and you had Gen Xers growing weary of the style and infrequency of the yearly evaluation. It felt too formal, too delayed and, in a way, insincere. Xers had different objectives and priorities from their Boomer predecessors. The old model wasn't working for them, so they shook things up by asking for more regular and transparent feedback.

Enter Millennials. They're the first generation in the workforce that grew up with the Internet. It has shaped who they are and what they expect, and they're bringing those new expectations into the working world. To stay competitive, companies have to adapt and adopt a progressive feedback structure. The ones leading the pack are those whose leaders recognize that their talent development strategies need to evolve with the changing demographics of their workforce. Successful feedback and reviews are absolutely critical. Oftentimes an employee's exit can be traced back to a poor review session with his manager. If you're not rethinking your review session to appeal to Millennials' unique needs, you're going to slowly (or quickly) see your turnover numbers creep up.

Don't be afraid to examine your current review structure and ask questions. Your review policy should be a living, breathing, evolving thing. Has it been touched in the last ten years? Five years? Past year? Do your managers give both formal and informal feedback? Is there flexibility in feedback frequency, or is the rate static? Do you customize your approach based on the generation and/or the individual's preference? Are you staying abreast of what your competitors, as well as the best-of-the-best, are doing? If you answer "no" to any of these questions, read on.

WARNING

If you make a 180-degree shift in the way things used to be done, you're going to face an unhappy flood of Xer and Boomer employees. Make sure you're giving people a few options. Maybe your Xers don't want a weekly check-in and once a month serves them just fine. Don't ever assume; take the time to ask. And always keep in mind that change is hard, and in the workplace, if you're trying to retain *all* generations, evolution trumps revolution.

Knowing what works for Millennials

When strategizing about how to deliver feedback to Millennials, don't spend sleepless nights daunted by how much you need to change. Yes, Millennials are wired a bit differently, but at the end of the day, they're just people. To make things easier for you and more valuable for them, it's helpful to get a handle on understanding what works for them. Chances are you've got a pretty good grasp of how to communicate with Baby Boomer and Gen X employees, but start thinking (or asking!) about what works for Millennials before you sit down for a review.

Ask them to self-evaluate before they pontificate

One of the first steps to make a review session work for Millennials is to give them time to think and evaluate first. This practice is not uncommon to Millennials — they've likely been doing it from elementary school all the way through their MBA programs — but that doesn't mean they do it without prompting. Sitting down and listing all the things you've done right and wrong isn't necessarily a fun task for any generation, but it certainly is worthwhile. Prior to an informal or formal review session, ask Millennials to reflect on their performance.

Ask yourself whether you know what to say

While it may seem obvious, do your best to think before you speak. Consider phrases/words/thoughts commonly used in the workplace that should be avoided and replace them with something more savory.

Don't Say	Do Say
Three month ago . . .	Last week or a couple of hours ago . . .
Why do you need so much feedback?	How much feedback do you prefer?
What could you have done differently?	What did you do well and what would you change?
Back in my day . . .	What has worked for me may or may not work for you . . .
Let's talk about your weaknesses . . .	Let's focus on your strengths . . .

Ask them

Yup. That is it. Just plain ask them how they like their feedback. In all likelihood they have lots of thoughts on the topic. But you can't forget that, though they belong to the Millennial generation, each employee is an individual. Take the time to have a conversation with them about how they prefer to receive feedback. Come to the meeting prepared with a proposed review session and format. Ask them for their thoughts, amend as necessary, and go from there. If you're feeling adventurous, ask them whether they need anything different from you as a mentor.

Differentiating between formal and informal feedback

Feedback sessions lie on a moving scale of formality, where all levels are equally important, but knowing when and how to go about each one . . . well, that requires a dash of experience with a pinch of emotional intelligence. That said, Millennials show a marked preference for the informal end of that scale. They're an inherently informal generation because they grew up in an environment that allowed for constant and candid communication. Facebook, Twitter, and Instagram all allow Millennials to give feedback on people's lives with a thumbs up/heart icon/emoji or comment. An acquaintance might post a recent picture of a vacation in Spain, and the response might be "Whoa, Jordan, those bullfighters are impressive. Looks fun!" Even if they've spoken to Jordan only a handful of times, they're comfortable commenting (in a way, giving him feedback). They're so accustomed to constantly giving and delivering feedback via these informal platforms that, to a Millennial, informal is the new normal, to the point that very formal feedback can stir up anxiety and feel a bit uncomfortable.

In stark contrast, other generations grew up in an environment when the norm was being left alone to fend for yourself unless something was going terribly wrong. In the workplace, older employees wait for the formal review process and use it as a scale to track progress over time. In this format, you condense a half year or year's worth of comments into a couple-hour time block. The window for feedback is typically opened for that brief period of time before being shut again for all but the most immediate and/or pressing needs. Politically correct language and documentation are standard, as well as professional attire and thorough preparation for every single review session.

There's clearly quite a difference between the formal standard that Xers and Boomers are accustomed to and the more informal check-in that Millennials hunger for. In all likelihood, all your employees — whether they're 25 or 68 — prefer a healthy mix of the two (with Millennials tipping the balance in favor of the informal). To make sure that you deliver, you must first understand what differentiates the formal from the informal.

Formal feedback looks like this:

>> The review is often scheduled months in advance.

>> Pre-work is a prerequisite.

>> The review room is organized in a specific way (for example, the manager deliberately sits across from the employee).

>> The review always takes place in person.

>> It lasts for a set period of time, typically one to two hours.

>> Criticism is carefully couched, using phrases like, "This is an area of opportunity."

>> Professionalism and polish in communication and dress are expected.

>> The review is meticulously documented.

>> Communication is (mostly) one-directional.

>> Extended periods of time lapse between sessions.

Informal feedback, on the other hand, looks more like this:

>> Feedback is delivered instantly or within a couple hours or days.

>> Little or no pre-work is required.

>> A public place or open office is often preferable to a closed-door office.

>> Virtual communication is an acceptable alternative to meeting in person.

>> Time frames are short and flexible, typically 5–15 minutes.

>> The style of communication is casual and open — direct, but not abrasive.

>> There are no expectations regarding decorum or dress.

>> Documentation is scant, aside from determining next steps.

>> Communication is two-directional.

>> Flexibility is key in finding time that works, which may often be determined on the fly.

REMEMBER

Each individual may prefer feedback that is particular to his career and lifestyle, so what works for one person won't necessarily work for another. It will take a bit more work upfront, but make sure to curate your approach based on the needs of the individual.

Determining the right frequency

It's no secret that Millennials want constant feedback. Of course they do — they've grown up in an instant world and know that the sooner they learn something needs fixing, the sooner they'll be able to fix it. The work environment, however, isn't necessarily designed to accommodate that model, at least not at the present. HR policies, overscheduling, and lack of resources can all get in the way of instant communication and evaluation. As a manager, you work with the tools at your disposal. Keep the lines of communication open with both your higher-ups and your direct reports. To ensure that you're determining the right frequency — one that works for you, your employee, and your organization — follow these three steps:

1. **Ask.**

   Get a gauge of how often the Millennials you're managing want your thoughts. You will find that it varies from person to person, and you'll save valuable time that might be lost in making assumptions.

2. **Research.**

   Seek insight from fellow leaders about what works for them. How often do they meet with their teams, and how rigid or flexible is that schedule? You can even take it a step further and track what trends and best-in-class examples are being referenced in the news and apply those concepts to your own practice.

3. **Act.**

   After asking and researching, set a plan into action. Pilot a feedback timeline for a month and then review until you find what works.

WARNING

The following are signs that the frequency may be too high:

>> When you meet with your direct report, you have trouble coming up with a review topic, whether the feedback is good or bad.

>> You spend all the review session talking about your personal lives.

>> Your own work is suffering.

>> The Millennial keeps cancelling your sessions.

>> There's not enough time between your conversations to see positive changes in performance.

>> You're bored.

>> They're bored.

TIP

At most, stick with a default frequency of once a week. Younger generations will favor informal feedback in the moment, but in many cases that just may not be practical. Instead, as a base, schedule one-on-ones regularly for 15–30 minutes. Set a time and a location, and make it a habit. That way you and your reports will grow accustomed to these check-ins. It's up to both of you to assess and readjust the necessary frequency from there.

Mastering the compliment sandwich (hold the cheese)

Some time ago, in a land of corporate masterminds, a brilliant and deceptively simple idea emerged from its cocoon: The compliment sandwich. Here's how it works:

>> **The slice of bread:** A specific, positive assessment on a recent accomplishment.

>> **The cheese:** A nice, vague compliment; for example, "People seem to like you".

>> **The meat or black bean patty:** All the things that really need work because, whoa, have you missed the mark.

>> **The lettuce:** One more quick criticism that is minor but matters for future reference.

>> **The slice of bread:** But, really, overall you're doing pretty well here.

Sure, there are flaws to this method, but the intent here is spot-on. Most people will freeze up if your review opens with everything that they've done wrong. A compliment to kick things off creates a pleasant, nonconfrontational

Supercharging Your Feedback Loop

environment for the meeting, and closing with positive feedback lets the employee leave feeling motivated (rather than wondering if he'll ever be able to do anything right). Millennials want nice thick slices of bread on their sandwich — more so than other generations — because they've been fed positivity and encouragement their entire lives. This is in direct juxtaposition to Gen Xers, who are known for a "hold the bread, extra meat" mentality. They favor an honest, direct, transparent, and anti-fluff feedback model where "area of opportunity" is a cringe-worthy phrase that is better substituted with what you actually mean "weakness." That's them, though, and that mindset doesn't always work well for Millennials.

TIP

Though Millennials want that compliment sandwich, you must tread carefully because they are allergic to inauthenticity. The worst thing that can happen is that the sandwich turns into an overcooked, inedible mess that's full of falsities. Too often, people take the compliment sandwich approach without understanding that it's really easy to read through the vague compliment cheese. If this is paired with a specific criticism of work, the next generation will naturally assume that all you're doing is trying to get to the bad stuff. So make sure your compliments are valid, or hold the cheese. You could also consider throwing out the sandwich all together and adopting one of these alternate approaches:

>> **Stop, continue, grow.** Meet with a Millennial on a regular basis and discuss two or three processes/behaviors to stop doing, two or three to continue, and two or three that can be improved upon. This allows for all ingredients of the sandwich but lays it out in a more transparent way — an open-faced sandwich, if you will.

>> **Cheers, perseveres, and keep clears.** Cheer the Millennial for a job well done, outline the areas she needs to keep pushing through (or persevere), and lay out the things or behaviors she should steer clear of going forward.

>> **The good, the bad, and the ugly.** Highlight the wins; point out the areas that have been, simply put, rather bad; and then pinpoint the areas that start as ugly ducklings but can turn into swans with just a bit of growth and change.

TIP

A little humor goes a long way with Millennials. If you've got some tough feedback to give, of course, give it the gravity that it requires, but if you come in with a doom-and-gloom attitude, you'll scare the wits out of them. Crack a joke or two, or share a story about how something went wrong in the past that's now a bit humorous in hindsight.

Avoiding the "participation trophy" mindset

Millennials have earned the dubious honor of being labeled the "trophy generation." Maybe you've thought to yourself, said out loud, or overheard someone else say,

"I just can't deal with this 'everyone gets a trophy' thing! Why do the Millennials I manage expect praise for just doing their job?!" As is usually the case, there is more to this whole participation trophy thing than meets the eye.

How Millennials feel about the rewards for trying

To let you in on a not-so-secret secret, Millennials didn't ask for any of the trophies or certificates that they received. Most Millennials were raised by Boomer parents who gave them out because the self-esteem movement was in full storm. The feel-good rewards for effort prevalent in the 1980s through 2000s were a reaction to the earlier feel-not-so-good era of command-and-control parenting styles.

Today, Millennials are none too happy to be referred to as the trophy generation because even though they probably did get a certificate for "best character" at the senior-year award ceremony and/or a basketball ribbon that read "participant," they're not proud of it. They may even deny that the trophies and ribbons impacted them because they are only too well aware of how ridiculous they were (it's been an incessant source of scorn, teasing, and mockery since they entered the working world). Though they may deny it, these participation awards did impact Millennials . . . but that doesn't necessarily have to be a bad thing.

Give them accomplishment (not participation) recognition

Millennials don't expect a trophy after completing every assignment, but they do want recognition of their efforts and praise for a successful finish. They do understand rejection; many of them learned what that felt like when they graduated into a recession economy. They're wary of underperforming and are looking for the encouragement that was the status quo of their youth. The praise doesn't have to come in the mindset of, "You tried really hard; here's a ribbon." Acknowledge that Millennials need more encouragement, but do it authentically. To them, a "no news is good news" mentality likely won't fly.

The dark side of the participation award

No one ever thinks about the flipside of this participation trophy thing. When everyone gets a trophy, the winners actually end up losing. By watering down the meaning of the award, it makes the win feel that much less satisfying. Millennials want that win, and they want it to mean something. If you praise them always, even when what they're doing sucks, you're doing them and yourself a disservice.

Ditching the "but I had to figure it out on my own" mindset

You may remember a time when, upon receiving tough feedback, you took it and figured out, on your own, how to improve your performance. While that may work in an authoritarian-leaning work environment or for a very independent generation like Gen X, the next-generation worker has different expectations. Millennials grew up with coaches, teachers, and counselors who consistently helped them grow and change for the better, constantly offering techniques and skills to help them confront challenges. If they lost the tennis match, their parents didn't say, "Well, you lost; now go figure out what you can do to be better." Instead, they said, "Well, that's too bad. What do you think you could've done differently to win? Here's what I would suggest. We can work on your backhand over the weekend. Now let's go get some pizza."

Like it or not, as a manager, the onus is on you to help set Millennials on a course for improvement. When Millennials look at their careers, they don't see themselves as solo players but as part of a team, and you're their coach. Instead of delivering feedback with the expectation that they will figure it out on their own, ditch the "do-it-yourself" mindset and come prepared to help them figure it out.

TIP

Here are some ways to help Millennials help themselves:

>> When delivering feedback on areas of improvement, present them with a framework restricted by deadlines and to-do lists.

>> Check in on the framework regularly so that you (and your Millennial employee) can track progress over time.

>> Be clear about what you want changed, how you want it changed, and when you want it changed by.

>> Give them a list of resources other than yourself, including websites, training tools, and other employees.

>> Offer small carrots along the way that they can "unlock" as rewards for improved performance, for example, a $5 gift card to their favorite coffee shop.

>> Avoid sticks (harsh punishment). Millennials will not react favorably, and you'll end up demotivating them.

>> Whenever you deliver tough news or commentary on performance, follow it up with a proposed plan of improvement.

You may be thinking that this sounds like a lot of hand-holding or is even a counterproductive (and time consuming) way to get the most out of your employees. While those thoughts are not entirely unwarranted, adopting structured, prescriptive styles of feedback delivery that can be measured over time will help you set Millennials on a fast-track to independent and excellent work. The more time you invest upfront, the more streamlined and hands-off you can be with them in the future. For now, a structured plan of improvement is one of the easier processes to adopt to prevent a Millennial asking (or singing), "Should I stay or should I go?"

Seeing what the best of the best are doing

Since annual reviews grew in popularity in the 1960s and 1970s, there have been standout companies and CEOs that have served as forward-thinking examples for others to model their own reviews on. Now, even those progressive companies are changing their ways. When it comes to feedback and reviews, there's no one-size-fits-all approach. As a leader, you can sift through the best-in-class examples to uncover and adopt either general overhauls or specific changes that make sense within your performance evaluation process.

General feedback considerations

Before overhauling everything about your feedback model, you may want to examine the most basics elements that, when shifted, appeal more to the Millennial demographic. While these shifts may be large (eliminating the annual review that you have 30 years of records for in an HR basement), it may be the most seamless shift you can make.

>> **The death of the annual review:** Though in many environments a case can still be made for the formal, annual feedback process, some large organizations are finding that it's too time consuming and just doesn't deliver the desired results. There are no sacred cows in the workplace of the future. Ask yourself whether your company is properly using the annual review and — more importantly — whether it's still the best use of time. There may be some micro versions that accomplish the same thing without stirring up such a big to-do.

>> **The 360 approach:** It's no longer enough for feedback to go in one direction — it needs to come from all positions in the company. Your manager is not the only person who may have constructive comments, and for Millennials, the more feedback from the more people, the better (within reason of course). Work is affected by everyone, not just one person. Many organizations have approached this more holistic, democratic approach to soliciting and receiving feedback.

Specific feedback considerations

If you're feeling creative, innovative, and bold about embracing changes to your feedback methods, then adopting versions of these examples may be best for you and your company. The following companies adopted unique feedback models to deliver specific results, and most are reaping the rewards. Maybe you'll read these and it will spark a unique idea of your own.

>> **Kayak.com's five-word performance review:** The process is simple. You meet in an informal environment like a coffee shop or restaurant. Either the manager or employee can request feedback that boils down to five words (two negative, two positive, and one of your choosing). You go over the words together and then decide what to do from there.

>> **GE's switch from "rank and yank" to "PD@GE":** When GE was under CEO Jack Welch's reign, it was famous for substantially growing in business, serving as an example for Six Sigma, and setting a precedent for the "rank and yank" or "vitality curve" model that placed employees on a bell curve. If you were in the lowest 10 percent, you were fired. Over time, that model has changed drastically into the more-current version, which reviews employees using an app that constantly grades their priorities as either "continue doing" or "consider changing."

>> **Pixar's "Plussing":** Pixar is becoming feedback famous for adopting a simple method: Any word of feedback requires constructive criticism. If you're going to deliver a criticism, it has to be followed by a "plus," an idea or suggestion that will help improve the original idea.

The reality is that the feedback and review process has to work for you and your team. Determine a plan that makes sense for your organization, and don't be afraid of testing it. When considering a new review method or technique, take these steps:

1. **Do the research.**

2. **Poll those you're leading and managing to see what works for them and what they feel is lacking.**

3. **Propose a vision for what could work and get insight from others.**

4. **Decide on a course of action and test it over a set period of time.**

5. **Reevaluate and course-correct (if necessary).**

WARNING

Many large, big-name organizations are adopting all kinds of fancy apps to make instant feedback less complicated and more painless, but it's just not that easy. One particular app allows employees (younger ones, let's be real) to send emojis throughout the day that express how they're feeling about work. A novel concept, but chances are high that if you present this new app to a room full of next-generation employees, they're going to sigh, roll their eyes, and put on a smile to please the leaders who are trying just a bit too hard to reach them. Flashy and new doesn't always mean best-in-class. Consider all angles before implementing drastic change.

Realizing that Feedback Is a Two-Way Street

The organizational structure has been flipped, spun three times, and pushed through a reinvention machine right along with the communication ladder. There is no one way to move around in an organization, move up the ladder, or get the job done. Feedback and communication are also multidirectional as the world shifts to accommodate a more networked model of work. Communication doesn't just flow from the top down; it can flow upwards, sideways, horizontally, or any which way. Instead of accepting a chain of command, Millennials push for a multi-directional model. The model is now a free-flowing structure rather than the linear start-stop of the past.

Do you have feedback for your Millennial employees? Yes, of course you do. And you can be fairly certain that they have thoughts they'd like to share with you too. Rather than shutting off the possibility of a symbiotic back-and-forth relationship, open your eyes to the feedback model that Millennials are hungering for — no longer a one-way street, but a two-way highway of information.

Ignoring your inner voice ("But in my day, I never gave my manager feedback!")

Back in the day, freely giving your opinion to anyone in a senior level could be quickly followed by a not-so-pleasant conversation of "this is just how things work around here" or "please pack up your things and go." Logically, it's still a bit unsettling when a younger generation challenges authority confidently and candidly, either in person or virtually. But Millennials grew up in a world that invited them to regularly question the status quo — disruption and innovative ideation were rewarded from a young age with gold stars and high grades. Social media gave them a platform to communicate with the President of the United States or the CEO of a local organization as easily as they would connect with their best friend.

REMEMBER

Before getting too frustrated by this mindset around authority, understand that Millennials want to give their manager feedback because they want to perform to the best of their abilities. Some of that may come down to not what they do *for you* as a leader, but what you do as a leader *for them*. With the best intentions, they hope that by providing feedback to you, you can become a better manager to them, which will in turn make them a better employee and ultimately have a positive impact on the company and the bottom line. This two-way communication, though substantially divergent from practices of the past, can be a powerful gift if both sides approach it thoughtfully and respectfully.

Soliciting valuable input

Creating an environment that doesn't shut down, but rather encourages, mutually beneficial feedback and feed-forth is only the first step. Next is ensuring that the two-way communication is productive. While vague questions like "How can I be better?" or "What are three things I can do to change?" are well-intentioned, they're too broad to elicit valuable feedback. One of two things can happen: The floodgates are opened (see the next section), or unhelpful and vague comments dominate the conversation.

TIP

To ensure that you're receiving the most helpful feedback as a leader, create some structure around how you like to receive feedback. One idea is to create an input form with a clear structure. This will make the Millennials' job manageable and straightforward, and it will shield you from the flood of unwanted, unproductive, or way-too-candid feedback that you may receive otherwise. It could be as simple as asking, via email, for five specific pieces of feedback regarding your involvement with recent projects or initiatives. Or you could ask for three high-lights about what went well in the past months and three lowlights about where they wish things had gone differently. If you prefer an even more structured approach, you can present employees with a feedback form after a project or a time period for annual/semi-annual reviews.

Stopping (or at least controlling) the floodgates

Asking Millennials for input is an excellent move in the right direction, but there is the risk that once you crack open that window, the feedback won't stop, lines will be crossed, or opinions will start coming out of turn. To ensure you have control over the feedback gates, take a creative and intentional approach when you solicit a Millennial's opinion. You may not be a manager who wants the constant drip-drip-drip of feedback, and that's totally fine. Communicate your expectations, and don't be afraid to be prescriptive in designating clear places and times for that feedback to be delivered. Consider the following options:

>> **Hold a Millennial open forum.** Many leaders have taken it upon themselves to create a venue for a group of Millennials to give feedback together. You could host an off-site meeting every year with employees under 40 to hear, directly from the source, whether the trends that others say about Millennials are true for your company too. This forum can also be run by an outside consultant if you feel like your staff won't open up to your own organization's senior leaders.

>> **Upgrade the anonymous tip box.** Sometimes employees have feedback that is more global and that you may have little power over. Instead of an anonymous suggestion box that may attract the ever-so-lovely "I hate your shoes" type of commentary, designate a wall in your office as the suggestion board (like a big white-board wall). They'll be less likely to give useless or over-critical feedback and instead will be thoughtful about what they recommend. This new process may get off to a slow start — it's public, after all — but you can lead the way and empower them by kicking it off with a few ideas of your own.

>> **Set clear boundaries.** You have no way of knowing how your employees will react before you seek their insight, so set expectations as clearly as you can about what's acceptable feedback and what is crossing a line. If you feel like a Millennial steps over the boundary, be honest about it. Every moment is a coaching moment.

>> **Ask for proof.** When you ask for feedback on your performance as a manager, the intention is not to make yourself a target for any and all comments, either hurtful or positive. If they're giving you feedback, ask them for examples to back up their statements. "You never take the time to check-in with me" is far less valuable than "in the past month, we have had only one 15-minute check-in." By asking for examples, they'll need to think and be deliberate about the kinds of comments they give you, rather than just go through a laundry list that may be half based in reality and half a reflection of perception and nothing more.

Acting More Like a Coach Than a Boss

Millennials usually don't leave a bad job or company; they leave a bad manager. In those situations, it's likely that the manager was acting too much like a stereotypical "boss" character — driving employees too hard, blaming others when things went wrong, and seeking a workhorse to do his bidding and earn company dollars year after year. Okay, this may be the worst depiction of a boss, but it can ring true to anyone who's felt like she's had one who's too tough.

In today's work world, these bosses will lose the popularity contest with all generations, especially Millennials, because this generation grew up with coaches who knew how to give tough feedback, helpful encouragement, and, yes, also a few trophies. To them, an ideal leader is constructive, acts like a role model, and rallies you to push a boulder up a hill versus a boss who criticizes how you're pushing.

REMEMBER

Imagine the best coach you've ever had, whether it was in tennis, basketball, or on the debate team. Coaches are mentors and guides whose intent is to make you stronger and better than you were before. Assume this mindset, and you'll be a better leader to Millennials without even knowing it. They're seeking a coach at work who can behave authentically, listen like a trusted confidant, and push like Coach Taylor (a reference for you *Friday Night Lights* fans).

Troubleshooting Common Feedback Issues

If you've ever struggled giving a Millennial feedback, you're not alone. It's hard. There is no one way to do it, and it doesn't always get easier with the more people you've led or managed; however, one thing is true. Whatever you're feeling, you're not alone. Others have felt your pain, your strife, and your desire to be better. A Millennial is just as much of an employee as someone from any other generation though, so there's no getting around this. Here's a brief guide on how to navigate the ins and outs of feedback with Millennials.

The delivery of tough feedback

No matter the generation, level, or age, delivering tough feedback is rarely a fun process. It can lead to a defensive attitude, a reluctance to change, or even a desire to leave. But everyone deserves the opportunity to identify and improve on sore spots, and you're entitled to the opportunity to improve your team and fix problem areas. The way Xers prefer to receive difficult feedback (they most likely want you to rip off the Band-Aid as quickly as possible) doesn't necessarily work best for Millennials.

The challenge

When you deliver tough feedback to Millennials, you worry that they're worrying. You may be nervous that they're starting to think too hard about what they need to do differently. Chances are that what you thought was a helpful conversation became one of their worst work moments ever.

Possible cause

Millennials were raised in the self-esteem movement and weren't given the tools for handling criticism at a young age. While other generations learned how to let it roll off their backs or deal with it and move on, younger generations internalize the feedback, all while merging their personal lives with their professional lives.

The remedy

TIP

If they're internalizing your feedback, it typically means they care . . . a lot. They likely view you as someone whom they want to impress. Maybe they view you as their confidant and coach. It may not seem like it in the moment, but this is actually good, so here's how you can move past the discomfort:

» Get comfortable knowing that the situation may get tense or awkward.

» Don't waste time getting to the tough feedback.

» Deliver your critiques in an appropriate time frame, the sooner the better.

» Provide a structured road map to improve.

» Follow up with next steps.

» Be a voice of encouragement along the way.

What to do if a Millennial cries

It's most managers' and leaders' worst nightmare — what happens if a Millennial starts blubbering, you panic, and you don't have tissues to provide for them? Okay, not all Millennials cry, that's an exaggerated depiction of what truly transpires. But it's more likely to happen with this generation, especially in their earlier years at work. You better start prepping now if you haven't already.

The challenge

Millennials can sometimes internalize evaluations and react defensively or sensitively, occasionally resulting in watery eyes, drops of tears, or a minor breakdown. This outcome can prevent a productive review session if what you intended as helpful words of change were instead heard as scathing criticism.

Possible cause

Millennials grew up in an environment that asked them to be vulnerable and open with their feelings, whereas other generations learned early on how to control their emotions and keep their poker faces intact. Additionally, Millennials may be taking feedback personally, not just professionally, and a comment about their work may be heard as a comment about them as a person.

The remedy

TIP

Although the tears may be distracting, confusing, and even a bit frustrating, you can take these simple steps if a Millennial is crying:

>> Don't automatically get frustrated.

>> Don't draw too much attention to the tears.

>> Continue with your thought.

>> Ask if there's anything the Millennial wants to say.

>> Welcome the option to talk later.

>> Don't respond with pity or condescension.

What if Mom and Dad get involved?

Millennials have a close bond with their parents and view them as trusted allies and quite possibly even friends. Sometimes this relationship can go a bit too far if the doting parents become meddlesome in the work environment. It started when Millennials were young, and it's very different than the way their parents were raised.

Millennials are growing up and becoming more independent from their parents — especially older Millennials who have been in the workforce for well over a decade. Luckily, that means fewer calls from Mom and Dad. But when it comes to younger Millennials and even the generation after them, their folks may still be around for support — much to the chagrin of managers.

The challenge

Millennials' parents may overstep and contact a work environment to discuss a feedback session gone wrong, amongst many other things. It comes across as unprofessional, annoying, and inappropriate.

Possible cause

In many cases, your Millennial employees may not know that their parents are calling. They likely discussed the situation with their parents, asked for advice, and may be seeking a solution, but the parents took it upon themselves to help solve the problem for them. Your Millennial employee likely didn't set his parents on you like a pack of Rottweilers.

The remedy

TIP

Consider some damage control and prevention before griping about meddlesome Boomer parents.

» Thank the parents for their interest, but let them know you need to speak directly to their Millennial child regarding anything work-related.

» Ask the Millennial about the incident.

» Explain to the Millennial why his parents' involvement can actually be hurtful, not helpful, to his career.

» Confront it and move on.

» Don't hold the incident against the Millennial or use it as a reason to think poorly about him.

» Use the close parent-child relationship in a positive way to boost your company's employer status. Consider creating an environment that welcomes parents to the office in a "bring your parents to work" day. This can be a great marketing strategy.

I think my Millennial is about to quit . . .

If Millennials leave an organization, it can likely be traced to the last time that they received feedback. You don't want that last review session to be the ultimate reason that a Millennial decided to leave the organization.

The challenge

A Millennial receives a firm review, and rather than planning how to change her behaviors or work, she starts plotting her exit to find a workplace she feels will be more conducive to her growth and career improvement (or hurt her feelings less).

Possible cause

If Millennials receive critical feedback without a clear structure of how to improve, they'll feel deflated instead of motivated. If weaknesses are focused on more than strengths, Millennials may be wondering whether they do anything right. *What are my contributions? Why am I even here?* While other generations wouldn't have dreamed about leaving their job without finding another one, Millennials believe that it's worth it if they don't have to sacrifice more of their life in a job that makes them unhappy.

The remedy

TIP

Move quickly and swiftly if you want your Millennial to stay:

>> Schedule an informal meeting.

>> Have an honest check-in and provide the option of a follow-up check-in.

>> Give the Millennial the opportunity to give you feedback (as described earlier in this chapter).

>> Ask whether a clear structure is in place for the Millennial's growth and improvement (if not, put one into action).

>> If things aren't going well for you or the Millennial, consider that it may be time for the Millennial to leave.

Chapter **4**

Motivating Millennials — Generation "Why?"

"What gets you out of bed in the morning?" It may sound simple, but garnering this information about what motivates each person is vital to understanding how to work with and retain employees.

Put the question out there and you get a whole spectrum of responses from individual to individual, as can be expected, but there are resounding similarities across the generations: connecting with great colleagues, challenging work, feeding the dog (and themselves), paying the bills, funding a vacation, and so on. Everyone, no matter the generation, wants fruitful, meaningful work — any manager or leader would agree to that. If, however, you want to level-up your managing skills, you need to understand not only the similarities but also the important differences among what motivates each generation. By understanding these nuances, you can collect the right tools to properly light a fire under your direct reports, regardless of what generation they belong to.

The thing is, managers have been working side by side with Boomers and Xers for quite some time and have already honed their spidey sense for the best tips and strategies to bolster motivation among these two groups. Millennials, on the other hand, especially the younger Millennial hires, are a bit more of an agent unknown. Managers are discovering that they need some extra help to better understand the complexity of a generation that is motivated so differently from generations past.

This chapter sheds light on how to reward and inspire Millennials. It explores why meaning is so important to Millennials and why you should reexamine the value of the dollar and shift to creative nonmonetary rewards. You get an idea of what those rewards look like. Finally, you discover how to tap into strategies for building a strong community of friends and colleagues within your walls and retaining a generation that is notoriously slippery.

Managing for Meaning

One common complaint from managers about Millennials is, "Why is it that what motivated me isn't motivating them?" To fully understand the answer to this question, you have to travel back in time to see how the other generations were raised. By looking at the stark differences that have wired the Millennial mindset, you can see why this generation is so hungry for meaning, above almost all else, in their work.

REMEMBER

Millennials are always going to hunt for a job in which they are making a difference, but the way it's manifested can take a variety of forms. They can be making a positive impact on people's lives, animals' lives, or the community at large. It can be as big as contributing to the fight against climate change or as small as paying forward a cup of joe. Whatever the case may be, Millennials *need* to know: Do I make a difference in my work? Do I matter? Because if that answer is no, it's going to be nigh impossible for them to get out of bed in the morning.

Looking back across generations

Once upon a time, the Traditionalist generation raised their Baby Boomer children with one goal in mind: to achieve the American Dream. In pursuit of this goal, many Baby Boomers followed the traditional path of college, job, marriage, money, house, and family — hopefully, with a bit of fun along the way. For them, working hard was a badge of honor, and Baby Boomers put in the hours, effort, and sacrifices to earn the respect and success they aspired to. They worked themselves to the bone, fought hard for their wins, and didn't have the time or luxury to redefine what work looked like. They competed with millions of their peers to land and keep a job, and understood the harsh reality that if they didn't get a paycheck, they wouldn't eat — and neither would their family.

Some Baby Boomers achieved the level of success they so desired, but at what cost? They missed out on watching their kids grow up and abandoned personal hobbies and interests in exchange for more hours at the office. Yet, when the Great Recession hit, many Boomers saw their company loyalty repaid with layoffs and financial ruin.

Having experienced the dark side of the American Dream, Boomers naturally wanted to raise their Millennial children with a lighter mindset. They taught their kids that the paycheck didn't matter as much as using their time and talents wisely: "If you're going to work as long and hard as I have, you better do something that matters to you." If Millennials had a nickel for every time they heard that sentence, they'd be a wealthy (and debt-free!) generation.

This messaging from their parents is one part of the equation that led to meaning-hungry Millennials. The other part is what they witnessed happening in the world around them. Millennials saw institution after institution crumble. They experienced homeland violence in the form of a deluge of school shootings and the horrific terror attacks of 9/11. They watched Al Gore's *Inconvenient Truth* as preteens, to be only further haunted by a series of inconvenient and, frankly, disturbing truths as revealed by *The Daily Show* or *VICE* news. Their Boomer parents encouraged them with sentiments like, "You can be part of the solution. You can help make our world a better place." The message struck a chord, and it has been part of the Millennial psyche ever since. For Millennials, if they aren't actively contributing and impacting the organization or the world in a positive way, they aren't doing anything at all.

Picture for a moment a 28-year-old professional named Albus. He's intelligent, driven, creative, and ambitious. He has switched jobs multiple times in his career because recruiters have been knocking down his door (or direct messaging his LinkedIn profile) to capture his brilliance for their organization. Being so sought after and successful, you'd think that young Albie would feel great about his current situation. But what you don't hear or see is his expressed dismay at happy hour with his friends — he's confused. He confides to his friends, "I'm grateful for all this opportunity. But I just don't know if what I'm doing matters . . . I'm not sure I can work much longer in a job that does so little for the world." None of his roles have connected him to the bigger picture or left him feeling like he's made any societal impact. So for now, he continues to chase the dream of using his talents in a way that leaves the world a better place than he found it.

Connecting the dots for Millennials

For every naysayer who believes Millennials aren't unique because they want to have a meaningful job, you're right. Millennials are not unique in this regard. Young Boomers were a generation of activists driven to make the world a better place, and Gen Xers wanted to disprove their apathetic label as a misnomer and positively affect people's lives. Here are the two critical slivers of difference:

>> Other generations didn't, and still don't, need others to affirm how they're making a difference. Millennials struggle to see their footprints if they don't see the end results and the tangible way their work contributed to it.

>> While other generations were willing to wait to ascend into positions where power, influence, and money could effect the change they wanted to see in the world, Millennials want to make a difference from day one.

TIP

To ensure that you're keeping Millennial workers engaged and motivated, help them connect the dots. Show them how their job and its associated tasks positively impact you, your company, and the community. There are countless ways to approach this. Depending on your organization, your chosen approach will depend on budget, workforce, and industry. Luckily, you have options no matter what kind of work environment you manage in. Try one of these proven methods of connecting the dots for Millennials:

>> **The physical connection:** One large organization implemented a program called "Line of Sight." Its intent was to connect each employee's work to the mission. On a large wall in the company's headquarters, you can find your role in the organization and connect, via the web of other departments, until you reach the top where you'll find the company's mission displayed prominently. You're literally a cog in the machine — but unlike the negative connotations of this idiom, without you and others like you, the machine falls apart. It's a quick and effective way to impart meaning to any role.

>> **The family connection:** When the job is hands-on and laborious — think warehouse and facility work — connecting workers to a lofty human purpose can feel like a bit of a challenge. One organization found that even if they connected the product in the warehouse to the end consumer's positive experience, the messaging wasn't resonating with their employees. It was too anonymous and ineffective. They decided, instead, to make it personal. Each employee was asked to share a picture of his loved one and then fill in the blank, "I work hard so that _____." By connecting the mission to their loved ones, employees were able to see an end goal that was worth working for.

>> **The individual connection:** To capture just how purposeful everyone's job is, accounting firm KPMG launched the "Higher Purpose Initiative." They asked the employees themselves to connect the dots. The firm asked each employee to contribute to their *10,000 Stories Challenge* that demonstrated how each person found meaning in work. After accumulating an impressive 42,000 stories and realizing that the exercise was a runaway success, KPMG went one step further. They created internal posters and external advertisements

showcasing what had been shared. The results wove a story of engagement and increased loyalty and pride in the organization that resulted in them jumping 17 spots on the *Fortune* 100 list of Best Places to Work For.

>> **The peer connection:** Sometimes, connecting the dots doesn't require a formal program. Instead, it calls for a culture that invites others to share when they're doing something meaningful or working alongside someone else who is. If your industry doesn't have straightforward connections to the bigger purpose, focus instead on creating a culture that is so inviting that it becomes the driver in and of itself. Build a network of peers and colleagues who can lean on one another, encourage friendships, and create an environment where working for the betterment of the team becomes the main goal at hand.

Engaging in philanthropy

There is no quicker way to inject meaning into your organization than to become heavy participants in philanthropic endeavors. Truthfully, in the corporate world, embracing a robust giving stratagem is a solid plan no matter the organization (or the mission). From a PR standpoint, the past 30 years haven't been kind to corporate America. The media, including news outlets and Hollywood, have taken down the business world in a major way. Next-generation would-be employees are wary of "corporate greed" and loathe the possibility that they may have to "sell their soul" or "work for the man" to pay off their college loans.

To counter these negative stereotypes and fold in another layer of significance, you should make engaging in philanthropy a major objective. Step one is to establish these programs and make sure to include a few that really speak to Millennials. Step two is to yell it from the rooftops. If no one (specifically job-searching Millennials) knows you're actively participating in these programs, you might as well not be.

There are different ways to tap into philanthropy, but to get you started, try the following:

>> **Volunteering:** Is this one a bit obvious? Yes, a little. Is it incredibly important? Absolutely. You should be putting substantial effort into nurturing these programs. Offer a day of the year, fully paid, to engage in a volunteering opportunity of the employee's choosing. Better yet, as a fun company outing, sponsor volunteer events as a way to bring co-workers and departments together. You might even consider hosting special trips that employees need to apply for, and fly the selected few out to an exciting and international destination to do their voluntourism. (How's that for a good carrot?) Whatever your company's budget, you can find volunteering solutions that work for you and appeal to Millennials.

Millennials are a "pics or it didn't happen" generation. They want an active hand in the philanthropic process, and the more experiential and share-worthy the event, the better. Focus on collaborative and active events. That way they'll continue to build relationships with their colleagues, have something fun and interesting to share, and, through that sharing, hopefully attract others to your company.

>> **Active giving:** The idea of active giving is a slight tweak to your volunteering efforts. Millennials are a generation that have embraced health and wellness trends like social running events (think the Color Run or the Warrior Dash) and gamified fitness. Why not combine this healthy mindset with a philanthropic objective? You'll be simultaneously speaking to their desire to stay fit as well as their need to build community with a workplace of like-minded peers. Form a workplace team to participate in a charity 5K, or implement a push-up challenge that raises money for a local school. The opportunities are limited only by your imagination (and your fitness level!).

>> **Corporate giving:** There are countless ways that you can enroll in a corporate giving program, and if you haven't already, you should. Understand that Millennials will lose trust for your company if you don't. (Check out *Charity and Philanthropy For Dummies* by Karl T. Muth, Michael T.S. Lindenmayer, and John Kluge, published by John Wiley & Sons, Inc., to find out more about all the ways your company can donate.) Give your next-generation employees some say in where corporate dollars go — ask for their opinions and advice, put it to a company-wide vote, or invite them to control an entire portion of corporate budget.

>> **Paycheck donations:** This concept isn't new, but it's a great way for all employees to feel like they are giving back. For each check that your employees get, ask whether they want to donate a percentage or dollar amount to a selection of charities. Giving them the ability to choose is critical, because some may hold more value in your Millennials' eyes.

Your company's philanthropic efforts can function as one of your strongest marketing tools or as a deal breaker. Be transparent about what and who you're donating to, because if it's kept a secret only to be discovered later by some resourceful reporters, you'll lose trust —and not just from your Millennials. On the flip side, you could sway an unsure candidate to choose your organization over another by giving to an organization that shares her values.

Compensating the Noncompensation Generation

Millennials are a generation saddled with debt, which — to the untrained eye — might make them seem like the group most eager to chase the paycheck. Alas, fair reader, if only the Millennial motivation strategy was as easy as offering a regular pay increase. The truth of the matter is much more complex.

Why isn't compensation enough?

Millennials want to pay off their debt, but that alone isn't going to be enough to stay in one job for the paycheck. Why, you ask? Here are the top reasons:

>> **Their parents are hanging around as an invisible safety net.** You may have heard the term "Boomerang kids." It's no accident that "Boomer" is in the phrase. Is their kid's job unsatisfying? Do they need some extra time to find their "forever career"? Boomer parents are letting Millennials move home, often rent free, to give them the support and freedom to quit their jobs, do some soul-searching, recalibrate, and re-career so they can find the role that will be most fulfilling in the future.

>> **The future is far from guaranteed.** The events of 9/11 occurred in the middle of Millennials' preteen and teen years: It hit them where it counts and left a lasting impact on an otherwise optimistic generation. They learned firsthand that you never know what tomorrow will bring, so you better love and make the most of what you're doing right now.

>> **Money promises nothing.** Millennials watched their parents, their friends' parents, even their teachers and counselors lose homes and retirement accounts during the Great Recession. Sure, making money is one of their goals, but they're well aware that it can be easily snatched away with the next economic downturn, no matter how hard you've worked or how carefully you've saved. Interpersonal relationships, experiences, and even career skills are impervious to the economy's whims, and in Millennials' eyes, much more worthwhile investments.

While Millennials aren't as motivated by money as they are by meaning, general feelings of goodwill won't pay the bills. A smart compensation strategy can be the deciding factor in whether a Millennial chooses to stay or leave your organization. Women in particular are more likely to leave if they feel they aren't being fairly compensated, especially in relation to their male peers. Compensate smart, but don't make it such a high priority that all other motivation factors and rewards are forgotten. When you need to talk salary, do so tactfully and mindfully with help from this section.

The dollars and cents conversation

The term "compensation" is more all-encompassing to Millennials than just paper and coin. When recruiting, or during the interview process, show them that you take a multi-tiered approach to compensation. It's not just a transactional relationship where you send them paychecks for their time; it's more complex and nuanced. It's about investing in their development, building a culture of community and teamwork, and even providing support for their general health and well-being.

>> **Phrase that won't work with a Millennial:** "It's going to be tough work at first, but you'll see, it'll be so worthwhile when you start realizing how much money you're going to make!"

>> **Phrase that will work with a Millennial:** "We value our employees and invest in them not only with our compensation structure, but also with training opportunities and wellness programs, because we believe in developing well-rounded individuals."

The fairness conversation

Access to the Internet is synonymous with access to the truth (faulty journalism aside), which means that pay inequalities based on race, gender, status, and so forth are common knowledge. The youngest of the next generation in particular expect you to come clean about how you compensate. Additionally, they're looking for a structure that values their individual needs; they value the ability to customize everything, and compensation is no exception.

>> **Phrase that won't work with a Millennial:** "We believe in treating everyone fairly, so everyone has the same compensation structure."

>> **Phrase that will work with a Millennial:** "We are transparent and fair about our compensation structure. That's why we tell you the process that goes into it and invite your opinion when necessary (for example, if you're earning commission on top of a base salary)."

The comparison conversation

In the past, sharing and comparing information about salaries would have been absolutely unthinkable and considered a major breach of propriety. Older generations can be completely taken aback when they see that Millennials are comfortable talking about many things not traditionally PC in the workplace, and that includes their salaries. It isn't uncommon for them to chat about what they took home last week or their latest commission check. They grew up grading each other's homework in class, so it only makes sense that compensation has the potential to go public as well. You won't be able to control what they're saying to one another, but you can help turn the tide of the conversation.

>> **Phrase that won't work with a Millennial:** "I can't believe you are comparing your salary with others. What they are making has nothing to do with you."

>> **Phrase that will work with a Millennial:** "Many behind-the-scenes factors go into calculating individual compensation structures. Let's focus on how we can help you achieve your goals."

COMPENSATING LIKE A BOSS

Compensation is so much more than meets the eye. To pay like a pro, don't view compensation myopically, but open your eyes to the "total rewards" structure. Think about how to reach Millennials beyond just throwing more money at them (which is likely to be a foolhardy approach anyway). Build in commission options, additional perks, and training opportunities, all filtered through the Millennial lens:

- Benefits are part of the compensation package, and Millennials will expect a robust benefits package that includes a wellness focus. (Give wellness programs the attention they deserve. They're highly sought after by the Millennial generation.)

- Millennials value salary over high commission structures. For example, a 70/30 commission structure is better than a 30/70 one.

- Flexibility in how, where, and when they work can be enormously motivating.

- Pump up the perks. Little, seemingly insignificant perks can go a long way.

- Get creative with your compensation. Everyone offers the gym discount, but maybe your organization is the only one to offer participation in a yearly triathlon or yoga retreat.

What is it with YOLO?

Thanks to rapper/singer/songwriter Drake, the next generation has adopted a popular motto that captures the essence of how they're living their lives: YOLO, or "you only live once." The mentality is not a new one — "tomorrow isn't guaranteed," "carpe diem," and "live in the moment" are all iterations of the same mindset — but Millennials have taken the message to heart. Naturally, this may lead to some genuine frustration from other generations that have invested a lot of time and care into carving out a successful and comfortable future for themselves, often sacrificing comfort in the present moment in order to play the longevity game. Millennial behavior can seem erratic — as if they're wearing YOLO blinders — that leave them with a shortsighted mindset that results in impulsive decision-making.

Some common frustrations about Millennials that can be explained by YOLO include the following:

>> Leaving a job without having another one lined up.

>> Leaving a high-paying job for one they enjoy more, but pays less.

>> Changing career paths only a couple of years into trying one path.

>> Spending instead of saving.

>> Renting instead of owning.

>> Prioritizing hobbies and personal endeavors over work.

WHERE YOLO COMES FROM

The Great Recession taught Millennials that corporations can't be trusted, buying a home isn't always the best decision, and saving may lead to losing. Add to that all the tragedies Millennials witnessed growing up — from 9/11 to movie theater shootings to the Boston Marathon bombings — and we have a generation that wants to live for today.

Rather than griping about why this mindset is counterproductive, celebrate how passionate it makes Millennials in the moment. While it may be a loss for some organizations as employees leave money and prestige for a meaningful career, others will tap into the enthusiasm Millennials bring to the day-to-day and the tasks at hand.

Rewarding Millennials

Past rewards structures were designed for employees who valued longevity and time above all else: pay increases and additional PTO (paid time off) aligned with the time spent with a company. Anniversaries were rewarded with cake and selecting a gift item from the company's anniversary catalog. Though some companies still offer similar rewards programs, they may need to consider reinventing these programs in the next 5–20 years. That's not to say that those who take pride in the time they've spent with an organization shouldn't be honored and recognized for their loyalty — they absolutely should. But you should also take the time to reward employees who've done an incredible job for the company within three short years. The workforce shift from seniority to meritocracy is too crucial to ignore, and there are absolutely ways to reward both preferences.

Making the most of the almighty dollar

TIP

Just because Millennials are motivated by many things beyond the dollar doesn't mean that money is unimportant or that they want to be paid in feelings tokens. Using monetary compensation as a reward can be energizing — if executed correctly:

>> **Commission:** Compensation structures are so industry- and position-specific that they deserve their own book, but throw on a generational monocle and you'll see this: Millennials, in general, prefer the reliability of salary balanced with commission rather than the unpredictability of commission balanced with salary. The economy has been too volatile for Millennials to risk steady income or pay rooted in the whims of others.

GOODBYE FANCY PEN, HELLO SABBATICAL

You may be surprised to hear that the generation that received a whole display-case worth of trophies growing up isn't looking for the same kind of rewards in the workplace. Plaques for good performance will be shoved into some dark corner of their closet along with the other stuff they don't know what to do with. The recognition they're looking for lies less in the tangible and more in the experiential. Can they take a sabbatical so they can cross "backpack through Southeast Asia" off their bucket list? Maybe they are given more freedom to work from home. Either way, ditch the tangible stuff. Well intentioned as it may be, odds are it'll end up in the trash someday.

>> **Salary increases:** Millennials expect more than the standard pay increase year after year. If they feel a bigger bump isn't in their future, they'll look elsewhere. For them, it's not about seniority; it's about meritocracy. Debt, "adulting" (purchasing a home or starting a family), and saving are still top of mind for Millennials. A decent raise could mean the last student loan payment or putting down an offer on a house.

>> **Bonuses:** For decades, bonuses have been a motivational tactic and rewards marvel. Regardless of the occasion, few will turn up their noses to an extra chunk of money (if you do know those people, please introduce them — they sound like fascinating case studies). However, take heed when giving Millennials a bonus and be sure to offer them choices. For example: Give them the option to choose cash or an experience (concert tickets, a trip, and so on).

Rewarding the individual versus the team

TIP

Carrots and sticks are the age-old ultimatum when it comes to motivating your team. While the stick method is the mother of all fear-based incentives, maybe subjecting your workforce to potentially terrifying ultimatums a la *Law and Order* isn't the best way to go. Instead, dangle a delicious and rewarding carrot that depends on group effort. Millennials will be more incentivized if they know their hard work will benefit both them *and* their teammates. While this next generation takes pride in individual accomplishment, they are more driven by team wins. Motivate and reward the team with some clever tactics:

THE SALARY VERSUS COMMISSION DEBATE

For Millennials, life outside of work matters too much to be subject to the weekly stress of unlocking enough commission to make rent. Unlimited commission, balanced out with a lower salary, is much less motivating than a decent salary with some commission, giving them the flexibility to rely on salary if necessary. It buys them the peace of mind to enjoy their family, friends, and hobbies outside of work, without worrying about making ends meet. Some industries, like finance, have had to completely overturn their compensation structures. Under the stress of knowing that the majority of their income was reliant on commission, Millennials fled to other industries or to progressive firms that understood that for the next generation, financial peace of mind in the here and now trumps the competitive commission model of the past.

>> **Make it visual.** When a team can visualize a reward, it's easy for everyone to get on board. For example, if your team is attempting to reach a sales goal, put sticky notes on a wall in a creative pattern; as you make sales, employees can take turns peeling the sticky notes away.

>> **Include surprise rewards.** As a manager or leader, giving an unexpected reward can be the greatest way to motivate your people. For example, if you adopt the sticky-notes method mentioned in the preceding bullet, hide secret surprises underneath some of the notes. They can be as simple as a frozen yogurt outing or as big as a $100 bonus for each employee — either way, they're bound to put a smile on your employees' faces (and a pep in their motivation step).

>> **Attach it to emotions.** Sure, that sale brought in so many dollars for the company. But what if you knew that, in turn, that money helped pay someone's salary, who could then finally pay off his car loans? *That* gives a Millennial that lovely warm fuzzy feeling. Make the bottom line more human, and you'll give your team more reason to push forward.

Finding nonmonetary rewards that motivate

The struggle to find the perfect reward can be boiled down to one question: What will motivate beyond money? For many Millennials, cold, hard cash doesn't even come close to the top of their perks list. Instead, consider the following three categories of rewards, in order.

Category one: Career growth

The life stage of a twenty-something demands focus on professional growth and ambition. Sure, not *all* Millennials demand more work or responsibility — but the top recruits and future leaders do. Many are at a stage where they may be wondering, "If I can't learn or move up quickly, why am I here?" and they're turning to you to understand that. If it takes too long to gain purchase or the process is so bureaucratic that all they see are obstacles, they're going to be less inclined to stay motivated. Reward stellar work with a new title, responsibility, or level in the organization. Keep them on the career trajectory. A smattering of options for career growth includes

>> Promotion to a new position.

>> Rotation to a different department.

>> Access to an esteemed mentor.

>> Placement on an important project.

>> Appointment to leading an Employee Resource Group.

>> The green light on a passion project.

Category two: Autonomy

Millennials have a drive to control their workload and their schedule. Much like Gen Xers, they have an entrepreneurial bug and seek freedom to explore their endeavors and passions devoid of micromanagement and skepticism of their work ethic. If a Millennial does something well, reward him with more autonomy and trust. Do your best to hand over the reins and provide support as needed. Research shows that autonomy is critical across the board for the next generation, and especially for older Millennials.

Category three: Fun

To state the obvious, every generation wants to have fun at work. It's not like someone wakes up in the morning, looks in the mirror, and says, "Today will be different. Today, I'm not going to have fun. Really looking forward to it." That would be bizarre and, frankly, very sad. But Millennials may be more apt to associate fun with work and are interested in creating experiences with co-workers — inside and outside the office. Using good times as a reward not only shows that you care about their hard work but also motivates them to become an even more integral part of your organization. Here's a smattering of options for fun:

>> Participate in a group fitness class or boot camp.

>> Invite a group to a local concert.

>> Get nosebleed seats at a local sporting event.

>> Host a friendly competition in the workplace.

>> Take a team out to the newest lunch spot.

>> Have a YouTube video and drinks break.

>> Instagram your trip to the local fro-yo joint.

>> Invite your team to go on a scavenger hunt around the city.

>> Venture to a food or drink festival.

>> Set the calendar for beer o'clocks.

>> Pay for a classic happy hour.

Providing shareable work moments

Millennials have grown up in a #YOLO society with countless social networks to tend to (find out more about YOLO earlier in this chapter). From posting updates from your latest hike to liking your friend's five-course dining experience, leaving a digital footprint is ingrained in this generation. One side effect of this lifestyle is that Millennials are always on the hunt for the coolest, most daring, most share-worthy experience. The Great Recession made very clear the low value of goods and placed high value on experiences; Millennials learned early that an amazing experience will be emotionally rewarding long after the luxury of a new car wears off. The next generation looks to leaders to understand their desire for fun and experience — and the two go hand in hand. Create a sharable work moment by taking the following steps:

1. **Brainstorm a list of group events that cater to your team's interests, hobbies, and passions.**

   Is your team interested in sports? Do they love trivia? Use what you know (or ask, if you don't) to come up with recreational options.

   WARNING

   Understanding your team's passions is a great starting point, but don't forget to take into consideration their lives outside of work as well. For example, if the majority of your team is composed of parents, they might not find your evening wine tasting rewarding when they have kids to pick up and spouses to assist.

2. **Narrow down that list with restrictions and limitations.**

   Take into consideration budget, number of participants, location, timing, and so on. It may seem obvious, but making sure the event is in line with company standards — and that your team can actually attend — is rather important.

   WARNING

   When thinking about activities, take into consideration what your company can and will pay for, but also keep in mind what your team would like as well. Skimping on a reward is not only a dirty trick, but it also puts unintended pressure on your team to pretend it was worth their time. Too much extravagance, on the other hand, can make your team feel as if you're putting on airs. In addition, make sure your event fits into your team's schedules. If you know your team is likely to have a bunch of personal commitments throughout the workweek, try to make your event's end time flexible; those who need to head out early can do so without feeling guilty.

3. **Make it sharable.**

   The good news: If you've crafted the experience to fit your team, you're halfway there. They'll appreciate the time and effort you've put into make it picture perfect. The second half comes down to the little things that will take your event from "meh" to must-share. Take, for example, happy hours. They're a dime a dozen. But happy hours where attendees are taught how to craft their own cocktails by a mixologist? Shareable (and dang fun). Try to add a twist that can take your event from awesome to #awesome.

Helping Millennials find their squad

"There is no 'I' in team" and "two heads are better than one" are mottos Millennials grew up rolling their eyes at for their sheer level of insistence. They know the ins and outs of group-think, team projects, and peer networks. And guess what? They very much rely on their peers in the workplace today. At work, they have a mindset of: "If I'm going to be spending eight to ten hours with these people every day, why wouldn't I want them to be good friends?" Millennials don't want a hard divide between their personal and professional lives — they want to be their whole and authentic selves at work and at home, so their friends should be present in both spheres as well.

WARNING

Millennials may love surrounding themselves with like-minded peers, but that doesn't necessarily mean they all have the gift of initiating and developing relationships. Hop into an elevator with a Millennial and you won't be greeted with sparkling conversation or an instant friendship — instead, you'll find a laser-focus on the phone and a muttered, "Have a good night" as she rushes out the door. All that is to say that Millennials respond well to structured networking and social events to help initiate work friendships.

Giving 'em a buddy

All Millennials can benefit from a coach or, in the case of work, a Mr. Miyagi (a la *The Karate Kid*), a Han Solo (a la *Star Wars*), or a Frenchie (a la *Grease*). They want a colleague to take them under their wing. Providing them this champion or buddy at work gives them a point of contact for questions that may not be necessary to direct to their manager. It gives them the inside scoop into the written and unwritten rules of the workplace, and, as a bonus, their work buddy could become their actual buddy. If you want to develop a program around this concept, ask for peer-match volunteers and have them design the system. You may be surprised by what you get.

TIP

Whether the buddy system is formal or informal, keep a good pulse on close work friendships because they could lead to a thoughtful reward. Imagine a 26-year-old phenomenal employee named Maya, who is part of a rotational program: For three years, she spends six months in one location before moving on to the next. Each six-month stint means new people, new work, and new friends. When the three years are complete and you want to celebrate all her hard work, ask Maya whether she wants any of her past colleagues at the celebration and then fly them out for the big party. It may seem slightly excessive and over the top, but this is just the kind of reward that sets you apart from everyone else.

Offering up office extracurriculars

TIP

Aside from fun non-work-related experiences, consider work responsibilities and tasks as a way to get Millennials together and reward the group. Give them big responsibilities to show off their skills:

» Ask them to run a meeting or all-hands meeting with a theme to give them a little taste of leading.

» Create a task force of Millennials to solve generational challenges in the company.

» Host an all-company cook-off for employees to show off their culinary talents.

» Bring the philanthropy within your walls. Can your employees help with professional development for underprivileged kids? Or you could put on a silent auction, with all proceeds going to a local charity.

» Offer them the chance to mentor a brand-new hire. It'll give them an opportunity to show off some leadership skills and maybe even make a new work buddy.

Chapter **5**

Dropping Workplace Formalities

Seasoned employees feeling frustration toward the new kids on the block is not a new phenomenon. Traditionalists wrote off Boomers as hippies, Boomers denounced Xers as apathetic slackers, and just about everyone thinks Millennials are entitled narcissists who expect to be rewarded for just showing up.

When a Millennial, experienced or not, joins a team, questions mired in this frustration inevitably bubble up: Are you going to work as hard as I did? Why do you think you can work flexible hours? Are you incapable of putting down your phone? Why don't you show some effort and dress professionally?

The root of the problem here is pretty straightforward: Change is hard. Each generation brings different perceptions around what the work ethic looks like, the lines that should be drawn between workplace colleagues, and how to communicate effectively.

With so many preferences in the mix, trying to understand the correct workplace etiquette to employ can feel like an uphill battle. What seems appropriate to one generation (Millennials) can be seen as disrespectful to another generation (Gen Xers and/or Baby Boomers). This chapter takes a closer look at the shifting nature of workplace professionalism, from workplace attire, flexible schedules, and working relationships to social media usage, to help you unpack — and hopefully find a way to be at peace with — why Millennials would rather head to a café midday for a latte and some off-site work than partake of the break room's Keurig selection and finish working at their desk.

Distinguishing Between Formality at Work and Work Ethic

For decades, the close relationship between formality and work ethic has gone largely unchallenged. It has been a truth, almost universally acknowledged, that someone with a great work ethic surely exhibits all the outward signs of professionalism and proper workplace etiquette. As each generation has entered the workforce, it has fashioned its own version of what that work ethic and formality look like.

Checking out work-ethic mindset through the ages

For Baby Boomers, imagine the Mad Men–type work environment of the '60s and '70s: An eager, entry-level twenty-something respected all rules around dress, communication, and the clock. This respect, along with some extra hours and a solid work performance, meant that employee got ahead and avoided getting fired. The immaculate suits; long hours in the office; and flawless, perfectly formatted meeting agendas were all badges of a good employee with an impeccable work ethic.

Now imagine the Working Girl–type professional environment of the '80s and '90s: An ambitious, no-nonsense, power-suit-wearing college grad built trust and respect by knowing when and how to bend the rules. The new hire mastered the blurred line between casual and formal dress and earned respect through an efficient work style that resulted in getting more work done in a shorter amount of time.

Millennials have their own take on formality and work ethic. Simply put, they've tossed the formula that says formality = work ethic out the window. For Millennials, defined work hours, strict dress codes, and communication pleasantries are all good and well, but not essential to doing their job or even excelling at it. The three-piece suit and alphabetized memos can be easily replaced with jeans and instant messaging the boss, without sacrificing quality of work or determination to succeed.

For a snapshot of how formality has shifted through the generations, see Table 5-1.

TABLE 5-1   **Views on Formality through the Decades**

Issue	1960s and 1970s	1980s and 1990s	2000s and 2010s
What hard work looks like	Long hours Arriving early and leaving late Working weekends Never saying "no" Always willing to lend a hand	Fewer hours, working more efficiently Arriving right on time and leaving right on time Late nights only if necessary Work hard, play hard Prioritizing for the sake of balance	Working anywhere, anytime Results — not hours — prove the level of work Innovative processes reap the most rewards Work hard, play always
What to wear	What you wear reflects how much you care about your job "Dress for the job you want, not the job you have" IBM Blue suits	Professional attire is a necessary evil Bend the rules (will wear the suit but not the tie); shoulder pads and popped-collar polo shirts Business casual	What you wear has no influence on your work Dress for the day, not the job Jeans and Converse sneakers
Personal life versus professional life	*Work-life separation:* Who you are at work is not who you are at home	*Work-life balance:* Get all the work done first, then engage in light chatting at the water cooler	*Work-life integration:* What you see is what you get; who you are at work is who you are at home

REMEMBER

There is no golden generation. Every generation will have those bad eggs who don't work as hard as they should, but they will also have the overachievers who make everyone else look bad. The general attitudes toward balance and integration should serve as a summary to help you understand the complexities. That way you can weed out the difference between a just plain bad Millennial employee from one who shows promise but just happens to view work differently than you.

Unpacking the impact of dress code

Gone are the days when people had great expectations to "dress for the job you want and not the job you have." Sure, there are times you need to dress to impress, but what exactly does everyday "professional dress" look like now?

Certain industries have their own rigid expectations and guidelines (for example, finance and law still enforce rather strict dress codes that, in comparison, make Silicon Valley workers look like hipster peasants) but for the majority of the workplace, dress codes have shifted from business formal to business casual to casual.

THE NEED FOR AUTHENTICITY

A side effect of work-life integration is that anything appearing to be "put-on" or false can be met with hesitation, and even skepticism. Formal attire and communication can read as inauthentic to Millennials. Can you trust a suit? Can you trust politically correct conversation? Maybe. But maybe not. They can be read as a lack of transparency, and may lead Millennials to wonder what you're trying to hide. Just analyze the celebrities, role models, and bosses that Millennials respect the most — they're the ones who seem like they have nothing to hide. They're vulnerable, make mistakes, and admit to their own shortcomings. Look no further than Jennifer Lawrence as an example: Her shameless demeanor in interviews, her undeniable charisma, her fearlessness in just being herself — cursing, tripping, and being almost too candid, all on camera — and her vulnerable interviews in magazines are devoid of any pretense. This desire for authenticity seeps beyond celebrity and into nearly every Millennial workplace expectation.

Understanding the need to dress it down

Many Millennials ask, "Why does it matter what I wear? I can do just as well (and maybe better) if I wear what I want!" Why the sudden shift with Millennials? Well, for most of Millennials' lives, what was once defined by formality is now, instead, opting to reflect the latest trend and/or become markedly *not* formal:

>> CEOs can, and do, wear shower shoes on camera (looking at you, young Mark Zuckerberg).

>> Fine-dining servers wear jeans, plaid shirts, and suspenders if they're fancy.

>> Your "Sunday best" can describe your favorite jersey.

>> The whole notion of dressing up for a flight has been tossed out the window in favor of what can only be described as dressed-up PJs.

>> The athleisure (workout clothes worn in other settings) market has skyrocketed . . . Millennials are choosing stretchy over starchy.

>> What you sweat in costs more than what you impress in (yoga pants cost more than slacks).

Also keep in mind that Millennials grew up in a time when the news exposed countless industries, institutions, and people as corrupt or deceptive. Dressing down is arguably a reaction to that — it eliminates any potential for falsity. Informal-wear means more than just personal comfort; it's an appeal to authenticity. The perception is that you're not putting on airs, and you're not pretending you're something you're not. Who you are at home is who you are at work. You bring your authentic self to the workplace. What is a universal trend across this generation is a strong preference for freedom in the workplace to dress in a way that suits their personality and lifestyle, whether that be a nice summer dress, the trendiest new wear, or simple jeans and a tee.

REMEMBER

The next generation isn't going to give a round of applause to managers who allow casual Fridays. Though even this one day of casual dress is a large change for many organizations, it can give them a taste of what could be, and they'll wonder why you can't just extend this to every day. Dress matters less for success than it ever has before, and, arguably, clothes that make you happy and allow you to breathe may actually improve performance.

Setting a Millennial-friendly dress code

Don't think that because Millennials prefer informal dress, the best course of action is to throw out all your company standards and give them free reign to show up in their ripped denim and graphic tees. Instead, consider how you can move the needle and adapt what you already do in a way that doesn't sacrifice your company's culture. Don't be afraid to challenge the status quo of your dress policy in as objective and unbiased a way as possible. Gather a team of leaders to assess the options. But watch for the following two characters who will inevitably show up. If you can identify them beforehand, it's probably even best to try to avoid sending invites for this conversation, because they're not going to be valuable additions to the group:

>> **The hater:** He's not even listening to the conversation. He's annoyed that you're even considering "kowtowing" to these Millennial upstarts, and his goal at the meeting is to remain rigid and unbending, no matter how sound the logic may be. He's obviously not going to be super helpful.

>> **The groupie:** She loves Millennials and thinks they're the best thing to happen to your organization since email. Just like the naysayer, she'll be blindly willing to change whatever it takes to accommodate the next generation hires. Her perspective, far from unbiased, will only serve to further annoy those who may be more skeptical.

With your team of open-minded leaders assembled, ask yourselves these questions: Is a dress code absolutely necessary to get the job done? When was the last time it changed? Have you invited your employees' opinions about it? How much time and money would it take to change the dress code? Are there certain times when formality might be more appropriate than others?

Even if you have zero pull in your organization as far as being able to change policy around dress, don't fret. There are some things you can do to manage your own assumptions around dress code and also bend the rules to make the workplace slightly more accommodating for your Millennial direct-reports:

» **Don't make assumptions in interviews.** Just because some Millennials may seem underdressed, that doesn't necessarily mean they're not serious about the job. Don't let the few wrinkles in the pants, missing jacket, and tattoo sleeve distract you from the potentially brilliant mind that lies beneath. Listen, bias-free, to what she's saying. It's a far better indicator of future performance than what she's wearing. Of course, if you work at a firm with a very rigid dress code and casual wear is not welcome, consider telling candidates this before the interview so they can show up dressed appropriately.

» **Set expectations early.** The worst mistake you can make is getting frustrated by an unprofessionally dressed Millennial when you didn't articulate your preference in the first place. Believe it or not, growing up idolizing start-up culture does not an easy task of "acting professionally" make. Communicate expectations around dress clearly upfront. Because you know what they say about making assumptions.

» **Allow for flexibility where possible.** If you express how you expect your staff to dress, good for you for your clarity! If you can, try to embrace a "dress for your day" culture where your employees dress for the day that lies ahead. Are there meetings with the higher-ups on the calendar? Is it an all-email kind of day? Ask Millennials to dress up or down depending on the situation; that way they can add some dress-down days where it makes sense, without sacrificing all decorum.

» **Separate client code from office code.** If you happen to manage Millennials in a client-centric organization, then opt for a "dress for your client" code. Articulate the differences between what's okay with the client versus what's okay in the office. You should consider that more and more of your clients are Millennials themselves and may even appreciate a dressed-down version of the client meeting.

Most companies that get voted as "top places to work" buck corporate trends. Typically, the ones on these lists have accomplished the difficult task of dismissing outdated professional norms without ruffling the feathers of older employees. They also understand that "looking the part" is critical to the organization's brand and legacy. Before you put up the wall that resists change, step into a land of pure imagination and think of ways you can bring the look your company requires into the modern era. For example, if you ask employees to wear ties, might a skinny tie suffice? Or one with a fun print? If nice shoes are on the "must-wear" list, maybe retro sneakers can fit the bill . . . at least sometimes. . . .

MUCH ADO ABOUT TATTOOS

Millennials are getting inked en masse. One in three of them report having permanent body art. Even though members of other generations who took the plunge and got tattoos ensured that they were hidden, Millennials are sporting them publically and proudly as markers of their individualism. A generation that loves customization, they've now taken to customizing their own skin with designs that are emblematic of who they are and what they believe in. All the hullabaloo about tattoos being unprofessional falls on deaf ears, because ink or no ink, Millennials don't see it as a barrier to how they do their jobs.

If tattoos are just not going to fly in your environment, ask yourselves: Is it because they're inappropriate? Distracting? If so, why, and is there any room to change that perception? Unless your young employees have tattooed "bug off" across their foreheads or lewd/offensive images on their hands, in most cases, the tattoo shouldn't be an issue. Don't write off the tatted candidate just because you can't see past the tattoos. Simply ask Millennials to cover up the ink that's causing a stink, and explain that, *for now*, it's what would be best for the situation, the times, and the company. It's likely that in a few short years, as Millennials ascend up the ladder, more and more Fortune 100 companies will have heavily tatted CEOs.

REMEMBER

Avoid gender-specific guidelines because they're simply no longer relevant and will serve as a giant red flag to candidates. The next generation expects and demands equality in all matters of diversity, and enforcing gender-specific dress codes will deter them from your company. Opt for gender-neutral guidelines. You should also be cognizant of and sensitive to other matters of diversity like culture and religion (not to mention, it's the law!).

Turning off the clock: The impact of work hours

When Boomers entered the workforce, work was a destination. All meetings, calls, and daily tasks *had* to be done in the office because it's where all the workplace tools and trappings were kept. It was also the only place to show your manager just how dedicated you were by arriving early and staying late.

Due in large part to technology's seemingly limitless ripple effects, work nowadays is more about a state of mind than a designated physical space. The capability to work from anywhere, anytime, means that you're not restricted to the bounds of a 9 to 5 workday. Cue the debates about the merits of Millennials leaving early, staying late, requesting too much time off, and wanting to leave in the middle of the day to go for a run or to get their hair dyed blue.

For Millennials, it makes sense to weave work in with the personal. If you're a night owl and that's when you do your best thinking, why wouldn't you save a difficult assignment for late evening and take care of some errands in the morning? The end result will be better work, and isn't that the goal? In their minds, sticking staunchly to a set schedule isn't nearly as good a measure of an employee's drive and ambition as delivering exemplary results and innovative new ideas.

Testing out the flex schedule

This is what the next generation *hears* when a boss says, "We run the schedule this way because that's the way it's always been done, and at this point it'd be impossible to change":

>> No, you can't defer some of your duties to off-work hours.

>> No, we can't build a schedule that accommodates your other interests.

>> No, we'd rather you don't leave during the day for any reason other than a doctor's appointment or a pressing family emergency.

>> No, we don't believe you're working hard if we can't physically see you typing away at the office.

>> No, our culture doesn't allow for much flexibility; sorry if that makes you feel uncomfortable.

>> No, we aren't interested in considering you as a person versus a worker bee.

Summary? A lot of no's that can feel like a big slap in the face. Millennials start to feel like a resource that's being squeezed and forced into an inflexible model rather than flesh and blood human beings with needs that should be taken into account on a case-by-case basis. The answer is not to scrap all policy and revert all the no's to yes's, but it should serve as a wake-up call.

This equation is wrong:

Need for flexibility = lazy, entitled, bad worker

This equation is much closer to the truth:

Need for flexibility = different work ethic

If you feel like this only confirms what you've suspected, that it's yet another example of Millennial entitlement — this time around flexibility — it's easy to understand where you're coming from. But there's a difference between going home to goof off and going home to pour yourself, full force, into a project you're passionate about. If you want to find out which of the two is the case, try your hand at a little experiment: You may find the results are truly excellent work (with even more hours put in than if they'd restricted themselves to only the standard work schedule).

Follow these steps to test a flexible work schedule:

1. **Clearly define your expectations of "office hours," times when you would like your Millennial(s) to work from the office.**

   From there, you can decide together the "flex" part of the schedule.

2. **Hear out the objections, and invite ideas from Millennials if they have constructive solutions.**

3. **Make time and effort to try these solutions, with a "yes, and if" approach ("Yes, let's try this new arrangement, and if results aren't meeting expectations, we can revise our approach").**

4. **Review the results.**

5. **Come together to debrief the experiment and then decide to adapt, adopt, or cancel it.**

Checking your gut reaction

Before reacting unfavorably on impulse to a request for workplace flexibility, make sure you're actually hearing the Millennial's request. What does that look like? Say, for example, that you manage a stellar Millennial who is itching for a more fluid schedule. During a one-on-one meeting, your conversation goes something like one of the following two scenarios.

Scenario #1: The shutdown

You: "So, any questions for me before we end the meeting?"

Stellar Millennial: "I do have one — just curious — is everyone expected to be here until 5 every day?"

The question can lead to logical reactions: Are you saying you don't want to be here until 5? Do you think you don't have to work as hard? Do you want to work fewer hours? Needless to say, you feel a little frustrated. And rightly so. You put your boss hat on and give this sterile response:

You: "That is the expectation that we went over when you started, yes."

FLEXIBILITY FOR NONEXEMPT WORKERS

Managing Millennials who are either hourly employees or unionized adds layers of complexity to the work-ethic discussion. Flexibility is not a friend to rules, so you likely have fewer opportunities to bend. It's unfortunate but true. However, putting on a creativity hat to help you view the situation from different angles can turn these obstacles into opportunities.

Angle A: The resource repository

If you manage employees on the floor of a factory, rather than giving them breaks without resources, consider giving them tools to make the most of break times. One small-scale factory encouraged break times for book clubs or hobby time. They even went so far as to offer education sessions from the company so employees could choose to find more ways to add value to the organization.

Angle B: Empower to get power

Another company, after growing tired of people complaining about schedules, created a task force to solve the issue. The managers asked front line workers to make decisions for the whole company and, in turn, found a great solution that increased engagement and buy-in.

Angle C: If *Shark Tank* had a union sister

One organization's top manager told her employees that management sets aside a certain amount of budget for process innovation. If an employee had a good-enough idea to change a process that might help run work more efficiently, he could propose the idea and have at it. Rules, compliance, and bargaining didn't have to prevent flexibility; they could just as easily open the door to more creative flexible arrangements.

What did you accomplish? Complete shutdown. The Millennial likely feels embarrassed for bringing it up and confused as to why you wouldn't even hear her out on what may have been a perfectly reasonable request. After all, she's proven her work ethic and value to the company. Shouldn't her stellar performance be taken into consideration?

Scenario #2: The attentive manager

You: "So, any questions for me before we end the meeting?"

Stellar Millennial: "I do have one — just curious — is everyone expected to be here until 5 every day?"

Before freezing up and pondering all the reasons behind the question, you take a step back and inquire into why the question was asked in the first place.

You: "Good question but before I answer, I'm curious; why do you ask?"

Stellar Millennial: "I understand that a lot of people work that way here, but I feel like I'd be able to get more done if I could leave around 3 and work from a coffee shop. I'd be available via phone or email and could return to the office if there were any issues. Would that be okay?"

You: "Thanks for understanding our work environment. I'd love to give you that flexibility — let me check with the team first. If all are okay with it, then we'll have biweekly check-ins to make sure everything is getting done to your regular quality."

What did you accomplish? A few different, really positive things. First, you showed that you're willing to listen to that Millennial as an individual, with his own track record of performance. Second, you demonstrated a flexibility in management style, showing that you're willing to work with him to find middle ground that works for both parties. Nothing was promised, and no ground was given up. You simply listened to a reasonable request with a reasonable (and satisfying) answer.

Allowing yourself to reimagine work schedules

Many things are not as they appear at face value, and the same follows for seemingly frustrating requests for flexible scheduling. If any of the following flex schedule frustrations arise, please pause and allow yourself to rethink and cuddle up to the idea of a different working style:

>> **A Millennial requests extra time off.**

Worth reimagining because . . .

Past generations never had the luxury of asking for an extra week off during their first decade of work. Millennials have seen the effects of burnout in their parents, relatives, and friends and have read articles about countries with progressive work policies where employees spend less time working and more time vacationing. The result? Not just more fun pics on their Instagram account, but better work when they return. The next generation has seen the proven value of mental breaks; they're an opportunity to increase productivity and creativity. If time is money, time off is an investment. For both you and them.

>> **A Millennial asks for additional and alternative work duties before completing her day's to-do list.**

Worth reimagining because . . .

The greatest plight for any hard worker is to feel useless. If Millennials are at risk of feeling like their skills aren't being utilized, they may turn to ad-hoc projects to feel motivated. The generation raised on an overloaded schedule of extracurricular activities can feel most comfortable when set on a variety of tasks and projects.

>> **A Millennial arrives late/leaves early.**

Worth reimagining because . . .

When a Millennial gets to work an hour past the typical start time, chances are she's not trying to show you how disrespectful she is. Millennials show respect in the work they produce and the way they treat their employers and co-workers. They've adopted the concept of ROWE — results-oriented work environment — and taken it to heart. Before jumping to assumptions, just ask what they were up to. Maybe they had a networking breakfast, or perhaps they wanted to beat traffic and get in a few more work hours at their favorite café. Either way, if the work is getting done, is there any reason to stand on principle just to prove a point?

TECHNICAL STUFF

At a large medical device company, a manager had two Millennials who pushed to have some autonomy over where and when they worked. Open to new ideas, the manager gave each Millennial two weeks to try out his inventive way of getting things done. While Millennial One worked from a café two days a week and came into the office from 8 to 4:15 on other days, Millennial Two found respite in her home office for three days and came to the office from 9 to 6 the other two days. After two weeks, the manager regrouped with the pair and looked at results. Millennial One got more done in the two weeks and Millennial Two got less done. Reaching a compromise, the manager decided to allow all her reports one flexible day per week to work wherever he or she chose, and an 8:30–4:30 schedule the other days. If ever results weren't being met, they would be dealt with on an individual basis.

WARNING

Silicon Valley is heralded for policies that allow people to take unlimited vacation. Companies boast about cultures that let you work from wherever, whenever. While that may be beneficial to some Millennials, to others, it's crippling. Complete flexibility leads to a workforce where everyone is bound by the proverbial golden handcuffs — they sure are pretty and appealing, but you're chained. You may run the risk of vacation shame: people taking less vacation for fear of taking advantage of the system. In 2016, Alamo Rent A Car released their annual family vacation survey findings. Surveying 1,500 adults nationwide, they found that guilt over taking days off was widespread, with Millennials the most likely generation to feel bad about using their rightful vacation days.

Working hard or hardly working

TIP

Of all the stereotypes that exist about the next generation, and there are many, one of the most prevalent and most inaccurate is that Millennials are lazy and lack work ethic. Just because someone fails to conduct himself formally doesn't mean that he is unwilling or unable to work hard. Asking for an updated dress code, flexible schedule, or extra vacation day does not lack of ambition make. To be sure that you don't write off Millennials as lazy, try the following:

» **Don't lead with negative preconceptions.** Understand that most Millennials do want to work very hard and give you their all. Try not to assume that just because they're working differently, they aren't putting in solid effort.

» **Put yourself into a Millennial mindset.** Taking off your generational lens and seeing the world through another's is easier said than done, but it may be the key to relating to and connecting with Millennials.

» **Provide flexibility in whatever way you can — whether it's dress, work hours, or workplace.** Millennials are driven to work even harder when they're given the parameters in which they prefer to work. Minor changes you make can create a major impact with the next generation. A few minor fixes you can try:

- Focus on results, not hours or rules.

- Adopt the phrase "I'm flexible" into your vernacular.

- Share your story of work ethic and invite them to share theirs.

- Explain why certain rules or expectations are in place.

» **If you've tried the preceding tips but are still unsure, trust your intuition.** If you're reviewing these tactics and still can't find the answer you're looking for, ask yourself whether you've maybe hired a bad employee. If you're still unsure, maybe your struggles are really more about motivation and feedback, which you can read up on in Book 5, Chapters 3 and 4.

TIP

Millennials have their own heavy lifting to do. It's not the manager's responsibility to cater to the younger demographics without expecting anything from them in return. To help Millennials meet you halfway, ask them on a scale of 1 to 10 how comfortable they are with the standard work expectations and rules. Then ask them for suggestions about what you can do to help make that number higher. Offer mentorship and guidance to those who are seeking to change but explain that first they should

» Understand the work schedule policies and why they're in place.

» Talk through workplace expectations with a manager.

» Prepare an action plan and present it to their manager if they still feel strongly that a change is important.

REMEMBER

Maybe it isn't such a bad idea that Millennials push for fewer hours spent in the office. Studies and reports have shown that the biggest regret of older people is how much they worked. The United States consistently rates lower on the scale of overall satisfaction with life as the country with fewer vacation days, longer work weeks, and less paid maternity/paternity leave. Perhaps the hustle isn't so great, and just maybe Americans as a whole should stop taking pride in how busy we all are. Yes, there are countless other factors to consider like the economy, standard of living, and so on, but working fewer hours may be worth considering or at least discussing with your younger co-workers.

Drawing the Fine Line between Manager and Friend

In a hierarchical workforce dominated by Traditionalists, Baby Boomers, and Generation Xers, relationships between manager and direct report were incredibly clear: They were professional, the roles of power were explicit, and a solid distinction between work and home life left no confusion about what was inappropriate to share at work and/or at home. The traditional organization chart led a helping hand in defining the boundaries of that relationship.

As Millennials have entered the workforce, they've blurred all the lines that were previously commonplace and remained, mostly, unchallenged. Now, their cohort seeks colleagues that moonlight as friends. They hope for a manager who can either exist within or, at least, loop the perimeter of that friendship circle.

If you can get onboard with this pretty momentous shift in the manager-employee relationship, you'll be a step ahead of other managers in the retention game. Your employees will be more likely to trust you and feel even more incentivized to work hard for you.

REMEMBER

Drawing a line between manager and friend requires two things: your clarity on what kind of relationship you are comfortable with, and a willingness to clearly articulate if and when the line is crossed.

Telling Millennials when it's just TMI

Remember the taboo topics of conversation? The ones that would send any mother and/or father into a tizzy if they were brought up at the Thanksgiving dinner table with gram and gramps listening in? If you don't, congrats on your psychedelic childhood surrounded by hippies who freely spoke about the three major taboos: money, sex, and politics. Today, the next generation is not only willing to speak about those tabooed topics freely but will also gladly bring up all kinds of heretofore completely outrageous stuff to discuss in the workplace — their crazy weekends, the recreational drugs they may or may not have tried that one time, the latest messages from their Tinder dates, and so on . . . the list is long. To Boomers and Gen Xers who are unaccustomed to their level of oversharing, the first time it's heard can be quite the shock.

Take a look at Jay, an exemplary Gen X manager. His rapport with Millennial colleagues is impressive — they value his candor, sense of humor, and motivation to team development. Jay values their positivity, their ambition, and that they un-ironically laugh at his dad jokes. They all worked well together and were a top department in the company. Then one Monday morning, Nick, an eager 26-year-old, walked in and plopped into his chair. He was — in a matter of words — worse for wear. When Jay inquired about his disposition, Nick sighed, "Oh, man, I am so off today. I'm really hungover." That line between manager and friend? Consider it crossed.

TIP

When, or if, you are in a situation wherein you feel like Jay, take a step back and think about what you could have done differently to set a clearer boundary of what's acceptable and what's not. Then rest the situation that very moment — find a private place to make it clear when the line was crossed and why. Use the moment as a coaching opportunity to explain how you interpreted the exchange and how a senior partner or client might view it. Then, if you can, find a way to laugh about it because having a too-much-information moment can be thoroughly entertaining for everyone involved. It's not the end of the world if it happens a couple of times; it's a problem when oversharing becomes chronic.

Navigating social media

Every generation favors social media, but Millennials were the first to use it. Believe it or not, to a Millennial, making a relationship "Facebook official" is a big deal when it comes to work relationships, because they're sharing a big part of their personal lives. So, if they send you a friend request or try to follow you on Twitter, it's a sign of flattery, not a misguided step to pry into your private world.

That said, if you don't want them in that world, that's okay! If you, like many Xers, want your social media connections to extend no further than LinkedIn, then take the appropriate steps to set expectations:

1. **Determine what is on and off limits to you in the social realm.**

2. **Set your privacy settings on your accounts (purposefully or just in case).**

3. **Wait until they attempt to connect with you rather than putting the kibosh on it from the beginning.**

   For example, instead of saying, "I prefer not to be friends with any of my colleagues on social media" on Day 1, wait until you're sent a request and then kindly say, "I saw your request. Just so you know, as a general rule, I only connect on LinkedIn just so I treat everyone equally."

REMEMBER

If a Millennial is giving you access to her private life whether on social media or in person, you will probably learn things about her you never knew before. No, that doesn't mean you're going to hear in-depth stories about crazy weekends, but you will hear an earful about trips to the apple orchard, their Disney-themed parties (shouldn't that theme be reserved for kids?), and even what their friends are saying in negotiations at other companies. Instead of adopting concern at this exposure, use it as a point to connect with them. If something is questionable to their character in your organization, that's worth discussing. Otherwise, Millennials are self-aware enough to know that they're giving managers and leaders access to their political opinions on just about everything, and will hopefully refrain from anything that's not company-appropriate.

Explaining work social events to Millennials

As Millennials get to know their colleagues, walls come down. It's a lovely showcase of their comfort if they do the same with you, their manager, but it's not so lovely when they keep those walls down at the company holiday party or client networking event. Without a voice of condescension, let them in on your work social event dos and don'ts. First, if they exist, outline any company policies around social events ahead of time so the expectations are clear and set. Second, be the mentor you always wanted. For example, say:

"Word of advice at client events: Keep it to two drinks. You don't wanna be *that* guy/girl."

Or:

"Something I wish I would have known when I was your age is that if your manager or leader invites you to happy hour, they genuinely want to see you there. It looks good to your colleagues and leadership if you show up to get to know everyone."

Placing boundaries where needed

As the organizational structure has flipped and turned, so have the rules of hierarchy. No longer is the senior leadership team untouchable or unapproachable; the opposite is now the expectation for Millennials. You may have heard stories of Millennials emailing the CEO or popping into the senior VP's office for a "quick chat," and while these examples may seem outlandish, they're happening on a regular basis. While some leaders find this kind of behavior charming or impressive, they're usually in the minority. If you have Millennials charging to the top when they should be embracing more prudent behavior, explanations are in order.

For starters, explain why boundaries are needed:

>> **Describe the difference between ambition and desperation.** Millennials likely think they're taking the right approach, an impressive one in fact, without knowing that they're rubbing you the wrong way.

>> **Coach them on how to approach leadership.** To a Millennial, senior leaders aren't scary; they're just people. An audible scoff could be heard from them if people create a fear cloud when leadership passes by in the office halls. They won't automatically respect boundaries, so help them find an alternate path to be heard at the top — even if it's just a path through your voice as a messenger.

TIP

Making yourself accessible is a helpful strategy:

>> **Open the door.** The physical act of opening the door is less important than communicating your willingness to hear thoughts and ideas from all levels. Maybe you can attend a new-hire orientation just to answer anyone's questions. Maybe you can move your corner office to the middle of the floor in an open cubicle. No matter how you do it, make it known that you're open to input.

>> **Step up your social presence.** The next generation does not need to see you face to face to get their opinions across. An intranet or company Twitter account can open the conversation to change.

Channeling Your Inner Emily Post: Communication Etiquette

Unlike Baby Boomers and Gen Xers, Millennials weren't drilled on the ins and outs of etiquette while they were growing up: They're less likely to hold a door open for a stranger, shake your hand upon meeting, or refer to you as Mr. or Ms. so-and-so. It's not that Millennials are uncivil or rude; they just didn't learn the so-called rules of propriety because they weren't necessary in the society they grew up in. When they go to work, they may need basic training in etiquette and unwritten rules — a "Manners at Work Boot Camp," if you will. Rather than feeding a fire of frustration, prepare to train them on some basics:

>> Phone call dos and don'ts.

>> The proper way to write an email.

>> Phrases or slang to avoid.

>> When to send a thank-you card.

>> Turn around/response times.

>> Times to hug versus times to shake hands.

>> Requests for time off.

>> What to prioritize during the day.

Accepting the habit of multitasking and its side effects

Growing up in an era of technology at their fingertips wired the next generation's brain differently than generations past — their ability to multitask is unlike any of their predecessors. (*Note:* The act of multitasking is neurologically impossible, but switch tasking is not. "Multitasking" refers to the speed at which the younger generations are able to switch between devices and tasks at lightning speed.)

Millennials are on a mission to work hard to accomplish the day's tasks in due time but will pause to stretch their mind with a reading break, their body with a quick basketball game, or their social world with a ten-minute skim through the latest on Instagram and/or Snapchat. These mind and body breaks could make you draw conclusions about their unprofessionalism, but keep in mind that what may look like unprofessionalism to one generation is just another using their brain as it's wired.

Consider the following habits, side effects, and likely truths you may encounter, along with some handy coaching cues.

Using devices at meetings

The habit: Taking BYOD (bring your own device) too literally at meetings — phones and computers up and on.

The side effect: As Millennials (and they're not the only generation) check their phone or computer during a meeting, their colleagues and leaders feel frustrated. The Millennial appears distracted by personal or professional matters and disinterested in the conversation.

The likely truth: Yes, it's true that seeing the latest Snapchat story update is absolutely not important, but there is a laundry list of reasons why they may be checking their phone. If it's a text update, recall that Millennials' phone etiquette relies on fast responses because a delayed text response is rude, and that text may be from a fellow co-worker. Maybe they're checking for an email that hasn't yet come from a client or reading through documents to be extra prepared for the meeting.

The moment to coach: Checking a phone or computer in a meeting *is* distracting to the person speaking — if you say that it isn't, you're well accustomed to the habit by now. If necessary, make it a tech-free meeting or kindly ask them to close the computer and turn off the phone before every meeting.

Checking social media

The habit: Scrolling through social media while working.

The side effect: A surrounding colleague and/or manager assumes that the habitual Millennial is using company dollars to work on his personal life.

The likely truth: What may look like distractions to one person can be the exact activity needed to stay focused for others. When Millennials were teens, Friendster, MySpace, YouTube, Facebook, and Twitter came out in rapid succession. Checking them became a daily activity and pastime from a young age. Rather than view their occasional checking of Facebook as a misuse of company time, consider it an occasional, much-needed mental break.

The moment to coach: The best way to manage it is to establish trust. Say something like, "At company XYZ, we trust you. We trust that you aren't updating a Facebook page all day but know that you might check it occasionally, but not at the cost of your work or your team."

REMEMBER

There is a high probability that Millennials checking their social media are doing it for business purposes. They're scanning the company Facebook page or scoping out what the competition is saying on Twitter. Try to assume first that they're on social media for business reasons and second for personal ones.

Wearing headphones

The habit: Wearing headphones all day.

The side effect: Putting off an air of "I don't want human contact or conversation at work" and making other generations feel disrespectfully tuned out.

The likely truth: Although this could be seen as disinterest in human contact at work, it may be the most productive way to get things done. Via tech like Zunes, MP3s, Discmans, and iPods, Millennials have carried music around in their pockets since adolescence. While they survived CHEM 401 classes in college thanks to Pandora's study playlists, today they're tuning into Spotify's focus playlists to get their work done. Their headphones are a sign that they're getting down to business.

The moment to coach: It may be necessary to adopt a headphone policy: Headphones on signifies a "please don't interrupt my work" work mode. However, if it's urgent, send an instant message or email to have a necessary conversation.

Understanding (and accepting) why Millennials won't pick up the phone

Millennials are notorious for their fear of phone calls and refusal to check their voicemail. While it may be easy to make fun of this perceived lack of communication skill, they're already in on the joke. Many are aware of their awkward demeanor on a phone call and longingly look at the ease with which their Gen X and Boomer colleagues pick up the phone and converse. Join in on the fun and acknowledge all the reasons Millennials aren't naturally skilled at picking up the phone:

>> **Instant Messenger:** Millennials chatted with their friends after school on AOL and MSN Messenger (if you want to have a bit o' fun, ask your Millennial colleagues what their screen names were).

>> **Online dating:** Blind dates are essentially a fable for today's singles, and meeting someone in a bar or at church — once common ways of meeting partners — is now an adorable meet-cute story among Millennial friends. If meeting a partner — arguably one of the most primal things humans do — entails online conversation prior to meeting, then you can imagine that building rapport quickly in person doesn't come naturally.

>> **Small-talk shield:** Millennials grew up protected — the world was scary, and to stay safe, they were warned not to speak to anyone they didn't know. It has led to Millennials being a little weak on small-talk skills. For a fun social experiment, watch two strangers in their seventies meet versus two strangers in their twenties. The pair in their seventies pair will likely find some commonplace conversation and make nice, while the Millennials will introduce themselves, have a quick convo, and then resort to their phones. One way is not better than another, but they certainly are different.

Some Millennials prefer the phone — they find texting tedious and emailing slow. Older Millennials didn't even get their first cell phone until after graduating from college. Young Millennials and their successors prefer FaceTime to texting and phone calls. Don't stereotype too easily — one Millennial is not necessarily like another.

Just as you wouldn't make fun of a 70-year-old CEO who doesn't know how to use Snapchat, so too should you not make fun of a 28-year-old Millennial who gets anxiety every time she answers the phone. The worlds they grew up in were different, and they each have their own communication strengths and weaknesses.

Figuring out who needs to adjust

In nearly every situation, asking one generation to change everything for another doesn't work — adjustment needs to happen in every generation. Knowing who needs to adjust and when to do so can be tricky, but you can use Table 5-2 as a starting place.

TABLE 5-2   Common Formality Issues and Adjustment Recommendations

Issue	When the Manager Needs to Adjust	When the Millennial Needs to Adjust
Work ethic	The 8–5 schedule is producing results but not happy employees. Creative ways to find efficiency are possible.	The 8–5 schedule is necessary for clients and colleagues because being close to the phone/computer/client/patient is the only way to achieve results.
Dress etiquette	Your dress code feels antiquated or others in the industry are adapting their dress code. Or when blue jeans Fridays aren't even motivating anymore. Or when you ask your staff what they prefer and the majority responds that they want casual attire.	Clients expect a certain type of dress from you in order to do their business. Senior leaders have expectations, and moving up and around the organization demands their approval. Certain events require special dress.
Flexible hours	Focusing on results rather than the rules will usually produce superior work.	Their work is suffering in a results-oriented environment, and they need to just put in the hours as asked of them.
Communication etiquette	When communication isn't up to your standard but work is still getting done as asked, expectations may need to shift.	If behaviors consistently read as rude, inappropriate, or apathetic.

6

Who's the Boss? Becoming an Influential Company Leader

Contents at a Glance

IN THIS CHAPTER

» **Differentiating between management and leadership**

» **Identifying leadership-based engagement drivers**

» **Knowing why top leaders must buy in**

» **Identifying behaviors and traits of engaged leaders**

» **Recognizing the importance of training and coaching**

» **Identifying leadership best practices**

Chapter **1**

People Who Lead People: Engaging Employees through Leadership

ecent research by Dale Carnegie shows that employees' engagement levels rise when they believe in their senior leadership. Indeed, they feel most engaged when the company's leadership clearly communicates strategy and plans, connects with employees, and helps everyone feel part of where the organization is going. Leadership, then, is a key engagement driver. To find out how leadership begets engagement, read on.

Distinguishing Management versus Leadership

Often, people confuse the term *leader* with the term *manager*. But there's a big difference between them. A manager manages process, programs, and data. Leaders, on the other hand, guide people, build fellowship, and steer organizations to success (read: make money and grow). Leaders set the direction; managers follow the plan to get there. Yes, managers are indispensible when it comes to creating and monitoring policy. But leaders define and uphold an organization's principles. And leaders — more specifically, *engaged* leaders — really drive engagement in an organization.

Management plays an essential role in the stability of a company. In fact, it's critical for leaders to be effective managers as well as effective leaders. But because employee engagement entails a pervasive change in corporate culture, it unfortunately cannot be simply assigned to just any manager or management team.

Before you can get a handle on how leadership drives engagement, it's important to understand the difference between a leader and a manager. For help, see Table 1-1.

TABLE 1-1   Management versus Leadership

Management	Leadership
Management is about control.	Leadership is about trust and empowerment.
Management is about authority and hierarchy.	Leadership is about alignment and expertise.
Management involves discrete tasks.	Leadership's focus is on vision.
Management involves one-way communication.	Leadership involves two-way communication.
Management is characterized by following the plan.	Leadership is characterized by experimentation.
Management assumes a dominating perspective.	Leadership invites multiple perspectives.
With management, there is often one decision-maker.	With leadership, team input is emphasized.
Management is about measurement.	Leadership is about personal accountability.
Management focuses on quick decision-making.	Leadership focuses on wise decision-making.
Management sticks with the tried and true.	Leadership seeks innovation.
Management assumes the role of director.	Leadership assumes the role of coach and counselor.
Management seeks to satisfy employees.	Leadership seeks to engage employees.

Table 1-2 offers another way of looking at the difference between managers and leaders.

TABLE 1-2

Managers versus Leaders

Managers	Leaders
Take care of where you are	Take you to a new place
Deal with complexity	Deal with uncertainty
Are efficient	Are effective
Create policies	Establish principles

Surveying Leadership-Based Engagement Drivers

REMEMBER

How, exactly, does a strong leader engage employees? One way to answer that question is to mention three things a strong leader *doesn't* do: spread negativity, cynicism, and skepticism. Instead, strong leaders engage employees by offering the following:

>> **Trust:** You don't *get* trust unless you *give* trust. Strong leaders trust their employees. When employees feel trusted by their leaders, they're more likely to trust their leaders and be engaged. If employees don't feel trusted, they won't trust in return — and engagement will take a dive.

>> **Authority:** For employees, feeling confident that someone is in charge can lay the foundation for engagement. If employees are worried that no one's at the helm of the ship, engagement will suffer.

>> **Security:** Especially when the economy is suffering, security is key to engagement. Strong leaders leave their employees feeling like things will turn out okay, and in doing so, they boost engagement.

>> **Direction:** A key part of leading is knowing where you're going — you can't expect people to follow you if you lack direction. Engagement suffers when leaders lack direction.

>> **Vision:** Employees will be more engaged when their leaders have and convey a clear vision — one that inspires them to follow.

>> **Structure:** The organization's structure must be such that everybody knows the organization's boundaries. A lack of structure will quickly result in false assumptions, leading to disengagement.

>> **Clarity:** Employees must understand what's expected of them.

>> **A role model:** Employees need someone to look up to. Role models enable employees to pinpoint — and then emulate — behaviors that result in success.

>> **Reassurance:** All employees seek reassurance. They want to feel as if someone is looking out for them. Failure to provide this can lead to a reduction in both confidence and engagement.

>> **Cohesion:** Think of your team as a symphony. Although each person has her own part to play, everyone must be playing from the same musical score. This cohesion plays a big part in employee engagement.

>> **Inspiration:** Giving people a sense of purpose inspires them, enabling them to feel good about what they're doing.

>> **Recognition:** All employees want to feel that what they do matters. That's where recognition comes in.

Understanding That Leadership Starts at the Top

It's not enough for line managers to work to engage employees. When it comes to engagement, leadership must come from the top.

Most CEOs are far more comfortable working their left (analytical, sequential, objective) brains than their right (random, creative, subjective) brains. As a result, many CEOs attempt to delegate the primary responsibility for engagement to HR or some "soft skill" function instead of championing the cause themselves.

Unless you want your employees' engagement levels to go the way of the dodo, you must do all you can to prevent top leaders from delegating engagement efforts. With all due respect to HR, if it owns engagement, engagement will likely be perceived by employees as just another "flavor of the month" program. Senior leaders *must* support engagement to prevent employees from assuming it's a touchy-feely, lip-service-only, employee-satisfaction initiative.

CREATIVE + LEADERSHIP = CREATIVESHIP

These days, mere leadership may not be enough. What's often needed is a little something called *creativeship* — that is, creative leadership necessary to build a sustainable business model and culture. Creativeship enables businesses to engage employees and thrive in this new world of unprecedented technological advances, globalization, shifting economic drivers, government intervention, changing workforce demographics, widespread generational differences, and the emergence of corporate social responsibility (CSR) as a motivational driver.

Briefly, creativeship involves focusing on six key priorities:

- **Purpose:** Organizations must articulate both what they do and why they do it if they want to attract, hire, and retain top employees.

- **Engagement:** According to Gallup research, companies with high engagement levels are more than 200 percent more profitable than organizations with low engagement levels — which is why more and more leadership teams are asking their HR and organizational development (OD) staff to build engaged workforces.

- **Performance:** Creating sustainable cultures of performance at both the company and individual level is key.

- **Innovation:** Creating cultures of *innovation* fosters both engagement and sustainability. Companies fail when they stop evolving their products, services, and internal processes. That means investing today's cash to discover tomorrow's new technologies, products, services, geographies, and approaches.

- **Tri-branding:** Tri-branding occurs when organizations link their employment brand with their product or service brand, while at the same time leveraging third parties, including customers and suppliers, as brand ambassadors. The results are astounding!

- **Global growth:** The old business adage "grow or die" is at the core of creativeship. In this era of globalization and technological advances, companies need to understand that they'll perish if they don't evolve, grow, expand, and morph. Companies that are local need to think regional; companies that are regional need to think national; companies that are national need to think global.

If the CEO lacks the time or talent to champion engagement, your firm must identify someone else at the senior level to take up the charge. This person must be senior enough to lend credibility to your engagement efforts, and preferably have the ear and support of the leader. Regardless of personal preferences, all senior leaders must speak the language of engagement and behave in demonstrably committed ways. Top leaders must believe in and be able to articulate engagement.

REMEMBER

Holding leaders accountable for engagement levels in your firm is critical. Measurement is an important driver. Unless a CEO's board measures the CEO on engagement, the CEO may not have an impetus to lead any differently. Only when senior management is regularly measured and judged on engagement criteria (by reporting on engagement every quarter and communicating the CEO's performance metrics throughout the company) will they be motivated to measure up.

Although it's critical that senior leaders make the push for engagement, the things that drive engagement (see the preceding section) are largely the province of an organization's visionaries, role models, innovators, and counselors. These leaders may not be the most senior staff, hold the loftiest titles, or pull down the biggest salaries. But they make their mark on the company culture, inviting multiple perspectives and team decisions while retaining — and communicating — a strong sense of personal accountability.

Identifying the Behaviors and Traits of Engaged Leaders

Does this sound familiar? Mary is an exceptional engineer, so you promote her to be the department manager, and she fails miserably. Or, John is an outstanding nurse, so you promote him to be the nursing supervisor, and all the other nurses hate him. Or, Stephanie is your top salesperson, so you promote her to be the sales manager, and the sales team's quotas drop, big time.

Fact: It is actually quite rare for an outstanding employee in his job to also be an excellent *succession candidate* (that is, someone who could take over his boss's or his boss's boss's job). Why? Because the traits and behaviors needed to succeed as an engineer, a nurse, or a salesperson are often quite different from those required to be a successful leader. For example, an engineer probably doesn't need to be empathetic. But the person who manages the engineering department? That person probably does.

Strong people skills transcend technical capability. It's possible to successfully lead engineers, for example, without being one. One leader was asked to serve as chief operating officer of a global environmental consulting company, overseeing 2,000 engineers and scientists. The leader resisted, saying, "But I'm not an engineer!" The leader's boss responded, "We have 2,000 engineers and scientists who all think alike. You, on the other hand, possess the behaviors and traits necessary to *lead*."

The challenge facing many companies is that salaries and rank increase based on individuals' ability to leverage others to get things done. That's why upper managers make more money. In part because of this, a lot of people have aspirations to become leaders of people. But that doesn't mean everyone's good at it.

A few common leadership traits and behaviors

TIP

If you're considering hiring or promoting someone as a "people leader" in your organization, evaluate whether that person possesses the following traits:

>> Caring

>> Empathy

>> Energy

>> Equitableness

>> Expressiveness

>> Fairness

>> Honesty

>> Humility

>> Neutrality

>> Optimism

>> Passion

In addition, great people leaders

>> Communicate a clear vision for their part of the organization.

>> Translate their vision into motivating strategies and implementation plans.

>> Help people set short-term priorities in line with long-term goals.

>> Help direct reports understand how they contribute to the vision.

>> Recruit and hire talented, high-performing employees.

>> Clearly communicate performance expectations.

>> Manage and evaluate performance (including making the tough decisions).

>> Focus on *how* results are achieved as much as on *what* results are achieved.

>> Recognize and reward achievement when performance surpasses expectations.

- Base pay fairly on both quantitative and qualitative results.
- Provide clear, specific direction and give open, honest feedback — including positive feedback, when deserved.
- Place a high priority on coaching people.
- Create a continuous learning environment.
- Help others prepare for increased responsibility.
- Proactively look to promote from within.
- Work with employees to identify career-growth plans that link with business-growth plans (known as cross-training or professional development).
- Help less-experienced employees gain experience interacting with clients.
- Look to eliminate unnecessary work or obstacles to productivity.
- Proactively identify and develop a successor.
- Maintain open communication (see Book 1).
- Create an environment and culture that motivates and inspires, and then enables others to succeed.
- Inspire people to follow.
- Willingly share their best individual talent with others.
- Create and facilitate productive teams.
- Delegate and empower.
- Remain distant enough to be objective.
- Keep their promises and honor their commitments.
- Seek input before making key decisions.
- Encourage feedback.
- Listen.
- Treat people with dignity and respect.
- Respect the importance of other people's time.
- Work cooperatively with others to achieve common goals.
- Successfully manage conflict (see Book 2).
- Assess issues and come up with shared solutions to improve performance.
- Work effectively with peers and colleagues.
- Strengthen employee/manager relationships and build a stronger team (see Book 4).

>> Work effectively in a cross-cultural environment.

>> Appreciate the value of diversity (race, nationality, culture, age, gender, sexual orientation).

>> Adapt to cultural differences.

TIP

If you need to assess someone's leadership capabilities — or your own — try using a scale of 1 to 10, with 1 meaning "not at all" and 10 meaning "excels at this," to rate that person on each of these items.

Tips for defining success in your organization

Take a hard look at your organization. Who are your best managers? What are the traits and behaviors that make them so good? These are the traits and behaviors that define success in your firm, and the traits and behaviors you must cultivate in each and every line manager. Be prepared to make an investment in the development of people skills in the same way you would in the development of technical skills.

TIP

To determine what behaviors and traits are most important for your organization, gather a cross-sectional group of leaders and list the employees who consistently embody excellence at your company. (The actual number of names will depend on the company's size; target the top 10 percent.) It doesn't matter how junior or senior the employees are, or whether they're from research and development (R&D), retail, finance, or HR. Then start listing the behaviors and traits that make these individuals shine, making sure to limit your list to personal qualities rather than achievements.

For example, suppose an employee on your list, John, an architect, always comes up with the best numbers. Why? Is it because he's a great architect, which you could attribute to education and skills? No. It's because he's tenacious, creative, and resourceful. These are traits. In addition, John surrounds himself with the best people, chases clients the company never would have pursued otherwise, modifies his business development plan to incorporate new findings based on proposal wins and losses and subsequent contact with clients, and is dogged in following up and following through. These are behaviors.

If the people on your list all possess the same 15 behaviors or traits, you can assume these are the distinguishing characteristics you should be looking for in new hires and candidates for promotion. Of course, education and skills are important. But those are what's needed merely to get a candidate's foot in the door or to suggest adequate performance. You don't want adequate — you want *excellent*.

Here Comes the Train Again: Training Managers to Become Engaged Leaders

If you want to be a doctor, you have to attend years of medical school. If your goal is to be a pilot, flight school is likely in your future. Yet, people often receive zero training — zip — when tapped by their firms to start leading people. Incredibly, we act like anyone can do it!

Guess what? They can't. Sure, some people are natural leaders. They just have it. But most people need a little training . . . even if they think they don't. (Unfortunately, the ability to lead others is a trait that almost everyone thinks they possess. For example, someone who would never venture an opinion on a technical issue often has completely misplaced confidence in his or her communication and team-building skills.)

"Sure," you say. "In a perfect world, we'd provide training for every new manager. But here at XYC Corp., we're too busy trying to get product out the door. We don't have time!"

Wrong. You have to make time. Practically every research study in the history of the world lists people's relationships with their leaders — or, more precisely, their managers, who *should* be their leaders — as a leading engagement driver (good manager) or *dis*engagement driver (bad manager). (One 2012 study, by *Parade* magazine, revealed that 35 percent of U.S. workers polled would trade a substantial pay increase for seeing their direct supervisor get fired.) Heck, there's even an adage about it: "People join great companies, but they leave bad managers." And yet, organizations put scant resources in training these most-valued assets — the people we entrust to lead, motivate, and engage our employees.

REMEMBER

These people leaders can truly make or break your overall engagement efforts because they're perfectly positioned to transmit key information up and down the ranks.

The proper development of your firm's people leaders is one of the first "must do" items on your list. This should include supervisory training for first-line people leaders, who are often being asked to manage people for the first time. It's baffling that employees who need the most attention and leadership — entry-level staff — are often entrusted to managers who have, on average, the least experience, and who often lack the communication skills required to establish trust and create alignment.

REMEMBER

Trust is the first step toward capturing discretionary effort — the invaluable by-product of great leadership. If leaders withhold trust, they can hardly expect employees to trust the leadership in return. Leaders who trust their employees will soon see this trust reciprocated. (Flip to Book 6, Chapter 2 for more about trust.)

On the other side of the spectrum, senior leaders, who have honed their communication skills over the years and have loads of practice leading people, are most likely directing executives who are self-sufficient and independently motivated. In other words, those with the highest level of leadership skill and experience are leading people with nominal need, while those who lack leadership skill and experience are leading those with the greatest need. This situation can be a tremendous stumbling block to engagement. Clearly, if your first-line leaders are not in alignment with your company's engagement goals, your chances of success are slim to none.

Compounding this problem is the fact that line managers often achieve their position for the wrong reasons — chiefly tenure, technical ability, and personal ambition, rather than leadership ability. Few organizations consider "people skills" a core competency — let alone a requirement for advancement. But in order for your engagement efforts to work, these "soft" skills must be seen as a job requirement for managers. In addition, managers' effectiveness in engaging their staff must be measured. Otherwise, they simply won't make engagement a priority. Managers must be trained in, and evaluated on, leading people.

REMEMBER

An organization needs talented, skilled leaders of people at the line-manager level. If a person doesn't like to lead people or isn't good at it, that person should not be in line for promotion to management, period, end of story.

Of course, for a leader to be able to engage others, she must also be engaged. Indeed, according to a 2009 study by Sirota Survey Intelligence, Inc., disengaged leaders are, on average, three times as likely to have disengaged direct reports. A key first step to building engagement among first-line leaders is to treat them as part of the leadership of the company. That means making sure that even first-line leaders receive critical communication in advance of the general population. They need thorough information on the issue, policy change, or strategic plan in play, including what has already been challenged or debated. They also need the opportunity to ask questions of their own. And they may need time to digest a policy change and to think through how it should be incorporated into their group's work. Most of all, they must appear informed when they pass along the information to their staff. Otherwise, their authority is diminished.

REMEMBER

If line managers disagree with a corporate mandate, the proper forum for discussion is with his superiors, not with those lower in the chain. Agreeing to serve as a leader means forfeiting the right to vocal cynicism! That being said, effective managers also happen to be authentic, real, and transparent. Employees can see through a manager who engages in "corporate speak." Bottom line: Enthusiastically embracing a mandate is often a struggle when you know it may cause a disconnect with your employees. This is a fine line that managers have to walk.

Put Me In, Coach! Coaching for Engagement

A key aspect of leadership and engagement is coaching. Coaching may be provided by a manager, by a team leader, or by a formal or informal mentor. A coaching session could be an organized meeting or occur during a brief, informal conversation.

What is coaching, exactly? Simply put, coaching is about ongoing change and development. It's about helping others gain knowledge, information, and perspective to improve performance, develop competencies, build better relationships, enhance communication, enable different perspectives and insights, and identify and recognize strengths and potential.

A coach can help others explore new approaches to a problem, challenge them to take a risk, help them think of things differently, and assist them as they strive to complete a stretch goal. Coaches regularly provide direction, instruction, feedback, recognition, support, and encouragement to the individuals or groups they lead.

A quick guide to coaching

REMEMBER

Coaching is a continuous process, consisting of three primary steps:

1. **Set expectations and confirm a plan of action.**

   More often than not, issues in a conflict between a boss and an employee have their roots in a lack of expectations and objectives, and no plan in place to ensure regular follow-up. Typically, the boss has been vague with instructions, and then becomes upset when the employee interprets the vague instructions incorrectly. Almost always, the manager coaching the employee through the process would have resulted in a productive outcome.

2. **Observe performance and provide developmental opportunities.**

   Part of the plan of action should be to build in regular check-in points to make sure the employee has a go-to person for questions and input, and to ensure the employee is being developed to succeed. A manager who is willing to provide a stretch assignment can really engage an employee, but ongoing coaching will be required to ensure development.

3. **Solicit or offer feedback and provide direction, instruction, or perspective as needed.**

This step is so critical in coaching. Engaged managers create cultures where it's safe for an employee to ask for help, instructions, clarifications, and insight. People respond to positive recognition; an employee who receives positive reinforcement through coaching is more often than not going to excel.

All three steps apply whether the coaching is formal or informal:

» *Formal* simply refers to coaching or mentoring that occurs as part of the line organization (in other words, by "the boss"), by design (for example, as part of a formal mentoring program), or using company-approved tools (such as performance appraisal forms or 360 feedback instruments).

» *Informal* refers to coaching that a protégé seeks on her own or to coaching offered by a manager or mentor outside the official tools and process of the company.

Key communication skills

A key to coaching for performance and development is creating dialogue that encourages the "coachee" to self-reflect and disclose information about his or own performance. Honest, two-way discussion about progress toward goals and feedback on specific behaviors is the aim. Effective two-way dialogue involves the following:

» **Speaking:** Asking questions and giving feedback

» **Checking:** Checking for a response

» **Listening:** Using active listening skills

REMEMBER

Coaching is not about "fixing" people, or about the coach having all the answers. It's a give and take.

Effective coaching requires the following core communication skills:

» **Active listening:** This is a set of skills — namely, attending, following, and reflecting (that is, briefly restating, in your own words, the core of what the speaker has communicated) — that demonstrate that you understand the thoughts and feelings being communicated by the other person from her frame of reference. (Flip to Chapter 2 in Book 1 for an introduction to active listening.)

>> **Soliciting self-feedback:** To solicit self-feedback, you must ask questions to get the other person to reflect on his own performance. This helps the person think critically, leading to increased self-awareness and ownership of one's performance and development. Key questions include, "Specifically, what did you do well?" and "What would you do differently next time?"

>> **Giving feedback:** You must give feedback to reinforce or correct behavior, leading to greater results and effectiveness. (Chapter 1 in Book 2 introduces the topic of feedback.)

>> **Asking questions:** Asking the right questions can be incredibly powerful. Doing so can help people to think more critically, help them explore and solve their own problems, and lead to self-discovery — or, to quote Oprah, that "a-ha" moment. For best results, use *open-ended questions* (that is, questions whose responses tend to be sentences, explanations, or insights) to solicit self-feedback and facilitate insight and learning. Use *closed questions* (that is, questions that require no explanation or insight, and often result in single-word answers) to focus a conversation or to clarify information.

>> **Providing perspective:** A key aspect to coaching is helping your coachee find and understand additional information — to take a broader view of issues and challenges. You can use several lenses to view problems or opportunities. For example, you may discuss how other people or groups may view the situation. Also, discuss the multiple aspects and impacts of an issue — for example, by running what-if scenarios.

A few handy pointers

TIP

When it comes to coaching, keep the following tips in mind:

>> Before you start coaching, make sure there are shared expectations for the coaching discussion.

>> Keep the conversation focused and on track, and create two-way dialogue.

>> Solicit information from the coachee to find out how she self-assesses her own behavior, strengths, and areas for improvement.

>> Listen to truly understand the other person's unique points of view. Be an effective listener.

>> Provide feedback that is timely, specific, and objective.

>> Be able to deal with difficult situations, such as defusing and addressing defensive reactions to corrective feedback.

>> Ask effective, open-ended, clarifying questions, followed by silence, to allow your coachee to reflect and answer the question completely before moving on to the next question/subject.

>> Facilitate the process of brainstorming and problem solving in coaching discussions instead of just giving the coachee the answer.

>> Help others to understand and explore alternative perspectives when considering different actions or solutions to an issue.

>> Help others to feel re-energized, focused, and committed as a result of a coaching discussion.

>> Support your coachees in helping them develop their own action plan for their development. This should include setting short-term and long-term goals.

>> Instill a sense of accountability with employees by coaching them on success measures and following up on their progress.

TIP

To better understand your current coaching skills and capabilities, try ranking your skill level with regard to each of the preceding tips, assigning a score of 1 to your weakest skill and a score of 12 to your strongest skill. Use each number only once. After you've ranked yourself, look at the skills you ranked the lowest. These are the ones you probably need to work on. Don't forget about the other skills, however. Even the ones you ranked highest may require attention.

The GROW model

When planning a coaching session, whether formal or informal, consider using the GROW model. GROW stands for the following:

>> **Goal:** What is your goal? What do you want to achieve? To determine this, you might ask the following questions:

- What would you like to discuss?

- What do you really want?

- What is stopping you?

- What is important to you about this?

>> **Reality:** What is the current reality of your situation? You might assess this by asking the following questions:

- What's going on/getting in your way?

- What have you tried so far?

- What worked or didn't work?

- What decisions do you need to make?

>> **Options:** What are your options? To establish these, try asking the following questions:

- What might you do to reach your goal?
- What if that course of action doesn't work?
- What is another way of looking at this?
- What else do you need to take into consideration?
- What is another possibility or option?
- What is the upside or downside?

>> **Will:** What will you do or commit to? To tease out this information, consider the following questions:

- What will you do?
- When will you do it?
- What support do you need to accomplish it?

Do This, Not That: Looking at Leadership Best Practices

There are countless leadership best practices and traps to avoid. Indeed, whole libraries are filled with books on how to effectively lead people. Following are just a few practices that can make an immediate difference, are free to implement, and can be used by leaders at all levels with little training or skill. As you work to improve leadership skills, consider the "best practices" in this section.

I feel you, man

REMEMBER

Know what your employees like — and hate — both inside and outside of work. If you take away nothing else from this book, take away this: A top engagement driver is showing your employees you care about them as people. It takes all of two seconds to ask an employee how his weekend was, or how his daughter's dance recital went, or if his wife recovered from the flu. Obtaining and weaving this knowledge into your daily chit-chat with employees goes a long way toward engaging them.

If what your employees love (or hate) is different from what you love (or hate), suck it up. Act interested. Sure, it's a basic thing, but it goes a long way toward earning their devotion and ensuring their continued engagement. Besides, you may learn something!

Offering a hand up

Make employees feel as though you really care about their careers. Part of your job is to give your employees experiences at your firm that they couldn't have elsewhere — experiences that will make them more valuable. Sure, you hope your employees stay with your firm for a long time, but if the day comes when they need to move on to another company, that's okay. That concept may feel scary. After all, you're basically saying that your employees should feel free to take what they've learned with your organization and move on — maybe even to a competitor. But working to grow your talent, and communicating your efforts, is a great way to foster engagement.

REMEMBER

The "line of sight" for your organization is its purpose, values, vision, and strategic plan. In addition to this "macro" line of sight, there's also a "micro" line of sight that exists on an employee level. This line of sight is all about "What job do I currently have?" and "Where am I going?" The more concern you show for your employees' growth and development in their careers — their personal "lines of sight" — the greater the probability you'll have engaged employees.

You're not the boss of me!

Stop telling employees what to do. Instead, have them help come up with solutions. Often, when managers spot a performance issue, they simply tell the employee what she needs to do to improve. There's no interaction, no dialogue, nothing. A better approach is to make an observation and then shut your cake hole and let the employee talk. Whatever the solution turns out to be, you'll almost certainly get better buy-in with this approach.

TIP

Also, avoid describing how to do a project or task. Give your employee the destination, but leave the driving directions to her. Employees often have their own ideas about process, and those ideas are often quicker, more innovative, and more efficient than the "tried and true."

Recognize, recognize, recognize

REMEMBER

When it comes to engaging employees, recognition is one of the most effective weapons in a leader's arsenal. Experienced managers have learned what neuroscientists and child psychologists have known for decades: Positive reinforcement and recognition lead to the replication of positive results. (See Chapter 1 in Book 5 for details on rewarding employees in different generations.)

IN THIS CHAPTER

» **Getting a handle on ideas for building trust**

» **Defining trust and uncovering needs**

» **Earning loyalty and reducing social distance**

» **Leading by example**

» **Encouraging trust among the staff**

Chapter **2**

Establishing Trust

The key factor in a leader's ability to influence a group is *trust.* This chapter dives into the basic human needs fulfillment as outlined in Abraham Maslow's hierarchy of needs theory, explores the defining factors people deploy subconsciously when assessing others, and looks at what a leader can do to bolster trust within an organization. Additionally, you get a snapshot of the actions a team can take to create a trusting environment.

REMEMBER

Trust is a two-way street. Trust given is trust returned. It's a full circle of intention and way of being in the world. People follow those whom they trust. Keep this adage in mind: "People don't quit jobs — they quit leadership."

Surveying Ideas for Building Trust in Business

REMEMBER

Once again: The key factor in effective leadership and the ability to influence and move a group forward is trust. Trust *is* power. Tapping into this wellspring provides access to great talent, resources, and the ability to amplify productivity. A trusted company is rewarded by customer/client dollars, vendors who want to work with you, and a motivated team who will move mountains to accomplish tasks.

Trust is a rapport built on genuine connection with others and is the foundation from which everything flows. Therefore, establishing trust as a leader should be one of your main goals. Unfortunately, only 37 percent of the population believes CEOs are "extremely/very credible," which is similar to the 39 percent rate for government leaders. Ouch! Businesses were distrusted by 48 percent of those surveyed in the 2017 Edelman Trust Barometer report. Clearly, there's work to be done.

Repairing and reinforcing trust should be a priority for every company and its leadership. When looking at the major contributors that erode trust, you can look at core needs not being fulfilled. When people question the credibility of institutions, it erodes confidence in belief systems, and that makes them prone to economic and social uncertainty. When people don't feel they're being taken care of or looked out for by the institution, government, or business, they question the ability of authority to be aware of and meet basic needs.

Table 2-1 shows the percentages of those who say each attribute is important to building trust in a company.

People need to look at a leader's ability to bring about a marked increase in trustworthiness in an organization. Values-based leadership (VBL) is a big part of moving from a *Halt* environment (described later in this chapter) to one of growth and sustainability.

TABLE 2-1   **Ways for Businesses to Build Trust**

Attributes	% of Those Who Feel the System Is Failing	% of General Population
Treating employees well	72	62
Offering high-quality products and services	68	59
Listening to customers	67	58
Paying their share of taxes	66	56
Engaging in ethical business practices	65	56
Transparent and open in their business practices	65	55
Placing customers above profits	65	55
Taking responsible action to address issues	64	55
Communicating frequently and honestly	60	52
Protecting and improving the environment	60	52

Attributes	% of Those Who Feel the System Is Failing	% of General Population
Creating many new jobs	55	47
Profits remain in the country	56	46
Programs with positive impact locally	53	46
Addressing social needs in everyday business activity	53	46

Source: 2017 Edelman Trust Barometer www.scribd.com/document/336621519/2017-Edelman-Trust-Barometer-Executive-Summary - fullscreen&from_embed

Defining Trust and Needs in the Workplace

So what is trust, exactly? Is it telling the truth? Perhaps the words *ethical behavior* come to mind, or *transparency*. Those sound right. To better understand what defines trust in the workplace, though, consider Dr. Duane C. Tway Jr.'s three perceptions to contextualize trust:

>> **Capacity for trust:** The ability to trust others based on your experiences, interaction, and life wisdom.

>> **Perception of competence:** The evaluation of yours or others' skills and the ability to do the job effectively.

>> **Perception of intention:** The effect of words, actions, and deeds as positively or negatively impacting others.

This framework provides a compact assessment when it comes to trust. On a mostly subconscious level, people utilize these categories to determine the trustworthiness of those they date, hire, and follow, seamlessly. Wait — did that sentence say date?

TECHNICAL STUFF

Consider this example: When you're dating someone, you first wonder whether you can trust them. Past experiences will dictate the depth of your abilities to trust — if someone once cheated on you, chances are your trust threshold will be lower. Next, you assess your dating partner: Is this person suitable to be in a relationship with me (or anyone else)? Do they possess the capacity to fulfill my needs? Then, based on going out a few times, comes the assessment of everything from table manners, to how they speak to their mother, to how they treat coworkers and friends and engage others on social media, and so on. Your assessments create a perception of the other person's intention in the world to be positive or negative, stable or volatile, violent or gentle — and all factor into figuring out whether you should trust them. Your assessment may happen consciously or unconsciously.

Establishing Trust

A similar process takes place in a business environment:

>> The staff will make their own determination on how much they can trust you (or anyone in a position of authority).

>> From there, they will decide whether you have the skills and experience to do your job and therefore effectively lead the organization. You may be surprised just how much research they may do on you through networking and Internet searching.

>> Then they will watch you, listen to you, and assess your every move to determine the authenticity of your intention as "real" or not. They will interpret your body language (see Chapters 2 and 3 in Book 1) and evaluate your engagements with different team members (see Book 6, Chapter 1) to decide whether you're fair or whether you show favoritism.

The list of assessments can seem endless. Assessing others' level of trustworthiness is a survival mechanism deeply ingrained within everyone. It's very real.

The baseline needs of a human being come into play when establishing trust, as this section is meant to show. Trust is also the precursor to motivating people (see Book 6, Chapter 3). Snap one puzzle piece into the next to continue cement a powerful leadership position.

TIP

Building a foundation based on trust creates the power needed to move your organization forward. It's worth the time and attention because you'll reap massive benefits down the road.

Using Maslow's hierarchy of needs to determine baseline trust

The most widely known needs theory is Maslow's hierarchy of needs, developed in 1943. Abraham Maslow's concept of needs has been applied to such areas as politics, social impact of events, and workplace attitudes for good reason — it makes perfect sense. The theory was updated in the 1960s and 1970s, but still intact are Maslow's three levels of needs each human being experiences:

>> **Deficiencies:** Basic needs including fundamental physiological human needs such as food, water, health, shelter, and sex, but also, interestingly, employment, safety, and sociability.

>> **Growth:** Feelings of accomplishment, achievement, respect for others and self, esteem, prestige, connection, meaningfulness, and belonging are some examples.

>> **Self-achieving:** Self-awareness needs, achieving one's full potential, giving back, and helping others achieve self-actualization and transcendence.

REMEMBER

As a leader, you have responsibilities *to* your people: to be a guardian, to be of service to those you lead, to be generous, and to diligently safeguard their rights. Those may sound like lofty ideals. However, consider that your organization is the one that will fill an employee's basic deficiencies by providing gainful employment with fair wages, permitting them to pay their rent, buy food, and create a warm, safe, and dry environment for themselves and their families. That's reality — not a lofty ideal. Additionally, providing a safe, growth-oriented company culture fulfills the growth needs of feeling accomplished, prestige, connection, and so on.

The survival mechanism drives people to fulfill these levels of needs, partially, through their work. The depth of trust an individual feels depends on how well those needs are filled. Tway's framing of the three contexts (listed earlier in this chapter) provides the sequence toward establishing trust. As employees view you, their leader, and the organization as ones that treat everyone fairly, with esteem, affording them the dignity to create a life for themselves and their families, the sequence is satisfied.

Employees can and do assess and reassess trustworthiness at any time. Consistency in keeping their trust builds loyalty and forgiveness. When you stumble, they will forgive you and keep working because, after all, everyone makes mistakes. On the flip side, if you're consistently careless, they won't give you the benefit of the doubt if there are missteps — ever.

REMEMBER

As a leader/employer, you hold these needs in your hands; they are each individual's social and economic requirements to feel safe and secure. Although not every person can be hired, and not every person will be retained indefinitely, understanding the impact you have on his or her lives will, hopefully, provide the motivation for you to stay the course.

Shifting from Halt to happiness

A *Halt* environment is one where trust is in limited supply. A continued state of distrust creates tension. People feel defensive and are always "on guard." Staffers look over their shoulders to see who or what may be lurking behind a comment. They wait for the other shoe to drop, anticipating the thump as it hits the floor. It's a terrible company culture. The team burns out, and creativity atrophies. *Cultural entropy* engulfs the group with unproductive and often unnecessarily extra work, fostering resentment and discontent. This isn't a fun or inspiring place to work.

Note that although sometimes distrust *may* create an immediate, short-term gain or growth spurt for a company as staff compete internally for recognition and success, it is short-lived. VBL is very much against the idea of sowing mistrust to foster internal competition.

Sifting through theory, practical and applied, of how to build connectivity and trust comes down to a few basic components. People want those basic needs in the preceding section met, but they also want to be seen, heard, and recognized, and they want to do meaningful work, with the goal of giving back to others. Figure 2-1 shows the conversion of the original needs that Maslow defines into three categories of workplace needs.

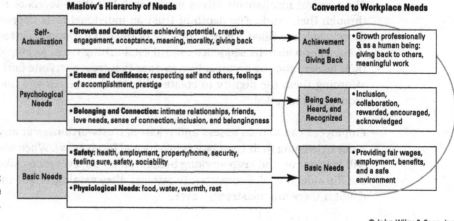

FIGURE 2-1: Needs conversion to the workplace.

© John Wiley & Sons, Inc.

When working with someone, ask yourself: Has this person been seen, heard, and recognized? You can frame this as regular team maintenance. It's not about breaking out trophies. The things that are often most meaningful and motivating to others are simple and cost very little. Providing a team member or colleague the opportunity to be an effective member/contributor to the team, to listen to what they say, and to recognize, verbally or through actions, that you've heard and seen them takes very little time.

Individuals aren't all the same; how they like to be recognized may vary. They may want to be allowed to

>> Share their ideas.

>> Support others through formal or informal mentorship.

>> Have their small successes celebrated on the road to larger achievements.

>> Be involved with problem solving.

>> Train for current and future roles.

Getting Others to Trust in Your Leadership

Balance is *power* — this is a concept all leaders should seriously consider. Being a balanced individual of sound mind, competence, and behavior is necessary. Those who exhibit erratic, unpredictable behaviors aren't considered trustworthy. Humans are built with an internal survival mechanism. If you spook them, they're not going to trust you. It's as if Halloween is happening every day when you have an unbalanced or overly emotional leader in the driver's seat. You just never know when they're going to jump out from behind a door and say boo. This type of behavior keeps everyone on pins and needles.

Exemplifying a balanced, even-keeled presence, with the help of the following sections, will provide the consistency necessary for trust to be established. Trust is the absence of doubt. When the team, vendors, and investors know that you'll consistently engage with them today and tomorrow in the same way you did yesterday, you're giving them that certainty.

REMEMBER

Be clear and be consistent in everything you do and how you do it.

Engendering loyalty

Trust is a partnership. It requires that all parties operate with the same intentions and by the same guidelines. It builds loyalty and commitment in the group. Throughout the years, countless teams have stuck together, even through some particularly difficult times, because they trusted their leader and one another. Commitment to one another and the process was the yield resulting from a bond of trust. Motivational speaker Brian Tracy sums it up well: The glue that holds all relationships together — including the relationship between the leader and the led — is trust, and trust is based on integrity.

What binds leaders and employees is a commitment to excellence and the knowledge that they can rely on each other. This connection takes time, experience, and continued repetition to cement in place.

TECHNICAL STUFF

Stella is a top-level leader of a large multinational pharmaceutical company. Her reputation for toughness has produced a highly productive group of managers and teams. She was once asked how she manages to balance her expectations and mobilize the teams to operate at such a high level. She smiled and said that the only way people work at this level is because they trust her and they trust each other: "Trust is the default engagement tool for us. Without trust, there is nothing else."

Reducing social distance gaps

Social distance is the belief in the difference between "us" and "them." To be sure, at times it's valid to make those distinctions when it's about context, not judgment. Social distance in the workplace, particularly now as the workplace is becoming more global, is the perception of power, distance, value, and belonging — who is "in" and who isn't.

In the case of leadership, social distance may be about which piece of real estate home office sits on. When there are multiple offices, there can be a territorial aspect to the perception of power — that where the leader works gains favor and priority. For example, if the leaders are in Baltimore, those working in the other offices located in Dallas, Dubai, Dublin, and Des Moines are prone to the isolating belief that they are secondary citizens and are less of a priority to the company. "Out of sight, out of mind" is the lament. It's easy to feel a sense of uneasiness or mistrust of those you don't see on a daily basis, or to create a sense of "them" being an enemy. The unknown isn't always something people can feel at ease with or trust. Therefore, it's important to address any social distance issues immediately.

TIP

Social distance in this case can be resolved through inclusion and communication:

>> **Unify:** Continually steer the focus back toward common goals, challenges, and opportunities.

>> **Puzzle pieces:** Illustrate, often, that each team in each office makes an important contribution to the total goal. Highlight these interlocking pieces to the leaders on the ground and the staff regularly.

>> **Consistently communicate with clarity:** Communication is a key attribute of a values-based leader. Communicate goals, missions, plans, and contributions regularly.

>> **Who, me?** Seek to find ways to include leaders and managers from other offices in your plans. Doing so amplifies your emphasis on inclusion and promotes a feeling among everyone that they are making contributions.

By using these skills, you'll be able to debunk the myth that there is only one central source of power and influence.

Setting Standards for Others by Example

At an annual meeting for a mid-sized company, the leadership team was rolling out initiatives and sharing the plan for their bright future. There was a lot of energy and applause throughout the morning. During a break, the ground-level leaders were happily engaging in conversation with team members, and the general feeling was one of optimism about the future. When they were asked why, the answer was that the leadership team would do what they said they were going to do. Although the fine details were still unclear at that moment, the teams weren't worried about the execution. They trusted the leadership because the leaders had been consistent in their behavior so far.

One of the highest awards a leader can receive is the trust of their people. When you do what you say you're going to do and do it consistently, your platform is a sure one. As this section explains, leading from the front, by example, motivates everyone around you to do their part.

Operating with self-awareness

Understanding your own motives for what you do — uncovering and keeping in check your trigger points to avoid projecting your *stuff* on others — is all part of being a self-aware leader. So is observing how you affect others. Much of this point goes back to the opening statements about being a steady, stable leader, but it's also about being emotionally intelligent and able to adapt and act in an appropriate manner.

Have you ever given a presentation and then looked around the room only to see mouths wide open or, even worse, everyone sitting with their arms folded and looking agitated? You look down at your notes and wonder what happened. Something triggered the response; your delivery, your tone, or the examples you gave may have caused a silent mutiny. The point is that you affected people negatively; this isn't about being a poor presenter.

A more common example is your attitude being projected onto a group. Perhaps there is an initiative you don't want to be part of or you don't believe in, but if that eye roll or quick negative quip slips out, you convey to those around you that you don't believe in it, you don't care, and it's nothing more than a nuisance. The team may respond with annoyance toward you if they believe in the initiative, or they may follow suit with your defiance. Either way, your example signals to them that public displays of defiance are acceptable. They may judge you for not being a team player.

Self-awareness is about understanding that you impact others, both knowingly and unknowingly. Keeping yourself in check to ensure that you don't negatively impact others takes self-awareness and discipline. Let's face it; everyone has bad days, is asked to do things they don't always agree with, or has to deliver bad news. As a leader, you're the lightning rod that influences these reactions.

REMEMBER

Set the standard: Equanimity always.

Avoiding exceptions yet remaining flexible

Making exceptions becomes a very fine line to walk at times. Compassionately engaging with the team means understanding that there may be circumstances beyond one's control to be addressed. This would fall under the category of flexibility, not exception — for example, allowing a parent to take an additional day off to care for a sick child even if their personal days have been used up. In one case, another teammate stepped up to fill the parent's workplace duties on that day, and even offered one of their own sick days to prevent the teammate from losing a salaried day off.

That's very different from an exception within the organization that favors one employee over another — for example, granting high performers exceptions to attend certain mandatory trainings, even though they need the required training. Delaying a required activity is one thing if they meet the requirement set for everyone else. When high performers show up and do what they're required to do, it's a powerful example to others in the organization that no one is better or more important than anyone else here.

If you're unsure whether you're playing favorites or making exceptions, all you have to do is listen to the complaining or resentful comments made by the surrounding staff.

REMEMBER

Set the standard: We are equals, without exception.

Sidestepping rumor mills and gossip hounds

The best way to circumvent the rumor mills, gossip, and conspiracy theories is to be transparent. Although it may not be appropriate to divulge sensitive information, it is important to dispense information such as financial results and plans for future correction and growth to the team and stockholders. When the information is out there in the daylight, it slows rumors. And do it in a timely fashion.

Delay only creates a sense of fear and uncertainty. Conveying certainty and transparency is key to gaining trust.

TIP

Water cooler moments will happen. It's inevitable. Humans will be humans. Put three people in a room together, and they will have three differing opinions and interpretations of a common event. Perception is a powerful lens through which people view the world, but everyone wears different glasses, and so opinions are formed that differ, sometimes mildly, sometimes wildly. It's just a fact. However, there are things you, as the leader, can do to help prevent rumor mills and gossiping in the workplace:

>> **Accept the elephant in the room.** Okay, so there's something going on. Everyone knows it. This is the action of *acceptance*. Recognize that it's happening and you're probably not going to be able to stop it. You can, however, slow the process down from becoming a canker sore.

>> **Gather the group.** Level with them: Yes, XYZ is happening. Let's wait before everyone jumps to conclusions. In the case of personal or interdepartmental rumors, be direct: "How about giving everyone in this situation the benefit of the doubt?" You ask them to reach into the compassionate side of themselves before creating a negative situation.

>> **Draw a line.** Plain and simple: "We don't gossip or spread rumors on this team. Although I can't stop you from speaking to one another, I do ask that you treat each other with dignity and respect, because this is what we stand for. If you must speculate, take it outside. Within these four walls, I ask that you refrain from this behavior."

Blowing off steam to defuse one's own fear, anxiety, or concern for security is normal and very human, but too much of it can erode trust by casting doubt into the minds of those around. Allow employees to have their process, but don't permit it to spread like wildfire and engulf the entire group.

REMEMBER

Set the standard: This workplace is a no-drama zone.

Encouraging others as a sign of trust

Trust given is trust returned. Encouraging others to do their job and to do it well is a form of encouragement. There may be a period of training before an individual can fly solo within their position, so train them well, encourage them to do it, and allow them to go for it.

REMEMBER

Set the standard: Encouragement is generosity amplified.

Mastering the thank-you

Old school? Yes. Good basic manners? Yes. Necessary to build rapport and trust with your team? Abso-freaking-lutely! Keep in mind that people want to be seen, heard, and recognized (refer to Figure 2-1). When a job is well done, an extra effort is made, or a new level is achieved, recognize your folks. Those famous two words go a long way. Dispense generously and often.

TECHNICAL STUFF

Have a look at the following stats (according to an article at Employee Benefit News: www.benefitnews.com/news/employee-personalization-drives-pre-nd-post-hiring-technologies). Clearly employees appreciate even the smallest expression of appreciation for what they do, but leaders don't see the need for it:

>> Twenty-two percent of senior decision-makers don't think that regular recognition and thanking employees at work have a big influence on staff retention.

>> Seventy percent of employees say that motivation and morale would improve "massively" with managers saying "thank you" more.

REMEMBER

Set the standard: Gratitude is our way of being.

Harnessing People Power

Your organization is made up of many parts, but the common thread is its people. When you harness the energy, talent, and skills of a group, amazing things can unfold.

Being an example sets the tone for the team — give them reason to trust you, and they will follow. You will be challenged or questioned at times. Just remember, a leader who gives trust receives trust. Allow your example to trickle down through the organization.

Following five engaging principles for the team

Building on your example, add the following simple ways of acting as a healthy team to the checklist, bearing in mind that trust still needs to be nurtured within all layers and levels of the organization:

>> **Be honest but not mean.** Be honest with your engagements. Always tell the truth — even little white lies can cause damage. Share and provide all relevant information, even if it puts you at a disadvantage.

>> **Dispense good judgment.** Use your best judgment when sharing information with others, but first ask yourself some questions: Is this necessary? Will it compromise someone else? And is it kind or judgmental? Treat others as you want to be treated and treat confidential information with confidence — not because it's compliant, but because it's the right thing to do.

>> **Be reliable and dependable.** People refer business to, share information with, and want to collaborate with those they know to be reliable and dependable. No one ever says, "I want to work with Joe because he's a lazy dude who never shows up on time." That's never going to happen. Show up for your team, on time, every time.

>> **Look one another in the eye.** When someone looks you in the eye, it's a sign of honesty and sincerity. It's a small, simple act of body language, a cue others pick up on immediately (see Chapters 2 and 3 in Book 1 for an introduction to body language). When you feel as if someone is untrustworthy, often it's because they don't look you in the eye. Additionally, studies have shown that eye contact of 30 percent or more of the time increases retention of the information shared — that's not even 20 seconds out of a minute.

>> **Embody the "fireman carry" attitude.** The seated fireman carry is a symbol of four hands interlocking. In 1964, a more stylized version of this image became the logo of financial giant Oppenheimer Funds to symbolize "Greater strength and support than any one individual can provide alone." This is the essence of the fireman carry attitude.

Unifying behind a common belief

Human beings enjoy being bonded together by a common goal or mission. Major religious organizations are founded based on belief systems. Civil servants such as firefighters, police, and military are also united by common missions. Companies have long done the same. Belonging is a big part of the human need. Being bound by goals, beliefs, or a common mission helps create a desire to achieve/win together.

Advertisers have long used slogans and catchphrases to create memorable brands, share key benefits, differentiate products from one another, and impart a positive feeling toward brands. Here are a few examples:

>> **Think Differently:** Apple

>> **Got Milk?** California Milk Processors Board

>> **Imagination at Work:** General Electric

>> **Every Little Helps:** Tesco

>> **There are some things money can't buy. For everything else, there's MasterCard:** MasterCard

As you've read this list, you may have smiled as you thought about your favorite catchphrase or slogan. Everyone has them. They create unity and a way of experiencing a brand, which also makes it feel like an exclusive experience. Either you're part of something, a club, group, brand, and so on — or you're not. So, why wouldn't you want to engender this same uniting, positive feeling under your brand of leadership? Does that sound complicated? Yes, it does. It sounds like it could be perceived as a massive marketing endeavor. But it really doesn't need to be complicated.

TIP

Here's the one uniting phrase used over again with great success: *We are all in this together!* You can't all be in it together unless you trust one another. This is a simple, useful slogan to rally people around you. It's all-encompassing. Dispense daily, when the team is up or when it's down. Share it at annual meetings, cross-divisional meetings, and everywhere the employees gather to gain focus. It's a reminder to them that they are to rely and can rely on each other. Set the expectation that they meet or even exceed your expectations.

Circumventing passive-aggressive personalities

One passive-aggressive apple can spoil the entire team.

Among the narcissistic personality types, the most common may be the passive-aggressive. You know the type: It's all about *them.* Passive-aggressive behaviors are not only maddening, but they're also subversive in nature. Consider the process of avoiding a confrontation (passive) but using *behind your back* conversations with others to tear down another person (aggressive).

WARNING

It's imperative that passive-aggressive behaviors be addressed. They can easily derail your efforts to establish trust and cast doubt and shame throughout.

Bypassing a passive-aggressive personality takes enormous patience and is an exercise in "compassion management." Individuals exhibiting passive-aggressive behavior usually do so because they have at some point in their lives experienced harsh criticism or they may feel their voices haven't been heard. There's no need to find the specific root of their behavior — just be aware enough to realize that the behavior stems from such influences in their lives. This awareness provides a glimpse into who they are and will lead you to approach the situation with compassion, circumventing a potentially explosive confrontation.

Passive-aggressive behavior creates an environment where people don't feel safe. For example, someone isn't sure if what someone else is saying to them is the truth or if the truth is only being told to others. Other examples would be the dreaded "cold look-through stare" in the hallway, or having a hello ignored, or a teammate agreeing to take on a task and then not doing it — even though everything else has been completed. It can be signaled by patronizing statements such as "Bless your heart." Backhanded compliments and a deep desire to be right are also part of this narcissistic profile.

TIP

As a leader, it's not always your place to address these situations. Although it could happen on a leadership level, depending on the ratio of staff to leadership, many issues will remain at the staff level. If you do need to address it, here are some tools to help you and your ground-level leaders and managers defuse these individuals:

>> **Keep your cool.** Avoid overreacting or permitting an attack on a personal level. Don't take the bait.

>> **Keep it at a distance.** You can't win nor please them, nor should you think you can. Simply agree to disagree but convey that the work still needs to get done — on time.

>> **Reflect.** You can't change them or their behavior. This is an opportunity to self-reflect: "Do I do this too?" or "Why am I trying so hard to make them happy or comfortable?"

>> **Adopt Mother Superior positioning.** Exemplify your best composure, sitting high and quietly without arguing. Think of that famous nun in a black habit, sitting, listening, and nodding. Behind that habit was a calm, cool, collected, and powerful presence who hardly had to say a word. It's very effective positioning.

>> **Utilize humor.** Laughter releases tension and forces people to breathe, which helps defuse anger naturally.

>> **Mind your language to prevent victim mode.** When in direct conversation, avoid using words like *you* or *your* directed at the individual. Rather, replace them with *I, we,* and *our.* Doing this can circumvent their perception that they're being attacked. (Find out why pronouns matter in verbal communication in Chapter 1 of Book 1.)

>> **Defuse resistance.** Offering a form of consequence for their lack of coopera-
tion will often break down resistance to taking on or completing actions:
"When this isn't done, the result is that there may be negative fallout around
your capabilities." Or: "When this situation isn't resolved, the unfortunate
fallout is that you may not be considered a team player, which will only have
negative long-term career repercussions." The consequence doesn't need to
be punitive, but the potential chain of events should be illuminated.

Chapter **3**

Motivating the Masses

Welcome to Motivation Central! Who you are as a leader makes a profound difference to your employees because you're the individual who sets the tone for the company. On-the-ground leaders also set the tone for your team.

This chapter provides you with a few different ways of considering motivation. The first is the basic human motivational theory, derived from needs-based principles discussed in Book 6, Chapter 2. Everyone has needs on a variety of levels, of course. Here you consider the needs most commonly seen in the workplace. When you know what these needs are and why people behave the way they do, it's much easier to take their cues. Knowing what someone desires on a deep level helps you motivate them. In essence, it's a reverse-engineering process.

The topics of purpose, meaning, and mission also interplay throughout this chapter. Your company has an overall direction, and robust social initiatives may be in place, but people still like personalization. One of the most compassionate things you can do for another human being is to take the time to really try to understand them. After all, there's a real reason — beyond a paycheck — that most people end up doing the jobs they do and sticking to a career niche. Subconsciously, they're addressing a deep need within themselves.

This chapter also considers how to motivate not just an individual but teams as a whole. There are a few ways to do this. One of the most powerful is to create an environment where team members motivate each other and teach each other in a supportive manner. There's no one size fits all, so choose what you feel you can accomplish first and start there. The goal is to provide you with options, insights, and statistics. Which path to take is your choice.

REMEMBER

As a values-based leader, you're self-aware, emotionally intelligent, and empathetic — not a soft and squishy plush toy, but a fierce leader who puts connection and engagement as priorities in your business. Taking the time to understand others is a demonstration of these attributes.

Peeking into the Human Motivation Theory

An entire chapter (Book 6, Chapter 2) is devoted to trust because it's the foundation from which all relationships form. Trust creates a stable environment and eliminates doubt that basic needs will be fulfilled, promoting feelings of safety. When trust isn't in place, doubt overtakes a group — and doubt is the killer of motivation. If the members of an organization don't feel that their leaders have their best interests at heart or are trustworthy, the general refrain becomes "Why should I bother?" When you have enough people saying that, it's safe to assume they aren't motivated. Often, their level of engagement is so low that you're not sure they're really working at all. They're just dialing it in for the day's pay. (Figure 3-1 shows the connection between trust and doubt.)

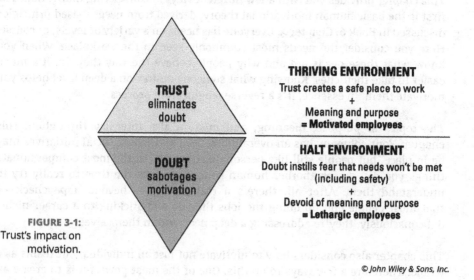

THRIVING ENVIRONMENT
Trust creates a safe place to work
+
Meaning and purpose
= Motivated employees

HALT ENVIRONMENT
Doubt instills fear that needs won't be met
(including safety)
+
Devoid of meaning and purpose
= Lethargic employees

TRUST
eliminates
doubt

DOUBT
sabotages
motivation

FIGURE 3-1:
Trust's impact on
motivation.

© John Wiley & Sons, Inc.

Human motivation most often stems from the needs system discussed in Book 6, Chapter 2. There are three categories:

>> **Deficiency needs:** The bare basics of life, including food, water, health, shelter, sex, safety, and employment.

>> **Growth needs:** Accomplishment, achievement, self-esteem, connection, and meaning.

>> **Self-achieving needs:** Self-awareness, giving back, and helping others.

When deficiency and growth needs are met, they increase the possibility that an individual can meet a self-achieving need. Having these needs met builds trust and esteem to accomplish whatever the individual wants to achieve. With that said, assume that deficiency needs are met and your employees are seeking to fulfill their growth and self-achieving needs. In the following sections, you can find out how to identify and understand the components that will motivate them.

Looking, listening, and categorizing

One of the attributes of being a values-based leader is the ability to listen and really hear other people by pausing long enough to get a sense of who they are. This chapter is about using that ability to learn how to identify what motivates them. Active listening is great (as you find out in Chapter 2 of Book 1), but getting at the intent behind someone's words is a sign of an empathetic leader. Everyone communicates in a way that reflects their deepest desires and motives. This section starts with basic classifications to help provide some framework for exactly what you're looking and listening for.

Noting the three things that motivate people

REMEMBER

In 1961, Dr. David McClelland looked deeper into needs and classified motivational principles into three more categories: power, affiliation, and achievement. According to this theory, everyone possesses one or more of these motivational triggers. One trigger is dominant, and the others vary in intensity:

>> **Power:** Those who are motivated by power like to plan and use that word a lot. Creating *the plan* is a way to ensure that they've secured power, authority, and/or control over a situation. Power-focused individuals fear a loss of power or the perception of lack of authority more than anything else. They'll keep a lid on anything that deviates from the plan. The lighter, brighter side of power is the thought process that a plan ensures others' safety. Safety, to power-focused individuals, means making sure that everyone is clear and moving in the same direction. They take ownership of this duty.

>> **Affiliation:** Here you have social butterflies, group leaders, and those who love being on the inside track. They're group-centric, want to be liked, and are often deemed social directors or ringleaders. Affiliation-focused individuals fear rejection. To be rejected would mean they've been excluded. Everybody wants to belong, to some extent, but those motivated by affiliation seek it as a means to exert their own form of power.

>> **Achievement:** Achievers are always focused on the next goal, sometimes even before the present goal has been achieved. They're always looking at what's next. They're motivated by the achievement of goals. Failure is their kryptonite. Their mantra is "Failure is not an option." It's important to know that these individuals often move from one goal to another without much of a pause. Another way to view this trigger is that these individuals like a challenge and thrive on having another mountain to climb or land to conquer.

Depending on their use, the triggers can be profoundly positive or destructive; there are always positive and negative aspects to everything. Someone with power needs may well be a mobilizing and unifying force behind a plan. And a control enthusiast may squelch the energy of a whole team with their need to be in complete control. Positive and negative possibilities exist within everyone.

Assessing yourself

Did you immediately recognize yourself as you read the categories in the preceding section? Most people do. Consider writing your perceived motivations on a sticky note and keep it in this chapter. But before you do, consider the questions in this section to further refine your assessment.

TIP

Working within the three categories in the preceding section, what would you consider to be your dominant motivational trigger? Ask yourself these questions:

>> What motivates you to come to work?

>> What's the reward you're really seeking?

>> Why this job and/or this company?

Forget preconceived notions, like the idea that wanting power is necessary to be a leader. Leaders come in many different forms, with different strengths. Some are more socially driven, relying on their connections and group influence to create success. A drive to achieve promotes the idea that they're highly focused. Whatever motivates you, knowing *yourself* can provide insights into your own behaviors, both known and previously unknown. Additionally, assessing yourself first creates a platform for understanding and compassion for yourself — and ultimately for others. Knowing why you react in a certain way in any situation will help you understand the same about members of your team (see the next section for details).

It's honesty time. No one else is looking at the notes you've made in this section. Regardless of which trigger motivates you the most, you can discern more about who you are and how you operate, and when you're feeling down or demotivated, you can usually find the answer in your dominant motivating factor not being fulfilled.

If affiliation is your dominant motivation, for example, having an inclusive, team-spirited, or community-centric form of expression in your leadership motivates you. However, exclusion in any form demotivates you. With this awareness, consider the importance of affiliation for you in your life. What does it bring you? Some answers can be acceptance, influence, and/or using that influence to gain something for either yourself or someone else. That can include simple things like networking through your circle of influence to help someone else find a job.

Assessing your team

After you assess yourself, consider your team and ask the same questions from the preceding section. Jot down those answers on a piece of paper or a sticky note. Put a star next to the one or two you think rank highest for your team and stick the note here in this chapter for now.

Keep in mind that motivation sometimes looks as if one stimulus moves a person forward, but if you look more closely, it turns out to be something completely different, or at least the context of it may become different. This is an important distinction to be made and one that will help you speak directly to those triggers. When you know the root cause, it's much easier to see through the weeds.

Consider the last staffer you engaged who seemed not to be "feeling it" any longer. They used to be engaged and motivated. What changed? What were they getting that's missing now? If you know the person well enough, you may be able now to look through the motivational trigger material in this chapter to figure out which one reflects who they are. Or you may need to have a conversation to learn more. Listen to what they say and how they say it. Notice what their body language cues are expressing (you can find help with this task in Chapter 3 of Book 1). Then re-motivate the individual by tapping into what they truly want. This is the reverse-engineering mentioned earlier. Here is one example of how to do this.

"Lila" was once a motivated, energetic part of the team, but recently she has been quiet and a bit withdrawn. You ask her how things are going. Her body language is a bit slumped, and she looks at her shoes a lot while you're chatting. After a little coaxing, she reveals that she just feels unhappy but she can't quite pinpoint why. Her work is still good and it's challenging, but it's just not . . . fun.

Lila's manager realizes that for the past 18 months, Lila was involved in a large-scale initiative bringing people from various offices together to problem solve a part of the business. Now Lila engages with only her manager daily. It becomes apparent that Lila misses the ability to set and reach goals in her work. The prior setting had her in a very structured type of work, and she loved it. Her manager realizes that Lila has really excelled every time she has been in that type of structure. Realizing that Lila needs that achievement in her work in order to feel fully engaged, her manager moves her work around to include others and asks her to lead structuring benchmarks and checkpoints for an upcoming project. Within weeks Lila perks up and is back to normal energetic self.

You find other means to reverse-engineer motivation in the nearby sidebar "Motivating Denise." Additionally, check out the example of Sam and his toy cars in the next section, which uses a slightly different tactic.

REMEMBER

Each process follows the same basic formula:

>> **Be observant.** Take the time to notice changes in your employee's connection to their work.

>> **Identify patterns.** Consider patterns of when the employee worked happily or excelled in certain situations.

>> **Identify the motivation.** Based on the pattern, is the motivating factor power, affiliation, or achievement?

>> **Reverse-engineer the motivating factor.** Give them what works for them — for example, if they like to achieve goal after goal, give them another goal to strive for. Otherwise you'll lose that person.

>> **Take action.** Redirect the employee's work into the form that works as a motivating tool: power people want to plan and be the authority, affiliation people prefer a community-driven environment, and achievement folks want to check off goal completions.

REMEMBER

When assessing others, consider the dominant behavior, but also be aware that there may be secondary motivational factors. People are multifaceted, not one-dimensional. So you'll probably be working with a dominant trigger and a secondary trigger. Look, listen, and watch the engagements of your team to see what really motivates them, and dispense your motivational remedies accordingly.

TIP

The great news is that once you know these triggers and how to recognize them, you'll be able to utilize them in many facets of your life. Consider practicing this concept on your friends, partners, and, yes, even your family. Your next holiday dinner together will be infinitely more interesting when you view everyone at the table through this filter. No, you're not being manipulative. You're honing your ability to understand others.

MOTIVATING DENISE

"Denise" is a big team player and an exceptional employee. She's always been viewed as an introvert, except when it comes to team activities. During those times, she shines and can mobilize the group. The organization promotes her to work with many work groups. But now Denise isn't part of one team that she feels is her own.

Her trigger is affiliation. She loves being *part of* a group. The new role may have seemed ideal for a social butterfly, but it disconnects her from that group/team environment of inclusion that makes her so happy. So, Denise begins to lag and doesn't seem to be motivated anymore. She does her work, but she isn't happy. Her manager realizes the disconnect for her, reassigns her to a lateral position within a work group environment, and voilà — she begins to excel again. Motivational issue resolved.

For another person motivated by affiliation, the social butterfly aspect of the role offered to Denise might have been perfect. Always consider that there could be several applications within each trigger. Customize to the individual.

Understanding that fear motivates more than anything else

Unfortunately, people are even more motivated by what they fear than by what they want. If you set a goal to do something — it doesn't matter if it's losing weight, saving up for a new car, or finding the perfect job — beware your internal saboteur. The severity of the sabotage depends on your perception of self. In some people, self-sabotage is more prevalent than in others, but no one goes completely unscathed.

Fear can manifest as defiance, procrastination, or self-doubt that you can do, be, or have something. Some may feel resigned to staying where they are now as the only way forward. People are likely to stop themselves from getting what they want without a cause/effect that's framed as losing something vitally important — the motivational trigger. This isn't a reference to threats, although fear-mongering has certainly been used as a menacing way of manipulating others.

Do you remember when one of your parents would tell your sibling something like, "Please clean up your toys, Sam"? (Of course they never had to tell you — this story is about your brother.) Sam would ignore the request. So they tried another tactic: "Sam, you love it when your room is clean. Don't you want to see all those fancy, fast racecars lined up on your shelf?" Sam's position on the matter didn't change. He loved his cars, but he still wasn't motivated to act. So, the third attempt: "Sam, please clean up — otherwise, there won't be time to go to Nancy's birthday party later. If you do it now, we can make it. But if you don't, then you won't have time to go because you'll be cleaning your room." If what he feared he would lose was important to him, he would finally clean his room. (If it wasn't, even that trigger wouldn't motivate him.) It turned out that Sam's trigger was affiliation. Your parents knew Sam loved playing with other kids and liked being part of a group, so nothing would stop him from going to that party.

The same is true for all people, even in the workplace. For example, if someone is motivated by power, the thought of not being able to lead, participate in an authority role, or be heard as an expert would be tough to entertain. To motivate someone fitting this profile, you could offer a cause/effect such as this: "Feeling powerless and frustrated by this situation will only make it worse. However, if you decide to participate in X change process, you'll be using your expertise to help everyone."

WARNING This is a big warning. This kind of motivation should never, ever be framed as a threat or delivered in a threatening tone.

TIP You can learn a lot from watching children's behaviors. The next time you see a child having a temper tantrum, ask yourself when and how *you* do that as an adult. Now, you probably don't throw yourself on the office floor and demand that someone get you a hazelnut coffee. However, everyone has an adult version of a tantrum, right? The next time it happens to you, ask yourself what you fear you're losing: Is it power, affiliation, or achievement?

Deciphering the money motivation myth

When leaders and managers are asked what they believe motivates their teams, the most common response is, of course, *money*. You may be wondering whether that's true about yourself and those around you. But is it really about money? Or is there something deeper going on?

Consider the meaning of money to those in the workforce, keeping in mind that philosophies about money vary from generation to generation. Offering money as motivation isn't *always* effective. Considering that a majority of your workforce is made up of GenXers and Millennials, knowing what money means to *them* will help you determine their priorities:

>> **Baby Boomers (born 1943–1960):** Money is a status symbol.

>> **Generation X (born 1961–1981):** Money is a means to an end.

>> **Millennials (born 1982–2004):** Money is today's payoff.

>> **Silent (born 1925–1942):** Money is livelihood.

>> **Homelanders (born 2005 and later):** Too early to tell, but maybe money is livelihood as well.

As you can see, money doesn't mean the same thing to everyone. That said, not everyone in a generation thinks exactly alike, either. But being aware of general attitudes about money can give you insight into the different thought processes. Unfolding McClelland's motivational triggers (see the earlier section "Looking, listening, and categorizing") will also help you understand what money may mean to different people.

Clearly, there's been a generational shift in mindset regarding the meaning of money. The current workforce of Millennials seeks financial means over career advancement. This jibes with their desire for a more experiential life over one spent acquiring stuff. They generate income to create a life and experiences they want, but they aren't necessarily interested in climbing the corporate ladder as Boomers were. In general, U.S. customer spending on live experiences and events has increased, indicating that it may not be just Millennials feeling the need to live life differently. Priorities have shifted. Living an experiential life is a motivator that can fall under any of the three motivational triggers in the same way money once did.

For example, a Millennial's deep desire for power may have more to do with the ability to control a situation and bring about a positive result at work, then have the flexibility to book their next trip to Vietnam, backpack to Machu Picchu, or swim with sharks around the Galapagos Islands. Millennials' translation of power is making a difference but also working to fund their adventures. Boomers may have the same desire to make a difference, but trends show that material possessions are more of their focus — a new house, a new car, or another item that projects the persona of success and power. The motivation may be the same (power), but the context of money, its use, how much is needed, and the projection of power are very different. So while power may be a Millennial's dominant motivator, money is secondary in creating their lives.

TIP

This shift from acquiring stuff to having experiences will continue to change the trends in workplace incentives. Consumer reports will indicate how deeply these desires grow within the culture. Stay tuned — and stay informed. What people spend their money on will tell you what their motivation may be. Think of it this way: Ask what a person wants to do with the money they make. Their answer will tell you whether they are motivated by power, affiliation, or achievement.

Helping People Find Their Meaning and Purpose Again

Feeling the need to be *useful* in this world is a major motivating factor for all generations:

>> An Intelligence Group survey found that 64 percent of Millennials would rather make $40,000 per year at a job they love than $100,000 a year at a job they think is boring. *Boring* to Millennials is a place where they're either unchallenged or disconnected from any meaning or purpose in the work they're doing.

>> A Clark University study found that 82 percent of Millennials said it was important for them to have a career that does some good in the world.

>> A Brookings University study said 63 percent of Millennials like their employers to contribute to social or ethical causes.

Considering that this group is already the largest generation in the population and soon will be taking leadership positions, meaning and purpose will be a more prominent focus than ever before. Meaning and purpose are increasingly key motivating and retention factors. Both GenXers and Millennials are deeply connected to a desire for meaningful work in the world. Cogent corporate social responsibility (CSR) initiatives that are organized and integrated will be increasingly key for motivation, as will the creation of shared values economy (SVE) structures that address human and social needs. The workforce wants to help resolve problems both in the world and locally by embodying the battle cry of "If not us, then who?"

REMEMBER

Helping people find their meaning and purpose is a motivational tool. Tap into their emotion in order to connect their hearts to the work they're doing.

Chunking it down: Bite-sizing purpose and meaning

You may be wondering how you would apply all this meaning and purpose stuff in your company. Theory can be fascinating, but practical application is the name of the game here. Not all readers may be leading massive corporations (yet!). What can you do about motivation, meaning, and purpose?

No matter where you are in your current organization, you can be a leader steeped in values and you can set a positive example for those all around you. Being motivated in your own work will help you motivate others. This is your opportunity to help your staff see what you see in the work you're all doing together.

Pull out a scrap piece of paper and follow along with Table 3-1. Break down what *your* business does. Whatever goods, services, or opportunities your company provides, list them out as shown for a few examples in the table. Remember, *every* product and service fills a need — if it doesn't, it won't be around for long. Consider the needs that your company addresses and add them to your breakdown. Making it personal, as in the third column, makes it really stick in your heart and your mind. Thinking about what your company does in this way creates an attachment or hook that in turn creates emotion around the meaning and purpose.

Emotion is the fuel. Passionate people are emotional people — they have energy, express their points with gusto, and fight fiercely for what they believe in. But sensitive people are emotional people, too. Their sensitivity often binds them to a specific cause, purpose, or meaning. There are many forms of emotion that form that bond. People may express it differently.

REMEMBER

Find your emotion. If you don't experience something emotional when you read the statements you develop in the third column, go back and try again. It needs to mean enough to inspire action or stay the course. This is your *why*.

TABLE 3-1 ## Bite-Size Purpose and Meaning Amplifications

Product or Service	What It Does	How It Fulfills Personal Needs
Directional app for use in the United States (for example, Waze or Google Maps)	Keeps user from getting lost and finds the quickest routes around traffic. Helps locate gas stations, places to eat, points of interest, and other fun places on their routes.	Helps people get to work and attend important events in their lives. Takes stress out of journeys. Makes traveling easier, richer, more fun, and more interesting.
Food business (Whole Foods, Fairway, Blue Apron, Hello Fresh)	Provides high-quality food and meals to the community.	Fuels and nourishes families so they can mobilize their dreams (including education, work, contribution to community, and engagement with others).
Clothing business (J. Crew, Madewell, Lululemon, Gucci)	Provides clothing and fashion for men, women, and/or children.	Makes people feel good about showing up in the world and experiencing the events of their lives. Enables a person to impress important people and be successful, such as on job interviews, and helps people feel confident in expressing themselves.

PURPOSE AND MEANING CONFESSIONAL

Meaning is highly personal. Consider the following statements:

- **Abraham, architect:** "I create homes that hold memories."
- **Sarandi, advertising executive:** "I show people how to get their needs met."
- **Sampson, financial professional:** "I give people peace of mind to know their loved ones will be taken care of even after they've gone."
- **Bryn, career coach:** "I help people realize their potential and get the job of their dreams."

Abraham, the architect, was raised in a small, modest home by a single mother. "We didn't have much growing up," he says, "but we sure had a lot of great laughs. I have so many wonderful memories. That's why I do what I do. I want to help other people to have a home where meaningful memories are created."

His is just one story revealing a meaningful and purposeful motivation. Sarandi, Sampson, and Bryn all have equally moving stories behind their statements. Every person has one.

Helping a team find its footing

The process described in the preceding section can be executed for a team within an organization or a small work group. In any case, it needs to be a collective process. Not everyone may agree, and some may be too shy to admit that they care enough to participate at all. That's a façade. Never forget that. Likewise, a defensive posture is usually a smoke screen to cover real emotion. Don't be fooled, and don't let such things stop you.

TIP

Ask team members why they're doing the job they do. Be prepared for several to say they need the money! That's fine. Ask them what they'll do with the money. This is a clue to why they are in their position. Remember, it's not the money but what they'll do with the money that is the underlying motivating factor.

Digging deeper will permit you to see why the work they do matters to them. Sometimes it's a connection to the CSR or SVE initiatives in place at the company — which is great! But they also want a job they find meaning in, whether they currently have that or not. Be inquisitive. Ask them questions about the work they're doing together as a team. Mold that into a motivating statement that unifies them. This isn't a slogan. What you're crafting is a *unifying statement*.

Keep it informal. Some teams come back with simple statements like "We make [stuff] happen" (you may imagine the more colorful word the team used!). That particular team is all about marketing research for Millennial companies, so that *would* be one way of saying they mobilize industries and companies, for sure. It was a completely authentic statement. Other teams have come up with variations such as "We take care of people as if they were our own family." Coming from a small team of healthcare professionals, this statement brought tears to the members' eyes as they nodded in agreement. It means something to them. And it motivates them to do their jobs every day.

REMEMBER

Unifying statements can really help those who may not be clear on the *why* of the work they do. Not every person can articulate it, but those around them share their experiences. People learn and gain clarity from others' experience.

Practicing and Reinforcing Motivation

The jury is still out on the best reward perks package. The workspace is constantly evolving and refining its approach, carefully balancing the desire of employees and the affordability of incentive programs for companies. This area will continue to be a moving target for the next few years. Millennials are redefining the workplace, so you'll have to wait and see what happens.

However, there is something you can do in the here and now, and it costs nothing. As you see throughout this chapter, empathy is essential to connecting with a team. Think back to the basis of what human beings want: They want to be seen, heard, and recognized. Often, you see what another person needs: a kind word, a little recognition, or maybe a reminder of what they really are motivated by.

Sometimes leaders and managers hold back such simple expressions of recognition and validation from an employee, considering them too "needy" or time-consuming. And without healthy boundaries, they'd be correct. Becoming the team's therapist *would* become a major time suck. That's not the intention here. The tools and insights provided thus far are a means to gain a glimpse into other people and help move them forward. This help isn't about participation trophies and gold stars being handed out to every team member. This chapter is suggesting a way to validate team members and inspire and motivate them.

Creating an environment where people can fail but learn from it

First, you can shine a light on a glaring issue that can cause a team to feel disempowered, fearful, and like a failure. That's when they're caught not knowing something they should know or they make a mistake. It's demotivating, even demoralizing for your dedicated employees. A workplace being a safe place to be is about more than just being healthy physically and mentally. There's an emotional component of safety that can be folded beautifully into the motivation of others.

Many years ago, Sarah Blakely, founder of SPANX, spoke at a conference and shared a story about sitting at the dinner table as a child every night. To paraphrase what she said: Her father would ask her what was her win and what was her loss for the day? After she told her dad about her loss, he would ask, "What did you learn from that?" You can adopt a similar practice with your team. (For details, see the next section and the later sidebar "Shifting the orchestra of discontent.")

REMEMBER

A mistake or misstep is only a failure if a lesson isn't learned from it. Don't dismiss negligent behavior, but when an honest error is highlighted in a constructive manner, it's less likely to occur again. Moreover, others can learn from these mistakes too. How do you wrap all this up into a tidy little delivery system? Keep reading.

Playing with pickup sticks: You can always find a solution

You may have heard the saying that everything you need is right in front of you. Clearly, when you're lost in turmoil — or if you're trying to motivate your team — that's not what you want to hear. But it's the truth. Playing pickup sticks is about working with what is scattered before you — your situation. Each stick represents a team member. Each stick has a certain amount of strength, but placing it together with other sticks creates something far stronger. Together we're better. Apart we're scattered.

Having team members teach and motivate one another creates a deep bond among them. It's never *only* the leader's role to motivate the team. They also need to do it for themselves and be willing to support others around them. You just need to show them how to do so.

SHIFTING THE ORCHESTRA OF DISCONTENT

Motivation isn't just the leader's job. The team plays a big part in creating a positive environment where others thrive. The leader can set up the environment for each person to win, but ultimately it's each person's decision whether to participate. Motivation occurs not just because a leader recognizes the team or taps into triggers — peers play a big part in the process as well.

As one particular team sat in a room together, they were asked to take out some paper and write down three highs, or wins, they had in the past week. It didn't matter how big or small it was — if it was an accomplishment, they should write it down. They went to work. Next they were asked to write down a couple of disappointments, missteps, or blind spots they'd experienced this week. Well, that went over like a ton of bricks. They said things like "Are you trying to get us in trouble?" and "Really? Is this an inquisition?" But after some reassurance, everyone went to work on their short lists.

Wins, of course, are joyful and full of laughter. But the group, without being cued, started taking notes on their wins and asking questions about how someone did what they did. Some team members said things like, "Now I know how to do this — thanks, dude." As they moved into the disappointments, missteps, and blind spots portion, they tensed up a bit. Finally one brave soul, "Meghan," stepped up. She was the newest team member. She shared that she'd made a mistake on an email she sent to a vendor. When prodded, she said, "Well, yeah, it was a mistake, and I'm not proud of it, but here's what I did to resolve the problem." The resolution she described took a lot of investigation. It was impressive. Everyone around her spoke words of support to her: "Wow, I would have never known that was the solution or where to get that! How did you figure this out?" Meghan exploded with pride as she explained her process.

Next up was the team skeptic, "Tina." "Okay, I'll play," she said. She admitted a misstep she had made that week. She wriggled in her chair and looked uncomfortable. Her manager jumped in and said, "Tina, no one thinks you're perfect. Mistakes happen. Do you want help fixing this issue?" She agreed after a bit of protesting. The group rallied and helped her. Tina's demeanor changed to become more open and less defensive.

After a few weeks of engaging with each other in this manner, team morale and motivation increased tremendously. They encouraged each other more. They became more open to being part of finding a resolution rather than allowing another team member to struggle.

Remember: People want to be seen, heard, and recognized. In this variation of motivating your team, you would be doing just that without getting into too many complexities. Not everyone may enjoy participating in the exercise, but they will learn a lot from observing the process.

Here's an exercise that has been used with great success. This isn't something you may need to do every week — perhaps only during times when people are feeling a little scattered or the team feels defeated. Set it up in an informal, relaxed spot in the office. Explain that you know they're working hard and you understand they may not always feel like they're getting very far. So it's time to play the high/low game:

>> Ground rules: no judgment, no retribution.

>> Ask team members to keep track of their highs and lows for the week. That should also include something from outside the office; it can be as simple as going to the gym three days this week or a major life event that may have happened.

>> Gather them together the following week. Ask someone to share one high for the week. Celebrate the high with congratulations.

But also ask for a low: a disappointment, mistake, misstep, or error. This one is usually met with caution. If they resist, ask them for an experience where they learned something new this week or a challenge they're stuck on.

>> Circle back around to a few of the highs. Ask what those lessons may have been: "What did you learn from this experience?" or "What did you learn about your abilities?"

Continue the conversation, encourage everyone as you go, and make it light. Do this exercise a few weeks in a row to help motivate them to see their contributions and where they can support their teammates. Thereafter, perhaps run the game once a quarter or as needed. Just don't wait to conduct this exercise until the situation is dire.

Pulling it all together

As you watch your team members engage in the exercise illustrated in the preceding section, you will notice patterns. Who loves the group interactions? Those people are motivated by affiliation. Who likes to be in control of the situation or becomes a bit bossy or defensive about not knowing something? Those are your power people. Who are the individuals who lock up with frustration over not winning or have a deep desire to just move forward? Those people are motivated by achievement.

REMEMBER

There is brilliance in all this. Come back around to the three categories shared earlier in this chapter: power, affiliation, and achievement. When you're really paying attention to your team (or spouse, family member, friend, and so on), you will know what motivates them — what it is they really crave in their lives.

(Side note: Knowing this information has also saved many personal relationships. Practice everything you discover about motivation on your family and see what happens.) It's not as hard as you think. When you know what someone really wants, it's not hard to give it to them:

>> **Those motivated by power:** Give them the chance to shine and to provide their point of view. They also like to keep people safe, so allow them to provide input on "efficiencies" — a code word for safety in a variety of ways.

>> **Those motivated by affiliation:** Give them the opportunity to work with others in groups and as in-house coaches. Recognize that they are social, so many of them can be very communicative. Job functions that allow them to use that skill make them so happy.

>> **Those motivated by achievement:** Give them a clear line to achieve their goals. When they've reached a goal, you must give them another one to strive for or you will lose their attention.

Chapter **4**

Thriving on the Challenges of Leadership

M ost people spend a huge amount of their time at work. It stands to reason, therefore, that work should make you feel good about yourself, give you a sense of personal mastery, and be fun. Unfortunately, many find work to be stressful, demotivating, and frustrating. Great leaders identify what motivates people and match their skills to those needed by the organization, thus creating a win-win situation. In order to create this situation, leaders need to be in a fit state to lead others.

Ideas about what makes a good leader have changed dramatically over time. In the 1920s and 1930s, trait theories argued that leaders were born. From the 1940s to the 1960s behavioral theories argued that you can be taught leadership — it is just a matter of adopting the right behaviors when attempting to lead. You can be autocratic ("I am the boss, do it this way") or democratic ("Let's decide how we should do this").

In more recent times, contingency theories (such as situational leadership) argue that no one leadership style is correct and that as a leader you need to adopt the correct leadership style for the situation. Transformational theories view leaders as agents of change. As a transformational leader you can "transform" the workplace via teamwork or team development, or by acting as an agent of change or a strategic visionary.

Human potential theories are the latest development and are concerned with the performance of the leader from a human perspective. These theories incorporate authentic leadership, resonant leadership, mindful leadership, and neuro-leadership. Human potential theories are concerned with maximizing your potential as a leader by being true to your values, and finding out how to work in harmony with yourself rather than trying to be something you're not. Mindfulness is a core element of human potential theories of leadership.

If you look at leadership theories over the last 70 years or so, you can easily see how each leadership theory has built on the last theory. You can also see why human potential theories are gaining in popularity. We live in a VUCA world — volatile, uncertain, complex, and ambiguous. This new world may go part of the way to explaining why some leadership theories are no longer effective. Yet many leaders, and you may be one of them, continue to base their leadership behaviors on outdated models. Why? Because like everyone else you probably do a fair amount of your work on auto-pilot. Over the years you've probably developed habits, which have been rewarding, and you repeat these patterns of behavior with little or no conscious thought.

Adopting new, human potential theories of leadership can be scary, as you discard the security blanket of your old methods of leadership and take a leap into the unknown of being yourself, and maximizing your potential as a leader. In this brave new world, you need self-knowledge and the courage to be true to yourself. In return, you can shed the heavy burden of trying to be someone you aren't in favor of being the best you can be.

Thriving Rather Than Surviving

Being a leader is a challenging role, especially in times of recession and economic crisis. Being a senior leader can also be a lonely and isolating experience. At times when you feel under pressure and uncertain about the future, you'll find keeping your team motivated and engaged tough. As a leader, you may also feel less inclined to seek support and guidance from your peers. Catastrophizing as thoughts spiral round and round in your head is all too easy.

Imagine missing a report deadline at work. In reality this situation is hardly life or death, is it? But your mind is likely to make up its own story about what's going on, blowing the matter out of proportion. Your caveman threat response can have a serious impact on your performance, health, and happiness. By practicing mindfulness and learning to observe thoughts as mental processes, you can change things.

Take the example of Dave and Ken, two middle managers from the same organization (names changed). Both applied for the same senior leadership role. An external candidate was appointed, so neither got the job. How they dealt with the situation was very different.

>> Dave's thoughts started to spiral down as he catastrophized about the situation. He tried to get on with work, but his mind kept on wandering to what went wrong at the interview, and how this might threaten his career.

>> Ken, however, applied mindfulness to his feelings of failure and rejection. He noticed himself starting to spiral down and his body becoming tense. He practiced mindfulness for a short while, calmly observing his thoughts without reacting or thinking about them further, recognizing the impact of his thoughts on his emotions, and then noticing how his body feels. He released the tension he felt and then focused his attention on the present-moment sensation of breathing. Ken returned to his work. He acknowledged feeling sad and a little angry about missing the promotion, but did not let these thoughts and emotions have a negative impact on his work and well-being.

This example graphically illustrates how mindfulness can help you, as a leader, pick yourself up after a fall, avoiding falling into a downward spiral of despair. Mindfulness also teaches you that the problem is never the real problem. Your perception and response to life's challenges is what can throw you out of the frying pan and into the fire.

Although many things are beyond your control at work, you always have a choice about how you respond. Choosing how you respond is empowering — it hands control back to you. Leadership can be challenging, and it's easy to forget to look after you. Here are three simple exercises that can help you balance work demands with the need to care for your well-being.

REMEMBER

For leaders, the ability to identify and overcome outdated mental programming without triggering the threat system is vital. If you're really serious about being a better leader, and thriving rather than surviving, you need to prioritize time to learn mindfulness and embed practice into every day you spend at work.

Soaking in the good

Think about the little things that make you feel good in life. Examples may include stroking a pet, hugging a loved one, someone appreciating something you've done, or seeing the first flowers of spring.

Ask yourself whether you can give these small pleasures a little extra attention. As you experience them, try pausing for a moment to really soak in the good they provide. Allow your body time to release feel-good hormones so that you can derive maximum benefit from these pleasurable experiences.

Soaking in the good is free and takes little time. It can also reduce your threat response, activating your parasympathetic nervous system, flooding your system with feel-good hormones. You may be amazed at the impact it has on your life.

Smiling

When you smile, you're telling your body that everything is fine. This simple action turns off your threat system. Your body immediately stops pumping adrenaline around your body, your blood pressure drops, and feel-good hormones such as serotonin are released.

Being kind to yourself

Do you find it easier to demonstrate empathy and kindness to others rather than yourself? Maybe you dismiss the idea of self-kindness as selfishness?

Sometimes you need to be selfish for your own preservation. Try to avoid beating yourself up for mistakes you make, things you get wrong, or things you should have done. Being kind to yourself can help reduce or eliminate the detrimental effects of fear, guilt, and shame.

Taking time out to consciously accept yourself and make friends with the person you really are helps you increase your happiness and creativity. This time out is especially important if you're a leader. Self-acceptance also helps to train your brain to work in approach mode rather than avoidance mode.

TIP

A befriending exercise such as the following helps you deactivate your threat system, making it easier to concentrate and gain a fresh perspective. Befriending yourself can be really hard when you first practice it, but it does get easier over time and is definitely worth working on. Follow these steps to cultivate kindness:

1. **Settle yourself into a comfortable, upright, dignified position, and focus your attention on your breathing for a minute or so.**

2. **Send yourself some kindness.**

    Imagine giving yourself a hug and accepting yourself exactly as you are — perfect in your human imperfection. Picture yourself surrounded by a warm glow of kindness.

3. **Send some kindness to a dear friend.**

   Thank them for their friendship and support. Wish them well and imagine them surrounded by a warm glow of kindness.

4. **Send some kindness to a neutral person — someone you've never met.**

   Wish them a happy life and send them kind thoughts. Imagine them surrounded by a warm glow of kindness.

5. **Send some kindness to a hostile person — someone who you may have argued with or who makes you feel uncomfortable.**

   Wish them a happy life and send them kind thoughts. Imagine them surrounded by a warm glow of kindness.

Being a More Mindful Leader

Human potential models of leadership all center around the concept of being the best you can be, maximizing your innate leadership qualities while being true to yourself and your values. All human potential theories incorporate mindfulness in some shape or form. This section briefly explores models and ideas around becoming a more mindful leader.

Authentic leadership

Authentic leaders are leaders who demonstrate the genuine desire to understand their own leadership behavior in order to serve the needs of the organization and its staff most effectively. Their behavior and decisions are based on strongly held values and beliefs. By upholding these values and beliefs, they increase their personal credibility and win the respect and trust of their team, colleagues, and peers.

Authentic leaders actively encourage collaboration and the sharing of diverse viewpoints, leading in a way that others perceive and describe as "authentic." Authentic leadership is all about leaders as individual people. It can be likened to a self-awareness approach to leadership and leadership development.

According to Bill George, former CEO of Medtronic and author of *Authentic Leadership* (Jossey Bass, 2004), authentic leaders are motivated by their mission, not your money. They tap into your values, not your ego. They connect with others through their heart, not their (sometimes artificial) persona. Authentic leaders should live their lives in such a way that they would be proud to read about their behavior on the front page of their local newspaper.

Defining the dimensions of authentic leadership

George defines authentic leadership as having five dimensions. Authentic leaders

» Understand their purpose

» Practice solid values

» Lead with the heart

» Establish connected relationships

» Demonstrate self-discipline

He believes that acquiring these five dimensions isn't a sequential process, but happens throughout a leader's life, often over a long time period.

Mindfulness is a key element of authentic leadership. It underpins all five dimensions described in the preceding list. It helps leaders increase their self-awareness and self-regulation. It helps them to be kinder to themselves and to protect their values.

Working out whether you're an authentic leader

TIP

This activity will give you an indication of how "authentic" your leadership style is. Score these questions as follows: 0 = not at all like me, 1 = a little like me, 2 = mostly like me, 3 = an accurate description of me.

1. I actively seek feedback to improve the way I communicate and work with others.

2. I always say exactly what I mean.

3. My actions are always fully consistent with my beliefs.

4. I always listen very carefully to others' views and opinions before reaching a conclusion.

5. If asked to do so, I can quickly and easily give a true description of how others view my strengths and weaknesses as a leader.

6. I never play games — what you see is what you get.

7. As a leader, I feel that I need to model behaviors that are consistent with my beliefs.

8. I recognize that others may not share my views on life and leadership, and am open to others' ideas.

9. I understand what motivates me, and the values that underpin my work as a leader and my life in general.

10. If I make a mistake I always admit to it and am ready to take full responsibility.

11. My values and beliefs have a huge impact on the decisions I make.

12. I actively seek out others' views to challenge the way I think about things.

Enter your scores in the following table:

Authentic Leadership Traits					Score for Trait
Self-awareness	1		2		3	
Transparency and openness	4		5		6	
Embodiment of values	7		8		9	
Seeking a balanced perspective	10		11		12	
Total overall score					

Interpret your trait score as follows:

0 = a trait you do not display or do not value

1–3 = a trait you can work to improve

4–6 = a trait you display

7+ = a trait you truly embody

To work out your overall score, add up the figures in the right-hand column. The authenticity of your leadership style is shown as follows:

0–13 = a low level of authentic leadership behaviors displayed

14–26 = a moderate level of authentic leadership behaviors displayed

27–36 = someone who leads with authenticity

TIP

If possible, repeat the exercise with one or more colleagues, peers, or members of your team. Don't forget to emphasize the need to be honest. Do your team members see you in the same way that you see yourself?

Resonant leadership

Resonant leaders are individuals who manage their own and others' emotions in ways that drive success.

The idea behind resonant leadership is that, rather than constantly sacrificing themselves to workplace demands, leaders should find out how to manage these challenges using specific techniques to combat stress, avoid burnout, and renew themselves physically, mentally, and emotionally. Many of these techniques are derived from mindfulness practices.

Resonant leaders

>> Are highly self-aware

>> Demonstrate a high level of self-management

>> Are highly socially aware

>> Are emotionally intelligent

>> Actively work to manage their relationships

Mindful leadership

The latest thinking on effective leadership suggests that leaders need self-awareness (a clear idea of what makes you tick, your strengths, weaknesses, beliefs, and motivations) and must be well-grounded and centered.

In addition, leaders need to be able to manage how their mind deals with multiple demands and constant connectivity so that they can maintain peak performance and well-being.

Mindfulness helps you to manage your mind by regulating and focusing your attention, making you more aware of your thoughts and emotions. Dan Siegel, clinical professor of psychiatry at UCLA School of Medicine and co-director of the Mindful Awareness Research Center, refers to mindfulness practice as "good brain hygiene," which is as important to your health as brushing your teeth.

TIP

If you want to explore this subject further, two key authors in the field of mindful leadership are Michael Carroll (*The Mindful Leader*, 2008) and Michael Chaskalson (*The Mindful Workplace*, 2011).

Practicing Mindful Leadership

As you process the continuous stream of information coming in from the world around you, your brain selects the things it deems most relevant and often dismisses the remainder. Academics and researchers argue that business performance is strongly influenced by this continuous stream of individual and organizational "meaning-making."

Mindfulness encourages a state of active awareness, openness to new information, and willingness to view situations from multiple perspectives. Adopting a mindful attitude allows you to suspend judgment until you have all the facts. Doing so refines your "meaning-making processes," giving you a more balanced view of the world around you.

This state of active awareness cannot be achieved by simply grasping the idea of mindfulness as an intellectual concept. To fully benefit from mindfulness, you need to regularly apply it to your workday practices. When you gain sufficient knowledge and confidence, you can help others around you by introducing a few simple mindfulness practices into their working lives. The following sections look at practical ways to incorporate mindfulness into your work as a leader.

Making mindful decisions

If you've been in a leadership or management role for any period of time, you're probably well versed in various models of decision-making. What you may not be familiar with is looking at your mindset and unconscious mental programming when making decisions. Your thoughts have a huge impact on how your body feels (for example, tension) and emotions (for example, happiness and fear). Similarly, holding tension or anger in your body has an impact on your thoughts. This impact is often unconscious, but can have a profound impact on the decisions you make.

A number of researchers have concluded that, when making decisions, emotions and negative information have a huge impact. Surprisingly, numeric information, analytic arguments, and logical arguments often have less impact.

By practicing mindfulness you become more aware of the different factors at play when making a decision, including the impact of your own meaning-making process, which leads to less subjectivity in decision-making.

TIP

Try this activity to improve your approach to making decisions. Follow these steps:

1. **Spend a few moments centering yourself in the present moment.**

   Focus on the sensation of breathing to make you relax and exist in the present moment.

2. **Clearly define the decision that you need to make.**

   Close your eyes, or hold them in soft focus (eyes looking down and three-quarters closed). Just sit with this question, using it as an anchor for your attention. Avoid the temptation to start making the decision or to think about it in any way; just keep on repeating the question in your mind.

3. **Imagine the question to be answered placed on a workbench in front of you for closer examination and study.**

   Spend a few moments exploring it, with kindness and curiosity. Consider the following:

   - Any negative information you may have associated with the decision — observing how this negative information impacts your thoughts or emotions.

   - Your emotional state in the present moment.

   - Any key numerical or statistical information that you may have.

4. **Open your eyes, evaluate all the information you have at hand, and make your decision.**

   You can now make a decision taking into account all the factors involved and being fully aware of any bias you may have initially felt.

Communicating ideas and expectations

The key thing to remember about mindful communication is that you're likely to spend a great deal of time on auto-pilot. You may be physically in the same room as the person you're communicating with, but at some point your mind is likely to wander elsewhere.

REMEMBER

As a leader, you need to make a real effort to be 100 percent present when communicating. You need to train your brain to notice when your mind wanders to the past or future or to matters unrelated, and gently bring it back to the present moment. In this state of present-moment awareness, you're better able to pick up verbal and nonverbal cues from your audience (see Chapters 1 and 2 in Book 1 for an introduction to these cues). You're better able to identify emerging areas of support and build on them. Similarly, you can pick up on areas of dissent and take time to explore or address them. Most importantly, people feel that you're really listening to them and that you value their time and input.

Mindfully encouraging others to speak up and contribute

A key part of being a leader is encouraging people to voice their thoughts and contribute to discussions and meetings. When you're in a mindful, present state of mind, you're better able to encourage people to share their ideas and support them in working collaboratively.

To improve the quality of your meetings, follow these steps:

1. **Remove anything that causes a distraction.**

   At the start of a meeting or collaborative working session, ask people to switch off their phones and so on.

2. **Set the tone for the meeting or working session.**

   You need to set the scene:

   - State clearly and concisely what you're trying to achieve.

   - Gain consensus from everyone present.

   - Reassure people that you're open to hearing their opinions and ideas (there's no such thing as a stupid question or suggestion). Back up this statement by making sure that you acknowledge and capture in writing every idea put forward.

   - Do not openly criticize someone's input (whatever you secretly think of it). Value that person by acknowledging their contribution.

3. **Create opportunities for everyone to share ideas and thoughts.**

   Don't expose people or put them on the spot. If they're initially too shy to contribute, be gentle and supportive.

4. **Recap what has been discussed and decided on so far to maintain direction and momentum.**

   At regular intervals, pause and give a brief overview.

5. **Make the final decision.**

   Remember that you're the leader and that the final decision rests with you. If this decision is different from the group consensus, always ensure that you thank everyone for their contribution, and let them know that you've really heard and considered their input.

Solving problems mindfully

Defaulting to old ways of thinking and behaving is all too easy when you're trying to solve problems — after all, they've served you well in the past. Mindful problem solving takes a more holistic approach. Follow these steps:

1. **Take steps to ensure that you're fully in the present moment.**

   Spend a few minutes doing a short mindfulness exercise of your choice (find some in Chapter 3 of Book 4), with your eyes closed or in soft focus.

2. **Place the problem you wish to solve on your "workbench" of the mind.**

    Try to picture the scene if you can. Observe how it makes your body feel and any emotions it invokes. Try your best not to judge these feelings and emotions as good or bad — just sit with them.

3. **Ask yourself the following questions.**

    After asking each question, observe the challenge sitting on your workbench and wait for an answer. Acknowledge each answer as it arrives.

    - How/why has the challenge arisen?
    - What factors are involved?
    - What are the possible solutions?

4. **Observe your answers with kindness and curiosity.**

    Avoid the temptation to drift away from the present moment by focusing on your answers. Observe any strong reactions that are elicited by any part of your exploration. Are you experiencing an emotion, for example excitement or fear? Is your body responding, for example, with a clenched jaw or fluttering in your stomach?

5. **Open your eyes and make a decision on the best way to solve the problem.**

    You can now make an informed and dispassionate decision, having considered all the facts.

6. **See the problem as a challenge.**

    Research suggests by reframing problems as positive challenges to learn and overcome, you're more likely to take a proactive approach and find effective solutions.

After practicing mindfulness regularly for eight weeks or longer you should be able to use techniques like this one much more rapidly, as you develop the ability to quickly tune into the present moment and observe things more objectively.

Creating a positive and inspiring workplace culture

As a leader, you're the one who sets the tone in the workplace. Being true to yourself and your values is important; that is, you need to be authentic.

If you truly value people's creativity and innovation, make sure that working practices reflect and celebrate these aptitudes. For example, your company could set up a system that identifies and rewards staff members who are innovative.

Google staff are allocated time each week to work on their pet projects or ideas that interest them. This freedom has led to the development of many of Google's most profitable products.

TIP

If you value mindfulness, and want to cultivate a more mindful workplace, consider

>> Offering staff mindfulness training in work time.

>> Setting aside space for people to get away from their desks or work areas to clear their minds and grab a few moments of mindfulness. Leading organizations are creating these spaces, and this privilege is highly valued and rarely abused.

>> Cultivating a culture in which staff members feel comfortable leaving their work area for a short time to practice mindfulness somewhere quiet.

>> Offering mindfulness drop-in sessions, possibly at lunch time, which people can join as and when they want to.

As Mahatma Gandhi famously said, "Be the change you want to see." If you want to encourage openness and honesty, be open and honest yourself. Many leaders paint a vivid vision of what an organization is like to work for, but fail to follow this vision through by making sure that the fundamentals are in place to make the vision a reality.

REMEMBER

Mindfully take a long hard look at your organization, and what it looks like from an employee's perspective. Does it really match up to the vision painted of it? Ask yourself what you can do to change things for the better, embodying your beliefs and values.

Coping with Stress and Pressure by Building Resilience

Did you know that a lack of control over your work can be a major source of stress? One study found that leaders experience the lowest level of stress in organizations. This low level may be in part because they have a high level of control over their work. While leaders do have a higher degree of control over their work than many other employees, the high pressure, fast-changing environment that most leaders work in can be a major source of stress. Stress is now reported to be the number one cause of workplace sickness and absence. A huge volume of research carried out over the last 40 years demonstrates the effectiveness of mindfulness to reduce stress.

Mindfulness can build your resilience in the following ways:

>> **It improves well-being.** It helps you gain more benefit from the pleasures in life and creates a greater capacity to deal with challenging events.

>> **It improves physical health.** Scientists have discovered many ways in which mindfulness can improve physical health. These ways include lowering blood pressure, reducing chronic pain, and improving sleep.

>> **It improves mental health.** Hundreds of research studies have concluded that mindfulness is effective in reducing stress, anxiety, and depression. It can also help with eating disorders, couples' conflict, and even obsessive-compulsive disorder.

>> **It helps you manage you mind better.** Make sure that you remember that you should be in control of your mind — your mind should not be controlling you! Creating a small gap between a stressful or difficult event and your thoughts puts you back in control

>> **It helps you to cope better with the difficulties in your life.** Mindfulness works, in part, by helping people to accept their experiences — including painful emotions — rather than reacting to them with sense of aversion and then avoidance. By approaching and exploring things you find difficult, their grip and impact on your life usually diminishes.

Although you can't always control the challenges and stressors that arise at work, you do ultimately have 100 percent control over how you respond to them. However, gaining this control can take practice.

Reading about mindfulness is all very well, but is no substitute for actually practicing it and hardwiring it into your brain. The best way to cope well under stress and pressure is to develop a regular mindfulness practice. After discovering and practicing the basics for eight weeks, as little as ten minutes formal practice each day can help you take control of your responses to life's challenges. Here are a few hints and tips to help you build your resilience.

Maintaining peak performance

The trick to maintaining peak performance is recognizing when your performance starts to drop off and taking steps to restore it. To maintain peak performance, try this exercise:

1. **Practice a body scan to identify the key areas of your body in which you hold tension.**

   These areas vary from person to person. Detecting tension in these areas can act as an early warning system, alerting you of the need to take mindful action.

At work you can do a three step body check at your desk. Here are the steps:

- Center yourself by focusing on the sensation of taking three slow breaths. Notice the sensations you experience, such as heat, cold, or tingling, when you focus your full attention on your feet. Pause to observe then repeat with your legs, followed by your bottom.

- Repeat the first step, focusing on your chest and internal organs, followed by your arms.

- Repeat the first step again, focusing on your neck and shoulders. Follow this with your jaw, nose, facial skin, and scalp. Finish centering yourself by focusing on the sensation of taking three slow breaths.

2. **Deal with any tension you detect in these key areas.**

   Try the following:

   - Breathing into them and then letting the tension go on the out breath.

   - Giving yourself a few minutes' break away from what you were doing by walking outside or from one area of the building to another or by leaving the office premises altogether.

   - Eating or drinking something mindfully. Spend a few minutes really experiencing the taste, smell, and sensations as you swallow the drink or eat the food.

   - Stretching at your desk — really experience the sense of stretching and moving your muscles.

   - Spending a few minutes focusing on sounds, with your eyes closed or in soft focus — just observe them as they arise and vanish without categorizing them or having to do anything.

3. **Return to your work.**

   Your improved performance more than compensates for the few minutes that you've spent practicing mindfulness.

Implementing mindful strategies for rejuvenation

Mindfulness teaches you how to manage your own mind. It shows you that you've a choice in how you respond to life. Just because you've always done things in a certain way doesn't mean that you have to continue to do so. Mindfulness is also about creating a balance in your life between things that nourish you and things that deplete you.

TIP

You may find that, when you get particularly busy, you drop things that seem unimportant such as playing a musical instrument, playing a sport, spending time with friends, or little pockets of time to yourself. The more you spiral away from being mode into doing mode, the busier you're likely to become. Here are a few mindful strategies you can try to rejuvenate your life:

» **Do a quick audit of the activities you do each day.** Note which ones nourish you (make you feel good or give you a sense of mastery or achievement) and which deplete you (sap your energy or make you feel bad).

» **Note whether your day includes at least a few things that nourish you.** Time spent on these things is an investment in your well-being and should be an important part of your day.

» **Recognize that some activities can both nourish or deplete you.** Decide what you can change (in your mindset or actions) to make certain activities more nourishing than depleting.

» **Spend a little time each day practicing mindfulness.** Set a time in your schedule, and don't let your busy workload rob you of this important investment in your productivity and well-being.

» **Do one thing a day mindfully.** Take a mindful shower, be mindful of your bodily sensations as you work out at the gym, or eat or walk mindfully.

» **Take a few minutes to pause and gain maximum benefit from something that you enjoy.** Savor every mouthful of that chocolate bar. See all the colors of that beautiful sunrise or sunset. Relish a hug from your children or loved one. Pausing to really experience things you enjoy in the present moment makes your body release feel-good hormones, which reduce stress and increase immunity and general well-being.

Chapter 5

Leading People, Change, and Strategy

Leading people and change are arguably the two most demanding aspects of a leader's work. This chapter explores how mindfulness can transform the leadership of people and change, and how the organization can become more mindful while still keeping a keen eye on the bottom line.

Leading Mindfully When Change Is the Norm

In the recent past, change projects at work were managed on the assumption that they had a distinct beginning, middle, and end. Arguably the most widely known model argues that after the initial shock and denial stage comes a feeling of loss, and in the final stage people start to experiment with the idea of doing something in a new way, eventually embrace it, and the new way of working becomes "business as usual." This model is great to bear in mind when major change happens occasionally, and there's time to embed changes and return to a state of business as usual.

Another commonly used model proposes that in the initial stages of change an organization prepares for change by breaking down old structures and ways of working, which causes uncertainty. In the middle stage, employees work to resolve the uncertainty and look for new ways to do things, and start to support and embrace the desired change. In the final stage (when people have embraced the change) comes further work to embed the new way of doing things into everyday business.

The problem with both models is that the pace of change for many organizations is now so rapid that there's rarely time to complete stage three (embedding and business as usual) before the next change is necessary. So just as the sense of loss and uncertainty starts to recede and people start to explore new ways of doing things, they're plunged straight back into shock, denial, and breaking down what they've only just built up.

It's no wonder that most change programs fail, and that change fatigue is costing the United States and United Kingdom economies billions each year.

Meeting modern-day challenges with mindful solutions

With little "business as usual," one change follows another and another, and little if any time exists to consolidate and embed each change.

Constant, "bumpy change" requires a new approach to leading change initiatives, centred on human processes of habit formation.

REMEMBER

While many change management projects focus on the steps necessary for organizational change, the Prosci ADKAR model focuses on five actions and outcomes necessary for successful individual change, and therefore successful organizational change. In order for change to be effective, individuals need

>> **A**wareness of the need for change

>> **D**esire to participate and support the change

>> **K**nowledge on how to change

>> **A**bility to implement required skills and behaviors

>> **R**einforcement to sustain the change

Knowledge and practice of mindfulness, together with some basic knowledge of how the brain works, on the part of both the leader and employees, makes this model even more effective. In the words of Jon Kabat-Zinn, father of mindfulness-based stress reduction (MBSR), "You can't stop the waves, but you can learn to surf."

Developing new change strategies

A head of operations — call him Dan — was faced with the necessity of cutting costs by 10 percent. He'd had to make similar cuts in the three previous years. Staff numbers had already been reduced, and working methods had changed and changed again. As a result, many staff were feeling disengaged from the company.

With help he identified that humans crave certainty, and certainty was in short supply. He speculated that many of the team were exhausted with the constant change, and probably felt threatened by the possibility of future changes that may reduce their status or security. He speculated further that many of his team were working in avoidance mode.

TECHNICAL STUFF

Depression often occurs after a period of prolonged stress. High levels of cortisol are released into the bloodstream and the right side of the brain becomes more active. Research by Davidson and Kabat-Zinn in 2003 concluded that, after practicing mindfulness for eight weeks, stressed workers showed a significant increase in left-brain activation (specifically the left prefrontal cortex part of the brain). A tendency toward right-brain activation can lead to an avoidance mode of mind; in contrast, left-brain activation is likely to promote an approach mode of mind. These modes of mind manifest themselves in the following ways:

Approach mode of mind (Promotion)	Avoidance mode of mind (Prevention)
Increased activation in the left prefrontal cortex	Increased activation in the right prefrontal cortex
Motivated by attainment of positive ends	Motivated by the avoidance of negative ends
Global processing	Local processing
Cognitive flexibility	Cognitive rigidity
Attentional flexibility	May lack ability to focus for prolonged periods
Flexible mindset	Rigid mindset

Embedding change individually and organizationally

Dan was concerned that the employees' experience of the last few years may make his next change initiatives even more difficult to implement. Dan knew that mindfulness training could help his staff become more resilient, increase their sense of positivity, and make them more likely to adopt an approach mode of mind in relation to the changes ahead.

Dan offered staff the option to attend mindfulness training in work time. The courses were publicized to staff as a personal development opportunity that could increase well-being and resilience in times of change. At the same time, Dan started to run focus groups on the challenges ahead to gain ideas about the best way forward. He was honest and open about the challenges that the organization, and specifically the operations department, was facing. He encouraged staff to take the lead in problem solving and solution finding throughout. All focus groups and problem solving forums started with a three-step focus break (see Chapter 3 in Book 4 for more on this), which served two purposes: It centered staff and focused attention on the task at hand, and it also helped him "model" mindfulness to his team.

Dan knew that habits, once formed, are stored in the primitive areas of the brain and are therefore repeated unconsciously, making them difficult to change. He knew that, in order to change habits, people need to be aware of them. At the start of the working groups he used light-hearted, fun activities to help staff become more aware of their habits and mental mindsets. This approach helped his team become more aware of their mental programming and defaults, and the fact that they could change them. Those who were attending mindfulness courses often chipped in with things they had been discovering about themselves, and their experience of doing things differently.

Once the way forward had been agreed and accepted by most members of staff, Dan made efforts to reinforce new ways of thinking and working, celebrating success and small wins along the way. Doing so helped to reinforce the new ways of working, which over time became "the way we do things round here." Within a few months the old ways of working and thinking were used less, and as a result they became less dominant, and most of his team seemed to replace them with the new habits.

TIP

Try these tips to make dealing with change less challenging:

>> Use mindfulness to help you to identify your unconscious habits and thinking patterns. Decide whether they're serving you well and, if not, consciously work to find new ways of acting and thinking. Repeat these over a two- to three-month period to form new dominant ways of thinking and acting that are more productive.

>> Use the ADKAR model next time you start to plan for an organizational change. Visit www.change-management.com for more information.

>> Habits take time to form, so organizational changes may be slow to be adopted. Help employees form new habits by providing opportunities to discuss, experiment with, and practice new ways of thinking, behaving, and working over a 8–12 week period. The more new habits are practiced, the stronger the neural pathways in people's brains become and the easier repeating the "habit" is.

>> Staff facing job loss need just as much support as staff making the transition to the new way of working. Mindfulness training can help those losing their jobs deal with the challenges that they're facing, giving them back a sense of control.

Creating Strategies That Allow the Organization to Flourish

In order to keep pace with change, you need to adapt your strategies. If you want to get ahead of change, a more strategic approach is needed. You have to anticipate trends and proactively define new and innovative ways forward. In order to do so, you must be agile and authentic.

Agility is now an essential leadership skill. The increasing speed of change demands that organizations need to become more nimble and flexible. Your ability to spot change on the horizon, anticipate what may happen next, and develop strategies in advance is vital.

Authenticity is another essential skill in times of volatile, unpredictable change. Your ability to create clarity by describing your vision and painting a picture of the future is more important than ever. You need to be able to lead with confidence and have the courage to take a stand. You need to build trust and confidence within your teams and be genuine in your communications. Change tends to cause anxiety and confusion. Your role as a leader is to bring a level of certainty about the direction of travel and evoke a sense of purpose for your staff.

Identifying organizational culture

If you really want to make radical changes to the way your organization operates, you need to gain a good understanding of its culture. Many tools and models are available to help you identify the characteristics of your organization's culture.

One way to work on cultural change is to identify subcultures that may exist within an organization and investigate why they may find it difficult to inter-relate. Rapid and constant change has a huge impact on organizational culture and can result in a "non-culture" — a kind of vacuum left where a cohesive culture used to exist. This vacuum needs to be filled with a new collective coherence.

Mindfulness helps you to step into the present moment and see what's really going on. This ability is useful when seeking to identify subcultures. You need to map the subcultures that exist and how these relate to each other. For example, manufacturing may have a completely different subculture than finance. Once identified, take time to celebrate the subcultures and encourage them to flourish. The idea behind this move is that you bring them out into the open and thus have a better chance of understanding of what you're dealing with. Trying to make a subculture comply with a corporate ideal often pushes it further underground, which makes it impossible to change. Giving people a unique subculture that they can be proud of often encourages that subculture to move closer to corporate intent.

Where a weak and dysfunctional subculture exists, try to give it a helping hand. Weak subcultures can seriously undermine organizational cohesion. Identify why confidence has been lost and help the business area add value to the organization once more.

The final stage of the process involves weaving together the diverse subcultures. By getting members of staff from different cultures working together on areas of common purpose, more areas of shared beliefs emerge. The shared cultural beliefs encourage subcultures to bond and form a web of shared beliefs. These webs can become strong, and equally as effective as the tightly woven, singular company culture of the past.

REMEMBER

Cultural change initiatives take time to embed — no quick fixes exist. As a leader, coming to grips with organizational culture can be the deciding factor between a strategy's or change initiative's success and failure. Ignore organizational culture at your peril. Be mindful that not all organizational cultures may be to your liking. Unless they're seriously detrimental to the organization, you need to let go of your personal feelings on the matter and spend your energy on getting the different subcultures to work together and establish more and more areas of common ground.

TIP

Most researchers believe human beings are more hardwired to cooperate than to compete. Gather together workers from different subcultures to work together on areas of common ground. Start the meeting with a three-minute focus break (see Chapter 3 in Book 4), explaining that participants will be working together for the next few hours, that you want them to gain the most from this time, and that this technique helps them clear their minds and allow them to do so. Get each participant to write down five things they feel need to be worked on — each written on a different piece of paper. Gather the pieces of paper and group them into themes and areas of commonality. These areas of common ground are the things to work on first.

Creating a collective vision for the future

Large organizations generally spend a considerable amount of time and effort on developing organizational visions. Branding and communication experts are drafted to help the top team define their vision for the future in a manner that will motivate staff and inspire belief, confidence, and desire in customers. Smaller organizations sometimes suffer from having no vision, or a vision that is too wordy, is difficult to remember, and feels unachievable. Visions are intended to paint a vivid picture of the organization and where it's heading. Less is often more. You need to make your organizational visions memorable and inspiring but also achievable.

Try using the following techniques to help you develop a vision for the future.

Step 1: Centering and visioning

Follow these steps for centering and visioning:

1. **Settle yourself in a room where you won't be disturbed.**

   Switch off your cell phone and your laptop (or at least the volume), and silence any device that may take your attention away from the task in hand.

2. **Sit in a comfortable, upright position.**

   Close your eyes or hold them in soft focus.

3. **Spend three minutes or so focusing your attention on the sensation of breathing.**

   Really feel the present-moment sensations of the breath entering your body and the breath leaving your body.

4. **Spend a further three minutes reconnecting with your body in this moment in time.**

   Check how your feet are feeling in this moment in time, followed by your legs, bottom, shoulders, and head.

5. **Open your eyes and capture on a piece of paper the five key characteristics representing how you'd like your organization to be in three to five years' time.**

   You can express these characteristics as words, pictures, or paragraphs of descriptive text.

Step 2: Identifying things you need to start, stop, and continue doing

Follow these steps to identify what you need to start, stop, and continue:

1. **Refocus your attention on the present-moment experience.**

Try to let go of the thoughts that are probably rattling round in your head. You've jotted them down, so nothing important will be forgotten.

2. **Spend two minutes focusing your attention on the thoughts in your mind — observing them as mental processes and then letting them go.**

3. **Spend a further two minutes focusing your attention on your breathing, as described in the preceding section.**

4. **Open your eyes.**

Read the "five characteristics" you jotted down and ask yourself, "In order to achieve this, what do we need to start doing, stop doing, and continue doing?"

5. **Jot down what comes to mind.**

Step 3: Checking your gut instinct and intuition

Follow these steps to check your gut instinct and intuition:

1. **Refocus your attention as in step 2 in the preceding section.**

2. **Open your eyes again and check what you've jotted down.**

Imagine what's on the paper becoming a reality, and hold that thought for a moment.

3. **Close your eyes or hold them in soft focus.**

Take five slow breaths. Now focus your attention on your body.

- How does your body feel in this moment in time? If you feel any tensions or sensations, where in your body are they being held?

- Do you feel any emotions? What are they?

- Are any thoughts popping into your head? What are they?

4. **Examine your experiences during this exercise.**

If you felt excitement and happiness and your body felt fine, you've probably got it right. If you felt fear or uncertainty, you may need to revisit your strategy.

This activity works well with a group. You can lead the mindfulness exercises and segue into and out of planning activities.

TIP

READING YOUR BODY

When in approach mode, you're more open to new and innovative ways of doing things. By practicing mindfulness for a few minutes at the start, and between each part of the task, you're more likely to come at the task with fresh ideas and clarity of mind.

Sensations held in your body can have a major impact on the decisions you make. If you're holding anger or fear in your body at an unconscious level, doing so can impact on your decision-making and planning, even if you're not aware of it doing so. In a similar way, tapping into your present-moment bodily sensations immediately after making a decision or plan can help you recognize how you really feel about it at an unconscious level. If you're happy, calm, or excited, the decision is probably right. If you're fearful, anxious, or uncertain, you need to examine why, and probably revisit your plan.

Developing strategies mindfully

Having defined a high-level vision, it's time to develop a strategy to make it happen. You need to gather key information into one place and summarize it into an easy to read format. You can use the model shown in Figure 5-1 as a discussion tool.

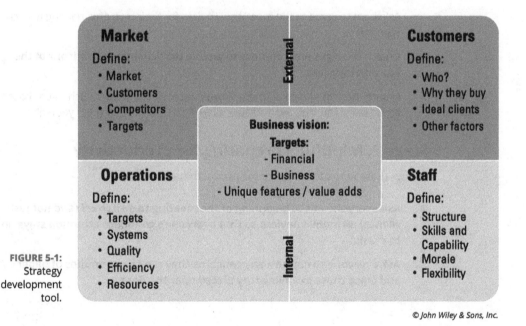

FIGURE 5-1: Strategy development tool.

© John Wiley & Sons, Inc.

Consider conducting a SWOT analysis for each of the segments in the model above, whereby you identify each segment's:

>> **S**trengths

>> **W**eaknesses

>> **O**pportunities

>> **T**hreats

You can take a mindful approach to this task as follows.

Stage 1: Getting ready

Get ready to develop strategies mindfully by following these steps:

1. **Decide on the best people to get the task done and invite them to a meeting.**

   Identify the mix of skills necessary to create an effective team.

2. **Send a copy of Figure 5-1 (or your own version thereof) to each participant prior to the meeting.**

   Ask them to come to the meeting with data for their own area relating to each segment.

3. **Create the right environment to enable participants to think out of the box and innovate.**

   Ensure that hot and cold drinks, slow-energy-release snacks, such as oat-based cereal bars, and fruit are available, even if you have to buy them yourself.

   TIP

Stage 2: Mindfully preparing for productivity

Follow these steps for prepare for productivity:

1. **Ask everyone at the beginning of the meeting to switch off (and not just silence) all mobile devices so that everyone's complete attention stays on the task.**

2. **Ask everyone to capture any concerns they may have on slips of paper and place these in a filing tray placed near the door.**

3. **Invite everyone to take part in a "centering" exercise.**

You may wish to explain to participants some of the science behind mindfulness exercises and why doing them is a good use of their time. Model mindfulness by leading the centering exercise as follows:

- Invite participants to close their eyes or hold them in soft focus.

- Invite them to focus their attention on the thoughts that enter their heads, to acknowledge them as "mental processes" and to let them go without starting to think about them or interacting with them in any way. Tell them that if their minds wander it's fine and when they notice this wandering happening to just gently escort their attention back to the present moment. Allow three minutes for this activity.

- Invite them to focus on the sensation of breathing, experiencing it as though for the first time. Allow two minutes for this activity.

- Invite them to focus their attention on any sounds they may be hearing — inside the room, outside the room, or even outside the building. Explain that the object of the exercise is to simply observe, not judge or react to the sounds. Allow one minute for this activity.

- Invite them to open their eyes, ready to work on creating a new strategy.

4. **Recap the overall vision that you're all striving to make reality.**

This vision should already have been agreed upon in previous meetings.

Ask those participants who do not wish to try the mindfulness exercise to just sit quietly and observe it.

TIP

Stage 3: Mindfully establishing the status quo

Establish the status quo with these steps:

1. **Appoint five chairpersons — one to focus on each of the five segments.**
Split the remaining participants evenly between the five groups.

2. **Explain that everyone will have the opportunity to contribute to all five segments.**

3. **Sound a bell to start the information sharing and capturing process.**

After 15 minutes, sound the bell again and ask each group of participants to move to a new chairperson. Repeat until everyone has had the opportunity to visit all five groups.

4. **Lead another short mindfulness exercise.**

   Use the three-minute focus break from Chapter 3 in Book 4.

Stage 4: Mindfully creating a new strategy

Follow these steps for new strategy creation:

1. **Share the information gathered.**

   Make sure that you, and the group as a whole, do not start to judge or categorize — just listen and absorb.

2. **Define as a group the strategies needed to achieve the business vision and targets.**

   Work your way around the segments one at a time.

3. **Thank the group for all their hard work.**

   Take responsibility for taking away the draft strategy and producing a professional document for sharing and further discussion.

Embedding new values and behaviors

When you have a clear idea of your organization's culture and vision and a clear strategy for the future, you need to make the plan a reality. The vision and strategy may call for staff to embrace new values, and almost certainly to adopt new behaviors.

Be mindful that old ways of working and behaving are likely to be deeply embedded, especially if they worked well in the past and people have enjoyed and been rewarded (by pay, recognition, or a sense of achievement) for working in this way. Don't expect staff to embrace your proposed changes with the same enthusiasm as you. For one thing, you have a head start. You've already started to rewire the way your brain thinks about working. As you've worked on creating the strategy, your brain has been busily storing new information and making new connections. You're aware of all the factors that led you to create the new strategy but your team is not.

When you're driving change you're likely to embrace it more quickly, even if you're not wildly enthusiastic about what it involves. Asking people to do things differently can generate all sorts of mental conflicts for them — many of which they may be completely unaware of. If accepted, new ways of doing things are eventually stored by the brain as habits, and these habits in time become more dominant than the work habit circuitry that they're currently using. The process of habit formation can be really slow. The more opportunities that you can create to explore and practice new ways of working, the stronger the brain's neural pathways (circuitry) become.

For some people, the perceived threat of the new way of working may prove too great and they default to old ways of thinking and behaving. Be mindful that they may not default on purpose as an act of anarchy; they may be largely unaware of how their thoughts, emotions, and habits are driving their behavior.

Mindfulness can be invaluable when you're trying to embed new values and behaviors. It helps you to develop awareness of your hidden mental world. It helps you develop the skill to observe your thoughts, emotions, and bodily responses. By developing this awareness, you're able to choose a wise response. As a leader, being able to respond to people and situations mindfully helps you manage yourself better when driving through difficult changes. Mindfulness can help you manage your well-being and deal with any personal difficulties or inner conflicts that arise. In addition, you'll be better able to observe when your team members are struggling and can then help them work better with their mind.

In times of change and uncertainty, be kind to yourself and your colleagues. Self-kindness can help you switch off your fight-or-flight response, making it easier to see things clearly and concentrate.

REMEMBER

How you feel about things is likely to have an impact on your behavior to others. Your behavior is likely to have an impact on how others feel, which has an impact on how they behave. By acting as a mindful role model, you make things easier for those around you, and you're likely to feel better too.

If you offer mindfulness training to your staff, it probably won't make an unwelcome change any more palatable. What it can do is help them to become more aware of what's going on in their mental landscape. This awareness gives them the opportunity to bring to the surface thoughts and behaviors that are making them unhappy, stressed, or fearful. Knowledge of what's going on in their minds allows them to take control of the situation. They can decide what to do next and focus their energy accordingly.

Creating a More Mindful Organization

Introducing mindfulness into your organization can lead to many benefits. Not only is mindfulness likely to improve employees' well-being, it may also make them more productive and creative. But does such a thing as a "mindful organization" actually exist?

In the 1990s, the concept of the "learning organization" was popular. The idea was that an organization would facilitate information sharing and learning for all members of staff and in this way continuously transform itself. Knowledge management systems were put in place to capture information and share it, and knowledge managers appointed to oversee the whole thing. The problem was that no one really knew what a "learning organization" looked like, so it was virtually impossible for organizations to know when they had changed into this mythical beast. While the idea was good, it became a never-ending journey — rather like that experienced by the crew in *Star Trek* — boldly going where no organization had gone before . . . with no clear final destination.

The idea of becoming a mindful organization may fall into the same trap. You will probably find it easier and more meaningful to focus on incubating pockets of mindfulness within your organization. Create spaces for staff to go and spend a few minutes in silence to refocus their efforts, and give staff permission to go to this place for short periods when they need to. Let mindfulness evolve within your organization, and leave the future to sort itself out. Who knows? In a few years' time many aspects of your organization may be transformed by mindfulness, but it's best to start with the present moment.

REMEMBER

Mindfulness can transform both your own and your employees' perception of change and how to manage it. Fortunately, your organization can become more mindful while still keeping a keen eye on the bottom line. Maybe you've done your own return on investment calculations. Introducing mindful work practices into your organization can be difficult when you occupy a junior role, but as a leader you can use your power and influence to change things for the better. You can choose to continue leading as you always have, or start to model some mindful behavior and start a quiet revolution. You've the power — the choice is yours.

Recognizing that looking beyond the bottom line is good for the bottom line

Research evidence suggests that mindfulness is likely to be good for your bottom line. Here are a few facts to consider:

>> **Stress is now the top cause of workplace sickness and absence in many countries.** Lost productivity costs money. Studies conducted over the last 40 years conclude that mindfulness is highly effective in reducing stress.

>> **Many workers are now so busy that they're in a constant state of fight or flight.** Practicing mindfulness can switch off the brain's fight-or-flight response, improving both well-being and the ability to be productive.

>> **A lack of focus and concentration can undermine work performance.** Research shows that mindfulness can improve focus and concentration.

>> **The ability to gain perspective and "see the bigger picture" is important — especially in times of change.** In recent years, seven independent studies have shown that mindfulness can help you see the bigger picture and set aside personal agendas.

>> **Research into mindfulness and decision-making demonstrates that mindfulness can help you make more rational decisions, not be "blinded" by past experiences, and come up with more creative solutions.**

>> **Mindfulness has proven effective in helping people manage their emotions better, develop a more positive outlook, and prevent burnout.**

Evaluating the return on investment (ROI) of mindfulness

Here's a strong argument for promoting and supporting mindfulness in the workplace: If, at a conservative estimate, 40 percent of participants in a mindfulness course for 12 people improve their productivity by 10 percent, that's equivalent to gaining an additional member of staff for two days a week.

Naturally the cost of mindfulness at work consultants varies, as do salaries and average staff absence levels. In addition, levels of productivity can be tricky to measure in many work environments. The question to ask yourself is, "What is the return on investment for an average training course?" Obviously, this is difficult to calculate.

Little research evidence suggests that spending on personal effectiveness courses or many of the generic "interpersonal" skills training classes actually has any impact on a company's bottom line. In contrast, a significant volume of research demonstrates that mindfulness does improve a wide range of desirable work skills such as relationships with colleagues and customers, focus and concentration, strategic thinking, decision-making, and overall resilience. It can also increase staff engagement and productivity.

REMEMBER

Although the bottom line is important, sometimes by looking beyond it and caring for your employees' well-being and making the workplace a great place to be, you gain greater commitment and buy in from your staff. Measuring the value of staff commitment and well-being is clearly impossible, but it cannot fail to produce a positive impact all around.

Mindfully improving employee engagement and retention

"Engaged employees" are fully involved in and enthusiastic about their work (see Chapter 1 in Book 4 for an introduction to engagement). This engagement motivates them to work in harmony with their organization. An employee's positive or negative emotional attachment to their job, colleagues, and the organization as a whole is important. Employee engagement is distinctively different from employee satisfaction, motivation, and organizational culture.

Mindfulness can improve employee engagement and retention. Practicing mindfulness leads to improved work engagement because it elicits positive emotions and improves psychological functioning.

Mindfully engaging staff

TIP

If your company runs an annual staff survey that includes questions relating to employee engagement, you could use these questions as a baseline. Try running a mindfulness pilot (with the full support of the senior management team and line managers), and compare current responses to those of previous years. You may be surprised at the positivity expressed by staff who have completed a mindfulness course compared with the attitudes of colleagues who did not attend.

Offer staff with a poor attendance record as a result of ill health the opportunity to attend mindfulness training. One company encouraged such staff to undergo mindfulness training in their own time. It resulted in a 51 percent reduction in sick leave, for a wide range of health conditions. Days off as a result of stress, anxiety, and depression dropped by 78 percent during the four years following the course and 55 percent of participants reported increased happiness at work.

Creating the right work/life balance for all employees

Working long hours does not increase your productivity; it usually decreases it. The same is true for staff members. Some organizations develop a working culture in which long hours are the norm. Employees feel that they need to be seen to be in the office for more hours than they're paid in order to fit in. Emails are often sent late at night, making other employees feel that they're in some way deficient because they're not working at that hour. In a similar way, some organizations expect staff to be in instant contact outside normal working hours.

As a leader, you've the power to support working practices that promote a healthy balance between people's personal and working lives.

Constant connectivity is bad for performance. Try introducing "no contact times" and encourage staff to switch off their mobile devices when away from work.

TIP

Keep an eye on the times that you and other senior managers send emails. If the working style that best suits you involves rest and relaxation after normal working hours and then a little time working in peace late in the evening or first thing in the morning, set your emails to send in normal working hours (you can easily set this system up). By doing so, you're not sending the message to others that they too have to be working late at night or early in the morning.

A lack of control over workload or working methods can be a major source of stress. Where possible, encourage workers to work in a manner that suits them. Encourage individuality, as long as core work hours are covered, work gets done, and targets are met.

TIP

Offer staff mindfulness training to examine objectively their current work/life balance and to establish a way of working that is more nourishing and rewarding for them personally.

Offer staff a "quiet room" to go to when they need ten minutes of silence to regain their sense of balance and improve their productivity. Doing so sends a positive message to staff that their need for a few minutes of quiet mindfulness is recognized; providing this area is so much better than employees sneaking off to bathroom stalls.

TIP

Index

Numbers

A

About the Authors

Shamash Alidina, MEng MA PGCE, is CEO of Learn Mindfulness International, offering training and teacher training in mindfulness for the general public as well as life and executive coaches, yoga teachers, doctors, nurses, and other health professionals. Shamash is the coauthor of *Mindfulness at Work For Dummies.*

Juliet Adams has spent most of her career working with organizations on leadership and strategic learning programs, organizational development, and change projects. She has worked on national projects for the police and several standards-setting bodies. She now runs her own successful consultancy, A Head for Work, specializing in new approaches to leadership and developing programs and e-learning content for leading organizations. She is the coauthor of *Mindfulness at Work For Dummies.*

Maria Gamb is founder and CEO of the coaching and training company NMS Communications, focusing on creating powerful leadership and happy, healthy organizations that thrive. As a former executive, she spent more than 20 years in corporate America directing and managing successful businesses valued in excess of $100 million. Her global experiences led her to write the Amazon bestselling book *Healing the Corporate World* (NMS Communications, 2010), which made her one of the few women to rank in the top ten of Amazon's Leadership category. Maria is a sought-after speaker, consultant, trainer, and retreat leader on the topics of values-based leadership and gender and team communication dynamics. She is the author of *Values-Based Leadership For Dummies.*

Bob Kelleher is an award-winning author, thought leader, keynote speaker, and consultant. He travels the globe sharing his insights on employee engagement, leadership, and workforce trends. Bob is the founder of The Employee Engagement Group, a global consulting firm that works with leadership teams to implement best-in-class leadership and employee engagement programs, workshops, and surveys. He is the author of *Employee Engagement For Dummies.*

Elizabeth Kuhnke is an executive coach, specializing in communication skills and personal impact. A former stage, television, and radio actor, she has designed university voice and movement programs and teaches acting skills to students and professionals. She is an accredited Myers Briggs Type Indicator (MBTI) administrator and Neuro-linguistic Programming (NLP) practitioner. She is the author of *Body Language For Dummies.*

Vivian Scott is a Professional Certified Mediator with a private practice in Snohomish, Washington. She has handled a variety of workplace cases, ranging from helping business partners end their relationship with dignity to creating a new working environment for a law firm. She has completed an extensive practicum and certification program with the Dispute Resolution Center of Snohomish & Island Counties, where she mediates on a regular basis helping parties resolve conflict in workplace, family, consumer, and landlord/tenant disputes. Vivian is a member of the Washington Mediation Association and spends much of her time advocating for meaningful resolution. She is the author of *Conflict Resolution at Work For Dummies*.

Dr. Christina Tangora Schlachter, PhD, is the CEO of She Leads, where she coaches leaders who are tired of too much firefighting and are ready to create meaningful change based on open and authentic conversations. Christina's matter-of-fact 12-week transformation process has helped thousands of leaders around the globe build rapport, speak honestly, and deliver results. She is the author of *Critical Conversations For Dummies*.

Marie Taylor was an executive coach, speaker, and facilitator of insight and learning. She established her own successful consulting and coaching practice in 2002 and was a coach for more than 18 years. She worked internationally, supporting leaders and their organizations to create success. An experienced facilitator and trainer, she worked with leadership groups in national government, technology and science-based start-ups, professional bodies, international corporations, TV, the arts, and nonprofits. She ran a successful leader-as-coach program, training leaders how to integrate practical coaching skills into everyday management. She was the coauthor of *Business Coaching & Mentoring For Dummies*.

Steve Crabb is an entrepreneur and business coach who has applied his professional coaching and business experience to working with individuals and organizations in order to bring about fast and lasting change in the name of business excellence. Specializing in stress management and business growth, Steve coaches and trains organizations, teams, and individuals to exceed their own expectations. He is the coauthor of *Business Coaching & Mentoring For Dummies*.

Hannah Ubl leads BridgeWorks' national research efforts, most recently overseeing the latest endeavor comparing Early Millennials, Recessionist Millennials, and Generation Edge. Whether running focus groups, diving into data analysis, interviewing a C-suite executive, or speaking one-on-one with every generation, her research has unearthed valuable tips, actionable solutions, and key marketing strategies for generationally diverse workplaces and clients. Hannah especially thrives when connecting quantitative and qualitative data to a message for the masses, overseeing the keynote speaking side of the business, and giving generational insight to numerous publications. She is the coauthor of *Managing Millennials For Dummies*.

Lisa Walden is the communications director at BridgeWorks. She is a seasoned generational expert who co-leads the conception of hard-hitting, forward-thinking, and incisive management and marketing insights. A sought-after expert who has been featured in publications nationwide, Lisa has lent her expertise to many of BridgeWorks' largest initiatives. She's led her team in developing a generational portal for a prominent national financial advising firm, helped a master-planned community design a Millennial-friendly neighborhood, and worked closely with organizations to develop impactful recruiting and retention strategies. She is the coauthor of *Managing Millennials For Dummies.*

Debra Arbit is CEO, integrator, and motivator at BridgeWorks, and she dedicates her time to the growth of the company and its clients. She continues to help organizations narrow generational divides, and her favorite clients are the ones with the most complex issues to solve. Debra has a passion for all things generations, but one topic close to her heart is how parenting styles have shaped Boomers, Xers, Millennials, and Gen Edgers. She is the coauthor of *Managing Millennials For Dummies.*

Publisher's Acknowledgments

Senior Acquisitions Editor: Tracy Boggier

Compilation Editor: Georgette Beatty

Project Manager: Chad R. Sievers

Production Editor: G. Vasanth Koilraj

Cover Image: © Chris Ryan/Getty Images